T0179724

Enterprise Process Management Systems

Enterprise Process Management Systems

Engineering Process-Centric Enterprise Systems using BPMN 2.0

Vivek Kale

CRC Press
Taylor & Francis Group
Boca Raton London New York

CRC Press is an imprint of the
Taylor & Francis Group, an **informa** business

CRC Press
Taylor & Francis Group
6000 Broken Sound Parkway NW, Suite 300
Boca Raton, FL 33487-2742

© 2019 by Vivek Kale
CRC Press is an imprint of Taylor & Francis Group, an Informa business

No claim to original U.S. Government works

Printed on acid-free paper

International Standard Book Number-13: 978-1-4987-5592-4 (Hardback)
International Standard Book Number-13: 978-0-429-45331-1 (eBook)

Visit the Taylor & Francis Web site at
http://www.taylorandfrancis.com

and the CRC Press Web site at
http://www.crcpress.com

To Girija,

my beloved muse and fellow traveler,

for her eternal encouragement, support, and inspiration,

without which none of my books would exist.

Contents

Section II   Road to Enterprise Process Management Systems

Section III Enterprise Process Management Systems

Section IV   Enterprise Process Management Systems Applications

List of Figures

List of Tables

Foreword

The success of an enterprise depends on the ability to support business processes well. However, many organizations struggle to transition from data-centric enterprise systems to process-centric enterprise systems. In fact, this is a much harder problem than what I expected when I wrote my first book on workflow management (WFM) in the 1990s. Therefore, I am glad to write the Foreword for the present extensive reference book on enterprise process management systems. The book focuses on Business Process Modeling and Notation (BPMN), which has become the industry standard in process modeling.

It is important to note that the idea to make information systems process-centric is not new. In the 1970s, people like Skip Ellis, Anatol Holt, and Michael Zisman had already worked on so-called office information systems driven by explicit process models. Ellis et al. developed prototype systems such as Officetalk-Zero and Officetalk-D at Xerox PARC in the late 1970s. These systems used variants of Petri nets to model processes. Another example from the same period is the System for Computerizing of Office Processes (SCOOP), developed by Michael Zisman. SCOOP also used Petri nets to represent business processes. Officetalk, SCOOP, and other office information systems were created in a time in which workers were typically not connected to a network. Consequently, these systems were not widely adopted. Nevertheless, it is good to realize that the vision still driving today's business process management (BPM) systems was already present in the late 1970s.

These office information systems evolved into WFM systems in the 1990s. The early WFM systems focused too much on automation and did not acknowledge the management aspects and the need for flexibility. These were followed by BPM systems that appeared around the turn of the century. These systems had a broader scope as compared with WFM technology, covering from process automation and process analysis to operations management and the organization of work. The trend to provide better management support is still ongoing in current systems. Over time, all systems started to use BPMN or variants of BPMN. This book on enterprise process management systems provides a detailed introduction to this notation and presents details on the different ways to realize such process-centric systems.

Looking to the future, I believe that the interplay between process management and data science will become of eminent importance. My new research group at RWTH Aachen University in Aachen, Germany is called Process and Data Science. We aim to combine process centricity with an array of data science techniques. Process mining is one of the key technologies we work on, and this is also mentioned in this book. Process mining aims to discover, monitor, and improve real processes by extracting knowledge from event logs readily available in today's information systems. The starting point for process mining is an event log. Event data can be used to conduct three types of process mining: process discovery (finding out what is really happing in the process and representing this as a process model ready for analysis); conformance checking (understanding where and why processes deviate and whether these deviations are harmful); and enhancement (extending models with performance and conformance information and generating process improvement ideas). Interestingly, process mining (as well as other data-driven BPM technologies) will help to improve collaboration between information technology specialists, management, domain experts, and workers. At the moment that the real processes are properly visualized, discussion can become more focused and fact-driven. Moreover, process mining supports digital transformation and the further digitalization of enterprises.

I hope you will enjoy reading this book by Vivek Kale. It combines business aspects with technology trends and pointers to methods. Organizations should use the present book to make their enterprise architecture more process-centric and to prepare for a wave of data science-enabled business improvement approaches.

Wil van der Aalst
RWTH Aachen University

Prof.dr.ir. Wil van der Aalst is a full professor at RWTH Aachen University who leads the Process and Data Science group. He is also part-time affiliated with the Technische Universiteit Eindhoven (TU/e). Until December 2017, he was the scientific director of the Data Science Center Eindhoven (DSC/e) and led the Architecture of Information Systems group at TU/e. His research interests include process mining, Petri nets, BPM, workflow management, process modeling, and process analysis. van der Aalst has published more than 200 journal papers, 20 books (as an author or editor), 450 refereed conference/workshop publications, and 65 book chapters. Many of his papers are highly cited (he is one of the most cited computer scientists in the world and has an H-index of 138 according to Google Scholar, with more than 85,000 citations) and his ideas have influenced researchers, software developers, and standardization committees working on process support. van der Aalst received honorary degrees from the Moscow Higher School of Economics (Prof. h.c.), Tsinghua University, and Hasselt University (Dr. h.c.). He is additionally an elected member of the Royal Netherlands Academy of Arts and Sciences, the Royal Holland Society of Sciences and Humanities, and the Academy of Europe. In 2017, he was awarded a Humboldt Professorship, Germany's most valuable research award (equivalent to five million euros).

Preface

An enterprise is not only expected to be effective and efficient but should also be able to adapt to the frequent changes in the market environment driven by technology, regulation, and competition—in other words, it should be agile. Enterprise agility has become even more important in these times of globalization, particularly in periods of continuous organizational change that are often caused by an increasing pace of innovation, collaboration with other organizations, new challenges in the market, mergers and acquisitions, societal changes, and/or technology advancements. The enterprises that can best respond to the fast- and frequently-changing markets will have better competitive advantages than those that fail to sustain the pace dictated by the process of globalization. This can be realized through enterprises acquiring better control and efficiency in their ability to manage the changes in their enterprise processes.

In the past few decades, all of us have witnessed a procession of different methods, tools, and techniques emanating from the information technology (IT) industry that have had a tremendous impact on the very nature and operations of enterprises. However, in midst of all this turmoil, one fact has remained constant: the existence of an abysmally low number of successfully implemented applications. The primary reason has been that the applications do not meet the expectations and needs of the business area(s) for which they were built, typically because of inadequate user involvement in the early phases of system analysis. The challenge identified was defining the system requirements correctly early on in the delivery process so as to minimize design, construction, and postimplementation repair.

One of the root causes identified for these problems was the inherent weakness of the phase in which requirements are captured and analyzed. This phase never seemed to get the requirements of the enterprise correctly, clearly, consistently, and completely. As a result, finished projects never seemed to deliver the promised functionality and had to be recycled for more analysis and development. Maintenance and enhancements were called for indefinitely and, thus, became harder to achieve as time passed by. Furthermore, because individuals change midway both on the development and user sides, system requirements also change and the whole process continues indefinitely. More specifically, there is a fundamental disconnect between the business and the IT/information systems people. Notwithstanding how much both of the parties try to bridge the gap, there is a fundamental divide between the perception of a business user and what the systems staff perceive—in effect, both classes of people speak different languages. Even when the systems personnel try to increase precision by using specialized methods and specification tools, the end-users are often never able to ratify the documented requirements completely because of unfamiliarity or discomfort with these very tools.

As organizational and environmental conditions become more complex, globalized, and competitive, data alone cannot provide a framework for dealing effectively with the issues of performance improvement, capability development, and adaptation to the changing environment. Conventional systems primarily store only snapshots of discrete groups of data at predefined or configured instants of time, along a business process within an organization. This predominating data-oriented view of the enterprise as implemented by traditional IT systems is the most unnatural and alien way of looking at any area of human activity. The stability of the data models, as canonized in the conventional IT paradigm, might have been advantageous for the systems personnel but, for this same reason, it is unusable (and, hence, unacceptable) to the business stakeholders within the organizations. Traditional systems could never really resolve the simple dichotomy of the fact that systems based on exploiting the unchanging data models, although easy to maintain, can never really describe the essentially dynamic nature of businesses. Business processes (and rules) were the other equally important portions of the reality that had been ignored by the traditional information systems. Unlike for the data-oriented view of the traditional systems, business users feel more comfortable with the process-oriented (and rules-oriented) view of the enterprise. They can not only readily identify with requirements captured in terms of processes (and rules) but can also feel more comfortable in confirming the veracity of the same. Service-oriented architecture (SOA) provides an opportunity for IT and the business to communicate and interact with each other at a highly efficient and equally understood level. This common, equally understood language is the language of business processes or enterprise processes in the form of Business Process Modeling and Notation (BPMN).

IT can fulfil its role as a strategic differentiator only if it can provide enterprises with a mechanism to prompt a sustainable competitive advantage—that is, the ability to change business processes in sync with changes in the business environment and at optimum costs. BPM solutions fundamentally are about accommodating change—accommodating changing business requirements that in turn require changing process logic, as well as changes in the system landscape brought about by mergers; system consolidations; and new technology, such as cloud computing. Faced with increasing demand from the business to deliver change faster, IT has long pinned its hopes on SOA's promise of service reuse. The services support a layer of agile and flexible business processes that can easily be changed to provide new products and services to keep ahead of the competition. These will be built on a foundation of SOA that exposes the fundamental business capabilities as flexible, reusable services. By packaging system functionality in reusable units with standard interfaces, IT could become more agile. Section II discusses SOA, which, along with the constituting services, is the foundation of modern EPMS solutions.

 Typically, SOA is inherently *bottom-up*, driven by the details of the underlying systems. The SOA architect tries to define service interfaces that will maximize reuse of system functionality. In reality, these services can rarely be simply snapped together to create BPM solutions because they rarely match up with the business requirements. Ideally, the process-driven application logic should not need to change to enable reuse or to accommodate changes in the underlying system landscape. This necessitates a *top-down* approach in which the business dictates and determines the required interfaces.

What Makes This Book Different?

The concept of processes is not new; what is unique in this book is *the process-centric* paradigm being proposed to replace the traditional data-centric paradigm for Enterprise Systems. Not being the normal book focused on a new technology, technique or methodology, this text necessarily takes an expansive and comprehensive look at end-to-end aspects of the envisaged process centric paradigm.

This book interprets the 2000s enterprise process management systems (EPMS) from the point of view of business as well as technology. It unravels the mystery of EPMS environments and applications as well as their power and potential to transform the operating contexts of business enterprises. Customary discussions on EPMS, do not address the key differentiator of these environments and applications from the earlier enterprise applications like enterprise resource planning (ERP), CRM, SCM, and so on: instead, EPMS for the first time, is able to treat enterprise-level services not merely as reusable discrete stand-alone services, but as Internet-locatable, *top down*, composable, and repackageable building blocks for dynamically generating real-life enterprise business processes.

This book proposes that instead of the customary data item in the traditional IT systems, the business process should become the smallest identifiable and addressable entity within any enterprise system. In other words, not the isolated data items or attributes of the entities of the traditional IT systems, but rather, it should be the processes (that access, create or modify the data item or attribute) that should become the focus of enterprise systems. Enterprise systems should be reengineered from the present data-centric architecture to a process-centric architecture. Hence, the reason to term the reengineered systems with a different name, namely, Enterprise Process Management Systems (EPMS). BPMN can not only capture business requirements: it can also provide the backbone of the actual solution implementation. Thus, the same diagram prepared by the business analyst to describe the business's desired "to-be" process can be used to automate the execution of that process on a modern process engine. This is achieved via a new process-centric architecture that preserves simplicity and stability in the business-oriented process-centric application layer while maximizing flexibility and agility in the underlying service contract implementation layer and vice-a-versa. This is achieved through a service contract implementation layer interposed between the process-centric application and the system landscape. The process-centric application layer never interacts directly with the underlying system landscape; instead, it always goes through the service contract implementation layer. The process-centric application is unaffected by changes in the underlying system landscape—what changes is only the logic of the service contract implementation layer. BPMN is used for both the process-centric application layer and the service contract implementation layer; in particular, to achieve these objectives, the latter is broken out into a stateful integration process and a stateless messaging process.

Here are the characteristic features of my book:

1. It enables readers to obtain a clear understanding of what EPMS really means and what it might do for them. The book presents process-centric EPMS as a better alternative to the traditional enterprise systems. It explains the context and demonstrates how the whole ecosystem works together to solve the main objectives of enhancing enterprise agility and flexibility, and sharpens the strategic focus.

2. It gives an introduction to the Enterprise Process Management Systems (EPMS) solutions that enable an agile enterprise.

3. Describes distributed systems and Service Oriented Architecture (SOA) that paved the road to Enterprise Process Management Systems (EPMS).

4. It addresses the requirements for agility by ensuring a seamless methodological path from process requirements modeling to execution and back (to enable process improvements).

5. It addresses the key differentiator of EPMS environments; namely, that EPMS, for the first time, is able to treat enterprise-level processes not merely as discrete standalone processes but rather as Internet-locatable, *top down*, composable, and repackageable building blocks for dynamically generating real-life business processes.

6. It introduces customer conversation systems that can enable sales closures through customer interactions rather than merely registering customer orders.

I have always been fascinated with the simplicity and facility with which end-users take to spreadsheet-based applications. There has always been a need for a spreadsheet-driven development methodology that would smoothly transition from requirements to implementation (and back). Chapter 12 presents the spreadsheet-driven spreadsheeter application development methodology for the development of processcentric application systems. This has been adopted from T. Damij (2001) and N. Damij and T. Damij (2014). I wanted to write a book presenting business process management and enterprise process management systems from this novel perspective; the outcome is the book that you are reading now. Thank you!

Finally, a remark on what this book is not about: although this book alludes to the current heightened priority on digital transformation of enterprises as its primary motivation, this is not a book on digital transformation of enterprises. Since this is a paradigm-changing book, hence, that itself is the focus of the book--the book cannot address everything within the two covers of a single book; it neither provides a framework nor a methodology on how to undertake a digital transformation initiative. But, yes, with this book we are fairly on the way —in effect, this book addresses the part on digital transformation of business processes. The journey started with an earlier published book Agile Network Businesses which is actually a book on network and e-Business business models. Author's last book *Creating Smart Enterprises: Leveraging Cloud, Big Data, Web, Social Media, Mobile and IoT Technologies* details the various technologies that are relevant for a digital transformation initiative. The author would need another book project to discuss the aspects of digital transformation of enterprise architectures (EA) before we are ready to tackle the subject proper of the digital transformation of enterprises. Epilogue gives an overview of the salient aspects of a digital transformation of enterprises initiative.

How Is This Book Organized?

Chapter 1 introduces the concept of enterprise systems and, in particular, ERP. After introducing the concept of ERP, the chapter highlights the tendency of ERP systems to reinforce the traditional silo-oriented operations of organizations. In the end, the chapter describes the importance of business processes in enabling flexible and adaptable enterprise-wide cross-functional integration.

Chapter 2 describes the framework for measuring business process performance in terms of the dimensions of timeliness, cost, and quality.

Section I: Genesis of Enterprise Process Management Systems

Chapter 3 reviews the basic concepts of systems thinking, systems science, systems engineering, and systems architecting. Knowing this basic information about systems helps in understanding the origin of the significance of enterprise architecture and the constituting business architecture, information architecture, application architecture, and technical architecture. This also provides the context for the significance of business processes in contemporary enterprises.

Chapter 4 presents enterprise architecture as a well defined practice for conducting enterprise analysis, design, planning, and implementation, using a holistic approach at all times, for the successful development and execution of enterprise strategy. This chapter describes the viewpoints, views, and perspectives that enable an enterprise architecture.

Chapter 5 describes the process views and perspectives that enable an enterprise process architecture. Analogous to the enterprise architecture frameworks for enterprise architecture described in Chapter 4, this chapter describes the workflow reference model (WfMS) as the reference process architecture for the enterprise process architecture.

Section II: Road to Enterprise Process Management Systems

Chapter 6 presents the basic concepts of modeling, enterprise modeling, and process modeling. The chapter presents several frequently used business process modeling languages including Petri Nets, Event-driven Process Chains (EPC), Yet Another Workflow Language, Unified Modeling Language activity diagrams, and BPMN.

Chapter 7 describes the characteristics of distributed systems and introduces distributed computing as a foundation for better understanding of cloud-enabled business processes.

Chapter 8 presents the definition and characteristics of SOAs, along with alternate approaches to realizing the vision of service-oriented systems, namely, Web services and Representational State Transfer services. One of the great potential advantages of solutions created using an SOA with Simple Object Access Protocol (SOAP) or Representational State Transfer (RESTful) Web services is that they can help resolve this perennial problem by providing better separation of concerns between business analysts and service developers. Analysts can take responsibility for defining how services fit together to implement business processes, while the service developers can take responsibility for implementing services that meet business requirements.

Integrating existing and new applications using an SOA involves defining the basic Web service interoperability layer to bridge features and functions used in current applications such as security, reliability, transactions, metadata management, and orchestration; it also involves the ability to define automated business process execution flows across the Web services after an SOA is in place. An SOA with Web services enables the development of services that encapsulate business functions and that are easily accessible from any other service; composite services allow for a wide range of options for combining Web services and creating new business processes and, hence, new application functionality.

Chapter 9 describes cloud computing's definition, presents the cloud delivery and deployment models, and highlights its benefits for enterprises. It highlights the primary challenges faced during provisioning of cloud services—namely, scalability, multi-tenancy, and availability. More importantly, the chapter leverages SOA to explain the cloud-based realization of business processes in terms of Web services.

Section III: Enterprise Process Management Systems

Distinguishing between BPM as a business program and BPMS as its subset realization into a software application, Chapter 10 first introduces the concept of BPM and its characteristics. It explains the concept of BPMS and its variation of enterprise process management systems being brought into focus in this book. In contrast to BPMS that reflect the "data item"-driven, reusability-focused *bottom-up* stance of the traditional IT view of the enterprise, enterprise process management systems embody the "business process"-driven, requirements-focused *top-down* stance of the information systems view of the enterprise.

EPMS promotes a world-view of process-driven or process-centric systems supported by a portfolio of systems like process bases, process warehouses, process intelligence, and process analytics. This book is a small step or at least an *expression of need* in that direction.

Chapter 11 describes BPMN 2.0, which is a graphical notation for modeling business processes. Using BPMN, business analysts can describe organizational processes in a way that can be understood by developers and system integrators, and that can serve as a blueprint for implementing the services and orchestrations required to support those processes. BPMN standardizes the notation used by business experts on the one hand and IT specialists on the other, thus finally bridging the gap between them.

Consequently, there is a need for a development methodology that would smoothly transition from requirements to implementation. Chapter 12 presents the "business process"-driven (or process-centric), requirements-focused, top-down-stanced spreadsheet-driven spreadsheet application development methodology for the development of process-centric application systems.

Chapter 13 discusses how BPMN 2.0 can not only capture business requirements but also provide the backbone of the actual solution implementation. The same diagram prepared by the business analyst to describe the business's desired to-be process can be used to automate the execution of that process on a modern process engine. The chapter also describes SAP Process Orchestration to give a practical context to the discussion presented in this chapter. This overview includes descriptions of SAP Business Process Management for addressing business process management, SAP Business Rules Management to address business rules management, and SAP Process Integration[*] for addressing process integration management.

Section IV: Enterprise Process Management Systems Applications

Chapter 14 explains the rationale for modeling business processes with queuing theory. In business processes, each activity of the process is performed by a resource (either human or machine); thus, if the resource is busy when the job arrives, then the job will wait in a queue until the resource becomes available. The chapter also introduces simulation as a technique that enables one to define and experiment with the imitation of the behavior of a real system in order to analyze its functionality and performance in greater detail.

Chapter 15 focuses on process improvement programs ranging from disruptive to continuous improvement programs: the first corresponds to business process reengineering programs, while the latter corresponds to programs like lean, Six Sigma and Theory of Constraints. The last part of the chapter focuses on the basic principle of time-based competition by discussing activity-based costing and comparing it with the more advanced concept of time-driven, activity-based costing.

Chapter 16 introduces the concept of human interaction management and compares its efficacy with BPM. It also presents the components of an effective customer interaction system—namely, automatic speech recognition, spoken language understanding, dialog management, natural language generation, and text-to-speech synthesis.

The Epilogue on *digital transformation of enterprises* highlights the real importance of business processes in the current context of heightened priority on digital transformation of enterprises. Conceiving the roadmap to realize a digitally transformed enterprise via the business model innovation becomes amenable only by adopting the *process centric view* of

---

[*] SAP SE, Walldorf, Germany

the enterprise—from the conventional *data-centric view* this would be an un-surmountable problem akin to hitting a brick wall at the Ms. Winchester's mansion.

Appendices I and II present an introduction to Business Process Execution Language and interaction architectures, respectively.

Who Should Read This Book?

All stakeholders of a BPM or EPMS project can read this book.

All readers who are involved with any aspect of a BPM or EPMS project will profit by using this book as a roadmap to make a more meaningful contribution to the success of their BPM or EPMS project.

The following is the minimal recommendations of tracks of chapters that should be read by different categories of stakeholders:

- Executives and business managers should read Chapters 1 through 10 and 14 through 16.
- Business analysts, enterprise architects and solution architects should read Chapters 1 through 16.
- Operational managers should read Chapters 1 through 11 and 14 through 16.
- Project managers and module leaders should read Chapters 1 through 15.
- Technical managers should read Chapters 1 through 16.
- Professionals interested in BPM should read Chapters 1 through 6 and 10 through 16.
- Students of computer courses should read Chapters 1, 3 through 13 and 16.
- Students of management courses should read Chapters 1 through 6 and 10 through 16.
- General readers interested in the phenomenon of BPM should read Chapters 1 through 10 and 14 through 16.

Vivek Kale
Mumbai, India

Acknowledgments

I would like to thank all those who have helped me with their clarifications, criticisms, and valuable information during the writing of this book; who were patient enough to read the entire or parts of the manuscript; and who made many valuable suggestions. I would like to thank Yatish Wasnik and Nitin Kadam for their comments and feedback on the book. I am thankful to Prof. dr. ir. Hajo Reijers, Prof. Dr. Jan Mendling, Dr. Paul Harmon and Dr. Mathias Weske for giving feedback on portions of the book. I am especially thankful to Prof.dr.ir. Wil van der Aalst for his feedback and writing the Foreword to the book.

In the beginning, I did not fully understand the meaning of "my wife being an inspiration or a muse." Eventually, I came to understand the phrase when the supreme irony dawned onto me: when Girija is away, I cannot work but, when she is there, I do not have time for her because—you guessed it right—I am too busy with my work. To say that the situation is patently unfair to her would be a gargantuan understatement. This or any other of my books simply would not exist without her help and support, and words alone cannot express my gratitude to her. I have no words to mention the support, sufferings, and sacrifice of my wife Girija and our beloved daughters Tayana and Atmaja. I am hugely indebted to them for their patience and grace.

Vivek Kale
Mumbai, India

Prologue

When Changing the Map Changes the Territory!

The concept of processes is not new; what is unique in this book is the process-centric paradigm being proposed to replace the traditional data-centric paradigm for enterprise systems. The traditional paradigm is covered in several publications including M. Weske (2012); A. H. M. ter Hofstede, W. M. P. van der Aalst, M. Adams, and N. Russell (Eds.) (2010); Jan vom Brocke and M. Rosemann (Eds.) (2014); W. M. P. van der Aalst and van Hee (2002); M. Reichert and B. Weber (2012); and M. Dumas, M. La Rosa, J. Mendling, and H. Reijers (2013). Though there may seem to be a lot of apparent commonality between these and the present book, the context is quite different. This book primarily focuses on exploring various aspects of the process-oriented paradigm as an alternative to the traditional data-oriented paradigm.

As it is not a typical publication focused on a new technology, technique, or methodology, this book necessarily takes an expansive and comprehensive look at end-to-end aspects of the envisaged process-centric paradigm.

Distinguishing between business process management (BPM) as a business program and BPM systems (BPMS) as its subset realization into a software application, Chapter 10 first introduces the concept of BPM and its characteristics. It explains the concept of BPMS and its variation of enterprise process management systems (EPMS) being brought into focus in this book. In contrast to BPMS, which reflect the "data item"-driven, reusability-focused, *bottom-up* stance of the traditional information technology (IT)-focused view of the enterprise, EPMS embody a "business process"-driven, requirements-focused, *top-down* stance of the information systems view of the enterprise. EPMS promote a world-view of process-driven or process-centric systems supported by a portfolio of systems like process bases, process warehouses, process intelligence, and process analytics. This book is a small step—or at least an expression of the need to move—in that direction.

As a preparatory step to EPMS, Chapter 5 describes the process views and perspectives that enable an enterprise process architecture. Analogous to the enterprise architecture frameworks for enterprise architecture described in Chapter 4, this chapter describes the workflow reference model as the reference process architecture for the enterprise process architecture.

This book proposes that instead of the customary *data item* in the traditional IT systems, the *business process* should become the smallest identifiable and addressable entity within any enterprise system. In other words, rather than the isolated data items or attributes of the entities of the traditional IT systems, it should be the processes (that access, create, or modify the data item or attribute) that should become the focus of enterprise systems. Enterprise systems should be reengineered from the present data-centric architecture to a process-centric architecture—hence, the reason to term the reengineered systems with a different term, namely, EPMS.

This is not as far-fetched as it may seem at the first sight. SAP SE's (Walldorf, Germany) move to introduce SAP S/4HANA can be read as a step back from the data-centric world view. This can be repurposed to enable SAP Process Orchestration (SAP PO) (along with the Eclipse-based Developer Studio) to become the cross-development workbench for S/4HANA to reengineer the data-centric functionality populating the traditional modules of FI-CO, SD, MM, PP, QM, and so on to a process-centric functionality.

In the earlier "data-driven" paradigm, batch mode systems did not create enough transaction data for justifying data mining or analytics. Even online systems including enterprise resource planning systems front-ended by functional menus did not generate enough data; correspondingly, the "reporting" was deemed to be good enough—it did not generate the need for analytics. Data mining/analytics took off only after the advent of Big Data caused by Web-based applications like social media and mobile.

In the "process-driven" paradigm focused on in this book, online enterprise systems front-ended by *functional menus* did not create enough process data for justifying process mining or analytics. This will happen only when enterprise systems are front-ended by *process menus* for which the enterprise system must be reengineered internally like the process-centric systems mentioned earlier.

The real significance of business processes can be understood in the context of current heightened priority on digital transformation of enterprises. Conceiving the roadmap to realize a digitally transformed enterprise via business model innovation becomes amenable only from the *process view* of the enterprise—from the conventional *data view*, this would become an unaddressable problem.

 With the advent of SMACT (social networks, mobile computing, analytics, cloud computing and Internet of Things), future IS/IT systems would need bigger portions of design thinking especially at the requirements stage. This book is also an exercise in an alternate design.

Author

Vivek Kale has more than two decades of professional IT experience during which he has handled and consulted on various aspects of enterprise-wide information modeling, enterprise architectures, business process redesign, and, electronic business architectures. He has been Group CIO of Essar Group, the steel/oil and gas major of India, as well as of Raymond Ltd., the textile and apparel major of India. He is a seasoned practitioner in digital transformation, facilitating business agility via process-centric enterprises and enhancing data-driven enterprise intelligence. He is the author of *Guide to Cloud Computing for Business and Technology Managers: From Distributed Computing to Cloudware Applications,* CRC Press (2015).

Other Books by Vivek Kale

Creating Smart Enterprises: Leveraging Cloud, Big Data, Web, Social Media, Mobile and IoT Technologies (CRC Press, 2018).

Enterprise Performance Intelligence and Decision Patterns (CRC Press, 2018).

Agile Network Businesses: Collaboration, Coordination and Competitive Advantage (CRC Press, 2017).

Big Data Computing: A Guide for Business and Technology Managers (CRC Press, 2017).

Enhancing Enterprise Intelligence: Leveraging ERP, CRM, SCM, PLM, BPM, and BI (CRC Press, 2016).

Guide to Cloud Computing for Business and Technology Managers: From Distributed Computing to Cloudware Applications (CRC Press, 2015).

Inverting the Paradox of Excellence: How Companies Use Variations for Business Excellence and How Enterprise Variations Are Enabled by SAP (CRC Press, 2015).

Implementing SAP® CRM: The Guide for Business and Technology Managers (CRC Press, 2015).

Implementing Oracle Siebel CRM (Tata McGraw-Hill, 2010).

Implementing SAP R/3: A Guide for Business and Technology Managers (Sams, 2000).

1

Enterprise Systems

Enterprise systems (ES) are an information system that integrates business processes with the aim of creating value and reducing costs by making the right information available to the right people at the right time to help them make good decisions in managing resources proactively and productively. Enterprise resource planning (ERP) is comprised of multi-module application software packages that serve and support multiple business functions. These large, automated cross-functional systems were designed to bring about improved operational efficiency and effectiveness through integrating, streamlining, and improving fundamental back-office business processes.

Traditional ES (like ERP systems) were called back-office systems because they involved activities and processes in which the customer and general public were not typically involved, at least not directly. Functions supported by ES typically include accounting; manufacturing; human resource management; purchasing; inventory management; inbound and outbound logistics; marketing; finance; and, to some extent, engineering. The objectives of traditional ES in general were greater efficiency and, to a lesser extent, effectiveness. Contemporary ES have been designed to streamline and integrate operation processes and information flows within a company to promote synergy and greater organizational effectiveness as well as innovation. These newer ES have moved beyond the back-office to support front-office processes and activities like those that are fundamental to customer relationship management.

1.1 Evolution of Enterprise Systems

ES have evolved from simple materials requirement planning (MRP) to ERP, extended enterprise systems (EES), and beyond. Table 1.1 gives a snapshot of the various stages of ES.

1.1.1 Materials Requirement Planning

The first practical efforts in the ES field occurred at the beginning of the 1970s, when computerized applications based on MRP methods were developed to support purchasing and production scheduling activities. MRP is a heuristic based on three main inputs: the Master Production Schedule, which specifies how many products are going to be produced during a period of time; the Bill of Materials, which describes how those products are going to be built and what materials are going to be required; and the Inventory Record File, which reports how many products, components, and materials are held in-house. The method can easily be programmed in any basic computerized application, as it follows deterministic assumptions and a well-defined algorithm.

TABLE 1.1

Evolution of Enterprise Systems (ESs)

System	Primary Business Need(s)	Scope	Enabling Technology
MRP	Efficiency	Inventory management and production planning and control	Mainframe computers, batch processing, traditional file systems
MRP II	Efficiency effectiveness, and integration of manufacturing systems	Extending to the entire manufacturing firm (becoming cross-functional)	Mainframes and minicomputers, real-time (time-sharing) processing, database management systems (relational)
ERP	Efficiency (primarily back-office), effectiveness, and integration of all organizational systems	Entire organization (increasingly cross-functional), both manufacturing and nonmanufacturing operations	Mainframes, mini- and microcomputers, client/server networks with distributed processing and distributed databases, data warehousing, mining, knowledge management
ERP II	Efficiency effectiveness and integration within and among enterprises	Entire organization extending to other organizations (cross-functional and cross-enterprise partners, suppliers, customers, etc.)	Mainframes, client/server systems, distributed computing, knowledge management, Internet technology (includes intranets, extranets, portals)
Interenterprise resource planning, enterprise systems, supply chain management, or whatever label gains common acceptance	Efficiency effectiveness, coordination, and integration within and among all relevant supply chain members as well as other partners or stakeholders on a global scale	Entire organization and its constituents (increasingly global and cross-cultural) composing the global supply chain from beginning to end as well as other industry and government constituents	Internet, service-oriented architecture, application service providers, wireless networking, mobile wireless, knowledge management, grid computing, artificial intelligence

MRP employs a type of backward scheduling wherein lead times are used to work backwards from a due date to an order release date. While the primary objective of MRP was to compute material requirements, the MRP system proved also to be a useful scheduling tool. Order placement and order delivery were planned by the MRP system. Not only were orders for materials and components generated by an MRP system, production orders for manufacturing operations that used those materials and components to make higher level items like subassemblies and finished products were also created.

 As MRP systems became popular and more and more companies started using them, practitioners, vendors, and researchers started to realize that the data and information produced by the MRP system in the course of material requirements planning and production scheduling could be augmented with additional data and used for other purposes. One of the earliest add-ons was the Capacity Requirements Planning module, which could be used in developing capacity plans to produce the master production schedule. Manpower planning and support for human resources management were also incorporated into MRP. Distribution management capabilities were added. The enhanced MRP and its many modules provided data useful in the financial planning of manufacturing operations; thus, financial planning capabilities were added. Business needs, primarily for operational efficiency and to a lesser extent for greater effectiveness, and advancements in computer processing and storage technology brought about MRP and influenced its evolution. What started as an efficiency-oriented tool for production and inventory management was becoming increasingly a cross-functional system.

1.1.2 Closed-Loop Materials Requirement Planning

A very important capability that evolved in MRP systems was the ability to close the loop (control loop). This was largely because of the development of real-time (closed loop) MRP systems to replace regenerative MRP systems in response to changing business needs and improved computer technology—that is, time-sharing replaced batch processing as the dominant computer processing mode. With time-sharing mainframe systems, the MRP system could run 24/7 and update continuously. Use of the corporate mainframe that performed other important computing tasks for the enterprise was not practical for some companies, because MRP consumed too many system resources; subsequently, some companies opted to use mainframes (now growing smaller and cheaper, but increasing in processing speed and storage capability) or mini-computers (which could do more, were faster than old mainframes) that could be dedicated to MRP. MRP could now respond (update relevant records) to timely data fed into the system and produced by the system. This closed the control loop with timely feedback for decision-making by incorporating current data from the factory floor, warehouse, vendors, transportation companies, and other internal and external sources, thus giving the MRP system the capability to provide current (almost real-time) information for better planning and control. These closed-loop systems better reflected the realities of the production floor, logistics, inventory, and more. It was this transformation of MRP into a planning and control tool for manufacturing by closing the loop, along with all the additional modules that did more than plan materials— they both planned and controlled various manufacturer resources—that led to MRP II. Here, too, improved computer technology and the evolving business needs for more accurate and timely information to support decision-making and greater organizational effectiveness contributed to the evolution from MRP to MRP II.

1.1.3 Manufacturing Requirement Planning II

The MRP in MRP II stands for "manufacturing resource planning," rather than "materials requirements planning." At this point, the MRP system had evolved from a material requirements planning system into a planning and control system for resources in manufacturing operations—an enterprise information system for manufacturing. As time passed, MRP II systems became more widespread and more sophisticated, particularly when used in manufacturing to support and complement computer-integrated manufacturing. Databases started replacing traditional file systems, allowing for better systems integration and greater query capabilities to support decision-makers, and the telecommunications network became an integral part of these systems in order to support communications between and coordination among system components that were sometimes geographically distributed but still present within the company.

1.1.4 Enterprise Resource Planning

During the late 1970s and early 1980s, new advances in information technology (IT), such as local area networks, personal computers, and object-orientated programming as well as more accurate operations management heuristics allowed some of MRPs deterministic assumptions to be relaxed, particularly the assumption of infinite capacity. MRP II was developed based on MRP principles, but incorporated some important operational restrictions such as available capacity, maintenance turnaround time, and financial considerations. MRP II also introduced simulation options to enable the exploration and evaluation of different scenarios. MRP II is defined as business planning, sales and operations planning, production scheduling, MRP, capacity requirements planning, and the execution support systems for capacity and material. Output from these systems is integrated with financial reports such as the business plan, purchase commitment report, shipping budget, and inventory projections in dollars. An important contribution of the MRP II approach was the integration of financial considerations, improving management control and performance of operations and making different manufacturing approaches comparable. However, while MRP II allowed for the integration of sales, engineering, manufacturing, storage, and finance, these areas continued to be managed as isolated systems. In other words, there was no real online integration and the system did not provide integration with other critical support areas, such as accounting, human resource management, quality control, and distribution.

The need for greater efficiency and effectiveness in back-office operations was not unique to manufacturing; it was also common to nonmanufacturing operations. Companies in nonmanufacturing sectors such as health care, financial services, air transportation, and the consumer goods sector started to use MRP II-like systems to manage critical resources. Early ERP systems typically ran on mainframes like their predecessors, MRP and MRP II, but many migrated to client/server systems where networks were central and distributed databases were more common. The growth of ERP and the migration to client/server systems really got a boost from the Y2K scare. Many companies were convinced of the need to replace older main-frame-based systems, some ERP and some not, with the newer client/server architecture.

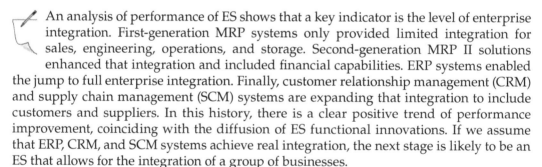 An analysis of performance of ES shows that a key indicator is the level of enterprise integration. First-generation MRP systems only provided limited integration for sales, engineering, operations, and storage. Second-generation MRP II solutions enhanced that integration and included financial capabilities. ERP systems enabled the jump to full enterprise integration. Finally, customer relationship management (CRM) and supply chain management (SCM) systems are expanding that integration to include customers and suppliers. In this history, there is a clear positive trend of performance improvement, coinciding with the diffusion of ES functional innovations. If we assume that ERP, CRM, and SCM systems achieve real integration, the next stage is likely to be an ES that allows for the integration of a group of businesses.

1.2 Extended Enterprise Systems

The most salient trend in the continuing evolution of ES is the focus on front-office applications and interorganizational business processes, particularly in support of supply chain management. At present, greater organizational effectiveness in managing the entire supply chain all the way to the end customer is a priority in business. The greater emphasis on front-office functions and cross enterprise communications and collaboration via the Internet simply reflects changing business needs and priorities. The demand for specific modules/capabilities in particular shows that businesses are looking beyond the enterprise. This external focus is encouraging vendors to seize the moment by responding with the modules/systems that meet evolving business needs. In this renewed context, ES enable enterprises to integrate and coordinate their business processes. They provide a single system that is central to the enterprise and ensure that information can be shared across all functional levels and management hierarchies.

ES are creeping out of the back-office into the front and beyond the enterprise to customers, suppliers, and more in order to meet changing business needs. Key players like Baal; Oracle Corp. (Redwood City, CA, USA); PeopleSoft (Pleasanton, CA, USA); and SAP SE (Walldorf, Germany) have incorporated advanced planning and scheduling, sales force automation, CRM, SCM, business intelligence, and electronic (e-) commerce modules/ capabilities into their systems, or repositioned their ES as part of broader ES suites incorporating these and other modules/capabilities. ES products reflect the evolving business needs of clients and the capabilities of IT, perhaps most notably those related to the Web. Traditional ES (i.e., ERP) have not lost their significance become because back-office efficiency, effectiveness, and flexibility will continue to be important. However, the current focus seems more to be external, as enterprises look for ways to support and improve relationships and interactions with customers, suppliers, partners, and other stakeholders. While integration of internal functions is still important and, in many enterprises, still has not been achieved to a great extent, external integration is now receiving much attention.

1.2.1 Extended Enterprise Systems Framework

The conceptual framework of EES consists of four distinct layers:

- A foundation layer
- A process layer
- An analytical layer
- An e-business layer

Each layer consists of collaborative components as described in Table 1.2.

1.2.1.1 Foundation Layer

The foundation layer consists of the core components of EES, which shape the underlying architecture and also provide a platform for the EES systems. EES does not need to be centralized or monolithic. One of the core components is the integrated database, which may be a distributed database. Another core component is the application framework, which also can be distributed. The integrated database and the application framework provide an open and distributed platform for EES.

1.2.1.2 Process Layer

The process layer of the concept is the central component of EES, which is Web-based, open, and componentized (this is different from being Web-enabled) and may be implemented as a set of distributed Web services. This layer corresponds to the traditional transaction-based systems. ERP still makes up the backbone of EES along with the

TABLE 1.2

Four Layers of EES

Layer		Components
Foundation	Core	Integrated database (DB)
		Application framework (AF)
Process	Central	Enterprise resource planning (ERP)
		Business process management (BPM)
Analytical	Corporate	Supply chain management (SCM)
		Customer relationship management (CRM)
		Supplier relationship management (SRM)
		Product lifecycle management (PLM)
		Employee lifecycle management (ELM)
		Corporate performance management (CPM)
Portal	Collaborative	Business-to-consumer (B2C)
		Business-to-business (B2B)
		Business-to-employee (B2E)
		Enterprise application integration (EAI)

additional integrated modules aimed at new business sectors outside the manufacturing industries. The backbone of ERP is the traditional ERP modules such as financials, sales and distribution, logistics, manufacturing, or human resources.

The EES concept is based on business process management. ERP has been based on "best practice" process reference models, but EES systems primarily build on the notion of the process as the central entity. EES includes tools to manage processes, design (or orchestrate) processes, execute and evaluate processes (business activity monitoring), and redesign processes in real-time. The business process management component allows for EES to be accommodated to suit different business practices for specific business segments that otherwise would require effort-intensive customization. EES further includes vertical solutions for specific segments like apparel and footwear or the public sector. Vertical solutions are sets of standardized, preconfigured systems and processes with "add-ons" to match the specific requirements of a specific sector.

1.2.1.3 Analytical Layer

The analytical layer consists of the corporate components that extend and enhance the central ERP functions by providing decision support to manage relations and corporate issues. Corporate components are not necessarily synchronized with the integrated database and the components may easily be "add-ons" instituted by acquiring third-party products/vendors. In the future, the list of components for this layer can be augmented by newer additions like product lifecycle management (ERP for the research and development function) and employee lifecycle management (ERP for human resources).

1.2.1.4 Electronic Business Layer

The e-business layer is the portal of the EES systems and this layer consists of a set of collaborative components. The collaborative components deal with the communication and the integration between the corporate ERP II system and actors like the customer, business partners, employees, and even external systems.

1.2.2 Extended Functionality

E-commerce is arguably one of the most important developments in business in the last 50 years, and mobile (m-) commerce is poised to take its place alongside or within the rapidly growing area of e-commerce. Internet technology has made e-commerce in its many forms (business to business, business to customer, customer to customer, etc.) possible. Mobile and wireless technology are expected to enable individuals to always access the Internet and make the provision "anytime/anywhere" location-based services (also requiring global positioning systems) a reality, as well as a host of other capabilities characteristic of m-business. One can expect to see ES geared more to the support of both e-commerce and m-commerce. The Internet and mobile and wireless technology should figure prominently in new and improved system modules and capabilities.

The current business emphasis on intra- and interorganizational process integration and external collaboration should remain a driving force in the evolution of ES in the foreseeable future. Some businesses are attempting to transform themselves from traditional, vertically integrated enterprises into multi-enterprise, "recombinant entities" reliant on core-competency-based strategies. Integrated SCM and business networks will receive great emphasis, reinforcing the importance of IT support for cross-enterprise collaboration and interenterprise processes. ES will have to support the required interactions and processes among and within business entities, and work with other systems/modules that do the same. There will be great need for business processes to span organizational boundaries (some do at present), possibly requiring a single shared interenterprise system that will do it, or at least communicate with and coprocess (share/divide processing tasks) with other ES.

Middleware, ASPs, and enterprise portal technologies may play an important role in the integration of such modules and systems. Widespread adoption of a single ASP solution among supply chain partners may facilitate interoperability, as all supply chain partners essentially use the same system. Alternatively, a supply chain portal (vertical portal), jointly owned by supply chain partners or a value-added service provider that coordinates the entire supply chain and powered by a single system serving all participants, could be the model for the future. ASP solutions are moving the ES within reach of SMEs, as it costs much less to "rent" than to "buy."

The capability of Web services to allow businesses to share data, applications, and processes across the Internet may result in ES of the future relying heavily on the idea of service-oriented architecture, within which Web services are created and stored, providing the building blocks for programs and systems. The use of "best in breed" Web service-based solutions might be more palatable to businesses, since it might be easier and less risky to plug-in a new Web service-based solution than replace or add-on a new product module. While the "one source" alternative seems most popular at present, the "best in breed" approach will be good if greater interoperability/integration among vendor products is achieved. There is a need for greater "out of the box" interoperability, thus a need for standards.

Data warehouses and knowledge management systems should enable future ERP systems to support more automated business decision-making and should be helpful in the complex decision-making needed in the context of fully integrated supply chain management. More automated decision-making in both front-office and back-office systems should eliminate/minimize human variability and error, greatly increase decision speed, and hopefully improve decision quality. Business intelligence tools, which are experiencing a significant growth in popularity, take internal and external data and transform it into information used in building knowledge that helps decision-makers to make more *informed* decisions.

 Greater interoperability of diverse systems and more thorough integration within and between enterprise systems is likely to remain the highest priority for all enterprises. An environment for business applications much like the "plug and play" environment for hardware environment would make it easier for enterprises to integrate their own systems and have their systems integrated with other organizations' systems. Such an environment necessitates greater standardization. This ideal "plug and play" environment would make it easier for firms to opt for a "best in breed" strategy for application/module acquisition as opposed to reliance on a single vendor for a complete package of front-office, back-office, and strategic systems.

1.3 Enterprise System Packages and Bespoke Solutions

In the past few decades, all of us have witnessed a procession of different methodologies, tools, and techniques emanating from the software industry that have had a tremendous impact on the very nature and operations of business enterprises. However, in the midst of all this turmoil, one fact has remained constant and that has been the lack of productivity improvements, irrespective of the extent and nature of computerization.

Right from the start, though, there was an even more basic problem in terms of the number of software applications that were actually completed and implemented successfully. Much has been written on the software crisis that engulfed information service groups in the 1980s. The reasons were multifold, as follows:

- With the advent of PC-like functionalities, users were becoming more aware and demanding.
- Consequently, applications were becoming bigger and more complex.
- Correspondingly, productivity was reducing rather than increasing.
- Software development times were increasing and cost and time overruns were fairly routine.
- Quality-trained professionals were always in short supply, resulting in increased costs for programmers; hence, systems development costs were ever-increasing.
- The mortality of systems was very high.

On average, out of the total number of IT systems under development, more than half used to be cancelled; of the remaining half, only about two-thirds were delivered. Half the delivered systems never got implemented, while another quarter were abandoned midway through implementation. Of the residual quarter of the delivered systems, half failed to deliver the functionality required by the management and were therefore scrapped. Only the remaining half of the systems was used after great modifications, which entailed further delays and costs in an almost neverending process.

One of the root causes identified for these problems was the inherent weakness of the phase in which requirements were captured and analyzed. This phase never seemed to

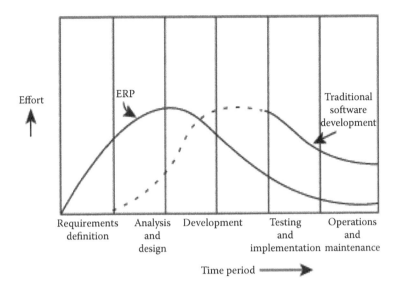

FIGURE 1.1
Comparison of efforts expended during ERP and traditional software development life cycles.

get the correct and complete requirements. As a result, completed projects never seemed to deliver on the promised functionality and had to be recycled for more analysis and development. Maintenance and enhancements were called for indefinitely and became harder to undertake as time went by. Because individuals often changed midway, both on the development and user sides, system requirements changed frequently and the whole process continued indefinitely. This is primarily because there is a fundamental disconnect between the business and the IT/information systems (IS) people. Notwithstanding how much both of the parties try to bridge the gap, there is a fundamental chasm between the perception of a business user and what is understood by the systems staff; in effect, both classes of people speak different languages. Even if the systems personnel tried to increase precision by using methodologies and specification tools, they were never able to ratify the documented requirements completely because users were unfamiliar with these tools.

Typically, surveys found that 50%–80% of the IT/IS resources were dedicated to application maintenance. The return on investment in IT was abysmally low by any standard of measurement and expectation. With IT/IS budgets stretching beyond the capabilities of most organizations, there was a compelling need for a radically new approach that could result in actual usable functionality that was professionally developed, under control, and on time (Figure 1.1).

The traditional software implementation involving the development of applications was characterized by the following:

- Requirement-driven functional decomposition
- Late risk resolution
- Late error detection
- Use of different languages or artifacts at different phases of the project
- Large proportion of scrap and rework
- Adversarial stakeholder relationships with non-IT users

- Priority of techniques over tools
- Priority of quality of developed software rather than functionality, per se
- Greater emphasis on current, correct, complete, and consistent documentation
- Greater emphasis on testing and reviews
- Major effort on change control and management
- Large and diverse resource requirements
- Schedules always under pressure
- Greater effort on projected or estimated target performance
- Inherent limitations on scalability
- Protracted integration between systems

Many alternate strategies were devised like computer-aided software engineering (CASE) and prototyping; however, none were able to cross this basic hurdle. CASE provided a more rigorous environment for requirement analysis and design and automated to a large extent the subsequent development of code, testing, and documentation efforts. The increased time spent on requirements definition with the users was envisaged to lead to systems that were closer to the user's actual requirements. On the other hand, prototyping was designed to address the requirement capture issue by making the users directly participate in the process of defining the requirements. This was mainly focused on the screen and reports design because these were the elements that could be visualized directly by the user. However, none of these strategies really resolved the problem. Packages like ERP and CRM adopted a totally different approach by providing the most comprehensive functionality within the package. Company personnel were only expected to pick and choose whatever was required by the company actually using the package. Thus, ES packages effectively short-circuited the whole issue of capturing requirements. The traditional project life cycle consisting of analysis, design, development, testing, and implementation was transformed to the ES implementation life cycle consisting merely of requirement mapping, gap analysis, configuring and customizing, testing, and implementation.

Figure 1.1 shows a comparison of efforts expended during ES and traditional software development life cycles.

This ultimately led to the ERP and ES revolution that we are witnessing today.

Unlike the traditional systems, the ES software implementations involving the implementations of preengineered, ready-to-implement application modules are characterized by the following:

- Primacy of the architecture, process-oriented configurability
- Primacy and direct participation of the business user
- Early risk resolution
- Early error and gap detection
- Iterative life-cycle process, negligible proportion of scrap and rework
- Changeable and configurable functionality
- Participatory and cohesive stakeholder relationships with non-IT users
- Priority of functionality over tools followed by techniques
- Quality of the functional variability and flexibility of the available functionality

- Greater emphasis on current, correct, complete, and consistent documentation of customizations
- Greater emphasis on integration testing
- Actual demonstration of functionality at all phases of the project
- Twin categories of resource requirements—functional and technical
- Schedules devoid of long-term cascading impact
- Demonstrated performance
- Larger span of scalability
- Efficient integration between systems

Off-the-shelf packages and especially enterprise-wide solutions such as ES were considered to be the best approach for confronting the software crisis of the 1980s. This was because of the following:

- ES ensure better validation of user requirements directly by the user.
- ES ensure consistent quality of delivered functionality.
- ES provide a cohesive and integrated information system architecture.
- ES ensure a fair degree of standardization.
- ES provide a consistent and accurate documentation of the system.
- ES provide outstanding quality and productivity in the development and maintenance of the system.

As companies are reporting their couple of decades of experience in implementing and operating on ES, a base of experience seems to support the fact that companies that plan and manage the use of ES are usually successful. It is no longer a matter of learning only new technology; it is now about applying the new technology effectively and addressing the problems of inertia and resistance to change across the enterprise. Today, the recognized management decision is not whether to use an ES but rather when to use an ES and which ES package to use.

1.4 Enterprise Resource Planning

In the early days, the most important systems in manufacturing companies were known as MRP-based systems. After two decades, MRP systems evolved into MRP II, but it was many years before ERP systems were first implemented, and these systems have continue to evolve since.

In the 1960s, MRP emerged with the rapid evolution of computers. The main emphasis of these systems was to manage inventory, and the use of MRP helped companies to control their inventory based on actual demand rather than reorder points. To do this, MRP used a set of techniques that took into account bills of material data, inventory data, and the master production schedule to predict future requirements for materials. A finished product was subdivided into its components and, for every component, a time schedule was developed. Based on this list, using computers, all necessary information required for the production of this specific product could be obtained in a very short time. The critical subcomponents could be tracked easily and, if necessary, could be obtained quickly to support on-time production. The critical path (time, resources, etc.) could be defined and orders could be organized in order to prevent time delays in the receipt of materials. However, even this simple procedure became tedious once the number of parts increased. Thus, a computer was essential to carry out these features of MRP. To sum up the benefits of MRP, it reduced the level of inventory a company needed to maintain, lowered production times by improving coordination and avoiding delays, and increased the company's overall efficiency.

In the 1980s, companies transitioned to MRP II. This system allowed manufacturers to optimize materials, procurement, manufacturing processes, and so forth, while at the same time providing financial and planning reports. The underlying idea behind the MRP II concept was to integrate MRP with further manufacturing functions and other business functions. MRP II was designed to assist in the effective planning of all of the resources available to a manufacturing company. Ideally, it addressed operational planning in units and financial planning in dollars and included a simulation capability with which to answer what-if questions. It included business planning, sales and operations planning, production scheduling, MRP, and capacity requirements planning, along with executive support systems that could be used to balance capacities and materials.

Toward the end of the 1980s, many business processes such as logistics, procurement, and financial accounting needed to be integrated to allow companies to operate at their maximum efficiency. Actually, software systems to automate each of these internal business processes already existed, and these were very efficient in their own areas. However, their relative autonomy and limited real-time interaction were major problems that had to be solved. The divisions did not exchange data with each other, or, even if they did exchange data, it was poorly coordinated, which caused substantial problems that decreased the efficiency of the systems. For example, it was impossible for accounting systems to exchange data with manufacturing systems, and the time lag for exchanging data was so large that it brought no benefits for either division.

1.4.1 Concept of Enterprise Resource Planning

The main focus of ERP has been to integrate and synchronize the isolated functions into streamlined business processes. ERP evolved considerably over the next 30 years as a result of continuous improvements in business management and the development of new information technologies. The ERP concept was first implemented at the end of the 1980s with the development of better client/server technology that enabled the implementation of an ERP system. ERP is a cross-functional enterprise backbone that integrates and automates many internal business processes and IS within the sales and distribution, production, logistics, accounting, and human resources functions of a company.

ERP not only coordinates multiple divisions but also requires companies to enter data only once for the information to be distributed to all of the integrated business processes. ERP systems consist of several integrated suites of software modules, which share common data and provide connectivity. Once the data have been recorded, they are available for all of the company's divisions. The information about the processes in the company is represented consistently and is up to date in all business divisions at all times.

There is a substantial difference between the concept of ERP and ERP systems. ERP is a concept of a much broader scope than the ERP systems that implement a subset of the tenets of ERP. In this chapter, after introducing the concept of ERP, the discussion will focus on leveraging the ERP-oriented capabilities of the enterprises.

1.4.2 Enterprise Resource Planning System

There is no generally accepted definition of ERP in the offerings in the market. Not only is there little agreement on what it really stands for, there is even less agreement on what constitutes an ERP package, how it should be used, the potential of productivity gain, the impact on the enterprise, the costs involved, the personnel needed, or the training required for the ERP personnel. Its characteristics are not limited to the ERP products and tools that are currently available in the market, and it is certainly not a technique or methodology. It is preferable not to attempt to contain ERP within a single set of current ideas but rather to look at ERP as a developing area of enterprise computerization with expanding boundaries. There is every reason to believe that the boundaries described for ERP in this book will be constantly enlarging in the coming years. Notwithstanding all this caveats, ERP could be defined reasonably as follows:

> An ERP software applications package is a suit of preengineered, ready-to-implement integrated application modules catering to all of the business functions of an enterprise and which possesses the flexibility for configuring and customizing dynamically the delivered functionality of the package to suit the specific requirements of the enterprise. ERP enables an enterprise to operate as an integrated enterprise-wide, process-oriented, information-driven real-time enterprise.

> ERP systems can provide this comprehensiveness and flexibility because, at the heart of the system, resides a CASE-like repository that stores all details of these pre-developed applications. These details include every single data item, data table, and software program that is used by the complete system. For instance, SAP has more than 800 application process definitions stored in about 8,000 tables within its repository. It also has additional support subsystems that help it to manage, secure, and maintain the operations of this package on a day-to-day basis. ERP systems are a major development based on the initial ideas about information engineering put forward by Clive Finkelstein in Australia around 1980. He crystallized the basic idea that systems analysis could be engineered. Information engineering approaches essentially treat applications development environment as an application in and of itself. The development can be designed and managed with an expectation that the users will request many changes; importantly, the systems are designed to accommodate such changes. The integrated application repository holds a full set of correlated information regarding the application, which also greatly facilitates documentation, testing, and maintenance. The major development of the ERP systems over the information engineering approaches was in terms of providing predefined, already-built-in comprehensive functionality of the application systems.

> The success of ERP packages is based on the principle of reusability. It is not a very new concept in the computer industry. The origin of reusability goes back almost to the beginning of the computer era in the middle of the last century

when it was recognized early that far too much program code was being written and rewritten repeatedly and uneconomically. Very soon, most of the programming languages provided for routines or packets of logic that could be reused multiple times within individual programs or even by a group of programs. Databases enabled the reuse of data, resulting in a tremendous surge in programmer productivity. Similarly, networks permitted reuse of the same programs on different terminals or workstations at different locations. ERP basically extended the concept of reusability to the functionality provided by the package. For instance, any ERP is based on the essential commonality that was observed in the functioning of companies within an industry. ERP systems built a reusable library of normally required processes in a particular industry; all that implementing ERP customers had to do was to select from this library all those processes that were required by their company. From a project effort and cost that was essential for the development and implementation using the traditional software development life cycle, ERP reduced the project effort and cost only to that associated with the implementation phase of the software development life cycle. A comparison of the traditional software development life cycle and postmodern ERP implementations is shown in Figure 1.2. Even though the cost of implementing ERP may seem higher than that for the traditional systems, ERP can be implemented sooner and, therefore, start delivering all of the possible benefits much earlier than the traditional systems. The fabled library of 800 best-of-class processes made available right from SAP R/3 (now SAP SE, Walldorf, Germany) is like building blocks or components that can be reused by any customer to build their system quickly and at a considerably reduced cost.

In the early 1990s, all software crisis situations underwent a dramatic change with the arrival of ERP systems. ERP systems changed the basic developmental model of implementing computerized systems within enterprises to that of implementing off-the-shelf, ready-made packages that covered every aspect of the function and operations of an enterprise. It provided an integrated set of functional modules corresponding to all major functions within the enterprise. It engendered the concept of implementing all of these modules as an integrated whole rather than in a piecemeal fashion. Although there have not been any published results as of yet, it became an accepted fact that enterprises that implemented ERP systems only for a part of their enterprises or only for a few select functions within their enterprises did not benefit greatly. Also, for the first time in the history of IT, ERP systems gave indication of the recognition of the fact that business processes of an enterprise were much more fundamental than time-invariant data characterizing various aspects of the enterprise. Furthermore, most importantly, ERP systems elevated IS from a mere enabler of business strategy of an organization to a significant part of the business strategy itself. Thus, ERP systems brought to an end the subsidiary and support roles that IT had played throughout the last few decades. However, in turn, the very nature of IS has also undergone a complete transformation (see Subsection 1.4.3.6). Implementation of an ERP within an enterprise was no longer a problem of technology; it was a business problem. ERP systems have been the harbingers of a paradigm shift in the role of the IS/IT function within an enterprise. The writing of this book was also motivated by the need to address these fundamental changes in the very nature of IS/IT activity within an enterprise.

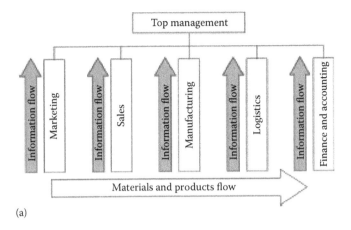

(a)

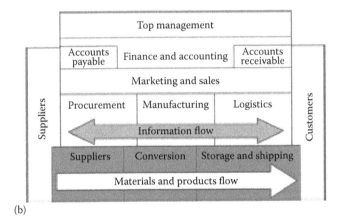

(b)

FIGURE 1.2
Information and material flows in (a) a functional business model and (b) a business process model.

1.4.3 Characteristics of Enterprise Resource Planning

The distinguishing characteristics of ERP are as follows:

- ERP transforms an enterprise into an information-driven enterprise.
- ERP fundamentally perceives an enterprise as a global enterprise.
- ERP reflects and mimics the integrated nature of an enterprise.
- ERP fundamentally models a process-oriented enterprise.
- ERP enables the real-time enterprise.
- ERP elevates IT strategy as a part of the business strategy.
- ERP represents a major advance on the earlier manufacturing performance improvement approaches.
- ERP represents the new departmental store model of implementing computerized systems.
- ERP is a mass-user-oriented application environment.

In the remaining part of this section, we introduce the concept of ERP and deal with each of these characteristics of ERP systems. There is also a need for a unifying framework that would bring together the various aspects of an ERP implementation. These include aspects of business competitiveness; information-based organizations; integrative and collaborative strategies; process-oriented, real-time operations; employee empowerment; information capital and knowledge assets; organizational learning; business engineering; change management; and virtual value chains and strategic alliances.

1.4.3.1 Enterprise Resource Planning Transforms the Enterprise into an Information-Driven Enterprise

All computerized systems and solutions in the past were using past-facing information merely for the purpose of referring and reporting only. ERP, for the first time in the history of computerized systems, began treating information as a resource for the operational requirements of the enterprise. However, unlike the traditional resources, information resource as made available by ERP systems can be reused and shared multiply without dissipation or degradation. The impressive productivity gains resulting from the ERP systems truthfully arise out of this unique characteristic of ERP systems to use information as an inexhaustible resource.

1.4.3.2 Enterprise Resource Planning Fundamentally Perceives an Enterprise as a Global Enterprise

In these times of divestitures, mergers, and acquisitions, this is an important requirement. Unlike some of the earlier enterprise-wide solutions available on mainframes, ERP systems cater to corporate-wide requirements even if an enterprise is involved in disparate businesses such as discrete industries (manufacturing, engineering, etc.); process industries (chemicals, paints, etc.); and services industries (banking, media, etc.). ERP enables the management to plan, operate, and manage such conglomerates without any impediments of mismatching of systems for different divisions.

Although it may seem to a minor point, ERP also permits the important functionality of enabling seamless integration of distributed or multilocation operations; we consider this aspect in the next section.

1.4.3.3 Enterprise Resource Planning Reflects and Mimics the Integrated Nature of an Enterprise

Notwithstanding the different ways in which many enterprises are structured and organized, enterprises function essentially in an integrated fashion. Across the years, the turf-preservation mentality has been rigidified even in the computerized systems deployed for the various functions. Under the garb of the fundamentally different nature of the activities and functions, a motley of IS had mushroomed within organization, reinforcing rather than lessening the heterogeneity of systems. This had led to problems of incompatibility, differing standards, interfacing issues, limited functional and technological upgrade paths, costly maintenance, high operating costs, costly training and support activities, inconsistent documentation, and so on. Instead of providing the strategic leverage necessary for the business operations of the enterprise, IS/IT systems became a constant drain on the enterprise and, truthfully, reduced their reaction times to the changes observed in the market space.

ERP with its holistic approach and its demand for integration dissolve all such efficiency-dissipating spurious processes not only in their IS/IT aspects but also in their actual functions. With a single centralized transparent, current, consistent, and complete database of all enterprise-related data, ERP in a masterstroke eliminated all wait times associated with all intracompany interactions. Integration as embodied in ERP eliminates many a non-value-added process. With its laser-like focus on best-of-business practices, ERP demonstrates glaringly the essential futility of routine bureaucratic mechanization within enterprises; it brings in consistency, discipline, and fast reaction times in the operations of a company. Thus, whereas finance may aim for minimizing stock, the purchasing function may want to maintain a buffer stock to avoid out-of-stock situations. Similarly, marketing may want production of more varied product models to cater to the requirements in the market, whereas production function will want to lessen the number of different kinds of products for reducing setup times and related costs. By promoting cross-functional processes and work teams, ERP offerings like SAP provides a powerful medium for supporting, reconciling, and optimizing the conflicting goals of different functions of the enterprises.

1.4.3.4 Enterprise Resource Planning Fundamentally Models a Process-Oriented Enterprise

As organizational and environmental conditions become more complex, globalized, and therefore competitive, processes provide a framework for dealing effectively with the issues of performance improvement, capability development, and adaptation to the changing environment. Process modeling permits the true comprehension of the characteristic structure and dynamics of the business. Business processes are the most important portions of the reality that had been ignored by the traditional IS. The traditional IT process modeling techniques, methodologies, and environments are a misnomer, for they truly model only the procedures for operating on the data associated at various points of the business subprocesses, which themselves are never mirrored within the system.

Conventional systems primarily store only snapshots of discrete groups of data at predefined or configured instants of time along a business process within an enterprise. This predominating, data-oriented view of the enterprise as implemented by the traditional IT systems is the most unnatural and alien way of looking at any area of human activity. The stability of the data models, as canonized in the conventional IT paradigm, may have been advantageous for the systems personnel but, for the same reason, they would have been unusable (and unacceptable) to the business stakeholders within the enterprises. Traditional systems could never really resolve this simple dichotomy of the fact that systems based on leveraging of the unchanging data models, although easy to maintain, can never describe the essentially dynamic nature of businesses. The lack of facilities for modeling business processes and business rules was the root cause of the resulting productivity paradox mentioned in the beginning of this section.

ERP systems for the first time recognized the fundamental error that was being perpetuated through these past few decades. Although many of the ERP packages still carry the legacy of the data-oriented view, the parallel view of business process and business rules is gaining prominence rapidly. This can also be seen to be the reason for the rapidly maturing groupware and workflow subsystems within the core architecture of current ERP systems.

1.4.3.5 Enterprise Resource Planning Enables the Real-Time Enterprise

ERP has engendered the earlier imagined-only possibility of a real-time enterprise. Even before the arrival of ERP systems, companies had witnessed the power and perils of operating an online system, which provided on-the-system direct registration of business transactions as well as immediate updates or postings to the relevant master and transaction data files. ERP has made this possible on an enterprise-wide scale and has realized tremendous gains in efficiencies and productivity by extending, as it were, the concept of just-in-time to the whole of the enterprise. Every system is a collection of many subsystems and processes, with life-cycle times of varying durations. A system that can respond effectively within the life-cycle time of some of the smaller life cycles can be considered to be functioning essentially in a real-time mode. As per this definition, for example, as far as the solar system is concerned, with reference to a life cycle of the Earth's rotation period of 365 days, forecasting the climatic conditions anytime within a period of 365 days could be termed as functioning in a real-time mode In analogy with this, for better appreciation of real-time responsiveness, enterprises could define enterprise standard time (EST). This could be defined based on the following:

1. A central reference location within the enterprise
2. An optimal cycle time in days or weeks suitable for all functions within the enterprise

All responses within the enterprise could be measured with reference to this EST. Enterprises that can cut down their EST relentlessly would be able to sustain their competitiveness in the market. This would become achievable to a large extent because of the instant availability of relevant information to all concerned members of the company provided by the ERP. Information is only relevant when it is available within a cycle of EST; information furnished after this period ceases to act as a resource and rapidly ends up being of value only for recording and reporting purposes. A continuous effort for reducing EST would result in a kind of customer responsiveness that would be unimaginable in earlier times.

Furthermore, the real-time responsiveness of the enterprise coupled with the earlier mentioned enterprise-wide integration also enables enterprises to have the powerful capability of concurrent processing, which would be impossible without ERP systems like SAP. Enterprises can obtain tremendous efficiencies and throughputs because of this ability to administer in parallel many a related processes that are not interdependent either fully or partially. In non-ERP enterprises, such closely related processes are typically done sequentially because they are usually handled by the same set of personnel, who may be obviously constrained to address them only in a sequence. An illustration of this could be an ad hoc analysis that may have to be done simultaneously on a set of POs and corresponding vendors/suppliers, deliveries, invoices, and so on. ERP systems like SAP can perform all these concurrently because of ready availability of all of the relevant, complete, and consistent information at the same time.

1.4.3.6 Enterprise Resource Planning Elevates Information Technology Strategy as a Part of the Business Strategy

The coming of ES heralded an enhanced role for IT systems. Indeed, they are no longer the support entities of the earlier years. If someone is under that illusion, they will pay a very high price, maybe even in terms of the corporeal death of the enterprise itself. Now, the real focus of IS/IT systems is on how to give the enterprise a competitive edge; such is part of the business necessities and priorities. Because of the complexity of increasing business change and uncertainty, good IS/IT abilities is business strategy incarnate!

This arises primarily from the fact that information itself has become a vital resource for an enterprise in the same league as the traditional resources like manpower, materials, money, and time.

1.4.3.7 *Enterprise Resource Planning Represents a Major Advance on the Earlier Manufacturing Performance Improvement Approaches*

ERP is the latest in the succession of approaches that have been adopted throughout the history of enterprises for the improvement of enterprise-level performances. ERP systems have realized the failed dream of improvements that were expected from the MRP II-based manufacturing resources planning systems of the 1970s. ERP systems have enabled combining the hard approach of MRP II with the much broader-scoped, soft approaches of world class manufacturing concepts that were widely adopted during the 1980s. The idea of world class manufacturing included such powerful approaches like just-in-time; total quality movement; benchmarking, lean manufacturing; human resource development movement; and, later in the 1990s, business process reengineering. Table 1.3 gives a list of major enterprise performance improvement movements during the last century. ERP systems provide the basic platform for devising techniques and tools for better implementations of the earlier approaches.

TABLE 1.3

Timeline of Performance Improvement Movements in the Twentieth Century

1690	Division of labor	Adam Smith
1890	Scientific measurement	Frederick Taylor
1900	Mass production	Henry Ford
1920	Industrial engineering	Frank Gilbreth and Frederick Taylor
1930	Human relations movement	Elton Mayo
1950	Japanese quality revolution	Joseph M. Juran and W. Edwards Deming
1960	Material requirements planning (MRP)	William Orlicky
1970	Manufacturing resource planning (MRP II)	Oliver Wright
1970	Focused factory	Wickham Skinner
1980	Total quality movement (TQM)	Philip Crosby
1980	Supplier-chain management (SCM)	
1980	Just-in-time (JIT)	Taiichi Ohno
1980	Computer-integrated manufacturing (CIM)	
1980	Optimized production technology (OPT)	Eliyahu Goldratt
1980	ISO 9000	National Standards Authority of Ireland
1980	World-class manufacturing (WCM)	Richard Schonberger
1990	Mass customization	Stan Davis and Joseph Pines II
1990	Lean manufacturing	James Womack, Daniel Jones, and Daniel Roos
1990	Business process reengineering (BPR)	Michael Hammer
1990	Enterprise resource planning (ERP)	
1990	Customer relationship management (CRM)	Frederick Riechheld
1990	Product lifecycle management (PLM)	
1990	Business intelligence (BI)	

1.4.3.8 Enterprise Resource Planning Represents the Departmental Store Model of Implementing Computerized Systems

The coming of ERP has been the death knell of the development model of IS systems and, along with it, has gone the concept of requirements capture, modeling languages, development of software programs, testing, and so on that have usually been associated with the conventional developmental model. In its place, for the first time, is the end-user-friendly model of what one could call the departmental store model of computerized systems. The reference here is to the fact that, rather than going through the complexities of specifying and getting a job done for you, you walk into a departmental store and, from the array of functional goodies on display, pick and choose the functionality required by you. An ERP is the analog of the great departmental store of functionalities or processes required within an enterprise. ERP makes the transition from the world of carefully engineered and running systems to, as it were, the world of consumers where the value of the delivered functionality is based not on its pedigree but only on what, how, where, and when it can be used gainfully.

This then is the final commoditization of the IS/IT products and services!

1.4.3.9 Enterprise Resource Planning is a Mass-User-Oriented Application Environment

Compared to the degree of involvement of functional managers and end users into traditional software project implementations, their participation in ES implementations may definitely seem unusual. ERP brings computerization to desktops and, in this sense, is an end-user-oriented environment in the true sense of the word. Unlike the traditional systems, where users accessed the system directly only in well-defined pockets within the enterprise, in ERP, end users are truly the personnel actually involved with the operations of the business. Because of the intense involvement of a sizable portion of the workforce of the company with the ERP implementation right from the beginning, the probability of them embracing the system and not struggling against it is much higher. They also act as the advocates and facilitators during and after the implementation phase.

1.4.4 Advantages of Enterprise Resource Planning

The implementation of ERP engenders the following business and technical advantages:

- Reconciliation and optimization of the conflicting goals of different divisions or departments; the transparent sharing of information with all concerned departments also enables cross-functional collaboration that is essential for the success of the millennium enterprise standardization of business processes across all the constituent companies and sites, thus increasing their efficiencies.
- The ability to know and implement global best practices.
- Alteration of the function-oriented organization toward a more team-based, cross-functional, process-oriented enterprise, thus leading to a more flexible, flatter, and tightly integrated enterprise.
- ERP provides a responsive medium for undertaking all variants on process improvement programs and methodologies including PI, process improvement, and business process.

- ERP also provides a responsive medium for quality improvement and standardization efforts including quality control, quality assurance, and TQM.
- ERP, being process-oriented, is a fertile ground for implementing activity-based management efforts, be it for budgeting, costing, efficiency, or quality.
- ERP provides the best conduit for measuring the benefits being accrued by the enterprises due to their implementation by monitoring the return on investment of not only money but also manpower, materials, time, and information. This could be in terms of various parameters like cost, quality, responsiveness, and cycle time. Thus, ERP could assist in the implementation of, for instance, the balanced scorecard within the enterprise.
- ERP systems, because they customarily implement best-of-class practices, provide the best means for benchmarking the organization's competitiveness.
- An ERP system enables an enterprise to scale up its level of operations drastically or even enter into different businesses altogether without any disruption or performance degradation.
- An ERP system ensures real-time creation of data directly during the actual physical transaction or processes by the persons who are actually responsible for it.
- An ERP system pushes the latest data and status to the actual operational-level persons for better and faster decisions at least on routine issues and empowers and gives ownership to the operational personnel at the level of actual work (this automatically does away with problems associated with collection of voluminous data, preparation, entry, corrections of inaccuracies, backup, etc.).
- An ERP system prompts the integration of data of the enterprise into a single comprehensive database.
- An ERP system enables online availability of correct and up-to-date data.
- ERP provides the most current, correct, consistent, and complete operational data that could be populated into the enterprise data warehouse for analysis and reporting.
- ERP greatly reduces the cost of maintaining systems. The vendor shoulders the responsibility of enhancing functionalities, providing technical upgrades as well as incorporating the latest country-specific regulations and statutory requirements.

1.4.5 Disadvantages of Enterprise Resource Planning

One of the biggest disadvantages of ERP is that, many times, it reinforces the silo-oriented functioning of the traditional functional organizations. For instance, the traditional functional silos of sales, production, purchase, and accounting get strengthened by the implementation of the corresponding SAP (Walldorf, Germany) functional modules, namely, SD, PP, MM and FI-CO, respectively. Although SAP (Walldorf, Germany) technically provides an enterprise-wide integration platform for all these modules, practically, the organization continues to function in the spirit of traditional functional silos.

ERP enhances team-based operations in the organization, but, often, these teams remain confined to the traditional functional silos in that they do not cross the boundaries of the functional departments. ERP implementations render the personnel enabled for system-based operations but do not necessarily do so for collaborative operations especially across traditional departmental boundaries. These limitations also arise out of their user profiles mapped into the SAP system that limits and enforces their authorization and access to data, information, analysis and business intelligence only to the confines of their functional departmental responsibilities.

Driven by issues of accountability and governance, even the biggest payoff of implementing ERP systems—the ability to monitor operational activities, critical performance parameters, productivity, value drivers, profitability, and returns on investment—get similarly thwarted because of the constricting user profiles. These issues are discussed further in the next section.

1.5 Enterprise Business Processes

Businesses take inputs (resources) in the form of material, people, and equipment and transform these inputs into goods and services for customers. Managing these inputs and the business processes effectively requires accurate and up-to-date information. For example, the sales function takes a customer's order and the production function schedules the manufacturing of the product. Logistics employees schedule and carry out the delivery of the product. If raw materials are needed to make the product, production prompts purchasing to arrange for their purchase and delivery. In that case, logistics will receive the material, verify its condition to accounting so that the vendor can be paid, and deliver the goods to production. Throughout, accounting keeps appropriate transaction records.

Most companies traditionally had unintegrated IS that supported only the activities of individual business functional areas. Thus, a company would have a marketing information system, a production information system, and so on, each with its own hardware, software, and methods of processing data and information. This configuration of IS is known as silos because each department has its own stack, or silo, of information that is unconnected to the next silo. Silos are also known as stovepipes. Such unintegrated systems might work well within individual functional areas, but to achieve its goals, a company must share data among all of the functional areas. When a company's IS are not integrated, costly inefficiencies can result. For example, suppose two functional areas have separate, unintegrated IS. To share data, a clerk in one functional area needs to print out data from another functional area and then type the information into her area's information system. Not only does this data input take twice the time, it also significantly increases the chance for data-entry errors. Alternatively, the process might be automated by having one information system write data to a file to be read by another information system. This would reduce the probability of errors, but it could only be done periodically (usually overnight or on a weekend) to minimize the disruption to normal business transactions. Because of the time lag in updating the system, the transferred data would rarely be up to date. In addition, data can be defined differently in different data systems, such as calling products by different part numbers in different systems. This variance can create further problems in timely and accurate information sharing between functional areas.

The functional business model illustrates the concept of silos of information, which limit the exchange of information between the lower operating levels. Instead, the exchange of information between operating groups is handled by top management, which might not be knowledgeable about the functional area (Figure 1.2a). In the quickly changing markets of the 1990s, the functional model led to top-heavy and overstaffed enterprises incapable of reacting quickly to change. This led to the view of a business as a set of cross-functional processes, as illustrated in Figure 1.2b. In the process-oriented model, the flow of information and management activity is horizontal across functions, in line with the flow of materials and products. This horizontal flow promotes flexibility and rapid decision-making and stimulates managers to see the importance of managing business processes. Now, information flows between the operating levels without top management's involvement.

1.6 Summary

This chapter began with a look at the evolution of ES, followed by the description of the extended enterprise systems. It then presents the characteristics of ES packages, which are examples of commercial off-the-shelf packaged systems. The latter half of this chapter details ERP systems. ERP systems enable the integration of heterogeneous and disparate business units, functions, and processes to coordinate, cooperate, and collaborate in aligning the business operations of the enterprise with its corporate strategy. After introducing the concept of ERP, the chapter highlights the tendency of ERP systems to reinforce the traditional silo-oriented operations of the organizations. The end the chapter describes the importance of business processes in enabling flexible and adaptable enterprise-wide, cross-functional integration.

2

Characteristics of Business Processes

A business process is typically associated with operational objectives and business relationships, for example, an insurance claims process or an engineering development process. A business process may be wholly contained within a single organizational unit or may span different enterprises, such as in the case of a customer–supplier relationship. Typical examples of processes that cross organizational boundaries include purchasing and sales processes jointly set up by buying and selling organizations, supported by EDI and value-added networks. The Internet is now a trigger for the design of new business processes and the redesign of existing ones.

This chapter focuses on business processes, which need to provide value to the customer. Value is usually defined in terms of the characteristics of the product(s) or service(s) that are output by the business process, namely:

- Timeliness, which is characterized by the speed with which a customer order can be satisfied; the objective is to minimize it. Timeliness depends on the process and its context. Timeliness in many service processes is the cycle time, where cycle time is the total time to process a single work item from start to finish. Timeliness in a made-to-order manufacturing system is mostly a matter of the lead-time between the customer order and the fulfillment of that order. Timeliness of an online retail store includes the response time to a customer request.

- Cost, which is characterized by the throughput rate of the processes; the objective is to maximize the throughput rate. Holding everything else as a constant, the more output a process can generate per unit time, then the lower the cost per work unit will be.

- Quality, which is characterized by the conformance to specification(s) of the output product(s) or service(s) to the satisfaction of the customer.

The degree of performance on the dimensions of timeliness, cost, and quality is ascertained by establishing a framework for measuring the process performance on a continuous basis.

2.1 Business Process

A business process is a set of logically related tasks performed to achieve a well-defined business outcome. A (business) process view implies a horizontal view of a business organization and looks at processes as sets of interdependent activities designed and structured to produce a specific output for a customer or a market. A business process defines the results to be achieved, the context of the activities, the relationships between the activities, and the interactions with other processes and resources. A business process may receive events that alter the state of the process and the sequence of activities. A business process may produce events for input to other applications or processes. It may also invoke applications to perform computational functions as well as post assignments to human work lists to request actions by human actors.

A business process is typically a coordinated and logically sequenced set of work activities and associated resources that produce something of value to a customer. A business process can be simply defined as a collection of activities that create value by transforming inputs into more valuable outputs. These activities consist of a series of steps performed by actors to produce a product or service for the customer. Each process has an identified customer; it is initiated by a process trigger or a business event (usually a request for a product or service arriving from the process customer) and it produces a process outcome (the product or service requested by the customer) as its deliverable to the process customer.

A business process has the following behaviors:

- It may contain defined conditions triggering its initiation in each new instance (e.g., the arrival of a claim) and defined outputs at its completion.
- It may involve formal or relatively informal interactions between participants.
- It has a duration that may vary widely.
- It may contain a series of automated activities and/or manual activities. These activities may be large and complex, involving the flow of materials, information, and business commitments.
- It exhibits a very dynamic nature, so it can successfully respond to demands from customers and to changing market conditions.
- It is widely distributed and customized across boundaries within and between enterprises, often spanning multiple applications with very different technology platforms.
- It is usually long-running—a single instance of a process such as the transformation of an order to cash may run for months or even years.

Business processes can be measured via performance measures such as time; cost; quality; and, hence, customer satisfaction. This chapter focuses on such characteristics of a business process. The presentation and approach in this chapter have been adopted from N. Damij and T. Damij (2014).

2.2 Process Performance

Process-oriented enterprises consider any enterprise or part of an enterprise as a process that converts input into output characterized by:

1. Inputs and outputs
   - Inputs are any tangible or intangible items that flow into the process from the environment.
   - Outputs are any tangible or intangible items that flow from the process back into the environment.

2. Flow units: A flow unit or job is an item that flows throughout the process. Depending on the process, the flow unit may be a unit of input, such as a customer order, or a unit of output, such as a finished product.

3. A network of activities and buffers: The concept of a network of activities and buffers describes specific precedence relationships among activities that are linked so that the output of one becomes an input of another, often through an intermediate buffer.

   • An activity is the simplest form of transformation; it is actually a miniprocess in and of itself.

   • A buffer stores flow units that have finished one activity but are waiting for the next activity to start.

4. Resources are tangible assets that are usually divided into two categories: capital and labor.

5. Information structure describes the information that is needed and available in order to perform activities or to make managerial decisions.

The process flow is a dynamic process that starts when an input (a flow unit or a job) enters a process and continues processing throughout different kinds of process activities and ends when it leaves the process as its output. Process flow measures represent important process analysis tools that can be used with the purpose of creating a better understanding of the business process discussed, discovering problems that exist within it, developing an improved version of the process or inventing a completely new process, and making a comparative analysis between the existing business process on the one hand and the improved or new one on the other.

The three key measures of the process flow are:

1. Cycle time or flow time, which is the time it takes to complete an individual flow unit or job from start to finish; it is the total time taken up by a flow unit within the process boundaries.

   It is evident from the above-given definitions of the process elements that each flow unit or job passes through a network of activities and buffers. Therefore, a flow unit at any time during its journey through a process could be found either undergoing a certain task performed within an activity, or waiting in a buffer for a next step.

   A typical cycle time of a flow unit includes value-adding and non-value-adding components such as:

   • Processing time (related to value-adding activities)

   • Inspection time

   • Transporting time

   • Storage time

   • Waiting time (planned and unplanned delay time)

 A flow unit usually spends only a small amount of time within value-adding activities as compared with the amount of time spent within non-value-adding activities or of the whole cycle time.

2. Flow rate or throughput, which is the number of jobs per unit of time; it is the number of flow units that flow through a specific point in the process per unit of time. Flow rates usually have different values at various points of time throughout the process.

3. Inventory, which is the total number of flow units present within the process boundaries; it is the number of flow units that may be found within the boundary of the process at any point of time.

   The inventory within the framework of the process depends on the difference between the inflow rate and outflow rate, because the inflow and outflow rates may differ over time throughout the process.

   The difference between inflow rate and outflow rate is given by

$$\Delta R(t) = R_i(t) - R_o(t)$$

where:
   $R(t)$ means the flow rate at a certain point of time t
   $R_i(t)$ means inflow; this is the flow rate of flow units that enter the process through its entry points
   $R_o(t)$ means outflow; this is the flow rate of flow units that leave the process through its exit points

With this, the following alternatives are possible:
   If inflow rate $R_i(t)$ > outflow rate $R_o(t)$, then the inventory increases at a flow rate of $\Delta R(t) > 0$
   If inflow rate $R_i(t)$ ¼ outflow rate $R_o(t)$, then the inventory is unchanged
   If inflow rate $R_i(t)$ < outflow rate $R_o(t)$, then the inventory decreases at a flow rate of $\Delta R(t) < 0$

4. Little's Law For a stable process, Little's Law defines the fundamental relationship between average inventory, average flow rate, and average cycle time in a stable process.

   a. Average flow rate or throughput is defined as the average number of flow units that flow through (into and out of) the process per unit of time. The average flow rate is a process performance measure that indicates the rate of producing the output of the process; the organization's ideal goal is that the process flow rate is equal to the demand rate.

   b. A stable process is one in which the average inflow rate is the same as the average outflow rate across an extended period of time; that is,

$$R = R_i = R_o$$

   c. The average cycle time is the average (of flow times) across all flow units that exit the process during a specific period of time. Since different flow units may have different cycle times for passing through the process, it is possible to calculate the average cycle time.

d. Average inventory is the number of flow units within the process boundaries at any point in time. Because the inventory within a process changes over time, it is possible to calculate the average inventory of a process.

Little's law states that, in a stable process, the average inventory equals the average flow rate times the average cycle time; that is,

$$I = R * T$$

2.3 Process Cycle Time

1. Theoretical cycle time: The cycle time of a flow unit within the process actually consists of the time taken by those activities, where the flow unit is processed according to certain works and the waiting time spent by the flow unit in different buffers.

   - The theoretical cycle time of a process is the minimum amount of time required for processing a typical flow unit without any waiting. It is the sum of the times of those activities that the flow unit passes through and where specific kinds of tasks are undertaken to process it.

   - Activity time is the time required by a typical flow unit to complete the activity once; the activity time differs from one flow unit to another.

   As the theoretical time cycle may be different for various flow units, the average theoretical time is computed as the average of the theoretical times of all flow units.

2. Critical path: A process flow is usually presented using a diagrammatic technique like a flowchart. A process flow or process flowchart may have many paths on the way from the start to the end of the diagram. Each of these paths may include different sequential or parallel activities, loops, and other possibilities. The theoretical cycle time of each path is equal to the sum of the times of the constituting activities.

   The longest path in the process flowchart is termed as the *critical path*; the theoretical cycle time of the process is actually the same as the theoretical cycle time of the critical path. All activities that constitute the critical path of the process flowchart are called *critical activities*.

   In cases where the process flowchart is complex and contains many paths, it can be difficult to compute the longest path of the process. A number of approaches have been developed to solve this problem, including the critical path method to determine the critical path of complex processes.

   The critical path is very important because its actual cycle time defines the cycle time of the whole process. This means that any delay in any of the critical activities causes a delay in the entire process, because the critical path is the longest path of the process. For this reason, management should pay special attention to the critical activities by providing them with all of the needed resources and monitoring their execution very closely. On the other hand, non-critical activities are not so decisive for the process cycle time because any delay caused by a noncritical activity could be more easily made up and such a delay usually does not cause a holdup in the whole process.

3. The critical path method is based on calculating a variable called the *slack time* of an activity, defined as the extent to which an activity could be delayed without affecting process flow time (i.e., cycle time). A critical activity is an activity whose slack time is equal to 0. Thus, the critical path consists of all those activities for which the slack time is equal to 0.

To determine the critical path, two schedules have to be calculated:

a. Forward schedule. A forward schedule is calculated starting from the first activity to the last one. This schedule calculates the earliest possible start time and the earliest possible finish time of each activity within the process. To compute the forward schedule, the variables Earliest Start (ES) and Earliest Finish (EF) can be calculated.

   i. ES means the earliest start time for an activity to begin after all of its predecessor activities have been completed.

   • For the first activity of the process, use the formula

$$ES = 1, \text{ where 1 means 1 time unit}$$

   • For other activities, use the formula

$$ES = 1 + \max(EF) \text{ of immediate predecessor activities}$$

   ii. EF means the earliest possible time for an activity to finish.

   • EF is calculated using the formula

$$EF = ES + d + 1, \text{ where d is duration time of the activity}$$

b. Backward schedule. The backward schedule is calculated in the opposite direction from the forward schedule; that is, starting from the last activity to the first one. This schedule calculates the latest possible start time and the latest possible finish time for each activity of the process. To determine the backward schedule, the variables Latest Finish (LF) and Latest Start (LS) can be calculated.

   i. LF means the latest possible time for an activity to finish without causing a delay.

   For the last activity, use the formula

$$LF = EF$$

   For other activities, use the formula

$$LF = \min(LS) \text{ of immediate successor activities} - 1$$

   ii. LS means the latest possible time for an activity to begin without causing a delay.

LS is calculated using the formula

$$LS = LF - d + 1, \text{ where d is the duration time of the activity.}$$

4. Slack time: The slack time of an activity is the amount of time that could be spent in addition to the duration time of the activity, without causing a delay to the start times of immediate successor activities.

   Calculating the forward and backward schedules enables us to compute the slack time(s) of each activity in the process using the formula

$$S = LF - EF = LS - ES$$

5. Cycle-time efficiency: Cycle-time efficiency can be obtained by dividing the theoretical cycle time by the average cycle time of the process. Therefore, the cycle-time efficiency is the ratio between the theoretical cycle time and the average cycle time.

   As the average cycle time includes the waiting time in the process flow,

$$\text{Cycle-time efficiency} = \text{theoretical cycle time/average cycle time}$$

2.3.1 Computing Cycle Time

As stated earlier, a flow unit on its journey from the beginning to the end of the process flow goes through a number of activities, as well as spending periods of waiting time in different buffers.

Cycle time can be computed in three different ways:

1. As the sum of the theoretical and waiting times

   Knowing the waiting time(s) spent in buffers of the process, the cycle time of a certain flow unit is:

$$\text{Cycle time} = \text{theoretical cycle time} + \text{waiting time}$$

   The average cycle time of a process can be obtained by:
   - Treating waiting in each buffer as an additional (passive) activity with an activity time equal to the amount of time in that buffer.
   - Adding waiting times to the theoretical cycle time of the appropriate path.
   - Obtaining the average cycle time of the process by finding the path whose overall length (activity plus waiting) is the longest.
2. Using value-adding and non-value-adding activities

   The activities of a process can be differentiated as value-adding and non-value-adding activities.
   - Value-adding activities are those activities that increase the economic value of a flow unit because the customer values them.

- Non-value-adding activities are activities that, while required by the firm's process, do not directly increase the value of a flow unit.

Since waiting is usually considered as a non-value-adding activity, the cycle time can be computed using the formula:

Cycle time = value-adding cycle time – non-value-adding cycle time

3. Computing the cycle time using Little's law

   It is possible to use Little's Law to compute the average cycle time of a process by finding the longest cycle time of the process flowchart—that is, by finding the critical path of the process.

2.3.2 Process Flow Aspects

2.3.2.1 Rework

A process flowchart may contain one or more segments of a number of sequential activities whose execution needs to be repeated several times, depending on a decision activity, where the value of a certain condition is defined. This is usually known as a rework or execution loop; each repetition of a rework loop is called a visit.

In cases of an inspection condition, the activities of the loop are not repeated the same number of times for each flow unit. Therefore, the average number of visits over all flow units is less than one visit. In such cases, the work content is calculated instead of the activity time. For reference, the work content of an activity is the activity time multiplied by the average number of visits at that activity.

The work content enables us to calculate a more precise estimation of the theoretical cycle time, in order to compute the critical path of the process.

2.3.2.2 Multiple Paths

There are a number of cases in a process flowchart where, after a decision activity, the process flow splits into two or more paths. The following general formula can be used to compute the average cycle time for a process flow that splits into multiple paths after a decision activity:

$$T = p_1{}^*T_1 + p_2{}^*T_2 + \dots + p_m{}^*T_m$$

where:
  p_i is the probability of following the flow of path i
  T_i is the sum of times of activities within path i
  m is the number of paths

2.3.2.3 Parallel Paths

There are also cases in which the process flowchart may contain one or more segments that are constructed from parallel activities. This happens when the output of a certain activity is needed as the input for a number of successor activities in different parallel paths.

The cycle time of the part of the process with parallel paths is represented by the maximum sum of times of activities in the parallel paths.

This sum can be computed using the following formula:

$$T = \max\left(T_1, T_2, \ldots, T_m\right)$$

where:
   T_i is the sum of times of activities within path i
   m is the number of paths

2.3.3 Process Capacity

An enterprise makes a decision concerning the improvement of their business processes based on the performance of the processes in terms of their throughput and process capacity. Considering that the average flow rate or throughput is defined as the average number of flow units or jobs that flow through the process per unit of time, the process capacity is the maximum sustainable flow rate of a process.

2.3.3.1 Resources

Since resources are essential for performing the process activities, the capacity of a process depends on the resources (e.g., capital and labor) that are used in the process. Moreover, every activity depends on the availability and ability of the resources required for its execution; while, for performing any activity requires one or more resources, every resource may be involved in performing one or more activities.

 A cost-effective means to increase capacity without increasing cost is to pool either demand or resources; when customer demands or resources are grouped together, such is called pooling.

A group of resources involved in carrying out similar kinds of activities is called a resource pool, which is a collection of interchangeable resources that can perform an identical set of activities. Combining resource pools into a single pool is called resource-pooling. Thus, resource-pooling means associating different resource pools into a joint resource pool in order to carry out a set of activities within a process.

Performing an activity may involve different resources and also a resource may be involved in processing a number of activities. Therefore, the sum of the working times that the resource spends in performing a number of activities concerning a flow unit that goes through the process is called the unit load of a resource. The unit load of a resource unit is the total amount of time the resource works to process each flow unit.

2.3.3.2 Theoretical Capacity

The determination of system capacity is a major enterprise design decision. System capacity is part of the operational strategy of the enterprise because the addition of large amounts of capacity requires a significant amount of time and money. Additional capacity is usually added by acquiring more facilities, expanding existing facilities, partnering with others who can provide capacity, or outsourcing operations. For short periods of time, capacity can be increased by working overtime; however, this is not sustainable over the long term.

Process capacity is how many products or customers the process can generate in a given time period. The theoretical process capacity is the maximum sustainable throughput rate for the process operating without interruption (e.g., no downtime due to maintenance, worker rest periods, and so on). To determine the theoretical process capacity, you need to know the maximum sustainable throughput rate for the process and the number of hours per day that the process can be feasibly operated.

In service industries, capacity may be determined as much by the arrival pattern of customers as by the availability and capacity of resources.

The capacity of the process is critically dependent on the availability of the resources. In reality, resources may be unavailable partly by reason of waiting, downtime, setup, idling, and other times. The theoretical capacity of a resource unit is its maximum sustainable flow rate if it were fully utilized (i.e., without interruptions, downtime, times wasted for setups, idling periods, and so on). Accordingly, the theoretical capacity of a resource pool is the sum of theoretical capacities of all resource units in that pool.

Since 100% utilization is not feasible, the actual process capacity will always be less than the theoretical capacity. Reasons for lost capacity include:

- Resource breakdowns: A machine may become unavailable due to a breakdown or a human resource may be absent.

- Preventive maintenance: Machines require regular maintenance to operate at maximum efficiency; this scheduled preventive maintenance makes the resource unavailable for processing. People may require periodic training (e.g., on an updated ERP system), which makes them unavailable.

- Process flow inefficiencies: A resource may become idle due to the unavailability of work. In a sequential line, if the work task in front of a task is slower, this unbalancing will cause starving at the task.

- Demand variation: As described earlier, the mismatch between demand and capacity can cause underutilization.

The flow unit on its way through different activities is processed by a number of resource pools with predetermined capacities; the pool with the lowest capacity is termed as the resource bottleneck of the process. Since the capacity of a process cannot be better than the process's bottleneck resource pool, this effectively makes it the defining capacity of the whole process.

The bottleneck resource pool is the key element to which the improvement teams should pay maximum attention in order to achieve the desired improvement of the process.

Assuming that we have a resource pool p with c_p resource units; the theoretical capacity of the resource unit, which in this case is also the theoretical capacity of the resource pool, is

$$R_p = \frac{c_p}{T_p}$$

where:
R_p is the theoretical capacity of the resource pool
c_p is the number of resource units in the pool p
T_p is the unit load of the resource pool

If the resource units in a certain resource pool do not have the same theoretical capacity, then the theoretical capacity of the resource pool is computed as the sum of all of the theoretical capacities of its constituting resource units, provided the following conditions are true:

1. The flow units are performed by resource units sequentially one by one.
2. The resource units are available the same quantity of time.

Load-batching and scheduled availability are important factors that have a real effect on the theoretical capacity of the process. Because different resources may have different working schedules, which may include shift work or a different number of hours per different days, the scheduled availability should be calculated in hours per week. Hence, these factors should be taken into the account when calculating the theoretical capacity by defining:

- Load batching as the ability of a resource unit to process a number of flow units simultaneously
- Scheduled availability as the quantity of time in which a resource unit is scheduled to perform a determined work

Thus, the theoretical capacity of resource pool p with c_p resources is

$$R_p = \frac{c_p}{T_p} * \text{load batch} * \text{scheduled availability}$$

2.3.3.3 Capacity Utilization

Capacity utilization measures the degree to which resources are effectively utilized by a process. Capacity utilization indicates the extent to which resources, which represent invested capital, are utilized to generate outputs (e.g., flow units and, ultimately, profits).

For each resource pool, capacity utilization of the process is defined as the capacity utilization of the bottleneck resource pool.

Capacity utilization of a resource pool can be calculated as

$$\rho_p = \frac{R}{R_p}$$

where:
R is the throughput
R_p is the theoretical capacity of a resource pool

The theoretical capacity can be improved by:

1. Decreasing the unit load on the bottleneck resource pool (i.e., work faster, work smarter)
2. Increasing the load batch of resources in the bottleneck resource pool (i.e., increase the scale of the resource)

3. Increasing the number of units in the bottleneck resource pool (i.e., increase the scale of the process)

4. Increasing the scheduled availability of the bottleneck resource pool (e.g., work longer)

2.4 Process Costs

The goal of an enterprise is to make long-term profits; therefore, understanding the cost of the process output is needed because profits equal revenue minus costs. Even for non-profit enterprises, the cost to deliver a product or serve a customer is a major performance parameter of the process. A *cost component* is any activity for which a separate cost measurement is desired. Example cost components are the materials consumed, inventory, labor, or overhead of the process.

Ways to classify costs include

1. As direct costs, which are those costs that can be directly and exclusively attributed to a particular cost object. Direct costs of the computer include the labor to assemble the computer and the components that go into the computer. The labor and components can be tied directly to a particular computer and they are exclusively done for that computer.

2. As indirect costs, which are those that cannot be directly and exclusively attributed to a particular cost object. To illustrate the difference, consider the manufacturing production of a computer. Indirect costs in this example are the management salaries and rent for the factory. Neither of these two cost components can be directly and/or exclusively attributed to a particular computer.

Cost allocation is the assignment of costs to the flow or work unit. Direct costs are traced to the work unit and assigned. Indirect costs cannot be traced to the work unit because they are common to many work units. Two methods are available to allocate indirect costs to the work unit. The first, more simplistic method is to identify a cost driver for the indirect costs; typically, all indirect costs are aggregated into a single cost driver called *overhead* that is charged as a percentage of the direct costs. Greater precision can be obtained by further differentiating the cost driver by (say) work unit type or department, or by defining cost centers, which are groupings of resources that have a single cost driver.

The second is a method called activity-based costing that attempts to allocate all indirect costs to activities based on the quantity of resources they consume. To illustrate, the computer manufacturer has the indirect cost of electricity. Normally, the cost of electricity would be aggregated with other indirect costs and uniformly allocated as described earlier. In activity-based costing, however, the enterprise determines how much electricity is consumed in the production of computers and assigns this number directly to the computer. Likewise, the area of factory floor used for computer production is determined and used to allocate the facility rental cost. Though activity-based costing can provide more accurate cost allocation, the primary limitation to its adoption is the difficulty of establishing a cost accounting system to support it.

Other ways to classify the process cost components are

1. As fixed costs, which remain constant for all levels of output. So, whether you serve a single customer per day or thousands, you incur the same fixed costs. Fixed costs are often set once a business is established. For example, once you purchase a building or sign a lease, then the fixed costs of rent and property taxes are determined and are difficult to change in the short-term.
2. As variable costs, which are the costs per work unit and therefore vary with the amount of sales.

 Labor can be a fixed cost or a variable cost; it depends on how the employees are paid. An accountant is a fixed cost if paid a salary, whereas a truck driver is a variable cost because the truck driver is paid per hour spent driving.

2.5 Process Quality

Quality can be defined from the two different perspectives, as follows:

1. Customer's perspective: The customer's perspective of quality is the degree to which a product or service satisfies the needs and expectations of the customer. This definition includes multiple dimensions of quality such as performance, features, reliability, durability, serviceability, aesthetics, and perceived quality. The definition is also contextual because the satisfaction of needs and expectations implies a value-orientation.
2. Enterprise's perspective: The enterprise's view of quality is the degree to which a product or service conforms to the specifications designed for the product or service. This view of quality is that the process produces no defects, and each product or service provided is consistent with little variability. This definition is a more objective engineering definition and provides a basis on which to control the processes generating the product or service.

These two notions of quality are inter-related: A product or service cannot meet customer needs unless the enterprise perceives those customer needs and designs a product or service to fulfil those needs—this is the quality by design idea. Then, in the delivery of the product or service, the enterprise must conform to the design specifications. Only by getting both the design and the delivery correct can an enterprise provide a quality product or service. Additionally, the enterprise needs to continuously work to improve the quality of its products and services.

To institute quality processes, an enterprise performs three main functions, as follows:

1. Design quality products and services by understanding customer needs and translating them into product and service specifications.

    The design of quality processes starts with understanding the customer's needs and expectations, often by asking them. When innovative ideas need to be introduced to customers first before they can understand and develop expectations for the new product or service, market research tools can be employed to ascertain customer needs and requirements. If the process output is primarily a service or has a large service component, then there are questionnaire instruments such as SERVQUAL designed to elicit customer perceptions of the service quality. Another commonly employed means to determine customer needs is via benchmarking with competing products/services. The benchmark lets the enterprise gauge itself against its competitors to see where it excels and/or where it falls behind.

a. The use of quality functional deployment methodology and tools provide a systematic way to take customer needs and design a product or service to fulfil those needs. The quality functional deployment methodology and tools translate the customer needs into the attributes of a product or service. The primary tool of quality functional deployment is:

- The house of quality, which is a matrix that denotes the strength of the association between a product or service attribute and customer expectations using a range from 0 to 9, with 9 indicating a very strong association.

- This matrix indicates the degree of correlation between product attributes as either weak, medium, or strong.

To use the tool, the enterprise must identify those product attributes that it can manipulate and then associate them with the customer expectations. Using benchmarking and other market analysis, the enterprise can prioritize the customer expectations that need improvement. The house of quality tells them what product attributes are most associated with those customer expectations.

b. Poka-yoke: To design quality into the product, the process that produces the product should be failproof. A Japanese word that has come to embody this idea is poka-yoke, essentially the foolproofing of a process. The observation is that process errors, mistakes, and variations can be attributed not to underperforming employees but rather to interruptions, fatigue, and other special causes. Using poka-yoke concepts, the process can be designed so that these errors do not occur.

- In manufacturing, you might design parts so that they can only be assembled in the correct way, thus removing the need for the worker to think about how the parts go together and possibly making an error.

- In service industries such as medicine or maintenance, checklists are used to remind the person to do all of the procedures for every customer.

Poka-yoke designs the process so as to eliminate the possibility of quality problems before they can happen.

c. Taguchi method: Another approach to designing quality products is the use of the robust design methods developed by Dr. Genichi Taguchi. Dr. Taguchi challenged the concept that a manufactured product simply meeting specifications was sufficient. He developed the quality loss function showing that any deviation from the target is undesirable. Normally, any value that fell within the lower and upper specifications was considered good. The quadratic loss function says that any deviation from the target value results in a loss—Dr. Taguchi's loss function is used in conjunction with the design of experiments to remove as much variation from the process as possible. It is also used to design robust products that will maintain small variation even when the process inputs or process itself are subject to variation.

2. Deliver quality products and services by having processes that produce no defects and demonstrate little variability.

The underlying principle of statistical quality control is that all processes exhibit variation in their output. Some of the variation is called *common cause* variation and is due to the inherent characteristics of the process. The common cause variation cannot be attributed to any particular problem or event. Other variation is the result of *special causes* that can be attributed to a specific problem such as a malfunctioning machine, fluctuations in temperature, or changes in the process inputs. Special causes typically cause greater variability than common causes, and the statistical quality control method seeks to identify and eliminate special causes.

Statistical process control uses control charts to monitor processes: it samples the critical measures of output quality and charts them to determine when they are in control or when they need intervention to correct potential problems. The design of a quality process involves instituting the correct feedback loops so as to constantly monitor and control the process. A control chart monitors the process and indicates whether it is in statistical control, meaning only common cause variation is present, or if there are any special causes that require process intervention. There are several different types of control charts that can be used, depending on the type of output variable being measured.

When the line falls out of the limits or is on one side of the mean for a number of sequential samples, then it is considered to be out of control. The control chart closes the feedback loop between the process output and the process. If the rope is seen to trend out of statistical control, then the employees are alerted to a special cause problem that needs to be investigated. Other tools such as fishbone diagrams and so forth are used to isolate the special cause so that corrective action can be taken. The usage of control charts helps to maintain process variability within a small range of values within which the variability is explained only by common cause variation.

3. Improve the quality of their processes by establishing continuous process improvement programs.

All enterprises should establish continuous process improvement programs that run parallel to the core business processes. Six Sigma is a continuous process improvement methodology that employs a data-driven approach to identify quality problems and reduce process variation in order to make the process perfect.

To perform continuous process improvement, the analysis teams need to identify improvement opportunities to:

- Eliminate waiting time (a waste)
- Eliminate wasted movement or effort
- Minimize inventory
- Eliminate repair and rework
- Minimize material movement

- Minimize inspections
- Reduce the variation of inputs, process, and outputs
- Reduce cycle time
- Improve machine reliability
- Improve flexibility of resources

Six Sigma uses an improvement process called Define, Measure, Analyze, Improve, and Control (DMAIC). Six Sigma uses extensive statistical tools to aid in analysis. The main tools used are process mapping, process capability tools, fishbone diagrams, pareto charts, hypothesis testing, failure mode effect analysis, design of experiments, and statistical process control. Six Sigma is usually performed as a project, where a problem is first identified and the project team subsequently follows the DMAIC process to improve the process. Six Sigma has become very popular in industry and certificate programs are available to qualify people as "black belts," indicating that they have gained and demonstrated adequate knowledge of the Six Sigma process and tools.

 The term "Six Sigma" refers to a process that produces no more than 3.4 defects per one million occurrences of the process, but its main goal is to act as a proxy for continuous improvement.

2.6 Measuring Process Performance

Figure 2.1 shows a categorization of process performance measurement systems. A process performance measurement system focuses on an individual business process, rather than on the entire company or an organizational unit. Traditional controlling looks mostly at the company as a whole, focusing on efficiency. The balanced scorecard and self-assessment concepts are placed in the same box, because of their common focus on

| | **Focus on** | |
	... the entire business or an organizational unit	... a single business process
Performance in a broad sense (efficiency and effectiveness)	Balanced Scorecard Self-Assessment	Process Performance Measurement Systems
Performance in a narrow sense (primarily measuring efficiency)	Traditional Controlling (e.g., Return on Investment, Economic Value Added)	Activity-based Costing Workflow-based Monitoring Statistical Process Control

FIGURE 2.1
Process performance measurement systems.

the whole company and their performance definition in a broad sense (i.e., efficiency and effectiveness)—although, their approach to measuring performance is quite different. Statistical process control, activity-based costing, and workflow-based monitoring are usually used for measuring a single process while focusing on efficiency aspects.

The determination of measurements and/or development of the measurement system(s) is often based on traditional, existing approaches at a company level that generally encompass both efficiency metrics and effectiveness metrics to determine performance. However, for process performance measurement systems, a process-oriented view of a business serves as the primary basis for their definition.

2.6.1 Concepts for Performance Measurement

As a part of business process management, process controlling related to measurement, analysis, and improvement of processes represents a loop that coordinates the execution of processes. Process performance measurement entails capturing quantitative and qualitative information about the process. Measurements can be obtained either through continuous or periodic measuring. Subsequently, the measurements can be transformed into performance figures, which thus translate unfiltered data into information about process performance, enabling the process manager to discharge their responsibilities related to process controlling.

2.6.2 Process Performance Measurement Based on Indicators, Measures, and Figures

Performance indicators for the assessment of process performance have to be defined in order for process performance to be determined accurately and must be continuously monitored by the process manager. The definition of a performance indicator can be based on the company's strategy, business process objectives, and/or strategic success factors. For example, a financial services provider may state as a business process objective the desire to secure "an increase in productivity by means of faster service provisioning." In this situation, in order to determine the level of goal attainment, two performance indicators can be identified: time (as an input factor) and service quantity (as an output factor).

Performance measures represent the operationalization of each identified performance indicator. This entails determining precisely how the performance indicator will be measured—that is, questions related to what, how, when, by whom, and where of measurements for each performance indicator must be addressed. For example, the performance indicator "time" might measure total cycle time, actual processing time, or something else.

Performance figures enable the summarization and representation of large amounts of data in a condensed and precise manner. They serve the management team as a valuable source of comprehensive information on the company's objectives and results. Performance figures represent those measurements, for which the process manager has determined objectives; consequently, comparisons between targeted and actual performance are possible. Performance figures are normally included in management reports. Therefore, a performance figure can be the measure itself (e.g., cycle time) or a combination of different measures (e.g., throughput efficiency equals the number of loan decisions per hour of cycle time).

2.6.3 Measurements to Determine Process Performance

There are many indicators available that can be applied for the measurement of company-specific process performance. In the early 1980s, companies defined indicators that focused primarily on efficiency and, to a lesser degree, on effectiveness: performance figures served to reduce costs rather than to improve profit-related issues. In order to avoid such a lopsided management focus, companies compensated by selecting indicators that were directly linked to their strategy and that in turn were linked to their business objectives and resources. This resulted in strategic performance figures that supported senior management in navigating toward the desired strategic direction.

Thus, the performance figures are highly dynamic and the selection of strategically important performance indicators is related to the notion of "critical success factors." In order to be successful, a company has to determine performance indicators and, subsequently, the performance measures and performance figures that are strategically relevant to their specific situation. Since measuring process performance starts with the identification of performance indicators, there have been numerous suggestions with respect to specifying the indicator groups of quality, time, cost, and flexibility.

In general, *quality indicators* describe the degree to which the actual product attributes and properties conform to the underlying product specifications. In the past, indicators often included costs for defect prevention, quality measurement costs, and costs related to failure rates. Currently, customer satisfaction serves as the major yardstick for measuring the quality of a product or service. Consequently, methodologies such as Six Sigma define indicators on the basis of performance-related customer requirements.

In general, *time indicators* are considered to be an indicator of competitiveness and process performance. Yet, within a just-in-time production paradigm, for example, production and/or delivery of production outputs at a premature or late point of time is considered to be a waste of time. Thus, the exact point of time is relevant, and an appropriate performance indicator would be the deviation from the targeted point of time. Within the field of research in optimized production technology, the main objective is seen in minimizing process time. Performance indicators and subsequent performance measures therefore include throughput time, actual processing time, waiting time, transportation time, and delivery time. In the time-based costing approach, time is viewed in yet another different way; namely, in terms of production costs.

In general, different cost factors provide the basis for *cost indicators*, for example, labor costs, information technology costs, production costs, product costs, service costs, failure costs, and so forth. A distinction can be made between fixed and variable costs. In addition, since the emergence of activity-based costing, indicators such as activity-based costs and subprocess- or process-related costs are also eligible candidates as cost indicators.

In general, *flexibility indicators* describe the degree to which a production or service process can be modified, including the timeline and costs associated with the restructuring of a production or service process. A further indicator for flexibility relates to the number of product or service components that can be exchanged within a given time. Moreover, process flexibility may also be viewed as dealing with output volumes or resource utilization.

2.6.4 Frameworks for Measuring Process Performance

Process performance is multidimensional; that is, process performance cannot be determined on the basis of a single indicator, such as productivity, but instead comes from

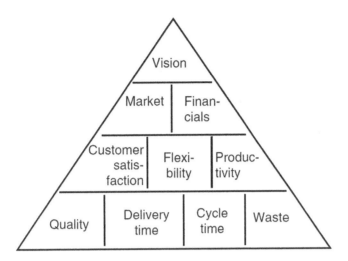

FIGURE 2.2
Performance pyramid.

the resultant of many different but interdependent indicators, measures, and performance figures that simply cannot be summarized in one single number.

As the entire company should be aligned with the wishes and requirements of its clients and other stakeholders, the performance measures have to be aligned with the objectives of the stakeholders, which undergo change depending on the adjustments that occur in the market environment, regulators, competitors, and the offered products and services. Thus, on an ongoing basis, the company's vision and the stakeholder-related objectives serve as a reference framework for determining and changing the measures of process performance.

The concept of the balanced scorecard is one of the best-known frameworks for developing an individualized measurement system and for determining processes and, hence, business performance.

The performance pyramid (Figure 2.2) framework stresses a hierarchical view of performance; that is, it considers the relationship between the following:

- Strategic performance (e.g., fulfilling the vision, market share, financial performance)
- Process performance (e.g., quality, cycle time, waste, or spoilage rate)

The layer connecting the two hierarchical levels depicts those performance indicators that impact both levels (e.g., customer satisfaction, flexibility, and productivity).

A framework for constructing a process-oriented performance measurement system is shown in Figure 2.3 and highlights the distinction between input, throughput, and output that is considered for determining performance indicators according to this classification. Process input factors include, for example, employees, plants, and equipment, as well as capital. The quality and quantity of these input factors can be a decisive factor in meeting customer requirements, which themselves represent an additional input factor. During the throughput phase, input factors are utilized and combined. The output consists of a product, a service, and financial results. The process performance is therefore determined through a measurement system that encompasses performance measures for input, throughput, and output.

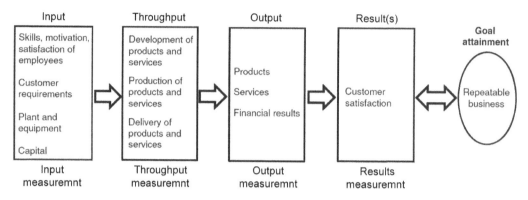

FIGURE 2.3
Framework for constructing a process-oriented performance measurement system.

2.7 Summary

This chapter started by identifying the characteristics of business processes, namely, timeliness, cost, and quality. The critical path is very important because its actual cycle time defines the cycle time of the whole process. This means that any delay in any of the critical activities causes a delay in the entire process because the critical path is the longest path of the process. It shows different approaches for computing the cycle time. The process capacity is determined as the maximum sustainable flow rate of a process. The bottleneck resource pool is the key element to which the improvement teams should pay maximum attention for achieving the desired improvement of the process. The pool with the lowest capacity is termed as the resource bottleneck of the process. Since the capacity of a process cannot be better than the process' bottleneck resource pool, this effectively makes it the defining capacity of the whole process. For any enterprise, the cost to deliver a product or serve a customer is a major performance parameter of the process. Similarly, quality is characterized by the conformance to specifications of the output product or service with respect to the satisfaction of the customer. The degree of performance on the dimensions of timeliness, cost and quality is ascertained by establishing a framework for measuring the process performance on a continuous basis.

Section I

Genesis of Enterprise Process Management Systems

An enterprise architecture is important to work with due to the complexity inherent in enterprise systems and in aligning the many subsystems so that they all work harmoniously towards the enterprise's goals. Enterprise architecture also provides the foundation on which enterprise integration is anchored. Business processes are crucial, as organizations adapt themselves to changing conditions. Management strategies, such as business process reengineering, process improvement, process innovation, and business process redesign have emerged to help organizations change their business processes promptly and dynamically according to the requirements of changing environments. The horizontal view of the business engendered by business process change practice represents a paradigm shift from the traditional hierarchical organizational structure. A process-oriented or process-centric stance adopts a horizontal view of organizations by emphasizing notions of processes, process owners, teams, and empowerment and deemphasizing hierarchical structures. As such, it represents an input–output activity view of business, as opposed to a functional, responsibility-centered structural view.

The traditional understanding of enterprise architecture has been presented in several publications including N. Rozanski and E. Woods (2012) and L. Bass and P. Clements and R. Kizman (2013). This section proposes process enterprise architecture in an analogy with the enterprise architecture; analogous to the enterprise architecture frameworks for enterprise architecture described in Chapter 4, Chapter 5 describes the workflow reference model as the reference process architecture for the enterprise process architecture.

Chapter 3 reviews the basic concepts of systems thinking, systems science, systems engineering, and systems architecting. Knowing this basic information about systems helps in understanding the origin of the significance of enterprise architecture and the constituting business architecture, information architecture, application architecture, and technical architecture. This also provides the context for the significance of business processes in contemporary enterprises.

Chapter 4 describes the viewpoints, views, and perspectives that enable an enterprise architecture. Enterprise architecture is a well-defined practice for conducting enterprise analysis, design, planning, and implementation, using a holistic approach at all times, for the successful development and execution of enterprise strategy.

Chapter 5 describes the process views and perspectives that enable an enterprise process architecture. Analogous to the enterprise architecture frameworks for enterprise architecture described in Chapter 4, this chapter describes the workflow reference model as the reference process architecture for the enterprise process architecture.

3

Systems Theory

To date, attempts to apply reductionism as well as the natural scientific method generally to social and organizational problems have not been satisfactory and have yielded only limited success. Systems thinking can be seen as a reaction to the failure of natural science when confronted with complex, real-world problems set in social systems. Systems thinkers advocate using holism rather than reductionism in such situations. Holism does not seek to break down complex problem situations into their parts in order to study them and intervene in them. Rather, it respects the profound interconnectedness of the parts and concentrates on the relationships between them and how these often give rise to surprising outcomes—the emergent properties.

Systems thinking uses models rather than laboratory experiments to try to learn about the behavior of the world and even then does not take for granted or impose any arbitrary boundaries between the whole that is the subject of its attention in the model and the environment in which it is located. Instead, it reflects upon and questions where the boundaries have been drawn and how this impacts the kind of improvements that can be made. Contemporary systems thinking also respects the different appreciative systems that individuals bring to bear in viewing the world and making value judgments about particular situations. In order to contribute to a holistic appreciation of the problem situation at hand, different perspectives on its nature and possible resolution should be encouraged.

3.1 Systems Thinking

A *system* is defined as a set of elements that have one or more relationships between them, while *systems thinking* is the process by which one seeks to understand those elements and relationships so as to be able to understand the behavior of the system as a whole. Systems are usually visualized graphically as a set of nodes with links or connections between them.

A system is more than the sum of its parts, particularly if it's large or complex. It may exhibit unique behavior(s) that cannot necessarily be inferred from the behavior(s) of its individual elements or any subset of them. In systems theory, it's important to have perspective, as a very small observer of a single element may be oblivious to larger interactions that might be clear to a giant observer of the entire system. The relationships between system elements can be:

- Strictly deterministic (i.e., controlled by physical or other laws)
- Completely stochastic (subject to chance)
- More complex

Where human decision-making is involved, some of the interactions can include behavioral effects as well.

Modeling a system can involve both art and science when the modeler seeks to decide what is to be included in a system abstraction and what is to be excluded. The boundaries of an individual system depend on the nature of the relationships that link the nodes and drive change. The relationships between elements inside the system are different from the relationships those elements have with elements outside the system. If understanding a particular system requires that its interactions with other systems be understood as well, a modeler might create a kind of meta-system in which the elements of the system may be systems themselves.

One of the most fundamental attributes about a system is its predictability, or the degree to which we are able to forecast the system's next state or states. This change in state might be:

- An inevitable response to endogenous vulnerabilities that are already present in the system
- An unanticipated response to an exogenous shock

A model without predictive ability has little value in managing extreme risk and can provide few insights that add value to the decision-making process. Conversely, a model with predictive ability may provide forecasts of possible future scenarios that are substantially different from those generated using other analytic methods and greatly aid in risk measurement and mitigation.

3.1.1 Systems Science

When scientific knowledge advances to the extent that there is a discrepancy between theory and practice, there is a paradigm shift, according to the eminent scientific historian Thomas Kuhn. Such paradigm shifts have also occurred with systems thinking.

The four paradigms of systems thinking described in this chapter are:

1. Hard systems thinking (HST) or functionalist approaches. Though there is wide diversity in the techniques embraced by HST, they all have certain common characteristics. First, they are essentially goal-seeking strategies using quantitative tools to achieve an optimal or near-optimal solution. Second, they need a clear definition of ends and the optimal means for achieving those ends. This characteristic is a handicap when a messy and complex situation has to be dealt with, which is inevitable in nearly all engineering and planning projects. Third, they are best-suited for tackling problems that don't involve human activity systems.

2. Soft systems thinking (SST) or interpretive approaches. This is a form of systemic thinking that understands reality as the creative thinking of human beings. It takes into consideration social reality as the construction of people's interpretation of their experiences and works with the aspirations of people's views, interpretations, and intentions. Although there are quite a number of soft systems methodologies that have been employed since the 1970s, we list below four that have been extensively used.

    a. Ackoff's interpretive planning
    b. Checkland's soft systems methodology

    c. Senge's fifth discipline

    d. Strategic options development and analysis

3. Critical systems thinking or emancipatory approaches. While many practitioners have hung on to and made good use of both HST and SST, it became obvious to them that emancipatory interests for dealing with inequalities, such as power and economic differences in society, were not being adequately considered by SST. As a result, critical systems thinking emerged in the 1990s to address these inequalities. Werner Ulrich, a Swiss planner inspired by Churchman, made a breakthrough by operationally addressing this problem.

4. Multimodal systems thinking (MST). The most recent addition to the family of systems thinking is MST, which has recently been adopted in Europe. Developed by J. D. R. de Raadt and his colleagues in Sweden, MST uses as many as 15 performance indicators to question the validity of decisions made by planners and policy-makers. Many of these performance indicators cover issues of sustainability as well as environmental and ethical issues.

3.1.2 Principles of Systems Science

The principles of systems science include the following:

1. The idea of systemness. Bounded networks of relations among parts constitute a holistic unit. Systems interact with other systems, forming still larger systems. The universe is composed of systems of systems.

2. Systems are processes organized in structural and functional hierarchies.

3. Systems are themselves and can be represented abstractly as networks of relations between components.

4. Systems are dynamic on multiple timescales.

5. Systems exhibit various kinds and levels of complexity.

6. Systems evolve.

7. Systems encode knowledge and receive and send information.

8. Systems have regulation subsystems to achieve stability.

9. Systems contain models of other systems (e.g., protocols for interaction with anticipatory models).

10. Sufficiently complex adaptive systems can contain models of themselves (e.g., brains and mental models).

11. Systems can be understood (a corollary of 9)—science.

12. Systems can be improved (a corollary of 6)—engineering.

Within the boundary of a system, we can find three kinds of properties:

1. Elements, which are the kinds of parts (things or substances) that make up a system. These parts may be atoms or molecules, or larger bodies of matter like sand grains, plants, animals, people, and so on.

2. Attributes, which are characteristics of the elements that may be perceived and measured; examples include quantity, size, color, volume, and mass.

3. Relationships, which are the associations that occur between elements and attributes. These associations are based on cause and effect.

 The state of the system can be defined by determining the value of its properties (the elements, attributes, and/or relationships).

   Systems can be classified as:

1. An isolated system, which has no interactions beyond its boundary layer. Many controlled laboratory experiments are this type of system.
2. A closed system, which is a system that transfers energy, but not matter, across its boundary to the surrounding environment. Our planet is often viewed as a closed system.
3. An open system, which is a system that transfers both matter and energy across its boundary to the surrounding environment. Most cosystems are examples of open systems.

Systems theory suggests that knowledge of one type of system can be applied to many other types. By studying interactions and connections between the pieces of a system, the gained knowledge can be useful when confronted with other problems.

3.2 Systems Engineering

The complexity of systems is increasing and the challenges associated with bringing new systems into being are greater than ever. Requirements are constantly changing in conjunction with the introduction of new technologies on a continuing and evolutionary basis; the life cycles of many systems are being extended, while, at the same time, the life cycles of individual and specific technologies are becoming shorter. Systems are also being viewed more in terms of interoperability requirements and within a system of systems context. There is a greater degree of outsourcing and the utilization of suppliers throughout the world, and international competition is increasing in the global environment. Available resources are dwindling worldwide, and many of the systems (products) in use today are not meeting the needs of the customer/user in terms of performance, reliability, supportability, quality, and overall cost-effectiveness.

The purpose of systems engineering (SE) is to support organizations that desire improved performance. This improvement is generally obtained through the definition, development, and deployment of technological products, services, or processes that support functional objectives and fulfill needs. SE is a comprehensive, iterative technical management process that includes translating operational requirements into configured operational systems—integrating the technical inputs of the entire design team, managing interfaces, characterizing and managing technical risk, transitioning technology from the technology base into program specific efforts, and verifying that designs meet operational needs. SE is a life cycle activity that demands a concurrent approach to both product and process development.

Systems engineering encourages the use of modeling and simulation to validate assumptions or theories on systems and the interactions within them. The use of methods that allow early detection of possible potential failures are integrated into the design process. At the same time, decisions made at the beginning of a project whose consequences are not clearly understood can have enormous implications later on in the life of a system, and it is the task of the modern systems engineer to explore these issues and make critical decisions. There is no method that guarantees that decisions made today will still be valid when a system goes into service months or years (or even decades) after it was first conceived, but there are techniques to enable anticipation and develop corrective measures that can address the envisaged challenges in future.

3.2.1 System Dynamics via Simulation Modeling

System dynamics is a computer-based simulation modeling methodology developed at the Massachusetts Institute of Technology in Cambridge, MA in the 1950s as a tool for managers to analyze complex problems. Using system dynamics simulations enables one not only to observe events but also see patterns of behavior over time. The behavior of a system often arises out of the structure of the system itself, and this behavior usually changes over time. Understanding patterns of behavior, instead of focusing on day-to-day events, can offer a radical change in perspective. It shows how a system structure is the cause of its successes and failures. System dynamics simulations are good at communicating not just what might happen, but also why.

 Providing the managers with more and more information is not necessarily the correct solution, since too much detail or complexity might do more harm than good. The behavior of a system is a consequence of its structure. Therefore, the only real changes we can make to a system are changes to the structure. Other changes to the system will soon be canceled out through the actions of negative feedback loops.

This structure is represented by a series of causally linked relationships, implying that decisions made within an organization have envisaged or unenvisaged consequences; some of these consequences will be visible immediately, while others might not be revealed even for several years. The primary assumption of the system dynamics paradigm is that the persistent dynamic tendencies of any complex system arise from its internal causal structure—that is, from the pattern of physical constraints and social goals, rewards, and pressures that cause people to behave the way they do and to generate cumulatively the dominant dynamic tendencies of the total system. A system dynamicist is likely to look for explanations of recurring long-term social problems within this internal structure rather than in external disturbances, small maladjustments, or random events.

The central concept that system dynamicists use to understand system structure is the idea of two-way causation or feedback. It is assumed that social or individual decisions are made on the basis of information about the state of the system or environment surrounding the decision-makers. The decisions lead to actions that are intended to change (or maintain) the state of the system. New information about the system state then produces further decisions and changes. Each such closed chain of causal relationships forms a feedback loop. System dynamics models are made up of many such loops linked together. They are basically closed-system representations; most of the variables occur in feedback relationships and are endogenous. When some factor is believed to influence the system from the outside without being influenced itself, however, it is represented as an exogenous variable in the model.

3.2.2 Changeable Systems

There is an ever-increasing need to develop and produce systems that are robust, reliable and of a high quality, supportable, cost-effective from a total life-cycle perspective, and that are responsive to the needs of the customer/user in a satisfactory manner. Further, future systems must be designed with an open-architecture approach in mind in order to facilitate the incorporation of quick configuration changes and new technology insertions and so that there is an ability in place to respond to system interoperability requirements on an expedited basis.

3.2.2.1 Increasing Complexity

Modern systems are more complex. Today's systems involve many science and engineering disciplines. New technologies (including information, biotechnology, and nanotechnology) create new opportunities and challenges. Interfaces are increasingly more complex and system integration is more difficult. To emphasize this complexity, new terms have been used; for example, systems of systems, system architectures, and enterprise systems. Table 3.1 illustrates the complexity of problems across dimensions of systems' decision problems.

3.2.2.2 More Dynamic

Systems interact with their environment and the needs of stakeholders evolve in concert with this interaction. Rapid changes in the environment require systems to be dynamic to continue to provide value to consumers of products and services.

3.2.2.3 Growing Security Concerns

Many systems face increasing security challenges due to threats from malicious adversaries ranging from hackers to terrorists. Information assurance, which is the activity of protecting data and its flow across communication networks, is a major concern of system developers and users. In a similar fashion, physical security is an important design criteria for many systems as well.

3.2.2.4 Rising Privacy Concerns

As systems become more complex, more interconnected, and face more security challenges, the potential for privacy violations increases. The protection of personal information in systems is now a major system challenge.

3.2.2.5 Increasing Interconnectedness

The Internet and advances in information technology (IT) have led to business-to-business collaboration and a global economy enabled by pervasive interconnectedness. Anyone can start a global business by establishing a website. Systems now have an international supply chain for electronic components; with this, increasingly, hardware development, software development, component production, and services are being done globally.

3.2.2.6 Many Stakeholders

The increasing complexity and interconnectedness has contributed to the rise in the number of stakeholders involved in the system life cycle. In addition to considering the perspectives of scientists, engineers, and engineering managers, system engineers must also consider the perspectives of functional managers (production, sales, marketing, finance);

TABLE 3.1

Complexity of Problems Across Dimensions of Systems Decision Problems

Problem Dimension	Low (Technical Problem)	Medium (Complex Problem)	High (Wicked Problem)
Boundary type	Isolated, defined; Similar to solved problems	Interconnected, defined; Several unique features and new constraints will occur over time	No defined boundary; Unique or unprecedented
Stakeholders	Few homogeneous stakeholders	Multiple with different and/or conflicting views and interests	Hostile or alienated stakeholders with mutually exclusive interests
Challenges	Technology application and natural environment requirements	New technology development, natural environment, adaptive adversaries	No known technology, hostile natural environment, constant threats
Parameters	Stable and predictable	Parameter prediction difficult or unknown	Unstable or unpredictable
Use of experiments	Multiple low-risk experiments possible	Modeling and simulation can be used to perform experiments	Multiple experiments not possible
Alternative solutions	Limited set	Large number is possible	No bounded set
Solutions	Single optimal and testable solution	Good solutions can be identified and evaluated objectively and subjectively	No optimal or objectively testable solution
Resources	Reasonable and predictable	Large and dynamic	Not sustainable within existing constraints
End state	Optimal solution clearly defined	Good solutions can be implemented but additional needs arise from dynamic needs	No clear stopping point

regulators, professional organizations; legal counsel; environmentalists; the government; community groups; and international groups, to name just a few of the many stakeholders with vested interests in the system.

3.3 Systems Architecting

Despite ever more sophisticated integrated circuitry and single-chip processors, hardware is not usually the source of systemic complexity and cost. The cost of software surpassed the cost of hardware long ago. Often it is the software that is the source of design and development problems—it is often costly to design, construct, and maintain in a timely and cost-effective manner. Systems engineering approaches and techniques have their origins in traditional hardware design methods and tend to abstract away systemic software design. Software design emerged in parallel with systems engineering, but focused on detailed code design concerns. However, what we see in terms of static structures like code is different from what we see when the code is compiled and is executing. This ethereal nature of software is why it is so difficult to design and construct software-intensive systems. Engineers and architects are constantly striving to find techniques, methods, and abstractions to design and analyze complex software-intensive systems—this includes the systemic software that enables the system to do what it is specified to do.

Traditional systems engineering approaches are viewed by many as inadequate for designing modern IT systems. Enterprise architecture merges many of the traditional systems engineering concepts with software design and engineering concepts. However, enterprise architectures tend to focus on business process engineering.

3.3.1 Systems Architecture

It is comparatively easy to build small, stand-alone applications with a few stakeholders and business concerns with no architecture and very little detailed design however, this approach does not scale very well. It is intellectually difficult to build large systems directly by focusing on detailed structures without an architectural design to provide a roadmap for detailed designers and implementers. Building large, complex software-intensive systems with many competing stakeholders and business concerns is a very different proposition requiring layers of coordinated design abstraction to guide implementation. It is very difficult to reason about and satisfy broad systemic properties in systems with high numbers of developers, customers, users, and other stakeholders without architectural designs to bridge the gap between system requirements and detailed software designs.

Architecture design is the place wherein engineers turn the corner from the requirements space to the design space. In terms of software design artifact, architecture is typically used to refer to coarse-grained designs that describe gross partitioning of a system into some collection of elements that can be code-oriented, runtime, or physical structures. Architecture provides a means to partition the system into elements that can later be designed in detail. The architecture can be scrutinized and studied to expose weaknesses prior to detailed element design and implementation. Finally, the architecture can be used to guide overall construction by serving as a prescription for how the elements can be assembled, resulting in a system with predictable properties and behavior.

TABLE 3.2

Comparison of Architectural and Detailed Designs

	Architectural Design	Detailed Design
1	Architectural design addresses the overall properties of a system and all of its elements such as performance, availability, scalability, modifiability, security, and others in addition to general functionality.	Detailed designs are concerned with specific computational properties and functionality provided by individual elements.
2	Architectural designs address the partitioning of the system into parts or elements and interaction among the elements. Architects focus on the external properties of elements, the ensemble of elements, and system structure.	Detailed designs address the implementation details of the part. Detailed designers focus on the internals of elements, structures, and algorithms utilized within an element.
3	Architectural design is declarative. Architects partition, design, and document system elements based largely on intuition and experience because an all-encompassing standardized, formal architectural specification language is not available. Architectural design principles guide the intuition of the architects and frame (or constrain) the work of detailed designers.	Detailed designs are executable in nature in that they are meant to be translated directly into code.

Systemic properties cannot be achieved through detailed-level design because they require broad coordination across most or all system elements. In cases where detailed code structures (e.g., objects, classes, functions) are designed first, the resulting system structure is large and flat, with numerous dependencies existing between parts of the system that are not well-understood. The overall systemic properties that emerge as a result of numerous software engineers designing small pieces of the system without the framework of structure provided by an architecture design will not be well-understood until the system is implemented.

Architectural design differs from detailed software design in terms of the concerns addressed. Table 3.2 presents a comparison of architectural and detailed design.

Designing the system's architecture is a critical first step in system construction because the architecture is used to ensure that the overall system objectives are being met. The system architecture frames the detailed design and construction of the parts that will make up the system and can help to identify potential functional and quality attribute issues. Through the architecture design, these issues can be addressed early on in the development process, minimizing downstream production costs and maximizing overall product quality.

Systems built without deliberately designed system architectures will possess emergent properties that will not be well-understood because they were not designed into the system. Properties such as performance, availability, scalability, modifiability, security, and so forth must be designed into the system to meet the needs of the stakeholders who will utilize, buy, and maintain the system. If not designed into the system, understanding and fixing systemic shortcomings in these properties can be problematic and, in some cases, impossible to remedy. Architectural design is required to frame the detailed design. Many broad systemic properties such as these cannot be retrofitted into the system after implementation because they are broad, cross-cutting concerns—these properties must be designed into the system from the very beginning.

Systems design is the process of defining the architecture, components, interfaces, and other characteristics of a system or component of a system where:

> The term "component" is used to refer to a physical part or element that is a member of the system.
>
> The term "interface" refers to the boundary of a component and the point of connection between components.
>
> The phrase "other characteristics of a system or component of a system" refers to the functional behavior of the system as well as the broad systemic properties it possesses, such as performance, availability, scalability, modifiability, and so forth.

There are many specific systems engineering approaches for translating a customer's need arising from a specific mission or business objective into an architectural design. The systems architecture frames the detailed design and construction of the parts that will make up the system and can help to identify potential functional and quality attribute issues. Through the architectural design, these issues can be addressed early in the development process, minimizing downstream production costs and maximizing overall product quality. Systems architecture is concerned with partitioning the system into components and identifying their responsibilities and rules for interaction to ensure that the necessary functional and quality attribute requirements are met.

Most modern system architectural design methodologies prescribe designing a system using hierarchical decomposition by first decomposing the system into components. These methods generally focus on functionality and use functional requirements to guide the decomposition. This process is recursively repeated on each component until off-the-shelf or easily designed and constructed components are all that remain. Once the elementary components of a system are defined, the detailed interfaces for each component can be defined and the appropriate engineer (or organization) for each component can proceed with the detailed design, implementation, and testing of the functional element(s). In principle, constructing the system then is accomplished by integrating the lowest-level components one level of abstraction at a time. Each level of decomposition becomes a level of construction and integration wherein the results of the previous level are verified and validated. Therefore, a key tenant of system engineering is that bottom-up integration is only possible with the existence of sound top-down design that begins with a robust systems architecture.

Architectural design is not a state of *being* but rather of *becoming*—it is a process. In the construction of software-intensive systems, there are many different kinds of stakeholders whose wants, needs, and expectations of the system will influence the design of the architecture. Focusing on users as the only stakeholder can cause an overemphasis upon functionality as a prime driver of system structure and thus may not be the best idea of systemic development.

Architectural designs can provide essential insight for engineers when designing software-intensive systems. Architectural designs identify the parts of the system, enterprise, or software and how they will interact to render a service. Design representations can be used to analyze the overall behavioral (functional) and nonbehavioral (nonfunctional) properties of systems, enterprises, or software. Behavioral properties include the essential functional requirements, whereas nonbehavioral properties include performance, modifiability, interoperability, and security, among others. These nonbehavioral properties are also referred to as quality attributes. Designers of systems, enterprises, and software must continually make trade-offs between behavioral and quality attribute requirements to achieve a balance acceptable to the stakeholder community. For example, some architectural design decisions might promote data throughput (performance) but undermine the ability to change the system (modifiability). Architectures allow designers to identify and reason about these trade-offs early on in the development so that these properties can be designed into the system, rather than fixing, tuning, or refactoring them after development.

Architectural requirements are not all of the requirements—they are those requirements that will influence the architecture utmost as it initially decomposes the system and selects the fundamental structures that will form it. These are easy choices to make, but they are difficult to get right. Although initial design choices are relatively easy to make, they are binding decisions and come with long-term impacts. Selecting the correct structure(s) is a critical first step in establishing systemic designs that satisfy functionality and the broader nonfunctional properties required of a system. The architectural design forms the scaffolding for the downstream detailed designers and implementers. Without clearly defining the architectural requirements before the initial design phase begins, it is nearly impossible to get the architectural design right.

3.3.1.1 Functional Architectural Requirements

Functional architectural requirements have the least influence on design. High-level functional requirements are best described with use cases. Although too cumbersome for modeling detailed requirements, use cases are excellent for discovering, analyzing, and documenting the functional requirements necessary for designing the architecture. Use cases are not models for functional decomposition, nor should designers use them to describe how the system provides services. Use case models describe what is needed in a system in terms of functional responses to given stimuli. A use case is initiated by an entity and then goes on to describe a sequence of interactions between the entity (or entities) and the system that, when taken together, model systemic functional requirements. Use cases may also include variants of the normal operation that describe error occurrences, detection, handling and recovery, failure modes, or other alternative behaviors.

Traditional use cases describe functional requirements in terms of actors and their interactions with the system. Each use case defines a set of interactions between actors and the system we intend to design. Use cases model system interaction with actors at a coarse-grained level of abstraction. This can help in establishing the scope of the project and in guiding architects through the critical initial decomposition and structuring of the system.

 Because use cases were popularized by object-oriented analysis and design methods (specifically Unified Modeling Language), they maybe were thought to be relevant only when using object-oriented methods and languages. However, use cases are not inherently an object-oriented modeling technique.

In use cases, the system is treated as a black box and the use case describes the requirement—what is needed—not how the system delivers the services. Use cases can also help to establish system context or scope; that is, what is inside the design space and what is outside of the design space. While functionality has less influence on structure, establishing a clear context is an essential first step in design. An unclear or poorly defined context can lead to severe design problems.

Use case models serve as a communication vehicle and encourage dialog between technical and nontechnical stakeholders.

3.3.1.2 Nonfunctional Architectural Requirements

Nonfunctional architectural requirements will have the most influence over the design. While functional requirements describe what the system must do, quality attribute requirements describe how the system must do it; however, both parts are required for a full understanding of the nonfunctional requirements. Take any given nonfunctional requirement and associate it with any number of operational elements. Together, it provides a fuller understanding of the requirement in terms of what must be done functionally and how it must be done in terms of a nonfunctional response.

Thus, to guide design choices and measure the fitness of the design, quality attribute requirements must be described with respect to some operational context. To do this, we will use nonfunctional scenarios to define more completely the quality attribute properties a system must possess. Nonfunctional scenarios describe some requirement in terms of the following:

- Stimulus, or the condition affecting the architecture. This can be an event, a user request for data, the initiation of service, or a proposed change to the system.
- Source(s) of the stimulus, or the entity (e.g., human, organizational, or technological) that is the source of the stimulus described above. There can be one or more sources.
- Relevant environmental conditions, or the conditions present in the system's operational environment during the receipt of the stimulus. Relevant environmental conditions can be diverse and will depend upon the stimulus, but examples might include "during runtime execution," "during initial development," "after deployment," "during peak load," "while seven hundred users are logged in," and so forth.
- Architectural element(s), or the element or elements of the architecture that are directly or indirectly affected by the stimulus. In early requirements-gathering, when quality attribute requirements are initially developed, the artifact is probably not known. However, after architectural design has commenced and is successively refined, the architectural element information should be added to the nonfunctional requirements information.
- System response, or how the systems stakeholders would like the architecture/ system to respond to the stimuli.
- Response measure, or a measure of how the system responds. The kind of response measure listed will depend upon the stimuli.
- For change/modification stimuli, we might have response measures that measure the cost of change in terms of time, manpower, cost, and so forth.
- For a performance stimulus, we might have response measures in terms of throughput, response time, and so forth.

The architectural design is critical to balancing these kinds of nonfunctional concerns before the steps of detailed design, implementation, or investment in upgrades to a software-intensive system. Compromise is made in terms of balancing systemic nonfunctional properties in the design. However, it is impossible to strike the optimal design balance if the quality attribute properties are poorly articulated, poorly understood, or remain unstated. If architecture is not informed of the exact nonfunctional requirements, they will rely on intuition or experience, or simply guess when making architectural choices to promote or inhibit various quality attribute properties in the system.

3.3.2 Enterprise Architecture

Enterprise architecture concepts evolved from the systems engineering community but are specialized to address the specific design concerns of very large, highly distributed IT systems and the organizations dependent upon them. Enterprise architecture frameworks are essentially design methodologies focused on business modeling, business processes, application functionality, and the technological infrastructure that supports the enterprise.

Many of the concepts embraced by the enterprise architecture community emerged from the commercial information systems (ISs) development that was taking place at IBM (Armonk, NY, USA) in the 1970s for large, distributed, business-oriented applications. These roots have given enterprise architectures a decidedly business and IT-centric flavor. John Zachman, an employee of IBM, was a key contributor to the company's information planning methodology called business systems planning. He applied concepts from traditional building architectures to the design and construction of business enterprises and the computer systems that empowered them. Zachman coined the term enterprise architecture and created the Zachman Framework for defining enterprise architectures.

The term framework is used to describe a prescribed set of steps and artifacts that are created as a course of designing an enterprise system or system of systems. Enterprise architecture frameworks (EAFs) embody design strategies and provide step-by-step guidance and even templates for designing and documenting the enterprise. EAFs prescribe a set of artifacts for specific enterprise stakeholders. Using an EAF, the enterprise architect creates various artifacts intended to be views of the system from the perspective of the enterprise stakeholders. Most EAFs identify a number of concerns that will guide the design of enterprises, such as:

- Business requirements: The business needs of the organization.
- Stakeholders: Those who will interact with the enterprise in some way.
- Business processes: A series of activities leading to the achievement of a measurable business result.
- Environment: Those conditions in which the enterprise must operate.
- Software: The standard software suite that is closely coupled to the infrastructure, such as operating systems, drivers, database systems, and so forth.
- Data: High-level data designs that describe the structure of an enterprise's data needs in terms of entities and relationships between entities.
- Infrastructure: The enterprise's general IT assets, such as networks, hardware, computing systems, routers, and so forth.

Today, there are many different EAFs for designing and constructing enterprise architectures; these include:

1. The Zachman Enterprise Architecture Framework
2. The Federal Enterprise Architecture Framework

3. The Treasury Enterprise Architecture Framework

4. The Popkin Enterprise Architecture Framework

5. Extended Enterprise Architecture

6. The Open Group Architecture Framework

7. The Department of Defense Architecture Framework

Key objectives of an EAF are to model the enterprise networks, databases, middleware, security, fault-handling, processing of transactions, and connectivity to the Internet so that customers can access services. The purpose of an EAF is to help enterprise architects manage the complexity of highly distributed systems of systems by providing techniques and methods to identify key stakeholders and their role in the enterprise; discover relationships between various entities of the enterprise; and, in some cases, map business processes to IT infrastructure. Most EAFs provide comprehensive documentation guidelines, templates, and frameworks for documenting the enterprise architecture.

Figure 3.1 shows the organization architecture consisting of business, information, application and technical architecture.

3.3.2.1 Business Architecture

The business architecture results from the implementation of business strategies and the definition of processes. This architecture dictates the functional requirements of business processes that determine the ISs that will operationally support the business. The core concept within the business architecture is the business process. A business process is a set of value-adding activities that operates over input entities producing output entities. These activities are either orchestrated by a central controlling entity or choreographed—the actual coordination mechanism is only relevant while detailing how the process is enacted.

Enterprise architecture	• Business processes and models • Business data • Organizational structure and relationships • Enterprise stakeholders • IT infrastructure
System architecture	• Identification of system context • Partitioning (hardware/infrastructure focus) • Identification of software requirements • Overall systemic functional requirements • Systemic integration and testing
Software architecture	• Identification of crosscutting design concerns (quality attributes) • Software functional requirements • Partitioning of software application(s) • Software and systemic integration and testing
Detailed software design	• Language features • Algorithmic efficiencies • Data structure design • Software application testing • Implementation of functionality

FIGURE 3.1
Organization architecture.

Although an organization always comprises multiple sets of coordinated activities, each may or may not be classified as an actual business processes. What distinguishes an arbitrary set of coordinated activities from a business process is the fact that the process necessarily adds value to a customer, whether internal or external to the organization.

An activity is performed during a specific period. As a precondition for its enactment, all of the business roles must be fulfilled by specific entities. These entities will be engaged in playing their roles for the duration of the activity. The activity postcondition is that all of the roles should have been completed by the end of the specified period.

An activity describes the business roles required of the organizational entities for its operation. These roles include:

1. The actor role. An activity requires one actor or a combination or team of actors to be executed. The actor represents a person, a machine or device, or an IS. An actor provides the services required for fulfilling the business role required by the activity.

2. The resource role. A resource is used as input or output of an activity during its operation. A resource is usually created, used, transformed, or consumed during the operation of the activity.

3. The observable state role. An observable state is a specific resource role that is used as a means to observe the status of an activity.

The major components for describing the business architecture are as follows:

- Business strategy: key business requirements, processes, goals, strategies, key performance indicators, business risks, and the business-operating model
- Business function: key business services, processes, and capabilities that will be affected by the organization architecture efforts
- Business organization: the high-level nature of organizational structures; business roles (internal audiences, external customers, and partners); the decision-making process; and organizational budget information

3.3.2.2 Information Architecture

The information architecture describes what the organization needs to know in order to run its processes and operations as described in the business architecture. It is an abstraction of the information requirements of the organization and provides a high-level logical representation of all of the key information elements that are used in the business as well as the relationship(s) between them. It defines a view on the business information that is independent of the application and technology architectures.

Business information is structured as a collection of informational entities. Entities describe various resources required by processes, including business, support, and management processes. An entity can result from the composition or specialization of other entities in the object-oriented sense. Entities have an identifier defined from a business perspective along with an associated set of roles with a related set of attributes; each role integrates its set of attributes into the entity. Thus, every entity has an overall set of attributes that results from the summation of attributes derived from each role the entity is able to play.

The principal components for describing information architecture are as follows:

- Information strategy: Information architecture principles, information governance and compliance requirements, canonical data models, industry data model support strategy, and dissemination patterns and reference models
- Information assets: A catalog of critical business data types and models (such as a customer profile, purchase order, product data, and the supply chain); relationships between such business data types; and all the processes and services that interact with these data

3.3.2.3 Application Architecture

The application architecture fulfills two major goals: supporting the business requirements and allowing efficient management of the organization's entities. To satisfy these goals, the application architecture should be derived top-down from the analysis of the business and information architectures.

The application architecture defines the applications required to enable the business architecture. This includes identifying how the applications interact with each other, how they will interact with other business integration elements, and how the application and data will be distributed throughout the organization. It typically includes descriptions of automated services that support the business processes and of the interactions and interdependencies between an organization's application systems, plans for developing new applications, and revisions of old applications based on the enterprises objectives.

The architecture of a business process support system is described using a structure of IS block. An IS block is then defined as an organized collection of services, mechanisms, and operations designed to handle organization information. Each block may state several attributes, such as availability, scalability (the ability to scale up performance), and profile-based access (the ability to identify who does what).

The application architecture defines the applications needed for data management and business support, regardless of the actual software used to implement systems. It functionally defines what application services are required to ensure entities and processes are supported in an acceptable time-, format-, and cost-related manner. Service is the aggregation of a set of operations provided by an architectural block. It can be seen as a generalization of the concept of web services. Service is composed of three types:

1. Business service, or a set of operations provided by IS blocks supporting business processes.
2. IS service, or a set of operations provided by an IS block to other IS blocks. This is used to aggregate multiple IS blocks.
3. IT service, or a set of technological services provided by the specific application platforms.

The principal components for describing application architecture are as follows:

- Application strategy: The key application architecture principles (e.g., build vs. buy, hosted vs. in-house, open source vs. commercial grade, open standards vs. .NET, etc.); application governance; portfolio management; and a set of reference application architectures relevant to the customer

- Application processes: A series of application-specific processes that support the business processes in BA
- Application services: An inventory of the key application services exposed to internal and external applications that support the business services
- Logical components: An inventory of relevant product-agnostic enterprise application systems that is relevant to stated business objectives
- Physical components: Actual products that support the logical application components and their relationships to relevant components and services in information and technology architectures

The granularity of abstraction required by an enterprise depends upon factors such as domain, scope, responsibilities, design and construction roles, and so on. Figure 3.2 shows increasingly more detailed abstractions that focus inwardly based on a frame of reference established by a higher abstraction. Each architecture in this example constrains the downstream architect and, although not shown here, detailed designers and implementers would be maximally constrained at the finest granularity of abstraction.

3.3.2.4 Technical Architecture

The technological architecture represents the technologies behind application implementation as well as the infrastructure and environment required for the deployment of the business process support systems.

The technological architecture addresses a large number of concepts since it must cope simultaneously with continuous technological evolutions and the need to provide different specialized technological perspectives, such as those centered on

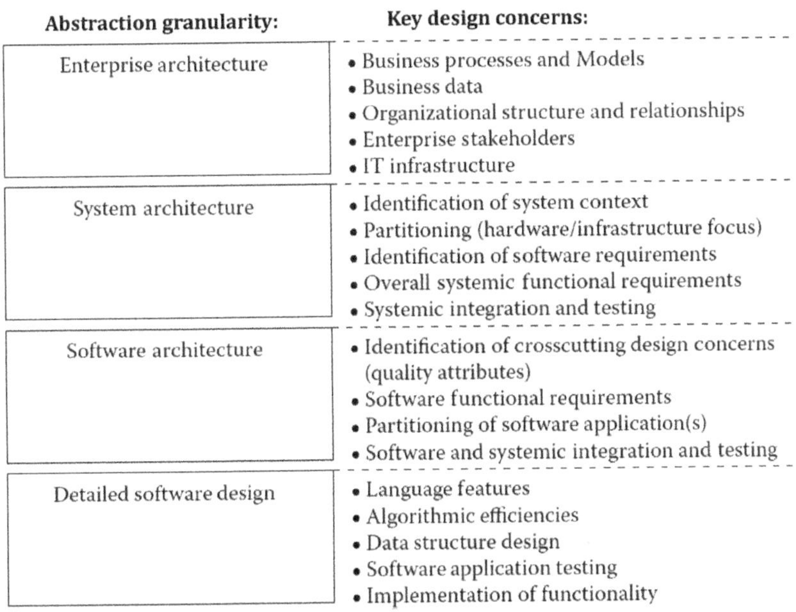

Abstraction granularity:	Key design concerns:
Enterprise architecture	• Business processes and Models • Business data • Organizational structure and relationships • Enterprise stakeholders • IT infrastructure
System architecture	• Identification of system context • Partitioning (hardware/infrastructure focus) • Identification of software requirements • Overall systemic functional requirements • Systemic integration and testing
Software architecture	• Identification of crosscutting design concerns (quality attributes) • Software functional requirements • Partitioning of software application(s) • Software and systemic integration and testing
Detailed software design	• Language features • Algorithmic efficiencies • Data structure design • Software application testing • Implementation of functionality

FIGURE 3.2
Abstraction granularity levels and the corresponding design concerns.

security and hardware. These concepts are abstracted as an IT block. An IT block is the infrastructure, application platform, and/or technological or software component that realizes or implements a set of IS blocks.

The principal components for describing technology architecture are as follows:

- Technology strategy, which comprises technology architecture principles; technology asset governance methodology; portfolio management strategy; and technology standards, patterns, and RAs. These assets and artifacts go a long way in strengthening and sustaining technology-driven business solutions.

- Technology services, or an inventory of specific technology services and their relationships as well as the business services, application services, information assets, and logical or physical technology components that realize such services.

- Logical components, or the product-agnostic components that exist at the technology infrastructure tier to support each technology service.

- Physical components, or the set of technology products that exists behind each logical technology component to implement the technology service.

3.4 Enterprise Processes

Enterprise processes are business structures that make up the enterprise. An enterprise might be composed of customer service, inventory, shipping, and production organizations. Business processes define how these entities interact, and identifying the enterprise business processes is the primary aim of most EAFs.

A business process is a description of the dynamic interaction of stakeholders and the flow of information between the various entities that compose the enterprise. Business processes drive the analysis and design of the enterprise architecture and are used to identify organizations, pertinent stakeholders, systems, data, and other entities relevant to the enterprise. In most enterprise methodologies, business processes are directly implemented or supported by IT infrastructures and systems.

Processes are means for identifying, documenting, and analyzing complex networks of human interactions with organizations and the IT systems they use to provide services, communicate, and generally conduct business operations. For instance, consider an organization whose business model is to sell products to other businesses via the Web, track inventory and shipping, manage customer relations, and so forth. This business model could be distilled into various business processes that describe the activities of the organization.

Business processes might describe the dynamic aspects of

- How a customer's order is processed.
- How the product is manufactured.
- How the inventory is updated.
- How quickly the product is delivered to the customer.

3.5 Summary

Systems thinking views the enterprise as a whole and assesses the system properties to try to understand the system behavior. This chapter reviewed the basic concepts of systems thinking, systems science, systems engineering, and systems architecting. Knowing this basic information about systems helps in understanding the origin of the significance of enterprise architecture and the constituting of business architecture, information architecture, application architecture, and technical architecture. This also provides the context for the significance of business processes in contemporary enterprises. Many of the current paradigms for enterprise improvement adhere to a system view including lean enterprise systems, total quality management, and supply chain management.

4

Enterprise Architecture

Among the first decisions that are made in an enterprise engineering project is what enterprise architecture (EA) to adopt. This chapter presents the concept of EA to support the analysis and design of enterprise systems. An EA is important to have when dealing with the complexity inherent in enterprise systems and to assist in aligning the many subsystems so that they all work harmoniously toward the enterprise's goals. EA provides the foundation on which enterprise integration is anchored.

Every enterprise can develop its own architecture independently. The problem with this approach is that developing an EA is an enormous undertaking fraught with the risk of omitting crucial elements, creating inconsistent interfaces between the views, and not finishing the project in a reasonable time period. Instead of developing an EA from scratch, an alternative approach is to start with a *reference EA*. A reference EA is a generic architecture that can be used as the starting point to derive an enterprise's architecture.

 The idea behind this is that an enterprise, by using a reference architecture, is more likely to include all relevant views in their architecture, will adopt best practices into their architecture, and will be able to create the architecture much more rapidly than if they did it from scratch. Additionally, the use of a reference architecture provides some insurance that the resulting architecture will be useful and completed on schedule.

4.1 Architecture

All computer systems are made up of the same three fundamental parts: hardware (e.g., processors, memory, disks, network cards); software (e.g., programs or libraries); and data, which may be either transient (in memory) or persistent (on disk or read-only memory) in nature. A computer system can be understood in terms of what its individual parts actually do, how they work together, and how they interact with the world around them—in other words, its architecture.

An EA provides a high-level design of the entire enterprise that will guide all other enterprise projects. An architecture represents significant, broad design decisions for the enterprise, from which all other design decisions should be consistent. Architecturally significant decisions are those that the architect (or architecture team) needs to make in order to address the concerns of strategy, structure, and enterprise integration. Architectural decisions include deciding how to decompose the enterprise into views, how to decompose each view into different abstraction levels, policies on technology usage, decisions on business culture to guide organizational design, and decisions on what modeling conventions to use.

The Software Engineering Institute (SEI) at Carnegie-Mellon University (Pittsburgh, PA) defines architecture as follows:

> The architecture of a software-intensive system is the structure or structures of the system, which comprise software elements, the externally visible properties of those elements, and the relationships among them.

EAs have the following major goals:

1. For the EA, its units, policies, processes, strategies, and technological infrastructure (e.g., IT systems) to successfully support all stakeholders in achieving short- and long-term business goals and objectives of the enterprise

2. For the EA to foster an alignment of the technological systems developed by and used by an enterprise with its business goals and strategic direction

3. For the EA to help an enterprise to learn, grow, innovate, and respond to market demands and changing basic conditions

4. For the EA foster and maintain the learning capabilities of enterprises so that they may be sustainable

4.1.1 Architectural Element

An architectural element is a fundamental piece from which a system can be considered to be constructed. Depending on the system being built, programming libraries, subsystems, deployable software units (e.g., Enterprise Java Beans and Active X controls), reusable software products (e.g., database management systems), or entire applications may form architectural elements in an information system.

An architectural element possesses the following key attributes:

- A clearly defined set of responsibilities
- A clearly defined boundary
- A set of clearly defined interfaces, which define the services that the element provides to the other architectural elements

4.1.2 System Structures

System structures are of the following two kinds:

1. The static structures of a software system define its internal design-time elements and their arrangement. The static structures of a system tell you what the design-time form of a system is, what its elements are, and how they fit together.

   Internal design-time software elements might be modules, object-oriented classes or packages, database-stored procedures, services, or any other self-contained code unit. Internal data elements include classes, relational database entities/tables, and data files. Internal hardware elements include computers or their constituent parts such as disk or central processing unit and networking elements such as cables, routers, and hubs. The static arrangement of these elements defines the associations, relationships, or connectivity between these elements. For software modules, for example, there may be static relationships such as a hierarchy of elements or dependencies between elements. For classes, relational entities, or other data elements, relationships define how one data item is linked to another one. For hardware, the relationships define the required physical interconnections between the various hardware elements of the system.

2. The dynamic structures of a software system define its runtime elements and their interactions. The dynamic structures show how the system actually works, what happens at runtime, and what the system does in response to external (or internal) stimulus.

   These internal interactions may be flows of information between elements, or the parallel or sequential execution of internal tasks, or, they may be expressed in terms of the effect(s) they have on data.

External properties manifest in two forms:

1. The externally visible behavior of a software system defines the functional interactions between the system and its environment. The externally visible behavior of a system (i.e., what it does) is determined by the combined functional behavior of its internal elements.

   This includes flows of information in and out of the system, the way that the system responds to external stimuli, and the published "contract" or API that the architecture has with the outside world.

2. A quality property is an externally visible, nonfunctional property of a system such as performance, security, or scalability. Quality properties tell you how a system behaves from the viewpoint of an external observer (often referred to as its nonfunctional characteristics).

   The quality properties of a system such as performance, scalability, and resilience (how it does it) arise from the quality properties of its internal elements. (Typically, a system's overall quality property is only as good as the property of its worst-behaving or weakest internal element.)

Quality attributes can be categorized into the following three groups:

1. Implementation attributes (not observable at runtime); these include:
   a. Interoperability: Universal accessibility and the ability to exchange data among internal components and with the outside world. Interoperability requires loose dependency of infrastructure.
   b. Maintainability and extensibility: The ability to modify the system and conveniently extend it.
   c. Testability: The degree to which the system facilitates the establishment of test cases. Testability usually requires a complete set of documentation accompanied by system design and implementation.
   d. Portability: The system's level of independence on software and hardware platforms. Systems developed using high-level programming languages usually have good portability. One typical example is Java—most Java programs need only to be compiled once and can run everywhere.
   e. Scalability: A system's ability to adapt to an increase in user requests. Scalability disfavors bottlenecks in system design.

    f. Flexibility: The ease of system modification to cater to different environments or problems for which the system was not originally designed. Systems developed using component-based architecture or service-oriented architecture usually possess this attribute.

2. Runtime attributes (observable at runtime); these include:

    a. Availability: A system's capability to be available 24/7. Availability can be achieved via replication and careful design to cope with failures of hardware, software, or the network.

    b. Security: A system's ability to cope with malicious attacks from outside or inside the system. Security can be improved by installing firewalls, establishing authentication and authorization processes, and using encryption.

    c. Performance: Increasing a system's efficiency with regard to response time, throughput, and resource utilization, which are attributes that are usually in conflict with each other.

    d. Usability: The level of human satisfaction derived from using the system. Usability includes matters of completeness, correctness, and compatibility, as well as a friendly user interface, complete documentation, and technical support.

    e. Reliability: The failure frequency, the accuracy of output results, the mean-time-to-failure, the ability to recover from failure, and the failure predictability.

    f. Maintainability (extensibility, adaptability, serviceability, testability, compatibility, and configurability); the ease of software system change.

3. Business attributes, which include:

    a. Time to market: The time it takes from requirements analysis to the date a product is released.

    b. Cost: The expense of building, maintaining, and operating the system.

    c. Lifetime: The period of time that the product is "alive" before retirement.

4.1.2.1 Attribute Tradeoffs

In many cases, no single architecture style can meet all of the quality attributes simultaneously. Software architects often need to balance tradeoffs among attributes. Typical quality attribute tradeoff pairs include the following:

1. Tradeoff between space and time: For example, to increase the time efficiency of a hash table means a decrease in its space efficiency.

2. Tradeoff between reliability and performance: For instance, Java programs are well protected against buffer overflow due to security measures such as boundary checks on arrays. Such reliability features come at the cost of time efficiency, as compared with the simpler and faster C language that provides the "dangerous," yet efficient, pointers.

3. Tradeoff between scalability and performance: For example, one typical approach to increase the scalability of a service is to replicate servers. To ensure consistency of all servers (e.g., to make sure that each server has the same logically consistent data), performance of the whole service is compromised.

When an architecture style does not satisfy all of the desired quality attributes, software architects work with system analysts and stakeholders to nail down the priority of quality attributes. By enumerating alternative architecture designs and calculating a weighted evaluation of quality attributes, software architects can select the optimal design.

4.1.3 Candidate Architecture

A *candidate architecture* for a system is a particular arrangement of static and dynamic structures that have the potential to exhibit the system's required externally visible behaviors and quality properties. Although the candidate architectures have different static and dynamic structures and share the same important externally visible behaviors (in this case, responses to booking transactions) and general quality properties (e.g., acceptable response time, throughput, availability, and time to repair), they are likely to differ in the specific set of quality properties exhibited (such as one being easier to maintain but more expensive to build than another).

An architecture style (also known as an "architecture pattern") abstracts the common properties of a family of similar designs. An architecture style contains a set of rules, constraints, and patterns of how to structure a system into a set of elements and connectors. It governs the overall structure design pattern of constituent element types and their runtime interaction of flow control and data transfer.

Theoretically, an architecture style is a viewpoint abstraction for a software structure that is domain-independent. Typically, a system has its own application domain such as image processing, a Web portal, an expert system, or a mail server. Each domain may have its own reference model. For instance, the model–view–controller is widely employed by designers of interactive systems. Such a reference model partitions the functionalities of a system into subsystems or software components.

 Architecture styles are important because each style has a set of quality attributes that it promotes. By identifying the styles that a software architecture design supports, we can verify whether the architecture is consistent with the requirement specifications and identify which tactics can be used to better implement the architecture.

In many cases, a system can adopt heterogeneous architectures—that is, more than one architecture style can coexist in the same design. It is also true that an architecture style maybe applied to many application domains.

The key components of an architecture style are:

- Elements that perform functions required by a system
- Connectors that enable communication, coordination, and cooperation among elements
- Constraints that define how elements can be integrated to form the system
- Attributes that describe the advantages and disadvantages of the chosen structure

For example:

1. In the data-centric style, the data store plays a central role and is accessed frequently by other elements that modify data.
2. In the dataflow style, input data are transformed by a series of computational or manipulative elements.

3. In the call-and-return style, functions and procedures are elements organized in a control hierarchy, with a main program invoking several subprograms.

4. In the object-oriented style, elements are represented as objects that encapsulate data and operations, and the communication among them is done via message-passing.

5. In the layered style, each module or package completes tasks that progress in a framework from higher-level abstractions to lower-level implementations.

Multitier architecture is commonly used for distributed systems. It usually consists of three element types, as follows:

1. The client element is responsible for graphical user interface presentation, accepting user requests, and rendering results.

2. The middleware element gets the requests from the client element, processes the requests based on the business logic, and sends a data request to the backend tier.

3. The data store server element manages data querying and updating.

All three types of elements are connected via a network (e.g., the Internet).

4.1.4 Stakeholder

A stakeholder in a architecture is a person, group, or entity with an interest in or concerns about the realization of the architecture. A concern about an architecture is a requirement, an objective, an intention, or an aspiration a stakeholder has for that architecture.

A stakeholder often represents a class of person, such as user or developer, rather than an individual. This presents some problems because it may not be possible to capture and reconcile the needs of all members of the class.

The important attributes of a software development project are often interpreted as a triangle whose corners represent cost, quality, and time to market. For example, a high-quality system would take longer to build and, hence, would cost more for completion. Conversely, it may be possible to reduce the initial development time but, assuming costs are kept roughly constant, but this would come at the expense of reducing the quality of the delivered software. One or more of these attributes are likely to be important to different stakeholders, and it is the architect's job to understand which of these attributes are important to whom and to reach an acceptable compromise when necessary.

A good architecture is one that successfully meets the objectives, goals, and needs of its stakeholders. Stakeholders (explicitly or implicitly) drive the whole shape and direction of the architecture, which is developed solely for their benefit and to serve their needs. Stakeholders ultimately make or direct the fundamental decisions about scope, functionality, operational characteristics, and structure of the eventual product or system.

 Describing architecture designs: the "4 + 1" view model, developed by Philippe Kruchten, is a way to show different views of a software system from the perspective of different stakeholders. It is especially useful in describing a complete set of functional and nonfunctional requirements. An alternative choice is to use architecture description languages to formally specify the structure and semantics of software architecture.

4.2 Viewpoints and Views

A view is a representation of one or more structural aspects of an architecture that illustrates how the architecture addresses one or more concerns held by one or more of its stakeholders. An architectural view is a way to portray those aspects or elements of the architecture that are relevant to the concerns with reference to this view.

An architectural description comprises a number of views; a view conforms to a viewpoint and so communicates the resolution of a number of concerns (and a resolution of a concern may be communicated in a number of views).

> A viewpoint is a collection of patterns, templates, and conventions for constructing one type of view. It defines the stakeholders whose concerns are reflected in the viewpoint and the guidelines, principles, and template models for constructing its views.

A viewpoint defines the aims, intended audience, and content of a class of views and defines the concerns that the views of this class will address. The objective of the viewpoint concept is to make available a library of templates and patterns that can be used off the shelf to guide the creation of an architectural view that can be inserted into an architectural description. They provide a framework for capturing reusable architectural knowledge that can be used to guide the creation of a particular type of architectural description.

1. Viewpoint catalog

   A viewpoint is defined with items like:

   a. Information, which describes the way that the architecture stores, manipulates, manages, and distributes information. The ultimate purpose of virtually any computer system is to manipulate information in some form, and this viewpoint develops a complete but high-level view of static data structure and information flow. The objective of this analysis is to answer the big questions around content, structure, ownership, latency, references, and data migration.

   b. Functional, which describes the system's functional elements, their responsibilities, interfaces, and primary interactions. A Functional view is the cornerstone of most architectural descriptions and is often the first part of the description that stakeholders try to read. It drives the shape of other system structures such as the information structure, concurrency structure, deployment structure, and so on. It also has a significant impact on the system's quality properties, such as its ability to change, its ability to be secured, and its runtime performance.

   c. Concurrency, which describes the concurrency structure of the system and maps functional elements to concurrency units to clearly identify the parts of the system that can execute concurrently and how this performance is coordinated and controlled. This entails the creation of models that show the process and thread structures that the system will use as well as the interprocess communication mechanisms used to coordinate their operation.

   d. Development, which describes the architecture that supports the software development process. Development views communicate the aspects of the architecture of interest to those stakeholders involved in building, testing, maintaining, and enhancing the system.

e. Deployment, which describes the environment into which the system will be deployed, including capturing the dependencies the system has on its run-time environment. This view captures the mapping of the software elements to the runtime environment that will execute them, the technical environment requirements for each element and the hardware environment that your system needs (primarily the processing nodes, network interconnections, and disk storage facilities required).

f. Operations, which describes how the system will be operated, administered, and supported when it is running in its production environment. For all but the simplest systems, installing, managing, and operating the system is a significant task that must be considered and planned at design time. The aim of the operational viewpoint is to identify systemwide strategies for addressing the operational concerns of the system's stakeholders and to identify solutions that address these.

2. Benefits

a. Management of complexity, which involves dealing simultaneously with all of the aspects of a large system and noting that such can result in overwhelming complexity that no one person can possibly handle. By treating each significant aspect of a system separately, such helps in conquering this complexity.

b. Communication with stakeholder groups, which takes into account that the concerns of each stakeholder group are typically quite different (e.g., contrast the primary concerns of end users, security auditors, and help-desk staff) and that communicating effectively with the various stakeholder groups is quite a challenge. The viewpoint-oriented approach can help considerably with this problem. Different stakeholder groups can be guided quickly to different parts of the architectural description based on their particular concerns, and each view can be presented using language and notation appropriate to the knowledge, expertise, and concerns of the concerned stakeholder.

c. Separation of concerns, which involves the idea that describing the many aspects of the system via a single representation can cloud communication and may result in independent aspects of the system becoming intertwined in the model. Separating different models of a system into distinct (but related) descriptions helps the design, analysis, and communication processes by focusing on each aspect separately.

d. Improved developer focus considers the idea that the architectural description is the foundation of the system design. Building the right system is enabled by separating out into different views those aspects of the system that are particularly important to the development team.

4.3 Perspectives

Many architectural decisions address concerns that are common to many or all views. These concerns are normally driven by the need for the system to exhibit a certain quality property rather than to provide a particular function; such properties are sometimes referred as a nonfunctional property. For instance, security is clearly a vital aspect of most architecture. It has always been important to be able to restrict access to data or functionality to appropriate classes of users and, in the age of the Internet, good external and internal security is even more important. There is an inherent need to consider quality properties such as security in each architectural view. Considering them in isolation does not make sense, and neither does using a viewpoint to guide the creation of another view for each quality property. Rather than defining another viewpoint and creating another view, we need some way to modify and enhance our existing views to ensure that our architecture exhibits the desired quality properties.

> An architectural perspective is a collection of activities, tactics, and guidelines that are used to ensure that a system exhibits a particular set of related quality properties that require consideration across a number of the system's architectural views.

The most important perspectives for large information systems include:

- Performance and Scalability (meeting the system's required performance profile and handling increasing workloads satisfactorily)
- Availability and Resilience (ensuring system availability when required and coping with failures that could affect this)
- Security (ensuring controlled access to sensitive system resources)
- Evolution (ensuring that the system can cope with likely changes)

The advantages of perspectives are:

1. A perspective is a useful store of knowledge, helping one to quickly review their architectural models for a particular quality property without having to absorb a large quantity of highly detailed material.
2. A perspective acts as an effective guide when one is working in an area that is new to them/when they are unfamiliar with its typical concerns, problems, and solutions.
3. A perspective is a useful memory aid when one is working in an area that they are more familiar with, to make sure that they don't forget anything important.

 Perspective should be employed as early as possible in the design of the architecture because such helps in preventing one from traveling down architectural blind alleys that lead to developing a model that is functionally correct but offers, for example, poor performance or availability.

1. Benefits

   Applying perspectives to a view benefits one's architectural description in several ways.

   a. The perspective provides common conventions, measurements, or even a notation or language that can be used to describe the system's qualities. For example, the Performance perspective defines standardized measures such as response time, throughput, latency, and so forth, as well as how they are specified and captured.

b. The perspective defines concerns that guide architectural decision-making to help ensure that the resulting architecture will exhibit the quality properties considered by the perspective. For example, the Performance perspective defines standard concerns such as response time, throughput, and predictability. Understanding and prioritizing the concerns that a perspective addresses helps one to identify a firm set of priorities to later decision-making.

c. The perspective describes how one can validate the architecture to demonstrate that it meets its requirements across each of the views. For example, the Performance perspective describes how to construct mathematical models or simulations to predict expected performance under a given load and techniques for prototyping and benchmarking.

d. The perspective may offer recognized solutions to common problems, thus helping to share knowledge between architects. For example, the Performance perspective describes how hardware devices may be multiplexed to improve throughput.

e. The perspective helps one to work in a systematic way to ensure that the relevant concerns are addressed by the system. This helps one to organize the work and make sure that nothing is forgotten.

2. Perspectives catalog

Figure 4.1 charts views versus the applicable perspectives

Table 4.2 describes perspectives in detail.

Perspectives are defined with details like:

- Applicability: This section explains which of your views are most likely to be affected by applying the perspective. For example, applying the Evolution perspective might affect your Functional view more than your Operational view.

- Concerns: This information defines the quality properties that the perspective addresses.

- Activities: In this section, we explain the steps for applying the perspective to your views—identifying the important quality properties, analyzing the views against these properties, and then making architectural design decisions that modify and improve the views.

- Architectural tactics: An architectural tactic is an established and proven approach one can use to help achieve a particular quality property (e.g., defining different processing priorities for different parts of the system's workload and managing this by using a priority-based process scheduler to achieve satisfactory overall system performance). Each perspective identifies and describes the most important tactics for achieving its quality properties.

- Problems and pitfalls: This section explains the most common things that can go wrong and gives guidance on how to recognize and avoid them (Tables 4.1 and 4.2).

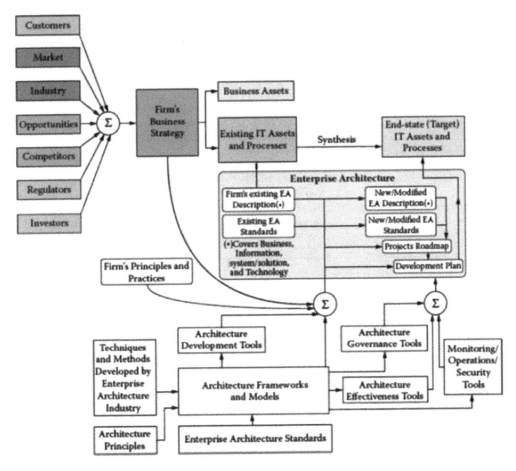

FIGURE 4.1
Charts views versus the applicable perspectives.

TABLE 4.1

Views versus the Applicable Perspectives

| Views | Security | Perspectives | | Evolution |
		Performance and Scalability	Availability and Resilience	
Functional	Medium	Medium	Low	High
Information	Medium	Medium	Low	High
Concurrency	Low	High	Medium	Medium
Development	Medium	Low	Low	High
Deployment	High	High	High	Low
Operational	Medium	Low	Medium	Low

TABLE 4.2

Perspectives Described in Detail

Perspective	Desired Quality
Security	The ability of the system to reliably control, monitor, and audit who can perform what actions on what resources and to detect and recover from failures in security mechanisms
Performance and scalability	The ability of the system to predictably execute within its mandated performance profile and to handle increased processing volumes
Availability and resilience	The ability of the system to be fully or partly operational as and when required and to effectively handle failures that could affect system availability
Evolution	The ability of the system to be flexible in the face of the inevitable change that all systems experience after deployment, balanced against the costs of providing such flexibility

4.3.1 Change Perspective

A snapshot of this perspective is as follows:

- Desired quality: The ability of the system to be flexible in the face of the inevitable change that all systems experience after deployment, balanced against the costs of providing such flexibility
- Applicability: Generally important for all systems; more important for longer-lived and more widely used systems
- Concerns: Magnitude of change, dimensions of change, likelihood of change, timescale for change, when to pay for change, development complexity, preservation of knowledge, and reliability of change
- Activities: Characterize the change needs, assess the current ease of change, consider the change tradeoffs, and rework the architecture
- Architectural tactics: Contain change, create flexible interfaces, apply change-oriented architectural styles, build variation points into the software, use standard extension points, achieve reliable change, and preserve development environments
- Problems and pitfalls: Prioritization of the wrong dimensions, changes that never happen, impacts of change on critical quality properties, lost development environments, and ad hoc release management

1. Applicability of the Change perspective

   The applicability of the Change perspective to the six views is summarized as follows:

   a. The Functional view may be informed by the Change perspective by enabling the functional structure to reflect the required change.

   b. The Information view may be informed by the Change perspective by mandating a flexible information model.

c. The Concurrency view may be informed by the Change perspective by dictating a particular element packaging or some constraints on the concurrency structure (e.g., that it must be very simple).

d. The Development view may be informed by the Change perspective by determining the impact on the development environment (e.g., enforcing portability guidelines).

e. The Deployment view may be informed by the Change perspective by defining impact on the Deployment view because system change usually affects structures described in other views.

f. Operational view may be informed by the Change perspective to the extent that it impacts on the operational view.

2. Tactics for enhancement

a. Contain change: Design a system structure so that the required changes are as contained as possible. A change starts to be a problem when its effects ripple through a number of different parts of the system simultaneously. For the interface dimension, for example, if an interface change requires a change to internal system interfaces, this is a much more serious problem than that of just changing the single software module that provides the external interface.

General design principles that can help in localizing the effects of change are:

- Encapsulation
- Separation of concerns
- Single point of definition

b. Create flexible interfaces: The specifics of creating flexible interfaces depend on the technology environment and problem domain of the concerned system. However, considering the degree of flexibility required of the important interfaces and how to achieve it is an important aspect of addressing the change concerns of the system. When designing the main internal interfaces of the system (and between the system and its environment), create them to be as flexible as possible. Some interface designs are significantly more resilient to change than others. For example, by using a self-describing message technology such as Extensible Markup Language to define message formats and allowing new message elements to be optional, messages can be extended with little or no impact on system elements that do not need to use the extended form of the interface. This approach is particularly useful for external interfaces if environment change is likely to be important for the system.

Such approaches are not without their costs, and these need to be evaluated in the context of the change requirements. To take interface flexibility to its logical extreme would involve dropping static typing of your interfaces altogether and establishing the types of all request parameters at runtime. However, such a flexible approach can be more difficult to understand and test and may be less efficient at runtime.

c. Build variation points into the system: This approach involves identifying system variation points locations wherein supporting a certain type of change is critically important and specifying a mechanism to achieve the change is required. A large number of specific software design patterns have been published that attempt to introduce some form of variation point (e.g., Façade, Chain of Responsibility, Bridge, and so on).

Some general approaches that can be useful include:

- Making elements replaceable
- Parameterizing operation with configuration parameters
- Using self-describing data and generic processing
- Separating physical and logical processing

d. Use standard extension points: Many mainstream information systems technologies provide standard extension points (such as the J2EE platform's ability to easily add support for new types of databases via the JDBC interface and for external systems via the JCA interface). For using such standard technology solutions, a number of flexible extension points are available that can adapted to meet the change requirements. For example, custom adaptors can be written to use standard application integration facilities to connect to in-house systems as well as the packaged applications they are normally used for. This avoids the designing and building of custom mechanisms for future integration into in-house systems.

e. Implement reliable changes: Since the effects of implementing a change cannot be assessed easily, the system must be exhaustively tested to confirm assumptions regarding postchange behavior.

Changes can be assured of reliability by:

- Software configuration management
- Automated build and release process
- Environment configuration management
- Automated testing
- Continuous integration

f. Apply change-oriented architectural styles: If there are significant requirements for system change, it may be worth considering the adoption of an overall architectural style that is particularly focused on supporting change. Metamodel-based systems provide a very high degree of flexibility in some problem domains (particularly database systems requiring significant schema evolution). Such metamodel-based systems can provide the ability to support very rapid change because instead of modifying the system implementation to change its behavior, it can just be reconfigured—which is usually a much faster process.

Metamodel-based systems are much more complex to develop and test than systems based on more static architectural styles. They are also inherently less efficient in terms of runtime performance, which can limit their applicability in environments where performance is a major concern.

4.3.2 Availability Perspective

In recent years, there has been a significant change in the way that most companies carry out their business, driven to a large extent by the Internet and the global operations of large organizations. Today's requirement for many systems is to be available for much of the 24-hour cycle. With the improved reliability of hardware and software, many expect that failures will be few and far between and that, upon failure, recovery will be prompt, effective, and largely automated.

A snapshot of this perspective is as follows:

- Desired quality: the ability of the system to be fully or partly operational as and when required and to effectively handle failures that could affect system availability
- Applicability: any system that has complex or extended availability requirements, complex recovery processes, or a high visibility profile (e.g., is visible to the public)
- Concerns: classes of service, planned downtime, unplanned downtime, time to repair, and disaster recovery
- Activities: capture the availability requirements, produce the availability schedule, estimate platform availability, estimate functional availability, assess against the requirements, and rework the architecture
- Architectural tactics: select fault-tolerant hardware, use hardware-clustering and load-balancing, log transactions, apply software availability solutions, select or create fault-tolerant software, and identify backup and disaster recovery solutions
- Problems and pitfalls: a single point of failure, overambitious availability requirements, ineffective error detection, overlooked global availability requirements, and incompatible technologies

1. Applicability of the Availability perspective

   The applicability of the Availability perspective to the six views is summarized as follows:

   a. The Functional view may be informed by the Availability perspective by enabling the business's ability to operate effectively. Functional changes may sometimes be needed to support availability requirements, such as the ability to operate in an offline mode when a communications network is unavailable.

   b. The Information view may be informed by the Availability perspective by considering the set of processes and systems for backup and recovery. Systems must be backed up in such a way that they can be recovered in a reasonable amount of time if a disaster occurs. Backups should not impact online availability, or, if they do, they may need to be scheduled to occur outside the bounds of the online day.

   c. The Concurrency view may be informed by the Availability perspective by incorporating features such as hardware replication and failover in the system that may entail changes or enhancements to the concurrency model.

   d. The Development view may be informed by the Availability perspective by imposing design constraints on the software modules. For example, all subsystems may have to support start, stop, pause, and restart commands to align with the system failover strategy.

   e. The Deployment view may be informed by the Availability perspective by mandating a fault-tolerant production environment (i.e., one in which each hardware component is duplicated and failover is automatic) or a separate disaster recovery site that can be quickly activated if the production site goes down. Per this view, the system may also dictate special software to support hardware redundancy or clustering.

f. The Operational view may be informed by the Availability perspective to allow the identification and recovery of problems in the production environment. There may also be a need for geographically separate disaster recovery facilities. Processes for main site failover, network failover, and data recovery must be designed, tested, and implemented. If the standby site is physically remote from the production site, processes are also required to move production staff from one location to the other or to deploy suitably trained staff at the standby site.

2. Tactics for enhancement

a. Select fault-tolerant hardware: Fault-tolerant computing platforms can continue to operate without interruption, even if a hardware component fails. These are typically implemented by means of redundant or duplicated hardware: each component—for example, the central processing unit, memory, disk, input/output port, and so on—is deployed in pairs and, if one of the pair fails, the other continues to operate while the fault is analyzed and the faulty part is repaired or replaced. Such platforms, although expensive, deliver a very high level of system availability and often allow hardware upgrades to be performed while the system is online. Redundant disk architectures (such as redundant array of inexpensive disks or mirrored disks) are a particularly common example.

b. Use hardware clustering and load balancing: High-availability clustering is a technique for protecting against failures by mirroring the whole computer rather than just a disk. In a clustered configuration, two or more identical computers (referred to as nodes) are deployed in parallel and share the total workload between them. If any one of the nodes fails, one of the remaining nodes takes over its workload and processing can continue (although the transactions that were in progress in the failed node at the time of failure may have to be resubmitted). This process is known as failover. Special software is required to manage the cluster. Some types of clusters (scalable clusters) can also be used to enhance performance due to their ability to reduce contention via replication.

A variety of different clustering configurations are available, depending on how the nodes are connected to shared resources such as memory, disk, and the communications network as well as what failover scenarios are supported. Whatever approach is chosen, incoming transactions must be allocated to one of the nodes. A technique called load-balancing performs this allocation and helps to ensure that the nodes are used to their fullest possible extent. Load balancing can be provided via hardware or, less commonly, software.

c. Log transactions: For a number of reasons, backups may not bring data (or a database) back to the state they were in at the point of failure. It is thus extremely useful to have a separate transaction log that can be replayed into the recovered database to bring it completely up-to-date. Such a capability may be provided by the storage mechanism, by front-end applications, or by underlying transaction management software. An added benefit of such transaction logging is that it can provide an audit trail.

    d. Implement fault-tolerant software: Software can also be written to reconfigure itself in response to changing conditions, for example, by allocating itself more resources (such as shared memory) when under load or by automatically disabling certain features if they malfunction and offering only partial service until the problem is rectified. This requirement is being addressed by cloud computing solutions.

    e. Implement software availability solution: Develop effective strategies to ensure the reliability and recoverability of the system, including:

- A robust strategy for data validation and dealing with rejected data
- A common strategy for detecting, logging, and responding to software errors
- A service to which error messages are logged and from which alerts and errors can be trapped
- The recording of full diagnostic information to help in subsequent analysis and repair

    f. Implement backup and disaster recovery solutions: Every system that manages persistent information (i.e., information that must be stored on stable storage and made available across system restarts) must include mechanisms for backing up this information by writing it to a separate storage medium from which the information can be recovered in the case of system failure (particularly, disk failure).

While the first mirroring architectures placed the disks physically near one another, you can now mirror onto disks at another location, possibly many miles away, by means of high-bandwidth, highly reliable fiber-optic networks. Such a distributed mirroring solution, while expensive, can also form part of one's disaster recovery architecture.

    Any backup solution must maintain the transactional integrity of the data so that, when the data are restored, they are left in a transactionally consistent state.

4.3.3 Scalability Perspective

The scalability property of a system is closely related to performance; however, scalability focuses mainly on the predictability of the system's performance as the workload increases. The performance of a computer system depends on much more than the raw processing power of its hardware, including the way that hardware is configured, the way resources are allocated and managed, and the way the software is written.

    A snapshot of this perspective is as follows:

- Desired quality: the ability of the system to predictably execute within its mandated performance profile and to handle increased processing volumes
- Applicability: any system with complex, unclear, or ambitious performance requirements; systems whose architecture includes elements whose performance is unknown; and systems where future expansion is likely to be significant
- Concerns: response time, throughput, scalability, predictability, hardware resource requirements, and peak load behavior
- Activities: capture the performance requirements, create the performance models, analyze the performance models, conduct practical testing, assess against the requirements, and rework the architecture

- Architectural tactics: optimize repeated processing, reduce contention via replication, prioritize processing, consolidate related workloads, distribute processing over time, minimize the use of shared resources, partition and parallelize, use asynchronous processing, and make design compromises
- Problems and pitfalls: imprecise performance and scalability goals, unrealistic models, use of simple measures for complex cases, inappropriate partitioning, invalid environment and platform assumptions, too much indirection, concurrency-related contention, careless allocation of resources, and disregard for network and in-process invocation differences

1. Applicability of the Scalability perspective

   The applicability of the Scalability perspective to the six views is summarized as follows:

   a. The Functional view may be informed by the Scalability perspective by revealing the need for changes and compromises to one's ideal functional structure to achieve the system's performance requirements (e.g., by consolidating system elements to avoid communication overhead). The models from this view also provide input to the creation of performance models.

   b. The Information view may be informed by the Scalability perspective by providing useful input to performance models, identifying shared resources and the transactional requirements of each. As one applies this perspective, one may identify aspects of the Information view as obstacles to performance or scalability. In addition, considering scalability may suggest elements of the Information view that could be replicated or distributed in support of this goal.

   c. The Concurrency view may be informed by the Scalability perspective to change the concurrency design by identifying problems such as excessive contention on key resources. Alternatively, considering performance and scalability may result in concurrency becoming a more important design element to meet these requirements. Elements of concurrency views (such as interprocess communication mechanisms) can also provide calibration metrics for performance models.

   d. The Development view may be informed by the Scalability perspective through a set of guidelines related to performance and scalability that should be followed during software development. These guidelines will probably take on the form of dos and don'ts (e.g., patterns and antipatterns) that must be followed as the software is developed in order to avoid performance and scalability problems later when it is deployed. This information will be captured in the Development view.

   e. The Deployment view may be informed by the Scalability perspective through crucial inputs to the process of considering performance and scalability. Many parts of the system's performance models are derived from the contents of this view, which also provides a number of critical calibration metrics. In turn, applying this perspective will often suggest changes and refinements to the deployment environment, to allow it to support the performance and scalability needs of the system.

    f. The Operational view may be informed by the Scalability perspective by high-lighting the need for performance monitoring and management capabilities.

2. Tactics for enhancement

    a. Optimize repeated processing: Most systems have a small number of common operations that the system spends the majority of its time performing. The resulting performance implication is that one should focus their performance efforts on that core 20% of the system.

        The goal of the performance engineering process is to minimize the overall system workload, as follows:

$$\text{System workload} = \sum_{l=1}^{M} (\text{operation cost})$$

That is:

$$\text{System workload} = \sum_{l=1}^{M} (\text{operation invocation} * \text{frequency of invocation})$$

The total workload for our system, for a unit of time, is the sum of all of the total operation costs over that unit of time (where we have n possible operations in our system).

        A system's operations are ranked by the total cost metric, and the performance engineering efforts are focused to optimize the operations at the top of this list first.

    b. Reduce contention through replication: Whenever there are concurrent operations in the system, there is a potential for contention. This contention is often a major source of performance problems, causing a reduction in throughput and wasted resources. Eliminating contention can be a difficult process, particularly when the contention involved is actually within the system's underlying infrastructure (e.g., an application server), rather than in the software over which there is a direct control.

        A possible solution for some contention problems is to replicate system elements, such as hardware, software, or data. This approach works only in certain situations, and a limiting factor is that the system often needs to be designed to take advantage of replication from the outset.

    c. Prioritize processing: A problem in many otherwise well-built systems can emerge when the overall performance of the system is within target, but some important tasks still take too long to execute. To avoid this situation, partition the system's workload into priority groups (or classes) and add the ability to prioritize the workload to the process. This allows one to ensure that the system's resources will be applied to the right element of the workload at any point in time, so the perception of performance problems is much less likely.

        A low-level example of this approach is the priority class-based thread and process scheduling built into most modern operating systems. When dealing with large information systems, this prioritizing usually involves identifying the business criticality of each class of workload. Those types of workloads that have to complete items in a timely manner for business to continue (such as order processing) are naturally prioritized over workloads that, while important, will not immediately impact business operation if they are a bit late (such as management reporting).

d. Minimize use of shared resources: As systems get busier and contention for shared resources increases, the waiting time takes proportionally more of the total elapsed time for tasks and contributes proportionally more to the overall response time. At any instance, a nonidle task running on a system is in one of two states:

- Waiting for a resource, either because it is busy (e.g., being used by another task) or not in a ready state (e.g., waiting for a head to move over a particular track on a disk or a software service to initialize)

- Making use of a resource (e.g., a hardware resource such as processor, memory, disk, or network or a software resource such as a message service)

Other than increasing the performance of resources that the task uses, a way to alleviate this situation is to minimize the use of shared resources by:

- Using techniques such as hardware multiplexing to eliminate hardware hotspots in the architecture

- Favoring short, simple transactions over long, complex ones where possible (because transactions tend to lock up resources for extended periods)

- Not locking resources in human time (e.g., while waiting for a user to press a key)

- Trying to access shared resources nonexclusively whenever possible

e. Minimize partition and parallelize: If a system involves large, lengthy processes, a possible way to reduce the response time is to partition them into a number of smaller processes; execute these subprocesses in parallel; and, when the last subprocess is complete, consolidate all of the subprocess outputs into a single result. Naturally, situations involving lengthy and expensive consolidation of subprocess outputs are suitable for this technique only if the consolidation cost is still small relative to that of the longer response time for the original process.

This approach is likely to be effective in a particular situations, depending on the following:

- Whether the overall process can be quickly and efficiently partitioned into subprocesses

- Whether the resulting subprocesses can be executed independently to allow for effective parallel processing

- How much time it will take to consolidate the outputs of the subprocesses into a single result

- Whether enough processing capacity is available to process the subprocesses in parallel in a manner faster than handling the same workload in a single process would be

 This approach is less efficient than using a single linear process (due to the partitioning and consolidation overheads) and achieves a reduction in response time at the price of requiring more processing resources.

If spare processing resources aren't available, parallelization is unlikely to be effective because the subprocesses will be executed one after the other and will be slower than the original design, due to the partitioning and consolidation overheads.

f. Make design compromises: Many of the techniques of good architecture definition that we have described in this chapter thus far can themselves cause performance problems in extreme situations. A loosely coupled, highly modular, and coherent system tends to spend more time communicating between its modules than a tightly coupled, monolithic one does.

Where performance is a critical concern, as a last resort, consider compromises in the ideal structure of design, such as:

- Moving to a more tightly coupled, monolithic design to minimize internal communication delays and contention
- Denormalizing parts of the data model to optimize access to data
- Using very coarse-grained operations between distributed system elements
- Duplicating data or processing locally to minimize traffic over slow communication channels

Making such a change may improve performance but is likely to have associated costs in terms of maintainability and possibly even ease of use. Thus, the desirability of these tradeoffs should be assessed carefully.

4.4 Enterprise Architecture Frameworks

A reference architecture is a meta-model, in that it is a model of how to model enterprises. It describes a structured set of models that collectively represent the building blocks of an enterprise system. Reference architectures embody the knowledge gathered, on a large scale, from a multitude of enterprise engineering projects.

The creation and description of a systems architecture from scratch can be a daunting task. Architecture frameworks simplify the process and guide an architect through all areas of architecture development; they provide a set of conventions, principles, and practices, which can be used by systems engineers to create such descriptions. There are a variety of different architecture frameworks in existence; they differ mainly with respect to their field of application.

The typical architecture framework has several benefits:

- It helps stakeholders to make decisions about enterprise design and operation.
- It provides users with some confidence that the use of the reference architecture will be successful in the current project.
- It facilitates communication of the enterprise design.
- It is applicable to a wide range of enterprise systems and scenarios.
- It establishes a common means to organize, interpret, and analyze architectural descriptions.

- It identifies architectural concerns, generic stakeholders, viewpoints, and abstraction levels.
- It encourages reuse.
- It provides a unified, unambiguous definition of terminology.

 There are several useful and not mutually exclusive principles to knowledge reuse, such as:

- Best practices: A concept used in knowledge management in order to capture and share the good solutions and lessons learned that are of value to the organization.
- Frameworks: A concept used in software development for providing building blocks for implementing generic functionality of a software system. A framework usually contains working code that needs to be changed and/or extended in order to fit specific application requirements. Examples of software frameworks include code libraries, tool sets, and application programming interfaces. The framework principle is also used in organizational setting as EA frameworks. These frameworks usually offer generic guidance for creating and managing EA as well as for the form in which an EA should be described. Examples of EA frameworks are the Zachman Framework and The Open Group Architecture Framework (TOGAF).
- Reference models: A system of models used to define concepts in a certain domain. The aim of reference models typically is to unify and integrate the body of knowledge in a certain area. Reference models are not directly seen as standards but rather often have a significant role in developing them. Reference models are frequently used for managing an established set of best practices and commonly available solutions (see Subsection 5.4 for a notable example of using reference models for business process management).
- Patterns: A concept for capturing and presenting proven reusable solutions to recurring problems initially used in architecture and later adopted to information systems analysis, design, and programming as well as organizational design.

4.4.1 Zachman Framework

The *Zachman Framework for EA and Information Systems Architecture*, better known under its short name the *Zachman Framework*, was introduced by John A. Zachman in 1987. It is considered to be one of the most important frameworks and influenced the contemporary understanding of EAs significantly. Many subsequent developed EA frameworks have employed the Zachman Framework as a foundation (Figure 4.2).

Zachman derived the framework from the world of classical (building) architecture and, hence, the names of the views and the perspectives relate to the terminology of architecture. The framework itself takes the form of a simple matrix, comprising rows and columns with intersecting cells that describe aspects of an entity. Usually, there are 36 cells as the matrix usually has six rows and always has six columns. The Zachman EA Framework is shown in Figure 4.3.

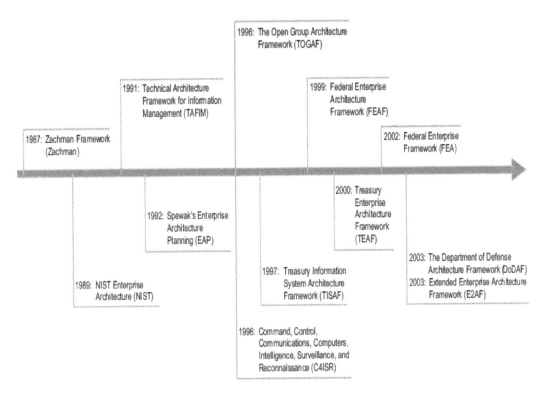

FIGURE 4.2
Development of EA frameworks.

The Zachman Framework has six types of view, as follows:

- Planner's View—Scope: This may be thought of as an executive summary for the project and will include aspects such as the overall size, cost, and relationship to the environment. This will help to define the scope and the context of the project.
- Owner's View—Enterprise or Business Model: This view represents the architect's plans that show a high-level view of the system from the owner's point of view. It includes the business entities such as the processes that need to be understood in order for the system to be used properly.
- Designer's View—Information Systems Model: This represents the interpretation of the owners' views into something that can be used by the designers. This will usually be more technically detailed view including data structures, behavioral aspects, partitioning, and so on.
- Builder's View—Technology Model: This view contains the same information as in the designer's view, but from the builder's point of view. Therefore, the emphasis will be on implementation issues and constraints such as tools, technologies, building materials, and so on.

	DATA What	FUNCTION How	NETWORK Where	PEOPLE Who	TIME When	MOTIVATION Why
SCOPE (CONTEXTUAL) Planner	Things important to the business	Process performs	Business locations	Important organizations	Events significant of the business	Business goals and strategies
ENTERPRISE MODEL (CONCEPTUAL) Owner	Semantic model	Business process model	Business logistics system	Workflow model	Master schedule	Business plan
SYSTEM MODEL (LOGICAL) Designer	Logical data model	Application architecture	Distributed system architecture	Human interface architecture	Process structure	Business rule model
TECHNOLOGY MODEL (PHYSICAL) Builder	Physical data model	System design	Technology architecture	Presentation architecture	Control structure	Rule design
DETAILED REPRESENTATION (OUT-OF- CONTEXT) Subcontractor	Data definition	Program	Network architecture	Security architecture	Timing definition	Rule definition
FUNCTIONING ENTERPRISE	Data	Function	Network	Organization	Schedule	Strategy

FIGURE 4.3
Zachman EA framework.

- Subcontractor's View—Detailed Specification: This could be the detailed designs that are given to the builders or programming team that are derived from the builder's view. In the case of off-the-shelf components, this would be the full specification for the systems or subsystems that are required. This view will also include any configuration, build, and deployment information that is required.
- Actual System View: This is the actual systems that are being developed or modeled.

The perspectives in the Zachman Framework are defined as follows:

- Data Description—What?: This is a classic structural view that shows the main elements and the relationships between them.
- Function Description—How?: This is a behavioral view that describes how each of the elements functions independently and also how they function together.
- Network Description—Where?: This view shows the deployment aspects of the system elements and any dependencies between them.
- People Description—Who?: This view shows the people involved in the view.

- Time Description—When?: This view shows any temporal, or timing, aspects of the system.
- Motivation Description—Why?: This view provides the basic rational or requirements for the view.

The Zachman Framework has seven basic rules that constrain the way the views and perspectives may be generated; these are described as follows:

Rule #1: The columns have no order. The columns, which represent the perspectives, have no particular order. For example, just because the "motivation description" is last in the list, it does not mean that it is either created after the other perspectives or that it has less of a priority. The number of perspectives must always be six, and this cannot be reduced or increased in number.

Rule #2: Each column has its own model. Each perspective has its own model, and this model will be represented by any number of diagrams, description, or other artifacts. Each perspective may also have its own meta-model that describes the structure of the model.

Rule #3: Each model is unique. Each model for the perspectives must be unique. It must be remembered that each model will have relationships with other models and must be consistent with other models.

Rule #4: Each row describes a unique perspective. Each of the rows represents a view of the systems from a particular point of view. Although there are usually six rows, there is no reason why there cannot be more than or fewer than this number, depending on the number of views identified. It is also usual for the views to be hierarchical in some way, so that the first row represents the highest level view and the sixth (or lowest) represents the lowest level of abstraction.

Rule #5: Each cell is unique. If each model is unique (rule #3) and each row describes a unique perspective (rule #4), then each of the cells should also be unique.

Rule #6: All cells combine to form a model. To have a complete model for any particular perspective, each of the models and, hence, cells, for that row must be present. Therefore, the combination of all of the cells in a specific row forms the model for that perspective.

Rule #7: The logic is recursive. The logical structure of the framework and its models applies to all instances of the entity that is being modeled.

The framework defines prestructured views and layers to represent an information technology (IT) enterprise. Unlike similar frameworks that often contain process models, the Zachman Framework does not prescribe any process or methodology. It focuses on the roles involved and assigns them to objects that shall be viewed from different perspectives. The Zachman Framework thereby provides a comprehensive tool to consider all relevant aspects, from all perspectives, while designing and developing an enterprise IT architecture.

4.4.2 The Open Group Architecture Framework

TOGAF provides an approach for designing, planning, implementing, and governing an enterprise IT architecture. The latest version is TOGAF 9.1, which was published on

December 1, 2011. The term "framework" is somewhat of a misnomer when it comes to TOGAF. TOGAF itself is not actually an architectural framework but rather a set of phases and associated processes in the form of an architecture development method (ADM) that will enable an EA to be created for an organization. TOGAF is effectively a management-based approach and, hence, focuses largely on management and planning, rather than the actual development of the architecture and its views. TOGAF does not define any particular views (although it does hint strongly at some) but instead focuses on how to manage the development and delivery of the architecture.

The EA is made up of four "architecture domains," which are as follows:

- Business architecture: This is the business strategy, organization, and key business process information that describes the business. The business architecture not only defines each of these elements but also the relationships between them.

- Applications architecture: This is the major logical grouping of capabilities needed to support the architecture.

- Data architecture: This forms the structure of an organization's logical and physical data assets and resources.

- Technical architecture: This is the description of the architecture that is to be produced, often referred to as the "future architecture." Usually, a number of technical architectures will exist that may then be evaluated before one is finally implemented.

The ADM is an iterative process covering all phases of EA development that is adaptable to the specific needs of any enterprise.

ADM is composed of the following phases:

1. The preliminary phase is executed once and sets the context for the whole project. This includes ensuring that buy-in is obtained from all relevant stakeholders defining any high-level architectural principles that will be applicable throughout the project. Any processes, standards, methodologies, and specific techniques that will be employed are identified at this point, so that it can be ensured that there are sufficient competencies in place. The basic scope and context of the architecture are defined, along with the validation criteria and any associated process that will be used to ensure that the architecture meets its stated goals. All roles and responsibilities are also stated at this point.

2. Phase A "architectural vision" is primarily concerned with defining the high-level requirements of the architecture and getting the formal go-ahead for the architectural work to be done. This will include the business requirements (such as business goals, business principles, and business drivers) and the constraints that will impact these requirements. The scope and main components of the baseline architecture are also defined at this point. The baseline architecture here refers to existing architecture when the current Phase A begins. In case the preliminary phase has just been run, there will be no architecture as such. The main stakeholders are identified at this point and their requirements are defined.

3. Phase B "business architecture" is the first of the four architecture domains that should be defined, as it drives the remaining three phases. The business architecture describes the product or service strategy (in terms of organization, function,

process, information, and deployment) based on the architectural vision that was generated during Phase A. As a general architectural principle, reuse is explored here to optimize the system development; the choice of tools may also be looked at.

4. Phase C "information systems" is concerned with developing the information and/or application architectural domains. The scope of Phase C is limited to the IT-related processes and the non-IT processes that are directly related to IT (support processes).

5. Phase D "technology architecture" is aimed at providing a complete description of the logical software and hardware capabilities that are used to support the information and application architectures. The technology architecture forms the basis of the implementation work.

6. Phase E "opportunities and solutions" has the main aim of planning the implementation of the architecture by looking at various solutions that may meet the requirements or any other opportunities that may be applicable. For example, decisions may be made here to decide whether to develop a solution or to go for a commercial off-the-shelf approach to realizing the components of the architecture. This phase will also decide the resources and budgets to be used, along with the high-level work packages or projects required to realize the architecture.

7. Phase F "migration and planning" is concerned with sorting the various projects or work packages associated with the architecture into some sort of order. This will depend on the priorities assigned to each project or work package and the dependencies between them. This will result in the production of a detailed implementation and migration plan.

8. Phase G "implementation governance" is when the actual projects are executed, and this phase is concerned primarily with coordinating and managing these projects to ensure that they deliver the architecture as needed.

9. Phase H "architecture change management" ensures that any changes to the architecture are managed and controlled in an effective manner. This phase effectively implements a change management process that applies to the architecture.

The TOGAF ADM is shown in Figure 4.4.

The TOGAF standard does not define or prescribe the form and look of its process outcomes (i.e., the deliverables that must be built in every phase during development). It could be a simple document containing a textual description, a textual and graphical description in a Wiki, or a model of the technical architecture in a modeling tool. Consequently, TOGAF is often combined with other view-oriented frameworks that have a Unified Modeling Language-based meta-model, which in turn does not have a full-fledged process or methodology.

4.4.3 Federal Enterprise Architecture Framework

The federal EA framework (FEAF) version 1.1 was published in 1996; a revised version 2.0 of FEAF was published in January 2013.

FEAF is primarily intended for EA development ongoing in federal agencies for the purpose of standardizing the development and use of architectures within and between these federal agencies. FEAF provides both, a structure (the Consolidated Reference Model) and

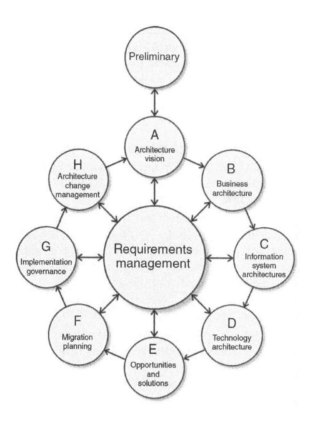

FIGURE 4.4
TOGAF ADM.

a methodology (the Collaborative Planning Methodology). The Consolidated Reference Model consists of six reference models and provides standardized categorization for strategic, business, and technology models. The Collaborative Planning Methodology is a full planning and implementation life cycle for federal EAs consisting of two main phases: (1) organize and plan and (2) implement and measure. There are frequent iterations within and between these phases.

4.4.4 Department of Defense Architecture Framework

The Department of Defense architecture framework (DODAF) version 1.0 was published in August 2003, eventually evolving into DODAF 2.0, which was released in May 2009. One of the major changes between DODAF version 1.0 and DODAF version 2.0 was the transition from a product-centric process to a data-centric process. DODAF is a view-oriented architecture framework that provides an organized meta-model-based visualization infrastructure for addressing specific stakeholders concerns.

The framework consists of eight main viewpoints that define specifies rules for constructing a view (perspective) on the system under development, including a set of relevant stakeholders and the purpose(s) for addressing their concerns. All DODAF views must follow a Unified Modeling Language-based meta-model (DM2) that defines specific types, semantics, relationships, rules, and constraints about how to build a DODAF-conformant system of a systems EA model.

In contrast to its very detailed meta-model, DODAF contains only a high-level, six-step phase model for dealing with the development process of an EA. If a more detailed methodology is required, a mapping of DODAF 2.0 views to TOGAF ADM deliverables is feasible.

4.4.5 Ministry of Defense Architecture Framework

The British Ministry of Defense architecture framework (MODAF) is a view-oriented architecture framework of which version 1.0 was released in August 2005. The last version, version 1.2.004, was released in May 2010.

Each viewpoint of MODAF offers a different perspective on the system of a systems project to support different stakeholder concerns and interests. MODAF 1.2.004 consists of seven different viewpoints: an All Views viewpoint, Strategic View viewpoint, Operational View viewpoint, System View viewpoint, Technical Standards View viewpoint, Acquisition View viewpoint, and Service-oriented View viewpoint. All of these viewpoints contain a different number of views; in total, there are 47 views.

1. The "All Views" viewpoint is created to define the generic, high-level information that applies to all of the other viewpoints. This will define key information, such as:
   - The scope of the architecture that is being defined by the architectural framework.
   - The purpose of the architecture that is being defined by the architectural framework.
   - A set of intended users and the views that will be generated. Not all the MODAF views will exist in a particular framework—the number of views, what they are, and how they are used will be dependent on the intended users of the framework. For example, a framework may consist of some strategic views and some operational views, and then this information may be used as part of the acquisition cycle as part of an invitation to tender. Organizations who intend to submit proposal for the tender may then be invited to respond (in part) by providing a set of system views that meet the operational elements defined in the operational views.
   - The environment in which the architecture will be deployed may be identified or described here to provide some context.
   - A defined set of terms in some sort of dictionary or ontology that must be used in the framework.
2. The Technical viewpoint contains two views that allow all of the relevant standards to be defined. This is split into two categories: current standards and predicted/future standards. Standards are an essential part of any architecture and it should be borne in mind that any number of standards may be applied to any element in the architecture.
3. The Acquisition viewpoint is used to identify programs and projects that are relevant to the framework and that will be executed to deliver the capabilities that have been identified in the strategy views. As well as the projects and programs themselves, the relationships, timing requirements, and dependencies between them are also identified. The views are intended to be closely coupled with the MOD's acquisition cycle, although no formal relationship between the

views and the acquisition artefacts is defined. This is clearly something that does need to be defined.

4. The Strategic viewpoint defines views that support the analysis and optimization of military capability. The intention is to capture long-term missions, goals, and visions and to define what capabilities are required to realize them. The capabilities, once identified, can then be described and the relationships and dependencies between them can be determined. These views may be used for high-level analysis, such as capability gap analysis, as well as as part of the acquisition process itself for defining the capabilities that must be delivered by the acquired systems and services.

5. The Operational viewpoint contains views that describe the operational elements required to meet the capabilities defined in the strategic views. This is achieved by considering a number of high-level scenarios and then defining what sort of elements, such as generic operational nodes and operational activities, exist in the scenarios. The operational views are solution-independent and do not describe an actual solution. These views are used primarily of part of tendering where they will be made available to supplier organizations and form the basis of evaluating the system views that are provided as the supplier's proposed solution.

6. The System viewpoint contains views that relate directly to the solution that is being offered to meet the required capabilities that have been identified in the strategic views and expanded upon in the operational views. Therefore, there is a very strong relationship between the system viewpoint and the operational viewpoint. The system views describe the actual systems, their interconnections and their use. This will also include performance characteristics and may even specify protocols that must be used for particular communications. The system views, however, do constitute the design for the solutions; they represent a specification of what the systems are, how they work together, and how they meet the required capability.

The MODAF meta-model (M3) defines a Unified Modeling Language 2-conformant stereotype profile that specifies the structure of the architectural information that is presented in the MODAF views. Even the standardized unified profile for DODAF/MODAF supports the modeling of MODAF-conformant EAs.

MODAF does not prescribe an official architecting process or methodology.

4.5 Summary

EA is a well-defined practice for conducting enterprise analysis, design, planning, and implementation, using a holistic approach at all times, for the successful development and execution of enterprise strategy. EA applies architecture principles and practices to guide enterprises through the business, information, process, and technology changes needed in order to execute their strategies. These practices utilize the various aspects of an enterprise to identify, enable, and achieve these changes. This chapter described the viewpoints, views, and perspectives that enable an EA.

The creation and description of a systems architecture from scratch can be a daunting task. Enterprise reference architectures or architecture frameworks simplify the process and guide an architect through all areas of architecture development; they provide a set of conventions, principles, and practices that can be used by systems engineers to create such descriptions. The latter half of this chapter described established architecture frameworks like the Zachman Framework, TOGAF, the FEAF, the DODAF, and the MODAF.

5

Process Architecture

An enterprise architecture is a high-level design of the entire business including its business processes. It describes the structure of the business processes, how they are coordinated with each other, and how technology supports them. It helps us to understand the business's complexity by showing how all of the different systems are linked together. Business process management (BPM) is a systematic, structured approach to analyzing, improving, controlling, and managing processes, with the aim of improving the quality of products and services. Common to most BPM definitions are the structured and analytical natures of BPM required to manage business processes and the cross-functional characteristics of the business processes that BPM handles. The integration link between the strategic organizational level and the task level enabled by business processes is important throughout the business planning, definition and measurement of *process performance* targets, and improvement actions. The integration link between the abstract strategic level and the operational tasks level enabled by business processes is important to guarantee a proper alignment between business intentions and their practical implementations.

The BPM approach is receiving major attention from the following

1. Business administration for the purpose of improving operations in organizations
2. Computer science communities for the purpose of investigating the structural properties of business processes and robust and scalable software systems to support the integration of business processes into complex information systems

Workflow systems are a subset of BPM systems that additionally have robust application integration, application development, process analysis, and richer process simulation and modeling capabilities. Workflow is broadly the automation of a business process, in whole or part, during which documents, information, or tasks are passed from one participant or entity to another for action in accordance with a set of procedural rules. A workflow process is made up of subprocess (a separate workflow process definition), activities, participants, flow control, and transition. The Workflow Management Coalition (WfMC), recognizing the need for standardization of the workflow products, created the workflow reference model (WfMS) that established a standardized terminology, a standardized set of functional components (e.g., process definition tool, workflow engine, workflow client application, invoked application, and administration and monitoring tool), and a set of interfaces that connected the various functional components.

 As described in Subsection 4.4, a *reference enterprise architecture* is a generic architecture that can be used as the starting point to derive an enterprise's architecture, including the process architecture corresponding to the constituting business processes. Similarly, this chapter posits that the WfMS is the reference process architecture for the enterprise process processes. This is analogous to the enterprise architecture frameworks described in Chapter 4.

5.1 Change

There are many different change management approaches and models. Here, we will discuss two of the more common models, namely, the Lewin's Change Management Model and the Deming Cycle.

1. Lewin's Change Management Model: It is recognized that people tend to become complacent or comfortable in a "freeze" or "unchanging/stable" environment and that they wish to remain in a "safe/comfort" zone. Any disturbance/disruption to this unchanging state will cause pain and become uncomfortable.

   Kurt Lewin, a psychologist by training, created this change model in the 1950s. Lewin observed that there are three stages of change:

   a. Unfreeze phase: In order to encourage change, it is necessary to unfreeze the environment by motivating people to accept the change. The motivational value has to be greater than the pain in order to entice people to accept the change. Maintaining a high level of motivation is important in all three phases of the change management life cycle, even during the transition period.

   b. Transition phase: This is where the change (plan) is executed and actual change is being implemented. Since these "activities" take time to be completed, the process and organizational structure may also need to change, as might specific jobs. The most resistance to change may be experienced during this transition period. This is when leadership is critical for the change process to succeed, and motivational factors are paramount to project success.

   c. Refreeze stage: This is when the organization once again becomes unchanging/ frozen until the next time a change is initiated.

2. Deming Cycle: The Deming Cycle is also known as the Plan–Do–Check–Act cycle; it is a continuous improvement model composed of four sequential subprocesses; Plan, Do, Check, and Act. This framework of process and system improvement was originally conceived by Walter Shewhart in the 1930s and was later adopted by Edward Deming. The Deming Cycle is usually implemented as an evergreen process, which means that the end of one complete pass (cycle) flows into the beginning of the next pass and thus supports the concept of continuous quality improvement.

   Deming proposed in the 1950s that business processes and systems should be monitored, measured, and analyzed continuously to identify variations and substandard products and services so that corrective actions can be taken to improve on the quality of the products or services delivered to the customers. To this effect, the details of the subprocesses are as follows;

   Plan: Recognize an opportunity and plan a change. Understand the gap between residents' expectations and what is being delivered; set priorities for closing gaps; and develop an action plan to close the gaps.

   Do: Execute the plan in a small scale to prove the concept. Implement changes and collect data to determine if gaps are closing.

   Check: Evaluate the performance of the change and report the results to the sponsor(s). Observe the effects of the change and test—analyze data and pinpoint problems …

Act: Decide on accepting the change and standardizing it as part of the process. Study the result; redesign systems to reflect learning—change standards and regulations where necessary; communicate it broadly; and retrain if needed.

3. Change the proficiency of business processes: The pace of change in the new digital economy puts demands on organizations to keep reinventing themselves in order to remain competitive. To be competitive, businesses must respond increasingly better and quicker. Recognizing this, many companies have made significant attempts to improve their business processes. In doing so, organizations have evolved from traditional functional hierarchies to business process-centered structures. This is because business processes are crucial as organizations adapt themselves to changing conditions. The continued interest in business processes can be attributed to the realization that, when properly designed, they can help an organization to achieve efficiency and effectiveness in its business operations. Management strategies, such as business process reengineering, process improvement, process innovation, and business process redesign have emerged to help organizations change their business processes promptly and dynamically according to changing environments.

The horizontal view of the business engendered by business process change practice represents a paradigm shift from the traditional hierarchical organizational structure. The hierarchy and function-based organization are vertical views of organizations that often involve decisions that translate down the hierarchy and result in choices that are best for the function, but not the organization. Cross-function linkage is achieved through work and responsibility handoffs to other functions. However, with time, functions and specialists multiply, as do the rules and bureaucracy to handle increasing contingencies.

The key concepts associated with hierarchical orientation are outlined as follows:

a. Environments are characterized by stability, limited uncertainty, and limited "consumerism"

b. People follow the structure and rules defined by virtue of their position and responsibilities

c. Markets do not change rapidly and the focus is not on flexibility, quality, service, or innovation

A process orientation adopts a horizontal view of organizations by emphasizing notions of processes, process owners, teams, and empowerment and deemphasizing hierarchical structures. Business process change integrates different views from quality, information technology, organizational change, innovation, and work redesign. As such, it represents an input–output activity view of business, as opposed to a functional, responsibility-centered structural view (Table 5.1).

Table 5.1 compares Hierarchical and Process-Oriented organizations.

4. Process-oriented organizations: A process-oriented organization is an organization that defines and manages business processes explicitly. This definition includes matrix organizations because they incorporate business processes in a manner similar to a pure process-oriented organization but with intersections across departmental responsibilities.

TABLE 5.1

Comparison of Hierarchical and Process-Oriented Organizations

Dimension	Hierarchical Firms	Process-Oriented Firms
Organizational structure	• Hierarchical organizational structure (based on functions/products) • Linear and sequential processes • Rigid bureaucracy • Organizational integration through structure • Protective organizational culture	• Networked organization based on cross-functional teams (process teams) • Parallel processes • Flexible adhocracy • Organizational integration through information • Productive organization culture
Human resources	• Fragmented, individual-performed tasks • Functional specialists • Expertise as a functional specialty • Compensation for skills and time spent • Advancement based on ability	• Holistic processes accomplished by teams • Case manager and process manager • Knowledge as an organizational resource • Compensation for results • Advancement based on performance
Information technology/systems	• Fragmented, function-oriented information systems • IT as a driver of business process change	• Integrated, process-oriented cross-functional information systems • IT as an enabler of business process change
Management practices	• Executives as scorekeepers • Managers supervise and control • Management by internal objectives • Function-wide suboptimization	• Executives as leaders • Managers coach and advice • Management by external objectives • Organization-wide global optimization

The ability to cope with incomplete and inconsistent requirements from clients and also with their continuous change is better handled inside a process-oriented organization than in a department-oriented organization because of the continuous focus of process-oriented organizations on the clients' needs (normally expressed in the higher percentage of internal resources allocated to directly satisfying the client).

In a more traditional arrangement, organizations are composed of departments, with each one having concrete but disparate responsibilities and tasks. This bifurcation may lead to an excessive focus on the departmental goals and tasks at the cost of missing the most important business driver: the client. Department-oriented organizations may face problems when they need to apportion the requirements of the clients (e.g., delivery quantities, schedules, or dates) within various departments. For instance, the organization may apportion goals as follows:

- "Delivery quantity" into the production department
- "Delivery schedule fulfillment" into the logistics department
- "Delivery quality" into the quality department

This trifurcated deployment of goals results in internal conflicts, like when the logistics department wants to deliver at a certain date some quantity of products that may face a quality risk. Resolving such internal conflicts will absorb precious resources, causing the organization to spend energy on internal discussions instead of converging onto the best solution for addressing the client's requirement(s).

The design, control, and improvement of the business process landscape of an organization can only be efficient and effective if there exists an enterprise-wide business process model defined, managed, and monitored with quantifiable indicators for the organizational operations.

Models of business processes are the basis for BPM. Process stakeholders can communicate about process structure, content, and possible improvements. BPM includes areas such as business process modeling, formal models, analysis and verification of business processes, process mining, and workflow management.

A BPM support system is a generic software system driven by explicit business process designs that enacts and manages operational business processes. A BPM system allows for the modification of the processes it supports, the deletion of processes, or the incorporation of new processes.

5.2 Process Architecture

This chapter describes the basics of process architecture and how the concept helps to bridge gaps between technical and business resources and enables people take an enterprise-level approach to process improvement. When everyone has the same understanding of strategy and how processes are connected and contribute to that strategy, process activities become synergized and productivity improves dramatically. Having a well-organized process architecture that is clearly understood across the organization that is linked with important corporate strategies and which is managed on a day-to-day basis is a key to the success of many a change effort.

Within any given company, hundreds, thousands, or even millions of processes exist in order for daily operations to occur. The way these processes are structured can help or hinder efforts to execute strategy. For an organization to function effectively, it is vital that it understands the structure of all of the business processes that exist and that create value (as well as which ones do not). How these processes integrate, communicate, and work together toward overall business goals is governed by process architecture. Having a business process architecture strategy in place can create a vital, unifying principle for successfully creating, introducing, using, improving, and maintaining organizational processes and ensuring all processes contribute to organizational goals and strategies.

Process architecture is the design and organization of business processes and related components into a unified structure and hierarchy. Process components, also known as process elements, describe the various units of a process. Examples of process components include departments, goals, systems, information, artifacts, triggers, inputs, outputs, data elements, and people—just about anything that can interact with a process or that is related to a process. Modeling these components and structuring them into a suitable hierarchy, tagging them for easy navigation, and enabling proper search capabilities allows users to connect easily with the process information they care about.

 Process architecture provides a visual representation of the processes and process systems within a company, offering executives and employees a bird's eye view of the activities of the enterprise and how they are all connected. By gaining an overall view of the enterprise, it becomes much easier for organizations to identify their strengths and weaknesses, enabling them to identify areas in need of improvement and offering them the ability to develop the strategies required to best exploit the strengths of the organization.

In addition to aligning perspectives and efforts across all levels and functions in a business, proper process architecture provides a number of benefits, as follows:

1. Process ownership: This ensures accountability for the improvement of end-to-end processes across the enterprise, including extended activities outsourced or in shared service areas.

2. Strategy creation: A comprehensive overview of the processes across a company can be an invaluable aid in the creation and adjustment of business strategies. By using process architecture to identify strengths and core competencies, executives can determine how to best move the enterprise forward.

3. Strategic alignment: This provides a line of sight between corporate strategies and frontline operational improvement activities.

4. Change management: This helps get employees ready, willing, and able to accept and embrace new ways of working, with the goal of involving people in the improvement journey, not just imposing process transformation on them.

5. Standardization: This serves as a guideline for process analysts to devise best practices for high-level and basic processes to ensure that all processes are aligned with the overall business strategy and are formatted and structured in a common fashion.

6. Costing: A company's process architectures can assist with highlighting areas of waste as well as where process outputs do not justify investment. These processes can then be remodeled or eliminated. Process architectures can also predict the cost of alterations to processes.

7. Automation opportunities: These help to identify processes or activities within processes that could be effectively automated to reduce the burden on staff members, as well as increase speed and efficiency.

8. Simplification: This enables process architectures to highlight redundant and complicated processes, allowing management to improve those areas and streamline the business.

9. Process visibility: This provides the ability to view and analyze end-to-end processes both individually and in the wider context of the enterprise in an intuitive way that everyone understands.

10. Performance metrics: This concept embeds key performance indicators within processes to provide immediate feedback on process performance and the potential impact of improvement initiatives.

11. Reduced cost: The simplification and automation of processes should ideally result in reduced operational costs for the enterprise.

12. Faster reactions: Simplification and increased automation should also result in quicker reaction to changing market conditions, allowing executives to rapidly adapt existing processes to new conditions.

13. Impact prediction: Process architectures can offer managers insight into how processes interrelate and into how modifications to any one process may affect downstream or synchronized processes. By understanding the impact a process change will have on its surrounding processes, executives can determine the best course of action for the improvement.

14. Training benefits: These provide a visual representation of the processes and procedures of an enterprise and can be a powerful training tool for new staff or for retraining existing staff. By using process architecture models, it is possible to reduce training and ramp time.

Process architecture is much harder to implement than most imagine. Very few employees can describe the connection between corporate strategies and the work their department performs. It takes an organized and concerted effort to turn high-level strategy into meaningful action.

5.2.1 Process Perspectives

Process architecture designs and organizes business processes and related components into a unified structure and hierarchy. It provides an overview of the various process systems, interfaces, interdependencies, rules, and other relationships within and between processes across a company and helps to align functional business objectives and strategies to process execution. Architecting the business processes entails looking at it through various perspectives or viewpoints.

1. Functional perspective: The functional perspective describes the processes themselves and their structures. Each process can be decomposed into subprocesses. It defines what has to be done—that is, relevant processes are defined. Besides the name (and identification) of a process, typically its purpose, goals, and so on are identified. Processes are elementary or composite: an elementary process cannot be decomposed anymore, while, in contrast, composite processes consist of so-called subprocesses. "Subprocess" is a role name and depicts nothing but another process.

2. Data and dataflow perspective: The data perspective describes which data (or documents) a process step consumes or produces. All inputs and outputs together build up the flow of data in the process model. Parameters are the most important data for a process; input parameters (e.g., IN, INOUT) are consumed by a process—that is they are read and used within the process—while output parameters (e.g., OUT, INOUT) are produced by a process. Process-related parameters should be distinguished from production data that stem from the application domain—they exist even if a process management system is not available. Parameters are created and known only by the process management system.

Dependencies between processes are defined through the production and consumption of data. Such dependencies determine a data flow between processes; that is, they determine the execution order of processes. Dataflow can be controlled by flow conditions: generally, data flow can adopt all flow patterns that are usually exclusively assigned to control flow.

3. Behavioral perspective: The behavioral perspective describes the order in which processes must be executed. It defines the dependencies between processes. However, in contrast to the concept of dataflow, wherein data embody the dependencies, the behavioral perspectives concentrate on modal dependencies between processes, as follows:

   • Temporal dependencies are relative control flow constraints: The start of a subsequent process must be delayed for two hours after the predecessor process has finished.

   • Causal dependencies are based on causes: A subsequent process can only be performed if the predecessor process has been performed successfully.

4. Organizational perspective: The organizational perspective defines persons or roles that are responsible for the execution of a given process. It determines the agents responsible and eligible to perform processes; an agent initiates the execution of a process. Typically, agents are humans who are selected to execute certain processes. However, when a process has to be performed in batch mode, a batch queue can also play the role of an agent. The core of the organizational perspective is the definition of the organization that defines the context for process execution. The organization consists of:

   • The population (including human and nonhuman agents)
   • The organizational structure

   Ultimately, it is the elements of the population that have to perform a workflow. They are often determined by evaluating the corresponding organizational policies that assign agents to the processes. Organizational policies often work on organizational structures.

5. Operational perspective: The operational perspective defines tools or systems that support the execution of a process. When a process is to be performed, it uses a specified set of tools, systems, and so on. Termed as systems process applications, they are also called within-elementary processes after they are initiated by agents. Process applications consume and produce data; thus, a data flow must be specified between them and the embedding elementary processes. Process applications are wrapped in order to provide a more general interface to the calling elementary processes.

5.2.2 Process Views

Service-oriented computing made an important shift from the traditional tightly coupled software development to loosely coupled software development. Software components or software systems are exposed as services; each service offers its functionality via a standard, platform-independent interface. Message exchange is the only way to communicate with a certain service. The interoperable and platform independent nature of services underpins a novel approach to business process development by using processes running in process engines for invoking from process activities (also called tasks or steps) the existing services. This kind of architecture is called as a process-driven, service-oriented architecture (SOA). The presentation and approach relayed in this section is adopted from Tran et al. (2009).

 In this approach, a typical business process consists of many activities, the control flow, and the process data. Each activity corresponds to a communication task (e.g., a service invocation or an interaction with a human) or a data processing task. The control flow describes how these activities are ordered and coordinated to achieve the business goals. As the number of services or processes involved in a business process grows, the complexity of developing and maintaining the business processes also increases, along with the number of invocations and data exchanges. In addition, this problem also occurs at different abstraction levels. However, the view-based framework is not just bound to these concerns alone. The framework is fully open and extensible such that it can incorporate other concerns—for instance, transactions, fault and event handling, security, human interaction, and so on.

This section presents the concept of architectural views for an SOA process. An architectural view is a representation of a system from the perspective of a related set of concerns. The architectural view concept offers a separation of concerns that has the potential to resolve the complexity challenges of an SOA process. In the view-based approach, perspectives on business process and service interactions are used as central views, in which each of them represents a certain part of the processes and services. These views can be separately considered to get a better understanding of a specific concern, or they can be merged to produce a richer or more thorough view of the processes and services.

Aiming at the openness and the extensibility, a basic view is defined called the core view as a foundation for the other views (Figure 5.1). Each of the other views are defined by extending the core view. The core view is the place wherein the relationships among the views are maintained; hence, the relationships in the core view are needed for view integrations. The core view provides a number of important abstract elements, specifically, View, Process, and Service. Each of them can be extended further. At the heart of the core

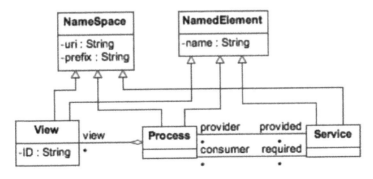

FIGURE 5.1
The core view.

view is the View element that captures the architectural view concept. Each specific view (i.e., each instance of the view element) represents one perspective on a particular Process. A Service specifies external functions that the Process provides or requires. A view acts as a container for view elements representing the objects which appear inside the Process. The view that represents concerns of a business process are mostly derived from the core view. Therefore, these elements of the core view are important extension points: the hierarchical structures in which those elements are roots can be used to define the integration points that are used to merge views.

Some important architectural views include:

1. Control-flow view: The control-flow is one of the most important concerns of an SOA process. A control-flow view comprises many activities and control structures (Figure 5.2a). The activities are process tasks such as service invocations or data

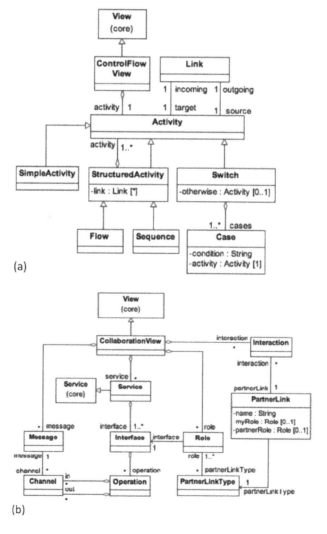

FIGURE 5.2
(a) The control-flow view; (b) the collaboration view.

handling, while control structures describe the execution order of the activities to achieve a certain goal. There are several approaches to modeling process control flows, such as state-charts, block structures, activity diagrams, Petri nets, and so on. Despite this diversity in control flow modeling, it is well-accepted that existing modeling languages share five common basic patterns: Sequence, Parallel Split, Synchronization, Exclusive Choice, and Simple Merge.

Entities of the Control-flow view are as follows:

- An *Activity* element is the base class for other elements such as Sequence, Flow, and Switch.
- Sequence: An activity is only enabled after the completion of another activity in the same sequence structure. The sequence structure is therefore equivalent to the semantics of the Sequence pattern.
- Flow: All activities of a flow structure are executed in parallel. The subsequent activity of the flow structure is only enabled after the completion of all activities in the flow structure. The semantics of the flow structure is equivalent to a control block starting with the Parallel Split pattern and ending by the Synchronization pattern.
- Switch: Only one of many alternative paths of control inside a switch structure is enabled according to a condition value. After the active path finished, the process continues with the subsequent activity of the switch structure. The semantics of the switch structure is equivalent to a control block starting with the Exclusive Choice pattern and ending by the Simple Merge pattern.
- A SimpleActivity element represents a concrete action such as a service invocation, a data processing task, and so on. Each SimpleActivity is a placeholder or a reference to another activity—that is, an interaction or a data processing task; the actual description of each SimpleActivity is modeled in another specific view. For instance, a service invocation is described in a collaboration view, while a data processing action is specified in an information view. Thus, every SimpleActivity becomes an integration point that can be used to merge a Control-flow view with an Information view, or with a Collaboration view, respectively.
- The StructuredActivity element is an abstract representation of a group of related activities. Some of these activities probably have logical correlations. For instance, a shipping activity must be subsequent to an activity of receiving purchase orders. The Link element is used in such scenarios.

2. Collaboration view: The collaboration view extends the relationship between Process and Service elements in the core view to represent the interactions between the business process and its partners (Figure 5.2b). The Service element from the core view is extended by a tailored and specific Service element that exposes a number of Interfaces. Each Interface provides some Operations. An Operation represents an action that might need some inputs and produces some outputs via correspondent Channels. The details of each data element are not defined in the collaboration view but instead in the Information view. A Channel only holds a reference to a Message entity. Therefore, each Message becomes an integration point that can be used to combine a specific Collaboration view with a corresponding Information view.

The ability and the responsibility of an interaction partner are modeled by the Role element. Every partner, who provides the relevant interface associated with a particular role, can play that role. These concepts are captured by using the PartnerLink and the PartnerLinkType elements, as are their relationships with the Role element. An interaction between the process and one of its partners is represented by the Interaction element that associates with a particular PartnerLink.

3. Information view: The information view involves the representation of data object flows inside the process and message objects traveling back and forth between the process and the external world (Figure 5.3a). Each Information view consists of a number of BusinessObjects elements. In this view, the BusinessObject element, which has a generic type, namely, Type, is the abstraction of, for example, any piece of information like a purchase order received from the customer or a request sent to a banking service to verify the customer's credit card. Messages exchanged between the process and its partners or data flowing inside the process might go through some transformations that convert or extract existing data to form new pieces of data. The transformations are performed inside a DataHandling object. The source or the target of a certain transformation is an ObjectReference entity that holds a reference to a particular BusinessObject.

4. Human view: The human view defines human roles and their relationships to the respective process and tasks (Figure 5.3b). Process elements that require human interactions are called as Tasks. Tasks may specify certain input values as well as a Task Description, and may yield a result that can be represented using output values. Roles denote abstract concrete users that may play certain roles. The Human view thus establishes a role-based abstraction. This role-based abstraction can be used for role-based access control. Role-based access control, in general, is administered through roles and role hierarchies that mirror an enterprise's job positions and organizational structure. Users are assigned membership into roles consistent with their duties, competency, and responsibility.

Examples for different roles are: Task Owner, or Process Supervisor. By binding the owner of a task to a process, the owner may complete the task by sending results back to the process; however, he or she may not be able to follow up on the process. Similarly, by binding the role of a Process Supervisor to a process, role-based access control can define that those users that are associated with the specific role may monitor the process execution.

Extension mechanisms: During the process development lifecycle, various stakeholders work at different levels of abstraction. For instance, the business experts—those who are familiar with business concepts and methods—sketch blueprint designs of the business process functionality using abstract and high-level languages such as flow-charts, Business Process Modeling and Notation (BPMN) diagrams, or Unified Modeling Language activity diagrams. Based on these designs, the information technology experts implement the business processes using executable languages such as Business Process Execution Language (BPEL), Extensible Markup Language (XML) Process Definition Language (XPDL), and so on.

According to the specific requirements on the granularity of the views, these views can either be abstracted (or refined) towards less (or more) concrete, platform- or technology-specific views using the extension mechanisms.

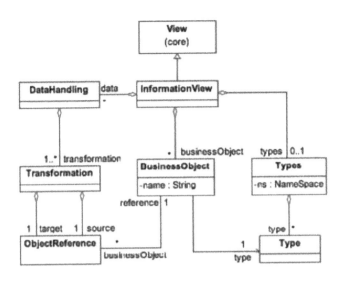

(a)

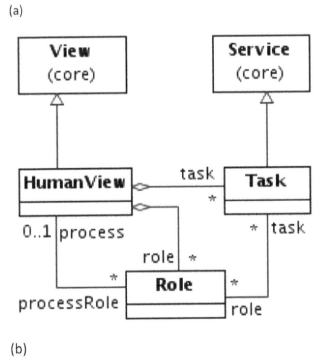

(b)

FIGURE 5.3
(a) The information view; (b) the human view.

A view refinement is performed by choosing adequate extension points and, consequently, applying extension methods to create the resulting view. An extension point of a certain view is a view's element that is enhanced in another view by adding additional features (e.g., new element attributes, new relationships with other elements) to form a novel element in the corresponding view. Extension methods are modeling relationships such as generalization, extend, and so on that can be used to establish and maintain the relationships between an existing view and its extension. For instance, the Control-flow view, collaboration view, and information view are mostly extensions of the core view using the generalization relationship.

Integration mechanisms: In our approach, the Control-flow view—as the most important concern in process-driven SOA—is often used as the central view. Views can be integrated via integration points to provide a richer or more thorough view of the business process. Typically, named-based matching mechanisms are utilized for integrating views; it is reasonable to give the same name to the modeling entities that demonstrate the same functionality and semantics. However, other view integration approaches such as those using class hierarchical structures or ontology-based structures are also applicable in the view-based framework.

View transformations: There are two basic types of model transformations: view-to-view and view-to-code. A view-to-view transformation maps a view conforming to a given meta-view to another kind of view conforming to another meta-view. View-to-code, or so-called code generation, produces executable code from a certain view. In the view-based framework, the view transformations are mostly view-to-code that take as input one or many views and generate codes in executable languages, for instance, Java, BPEL/Web Services Description Language, and so on. Numerous other code generation techniques are also available such as the combination of templates and filtering, the combination of templates and meta-models, inline generation, or code-weaving.

5.3 Reference Process Architecture: Workflow Systems

Workflows are useful for the coordination of interrelated activities carried out by organization members in order to execute a business process. According to the American Society for Quality, a business process is an organized group of related activities that work together to transform one or more kinds of inputs into outputs that are of value to the enterprise.

The term workflow is defined, according to the WfMC, as the automation of a business process, in the course of which documents, information, or tasks move from one participant to another in order to perform some actions in accordance with a set of procedure rules. When it is executed across an extended enterprise, it becomes a distributed workflow, in which different individuals participate in order to reach global objectives. In the work presented here, collaborative process planning can be considered as a business process that can be managed using distributed workflows.

A WfMS defines, creates and manages the execution of workflows through the use of software, running on one or more workflow engines. The software components store and interpret process definitions, create and manage workflow instances as they are executed, and control their interactions with workflow participants and applications. The following sections contain a review of the required components for a WfMS to bring the basic support to coordinating collaborations among distributed participants.

5.3.1 Basic Workflow Components

According to the WfMC, the basic items that must be represented in a workflow, to be complete and unambiguous for its execution in a WfMS, are as follows:

- Activity: A description of a piece of work that forms one logical step within a process. An activity may be a manual activity, which does not support computer automation, or a workflow (automated) activity.

- Participant: A resource that performs the work represented by a workflow activity instance. This work is normally manifested as one or more work items assigned to the workflow participant via a pending work list.

- Role: A mechanism that associates participants to a collection of workflow activities. A workflow participant assumes a role to access and process work from a workflow management system.

- Routing: A route defines the sequence of the steps that information must follow within a workflow. This element is fundamental for directing all of the activity work to the distributed participants, in order to guarantee the success of the information flow and decision-making.

- Transition rule: A transition rule is a logic expression that determines what actions need to be carried out, depending on the value of logic operators. The definition of transition rules implies multiple options, variations, and exceptions.

- Event: An occurrence of a particular condition (may be internal or external to the WfMS) that causes the workflow management software to take one or more actions. For example, the arrival of a particular type of email message may cause the workflow system to start an instance of a specific process definition.

- Deadline: A time-based scheduling constraint, which requires that a certain activity work be completed by a certain time.

All of these items can be represented in a workflow model definition that later can be interpreted and executed by a workflow engine. However, first, it is required to select a methodology to model the workflow items and their relations properly.

5.3.2 Types of Workflow

Workflows can be categorized into four types: specifically administrative, production, ad hoc, and collaborative. However, this categorization is not mutually exclusive; there are workflow processes that exhibit considerable overlap across these categories. In the case of the corresponding workflow products, also, there is a blurring of the lines among the various workflow types. Many production workflow vendors include capabilities to handle the other three types of workflow.

Administrative workflow products represent the lower end of the workflow product market. Administrative workflow is less structured and is usually based on a form, such as an expense report. While they are cheaper to purchase and are more flexible than a production workflow system, they have a lower degree of automation and generally do not have the integration and modeling functionalities of production workflow systems. Production workflow is the most rigorous of all the workflow types: it requires detailed routing and structure to be included in the workflow.

1. Administrative workflow: This is used to perform workflow processes with defined procedures, though not as structured as in the case of Production workflow, as each instance of the workflow can have a different amount of work associated with it. Administrative workflow arose from office automation. Office automation products [such as IBM Lotus Notes (IBM Corp., Armonk, NU)] first included

administrative workflow functions to manage these types of processes through emails and messages. An example of Administrative workflow is the process for an expense report approval. The employee would fill out the expense report which is then reviewed by an accounts payable clerk for ascertaining whether any items fall outside of guidelines. Once the expense report has been reviewed, it is approved and can be paid. In this example, the flow of work is well-defined, but the content of the work is different from one expense report to another.

 The same expense report approval process can also be implemented using a production workflow system. In the production workflow scenario, the employee would complete an electronic form. When the expense report has been completed, the system automatically routes it to the accounts payable clerk for review and approval. The differences in an administrative and a production workflow system are that Administrative workflow is simple to implement, unsophisticated, and uses email technology. Production workflow, in contrast, is sophisticated, can handle complex logic, and requires a high degree of process design.

2. Production workflow: This consists of highly automated workflow processes—the goal of a Production workflow is to automate the process as much as possible. This type of workflow began as a feature of the document imaging systems. The financial services sector uses document imaging for processing large amounts of transactions that are structured and repetitive, like in the case of loan processing or insurance claims. Any automation of these processes usually yields significant financial savings. To speed up the routing and processing of these paper-based forms, workflow was added to the document imaging system to help reduce process cycle time. Subsequently, the concept of routing documents and images has been expanded beyond the financial services sector.

   The WfMSs corresponding to Production workflows can be categorized into:

   a. Autonomous WfMS is a standalone system that does not need to function in conjunction with a business application. It can be used to manage workflow processes that involve an application and human participants. During runtime, an autonomous WfMS can invoke external business applications and pass data between different workflow participants. The integration of autonomous WfMS to other business applications usually requires application development.

   b. Embedded WfMS is a workflow system that is specific to a business application and which is used to perform workflow within the scope of the host business applications. Thus, an embedded WfMS requires a host system, such as an SAP enterprise resource planning (ERP) system. SAP Business Workflow (SAP SE, Walldorf, Germany) exists as a module of SAP ERP and uses the SAP's ERP infrastructure to perform its functions; additionally, it also offers the same user interface and operates in the same platform as the business application. Generally, use of embedded workflow does not require an application integration effort because it is already part of a business application.

       Compared to autonomous WfMSs, embedded workflow is easier to implement and maintain but cannot be used to manage complex processes that span multiple applications, as its use is limited to the events and triggers provided by the host business application.

3. Ad hoc workflow: This is implemented by a user to perform a string of actions that arise for a business scenario. This type of workflow is highly customized: every workflow instance is different and there is no predefined and standardized structure and routing. In other words, Ad hoc workflows are conceived for *Cinderella processes*. Every user can design a specific workflow for a business process. In an implementation of Ad hoc workflow, the sender determines the recipient who will receive the activities of the Ad hoc workflow; the recipient can then forward the workflow instance to other recipients. The workflow ends when there is no recipient to forward to.

The event–condition–action–alternative action scenario is one of standard formats for the workflow business rules. In event–condition–action–alternative action, the following are true:

- The event is the trigger that starts the business rule
- After the rule has been triggered, the condition is evaluated
- If the condition holds true, the action is taken
- If the condition is false, then the alternative action is performed

An example of an Ad hoc workflow with the rule is the process for checking customer credit. The event could be the receipt of a sales order by the account executive. The condition is the customer having good credit. If the condition is true, the action is to pass the order to *order fulfillment* for scheduling. If the condition is false, the alternative condition is to send notification to the customer regarding the credit problem. The recipient of the workflow could define his own subsequent Ad hoc workflow.

 The difference between an email and Ad hoc workflow is that, while email is only a message, Ad hoc workflow can also have actions and rules that can be included in the workflow. During design time, a user can specify actions that the workflow should undertake based on certain rules.

4. Collaborative workflow: This type of workflow involves a team of people working together. The participants in a collaborative workflow need to be able to share documents and to pass documents for review and comment. A Collaborative workflow would allow the participants to share design documents, comment on changes, and approve the changes.

An example of collaborative workflow process is the information technology project plan. Every project plan is tailored specifically to the project at hand. Revisions are usually made to the project plan. Another example of collaborative workflow is engineering change management. In this type of scenario, people from several functional departments are involved in reviewing and commenting on changes to a design.

The products that have been developed to cater to this workflow are generically called groupware. Unlike the production workflow system, collaborative workflow systems are not transaction-oriented. They usually do not create business transactions in backend systems.

5.3.3 Workflow Modeling

There are several emerging industry standards and technologies related to workflow modeling that consider all of the elements mentioned earlier. BPEL for Web Services is emerging as a de facto standard for implementing business processes on top of Web services technology. Numerous WfMSs support the execution of BPEL processes. However, BPEL modeling tools do not have the adequate level of abstraction required to make them usable during the analysis and design phases of high-complexity processes like collaborative product design, process planning, and manufacturing.

On the other hand, BPMN has attracted the attention of business analysts and system architects as a language for defining business process blueprints for subsequent implementation. The BPMN is a graph-oriented language in which control and action nodes can be connected almost arbitrarily. While BPMN is also supported by numerous modeling tools, none of them can directly execute BPMN models because they require the translation of BPMN to execute on a workflow enactment service with a workflow engine capable of executing BPEL directly.

5.3.4 Workflow Perspectives

Workflow modeling is aimed at specifying different perspectives of the application process and of the technical and organizational environments in which the workflow will be executed. This subsection describes the various perspectives that are relevant for workflow systems.

5.3.4.1 *Data or Informational Perspective*

The data perspective describes the data types involved, for instance data types for customer data or offerings. Besides the specification of the data types, data flow constraints between activities of a workflow are also described in the Informational perspective.

The data perspective consists of data flow between workflow activities. In particular, each activity is assigned a set of input and a set of output parameters; upon its start, an activity reads its input parameters and, upon its termination, it writes values it generated into its output parameters. These values can be used by follow-up activities in the workflow as input data. This transfer of data between workflow activities is known as *data flow*.

The modeling of data is required to permit workflow management systems to control the transfer of workflow relevant data as generated or processed by workflow activities during workflow executions.

By providing graphic language constructs to represent data flow between activities (such as the state information in a Petri net), the informational perspective can be visualized and used to validate and optimize application processes.

5.3.4.2 *Context or Organizational Perspective*

A major goal of workflow management systems is enhancing the efficiency of application processes by assigning work to "resources"—that is, persons or software systems as specified by workflow models. A WfMS requires information on the context that is organizational as well as on the technical environment in which the workflows will be executed.

Atomic workflows can be either automatic or manual. Manual atomic workflows are executed by persons who may use application programs to do so; automatic atomic workflows are executed by software systems without human involvement. Since a strict assignment of workflow activities to persons is not feasible in most cases, the *role* concept is defined dependent on the structure of an organization in which the workflow is executed. When an activity is about to start, the system uses predefined role information via *role resolution* to select one or more persons to perform the requested activity.

5.3.4.3 *Interaction or Operational Perspective*

The interaction perspective predominantly covers technical issues such as the invocation environment of application programs (including host and directory information of the executable program) as well as the definition of the input and output parameters of the application program and their mapping to input and output parameters of workflow activities.

Interaction perspective entails a sequence of steps as follows:

1. When persons are selected by role resolution to perform workflow activities.
2. When a person chooses to perform an activity, then the defined application program is started and the input data as specified in the workflow model are transferred to that application program.
3. When the person completes that activity, the output data generated by that activity are collected in the output parameters of the activity to be transferred by the WfMS to the next workflow activity, as specified in the respective workflow model.

5.3.4.4 *Processing or Functional and Behavioral Perspective*

The processing perspective covers the functional decomposition of activities as present in application processes; that is, it specifies which activities have to be executed within a workflow. Workflows typically have a tree structure such that the root node of the tree represents the top-level (complex) workflow, the inner nodes represent other complex workflows, and the leaf nodes represent bottom-level atomic activities.

Thus, per processing perspective, workflows are nested at all levels. In particular, workflows are partitioned into complex and atomic workflows, wherein complex workflows are composed of a number of (complex or atomic) workflows known as subworkflows.

The controlled execution of a complex workflow by a WfMS has to take into account interrelationships of the subworkflows covered in the subordinate *behavioral perspective*. This perspective specifies the conditions under which the subworkflows of a given complex workflow are executed. For instance, it could specify the branching of control flow depending on the value of the predicate(s). In general, the semantics of branches can be parallel, alternative, or controlled by predicates that are evaluated at execution time of the workflow.

5.4 Workflow Reference Model

The WfMC was created in 1993 to help standardize and coordinate the various uses of workflow. The charter of the WfMC was to develop interoperability standards and common terminology for use by the various workflow vendors. The WfMC recognized that because of the varied origins of the workflow products, there was a need for standardization for the various workflow products that were on the market. As mentioned in Subsection 5.3.2, Administrative workflow arose from office automation products [e.g., IBM Lotus Notes (IBM Corp., Armonk, NY)], while Production workflow arose from document imaging systems.

The WfMC created a WRM to address the standardization. The WRM divides the workflow system into five components: process definition tool, workflow engine, workflow client application, invoked application, and administration and monitoring tool. These five components interact with one another through the set of five interfaces. Figure 5.1 depicts the workflow components and the five interfaces.

The WRM provides the following three guidelines:

- Common terminology for the workflow product category: Without a standardized terminology, it is very difficult for customers to understand the workflow product segment. Not only is it confusing for the customers but also detrimental to the establishment of a workflow ecosystem of developers and consultants.

- The WRM is the functional components necessary in a WfMS: This serves as a guide for workflow product vendors to design their workflow products. By following this reference system module, the chances of product interoperability increase.

- Interfaces that connect the various functional components: The initial interface definitions are described in functional terms. Thus, they do not provide the technical specifications to allow for interoperability. The functional interface definitions provide the foundation for workflow system interoperability. Technical interface binding definitions were developed later that would allow different workflow systems to interoperate once they have implemented these interface bindings.

The components and interfaces of the WRM are shown in Figure 5.4.

5.4.1 Workflow Process Definition Tool

The process definition tool is a design tool that allows the workflow designer to design and model the workflow process. A typical process definition tool provides a graphical interface for the process designer to graphically design the business process. The process

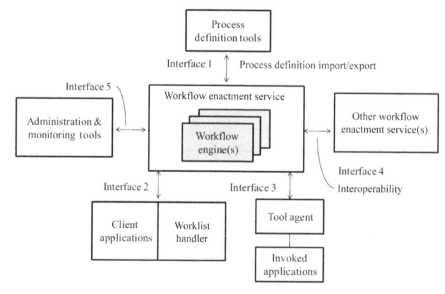

FIGURE 5.4
WRM components and interfaces.

definition consists of a network of activities and their relationships; criteria to indicate the start and termination of the process; and information about the individual activities, such as participants, associated information technology applications and data, and so on. The process designer would specify the steps, participants, and transitions between the different steps of the workflow process in the process definition tool. The result of the design activity is a workflow process model. The workflow process model is understood to be the representation of a business process in a form that supports automated manipulation, such as modeling, or enactment by a workflow management system.

Once the workflow process model has been designed, the process definition tool creates an output of the model using a process definition language. The generic format included in the WRM is the Workflow Process Definition Language (WPDL). The goal of the WPDL standard is to achieve interoperability of process models created using different process definition tool. As long as a workflow engine supports WPDL, that workflow engine can enact any workflow process model created using WPDL. In 2002, an XML form of the WPDL was published by the WfMC called XPDL. As a process definition language, XPDL contains process definition semantics that are understood by XPDL-compliant workflow engines.

1. Workflow process: The workflow process that is included in the calling workflow process is called a subprocess and can be nested further; that is, an XPDL workflow process could include another XPDL workflow process and so on. Thus, a complex process can be decomposed into a hierarchy of increasingly detailed processes. For instance, the order-to-cash business process can be decomposed into the order entry, order fulfillment, delivery, and billing subprocesses.

2. Activity: An activity is work performed by a specific resource. In XPDL, the mechanism to invoke a subprocess is through an activity that includes the execution of the subprocess definition. There are two types of activities: manual and automated. A manual activity is performed by a human participant and an automated activity is performed by a system participant. An automated activity usually invokes another application component and receives a response; it is also used for routing that has no resource assignment and to perform flow control. A flow control could be the implementation of an if–then–else statement in choosing the right activities to execute.

3. Participant: The participants in a workflow process could be:
   - An explicitly named human user: The participant of an activity is explicitly assigned using direct assignment. There is no additional logic needed to determine the appropriate participant for an activity during runtime.
   - A role defined in an organizational structure: The workflow engine references the organizational model with the role or the position specified in the workflow process model. The organizational model would contain the specific human participant assigned to the specified role or position. Using this mechanism, the appropriate human participant is not determined until runtime. The benefit of this approach is the extra level of abstraction between the role or position and the human participant. This helps to mitigate organizational changes (e.g., employee promotions) that would affect the workflow model if a direct assignment mechanism is used.
   - A position that is part of the organizational unit: Dynamic participant assignment uses the previous activities of the workflow to determine the correct participant. Another example is an activity to be processed by the

supervisor of the employee who executed a previous workflow activity. The system identifies the supervisor during runtime using the organizational structure. It routes the activity to the supervisor after the employee executes the previous activity.

- An information system: Programmatic assignments use programming to determine the participant assignment. Using a programmatic assignment, custom logic can be employed to determine the participant assignment. The participants are defined in an organizational model that might not be part of the WfMS. For example, an enterprise organizational structure might be stored in a Lightweight Directory Access Protocol product. In this case, the workflow process model would contain references to the organizational model in the external product.

4. Flow control: There are four generic flow control mechanisms, as follows:

- Sequential: Sequential routing is when one activity follows another activity and there is no branch in the workflow process. In sequential routing, there is only one thread that is being executed by the WfMS.

- Parallel: Parallel routing is branching in the workflow process such that multiple activities are performed concurrently. The decision for the branching could be conditional or concurrent. In conditional parallel routing, the process model specifies multiple branches at the point of parallel routing. Only the branches that satisfy predetermined criteria are undertaken. In concurrent parallel routing, all branches in the parallel routing are executed. In both conditional and concurrent routing, the branches could converge again to one single thread in a subsequent workflow step. Parallel routing could have more than one thread that has been executed by the WfMS for a workflow process instance.

- Iteration: Iteration determines how many times an activity or a group of activities are to be executed. As long as a condition is met, a block of activities is repeated during runtime. The condition could be specified as a loop with an explicit number of iterations or by using a while-loop construct. Using the while-loop construct, the workflow engine will repeat the activity block until the condition specified returns false.

- Nesting: This allows complex routings to be decomposed into a hierarchy of increasingly lower-granularity routings.

5. Transition: This defines the criteria for moving to the next activity and it is usually represented as a line from one activity to the next in the graphical workflow process model. Transition can be of two types: conditional and unconditional. A conditional transition is a transition that occurs only if the condition specified evaluates to true. If the condition evaluates to false, an exception branch could be specified for execution. Transition can be used to capture exceptions to a workflow process. In contrast, an unconditional transition is a transition that always occurs without exception.

 The process definition can be defined in a separate business modeling product, in which case interface 1 of the WRM is the conduit for transferring the business process definition to the workflow engine.

5.4.2 Workflow Client Application

Workflow client application is an application that requests services from the workflow engine including the retrieval of a worklist generated by the workflow engine for participants to execute. An example of this is the integration of a workflow engine to a workplace portal that acts as the workflow client application; this is required when an organization desires one single portal for users performing work. The workflow engine generates the work items assigned to specific users, which are retrieved by the workplace portal and then displayed to each user for action. Because of its role in handling work items, the workflow client application would need to instantiate a workflow process instance, execute a work item, and update the worklist in the workflow engine as to the status of a particular work item.

 The WRM has specified interface 2 for the interactions between workflow engine and the workflow client application.

5.4.3 Workflow Engine

The workflow engine is the runtime environment of the WfMS. The workflow engine takes the workflow process model from the process definition tool and enacts the workflow; that is, it creates process instances of the workflow process based on a trigger event for the creation of a workflow process instance. An event is a predefined circumstance the workflow engine is listening for: this could be the arrival of an email or the receipt of a leave request form. In an embedded WfMS, the trigger could be some status change of an application transaction. For example, the purchase_order.create event is raised anytime a purchase order is created; this event could in turn trigger the purchase order approval workflow to be enacted.

When a workflow process instance has been created, the workflow engine manages workflow relevant data throughout the life cycle of the workflow process instance. The data could be used to determine state transition, participant assignment, and the various conditions that might be involved in the workflow process. The workflow relevant data comes from the workflow engine, applications that participate in the workflow process, or the process definition.

 Application data are data in the applications that participate in the workflow process but are not available to the workflow process instance; this can be achieved through interface 3 of the WRM. Furthermore, a workflow engine can communicate with another disparate workflow engine through interface 4 of the WRM.

5.4.4 Invoked Application

Whereas the workflow client application requests services from the workflow engine, the workflow engine to perform work calls the invoked application. If we consider the workflow client application to be the frontend application that interacts with the users, then the invoked application is the backend application that creates business transactions. An example is the purchasing requisition process; an online request form completed by a human participant might trigger the process. In a workflow process, the invoked application is a system participant that usually performs a transaction as a result of the workflow process. Once the workflow engine has received the purchase request form, the next activity in the workflow process is to create a purchase requisition in the backend ERP system.

 The workflow engine would then invoke the ERP system through interface 3 of the WRM.

5.4.5 Administration and Monitoring Tool

This tool allows system administrators to manage the WfMS users, roles, and resources. If the resources are not part of the WfMS (e.g., Lightweight Directory Access Protocol to store the organizational model), the administration and monitoring tool allows for interaction with the Lightweight Directory Access Protocol tool. Other functions provided by the administration and monitoring tool include audit reporting, querying of process status, and updating active process instances. Workflow engines store all of the events and record updates to process instances in workflow logs. The administration and monitoring tool should be able to retrieve workflow logs for process instances that have completed and instances that are still in progress. These statistics provide data for process analysis, which can lead to process improvements. For process instances that are in the error state, the administration and monitoring tool should be able to restart or terminate those instances.

5.4.6 Workflow Reference Model Interfaces

In a heterogeneous environment, where the various components do not belong to one integrated product, the WRM provides definitions for five interfaces to integrate the various components of the WfMS. The WRM does not make assumptions about whether the various components of the WfMS are from the same vendor.

1. Interface 1 links the workflow process definition tool to the workflow engine. The original data format for this interface was based on the WPDL. The process definition tool would export a WPDL file and the workflow engine would be able to import the WPDL file. The interface definition was later updated to use XPDL. This new format is extensible because of its use of XML. The extensibility allows different vendors to add additional information to the process definition that can be used by the workflow engine that can understand them.

2. Interface 2 links the workflow client application to the workflow engine. It is a set of application programming interfaces (APIs) that the client application can invoke on the workflow engine. The client application is usually a front-end application with which a user would interact. Through interface 2, the client application can control workflow process instances, activities, and work items. The interface definitions include versions for the C programming language, Object Linking & Embedding, the Microsoft Common Object Model, and the CORBA interface definition language.

3. Interface 3 connects the workflow engine to the business applications invoked during the processing of the workflow model. The workflow engine can use a set of APIs on third-party applications. The functions provided by interface 3 include connection, disconnection, application invocation, status request, and termination of a running application. As with interface 2, the definitions of interface 3 include versions for the C programming language, Object Linking & Embedding, and the CORBA interface definition language.

 Interface 3 has been consolidated with interface 2 to form a workflow API.

4. Interface 4 enables integration between heterogeneous workflow engines by providing a set of APIs that one WfMS can invoke on another. The functions provided by the APIs include instantiation of a workflow process, querying the status of a running workflow process instance, starting a workflow activity, and

changing the status of a workflow instance. The initial version of the interface 4 definition used the Multipurpose Internet Mail Extension format for encoding the message that carries the request: it is an encoding protocol that allows a binary file to be enclosed in an email message. With the advent of XML and open standards because of Web services, there has been strong interest in interoperability in the entire technology industry. This led to the development of Workflow XML by the WfMC in 2000. Workflow XML is an XML-based protocol that allows one WfMS to invoke functions on another WfMS through the HyperText Transfer Protocol. Essentially, it is the XML-based binding function for implementing interface 4.

The Workflow XML message contains three parts:

- The message transport is an optional section wherein the sender can specify characteristics such as security; processing model (e.g., batch, asynchronous, synchronous); and message identification. This section does not need to exist for the XML to be a valid Workflow XML message.

- The message header section contains the message type (request or response), whether response is required, language (e.g., English), and the key to resources (e.g., the Internet address of the process definition).

- The message body defines the parameters for a response to or a request of an operation.

Workflow XML expands on the functions provided by interface 4 to include three groups of operations that one WfMS can request from another WfMS, as follows:

- The process definition group contains the operation to create a process instance. This operation allows a WfMS to instantiate a process instance of a previously defined workflow process model in another WfMS.

- The process instance group contains operations to obtain process instance data and to change the state of a process instance. The observer group is for a WfMS or a system resource to be notified of a status change of a process instance. Currently, there is only one operation, the change to the state of a process instance, defined in this group.

- An observer who has registered with a WfMS can receive notification when there is a change to the state of a process instance.

5. Interface 5 enables integration between workflow engines with the administration and monitoring tool. The WfMC defined the Common Workflow Audit Data 1998, which specifies the data a workflow engine should capture for the various events in the workflow process as follows:

- Process audit information specifies basic information (e.g., process instance identification number, process instance state, user) that needs to be captured when a process instance is started or changed. The individual workflow engine can define additional attributes that are recorded (with old values before the change and new values after the change) and are available for transfer using interface 5.

- Activity instance audit information captures information when an activity instance is changed and allows the workflow engine to define additional attributes available to interface 5.

- Work item audit information captures information when an work item is changed and allows the workflow engine to define additional attributes available to interface 5.

- Remote operation audit information section specifies data that should be captured when one workflow engine communicates with another workflow engine. The operations between workflow engines that need to be captured are start conversation, stop conversation, create process instance, change process instance state, change process instance attribute, get process instance attributes, process instance state changed, and process instance attribute changed. In each of these operations, the source and target workflow engines both need to record the information exchanged and data changed.

5.5 Summary

Enterprise architecture applies architecture principles and practices to guide enterprises through the business, information, process, and technology changes necessary to execute their strategies. These practices utilize the various aspects of an enterprise to identify, enable, and achieve these changes. This chapter described the process views and perspectives that enable an *enterprise process architecture*. Analogous to the enterprise architecture framework concept described in Chapter 4, this chapter described the WRM as the reference process architecture for the enterprise process architecture.

Workflow systems are a subset of BPM systems that additionally have robust application integration, application development, process analysis, and richer process simulation and modeling capabilities. Workflow is broadly defined as the automation of a business process, in whole or part, during which documents, information, or tasks are passed from one participant or entity to another for action, according to a set of procedural rules. The latter part of the chapter described the WRM.

Section II

Road to Enterprise Process Management Systems

There is an essential gap between approaches for modeling business processes and those for modeling information systems. Due to this gap, the translation of the business processes into an information system (and vice versa) and consequently the alignment of business and information technology has become difficult. There is a strong need for a methodology for creating a supporting information system that is based on the process architecture of an organization. This section addresses this requirement across its four constituent chapters. After introducing models and process modeling, this section describes distributed systems and the idea of service-oriented architecture (SOA), which paved the road to enterprise process management systems. It explains how cloud computing builds on virtualization to create a service-oriented computing model that can tackle requirements for flexible computing services, including both infrastructure and application workload requests, while meeting defined service levels for capacity, resource tiering, and availability. Finally, it leverages SOA to explain the cloud-based realization of business processes in terms of Web services. The traditional paradigm is covered in several publications such as R. C. Anthony (2016); P. Verissimo and L. Rodrigues (2001); T. Erl (2004); I. Graham (2008); and D.R. Ferreira (2013).

Chapter 6 presents the basic concepts of model, enterprise modeling, and process modeling. This chapter presents several frequently-used business process modeling languages including Petri nets, Event-driven Process Chains, Yet Another Workflow Language, Unified Modeling Language activity diagrams, and Business Process Modeling and Notation.

Chapter 7 describes the characteristics of distributed systems and introduces distributed computing as a foundation for better understanding of cloud-enabled business processes.

Chapter 8 presents the definition and characteristics of SOAs, along with alternate approaches to realizing the vision of service-oriented systems, namely, Web services and representational state transfer-ful services. An SOA with Web services enables the development of services that encapsulate business functions and that are easily accessible from any other service; composite services allow for a wide range of options for combining Web services and for creating new business processes and, hence, new application functionalities.

Chapter 9 describes cloud computing's definition, presents cloud delivery and deployment models, and highlights its benefits for enterprises. It highlights the primary challenges faced during the provisioning of cloud services, namely, scalability, multitenancy, and availability. More importantly, the chapter leverages SOA to explain the cloud-based realization of business processes in terms of Web services.

6

Enterprise Modeling

Implementing process-oriented architectures has proven to be difficult for many companies. Reasons for these difficulties include existing information technology infrastructures, which support functional organizations and hinder the transition toward process-oriented architectures. Implementing process concepts within organizations is only one step toward achieving an enterprise-wide focus on processes. In order to reap ongoing benefits from a process-oriented organization, continuous maintenance and control of the business processes is required. Process management deals with the efficient and effective execution of business processes. It consists of the planning, implementation, enactment, and controlling of processes and forms a life cycle that leads to continuous process improvement. Process management addresses the requirement of companies to stay adaptable to environmental and internal changes. Simultaneously, it helps companies to realize efficiency gains through the exploitation of cost-effective ways to produce goods and perform services.

There is a gap between approaches for modeling business processes and those for modeling information systems. Due to this gap, the translation of business processes into an information system (and vice versa) and consequently the alignment of business and information technology has become difficult. There is a strong need for a methodology for creating a supporting information system that is based on the process architecture of an organization. The practice of the last two decades shows the failure of software systems over and over again due to poor modeling: these systems failed not because of technical shortcomings but rather because they are not adequately supported by the underlying business processes. This chapter discusses processes from the systems point of view in Subsection 6.5.

6.1 Model

A model is a form of representing something: it is not a replication but rather an intentional selective construction of a new thing or system that has the purpose of representing another thing or system. A model is a simplification of reality in the sense that the model represents selected aspects of realty and ignores other aspects. No model is unique or exclusive, as there can be a multitude of them; furthermore, models are generally not correct or incorrect—it is only what it is with reference to the defining purpose of the respective model. The legitimacy or adequacy of a model depends only on the degree to which it accurately represents the purposeful view or viewpoint of the thing or system.

Typical characteristics of a model include:

- Abstraction: A model is a reduced description of the system.
- Accuracy: For the properties of interest, a model provides a true-to-life representation of the system.

- Understandability: Removing details that are irrelevant for a given view or viewpoint and specifying in a form that is intuitive enables easier understanding of the concerned system properties.
- Reasoning: A model helps with correctly analyzing and reasoning about the interesting but nonobvious properties of the system, either through some type of formal analysis or experimentation (e.g., by simulating the model on a computer).
- Inexpensiveness: A model is drastically cheaper to construct and analyze than the system.

Computer-based systems can be modeled using many different approaches, for example:

1. Data-oriented models view a system as a collection of data related by some types of attributes. The system is represented as a collection of entities related by attributes, properties, and classes. These models dedicate more importance to the organization of data rather than to the system functionality. The models of this type are widely used for developing data-centered systems, wherein the data-oriented perspective is very important. Unified Modeling Language (UML) does not have any kind of diagram that exclusively supports this perspective, since it favors object-oriented systems and does not promote the usage of diagrams primarily dedicated to data modeling. Nevertheless, it is possible to argue that UML class diagrams are partially data-oriented models. Entity relationship diagrams that define a system as a set of entities and the respective interconnections are suitable to represent data-oriented models.

    Object-oriented models, which can be viewed in a historical perspective as an evolution or extension of the data-oriented models, are multiple-view models, since they simultaneously use various models to address different perspectives (views) of the same system. UML, which represents a unifying notation of various development methods, includes a set of diagrams that allow the most relevant aspects of object-oriented systems to be described. Each diagram focuses on a given view of the system and obviously emphasizes some aspects and neglects others. The object-modeling technique methodology addresses the following three aspects:
   - The static structure (object model)
   - The reaction of the objects and the sequence of interactions (dynamic model)
   - The transformations of data (functional model)

2. Structure-oriented models allow the representation of the physical modules or components of a system and their interconnections. These models are dedicated to the characterization of the physical composition of a system, instead of its functionality. Block diagrams, UML deployment, and component diagrams are popular examples of languages used to represent structure-oriented models.

3. Activity-oriented models view a system as a set of activities related by data or execution dependencies. These models are well-suited to address systems where data are affected by a sequence of transformations at a given rate. Data flow diagrams, and flowcharts are examples of languages for representing activity-oriented models.

4. State-oriented models allow modeling a system as a set of states and a set of transitions. The transitions between states evolve according to some external stimulus. These models are adequate for systems in which the dynamic behavior is an important perspective to be captured. Finite state machines, statecharts, and Petri nets are examples of languages adopted to represent state-oriented models.

5. Heterogeneous models allow for the use of several characteristics from different languages in the same representation. A model is heterogeneous if it incorporates any combination of the characteristics of the four types of models described earlier. These models are a good solution when relatively complex systems must be modeled. Object process diagrams, control/data flow graphs, and program state machines are examples of languages for representing heterogeneous models.

6.1.1 Types of Models

Figure 6.1 shows the various types of models.

1. Descriptive: A descriptive model is used to describe or mimic a real-world phenomenon or system. With a descriptive model, one can reason about the properties or the behavior of the system. An example of this type of model is a model of the weather that allows meteorologists to forecast it. Since the model is simpler than the reality, reasoning with the model is also cheaper. In almost all natural sciences, including physics, biology, astronomy, and earth sciences, the models used by scientists trying to understand how the natural world behaves are descriptive in nature. Additionally, in engineering, descriptive models are used, for example, in reverse engineering scenarios when one wants to reason about an existing system without directly affecting it.

2. Prescriptive: A prescriptive model is used to define how a yet-to-be-built system is supposed to be. Prescriptive models are adopted as part of so-called forward

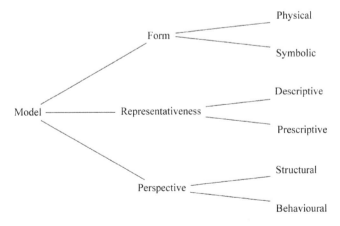

FIGURE 6.1
Classification of models.

engineering. Most of the models used in engineering are prescriptive. In software engineering, models created during the analysis stage describe the problem at hand, while design models, typically obtained from those analysis models, represent the system architecture and are used as blueprints for the implementation of the system.

3. Structural: A structural model is focused on the static aspects of a system. These models are used for describing the components or modules that are part of the system, so they serve for conceptualizing the system architecture. Class, component, and deployment diagrams, which are all supported by UML, are examples of diagrams that can be used for representing structural models.

4. Behavioral: A behavioral model emphasizes the dynamic, functional, and temporal aspects of the system. This type of models address the behavior of the system, being thus especially relevant in the analysis phase. Examples of diagrams that can be used to represent behavioral models include finite-state machines, Petri nets, and data flow diagrams.

5. Symbolic: These models are much more easily changed in comparison with physical models. By manipulating and changing the mathematical relationships, one can see how the model reacts and consequently how the system would react. If the model is relatively simple, then an analytical solution can be obtained by working out a set of mathematical relations. However, for complex systems, the respective mathematical models are also complex, which diminishes the possibility of an analytical solution. In such situations, the model can be analyzed by simulation— that is, by numerically exercising the inputs of the model to understand how the outputs are affected.

   The creation of a symbolic model requires:

   a. A set of signs (or symbols)
   b. A set of rules to operate on those signs

   A symbolic model contains a set of representations related to some phenomenon or system. The rules are used to manipulate the symbols and change the model, producing a sequence of representations of the modeled system. If the model is to be useful, then the manipulation rules must be valid not only in the context of the model but also in the context of the real system.

6. Physical: Typically, a physical model is a smaller representation of the original object (e.g., the solar system, a neighborhood, a building, an airplane, an automobile), but, sometimes, it can be larger if the original object is too small for humans (e.g., an atom, a molecule, a transistor). Interaction with a physical model allows one to obtain information about the properties of the modeled system. Scale models are special physical models in the sense that they seek to preserve the relative proportions (the scale) of the original object. In any case, usually, a physical model is not as accurate or complete as reality. Physical models are not very common in software engineering.

6.2 Modeling

Modeling is the process of identifying adequate concepts and selecting adequate abstractions to construct a model that reflects a given universe of discourse appropriately. Modeling permits the cost-effective use of the model in place of the real-world object or process for some purpose, such as simulation, construction effort estimation, and so on.

In a nutshell, modeling is related to abstraction, simplification, and formalization.

Modeling is the process of obtaining models. It can be considered as a transition from ideas to models in the prescriptive perspective, or a process that mimics the world in the descriptive one. Modeling is not a totally technical process. Actually, it is a combination of both science and art and includes some sort of creativity. The decisions made while modeling cannot be totally automated, but tools and guidelines can be supplied to make the process easier and to enable a higher likelihood of success.

6.2.1 Modeling Ontology

An ontology is an explicit representation of a shared understanding of the important concepts in some domain of interest. Ontologies are represented by conceptual maps that constitute a simple and well-known form of organizational knowledge. Conceptual maps use concepts, normally represented inside a rectangle, as well as relations between pairs of concepts that are expressed by a line that connects them and by connecting sentences that specify those relations.

This ontology considers two different separate perspectives:

- Reverse engineering employs descriptive models to model an existing system. Reverse engineering is a process of analysis in which the system is seen by means of a model. Figure 6.2a presents the ontology for the reverse engineering perspective.
- Forward engineering employs prescriptive models for modeling the envisaged system. Forward engineering is a process of synthesis wherein the system is developed starting from a model. Figure 6.2b presents the ontology for the forward engineering perspective.

The ontology presented is in compliance with the model of computation (MOC), which is a collection of rules that govern the semantics of the components and the communication among those components within a given domain. Classical examples of MOCs are dataflow and finite-state machines. The definitions of MOC and language are similar. Both refer to the components of a domain and the combination of those components to obtain the models or their representations. In fact, a language is the mechanism the software engineer uses to represent models (conceptualized according to a given MOC), using the adopted notation.

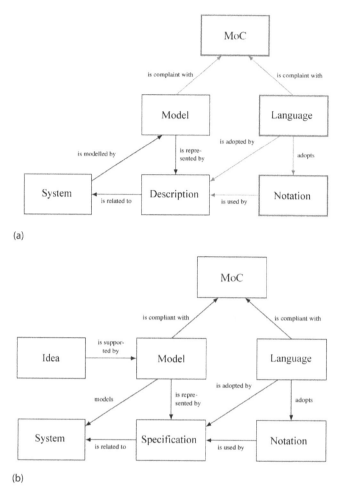

FIGURE 6.2
Ontology for a system. (a) Ontology from the forward engineering perspective and (b) ontology from the reverse engineering perspective.

MOCs are relevant for both languages and models. The accuracy of a particular modeling approach depends on the capability of the modeler to select the best-suited MOC—that is, the one that semantically best supports the characteristics of the system to be modelled. The modeler has complete freedom to select the MOC in such a way that it clearly conveys the essential features of the model, namely its concepts and relations. Often, the modeler does not directly select the MOC but instead chooses a language that conforms to it. The selected language defines the semantic limits of the system representation at the model level. The characterization of MOCs is of acute importance due to their impact on the accuracy of the models. If the MOC (and, consequently, the language) is not adequate, even if one is able to model what is needed, accidental complexity is introduced. For example, using finite-state machines as an MOC will make it very difficult to model a system that includes concurrency issues.

 Modeling corresponds to the activity of selecting a MOC in order to formalize, at the conceptual level, a given target system, while specification and description are related to the adoption of a language to represent, in a tangible form, the model of that system. A specification or a description that adequately represents the system depends on both the characteristics of the selected MOC for the modeling activity and the representation language—to avoid semantic mismatches and incompatibilities, the two MOCs should be compatible. In other words, the MOC used in the system modeling activity should be the same as that of the language.

6.3 Requirements of Modeling

This section describes six models that are essential for modeling software systems.

6.3.1 Domain Models

A domain model constitutes a description of the common properties and variables of the domain related to the system that is being developed. This model represents the things (entities or events) that exist in that domain; that is, it is a conceptual reference of the problem domain. The domain model enables describing and restricting the scope of the problem domain.

The domain model expresses enduring truths about the universe that is relevant to the system at hand, including:

- A definition of the scope of that domain, providing examples of systems or generic rules of inclusion
- A vocabulary of the domain (i.e., the glossary with the principal terms)
- A model of concepts that identifies and relates the concepts of that domain

6.3.2 Use Case Models

A use case model defines the boundaries of the system within the environment and specifies the functionalities provided by the system. A use case model is related to one or more requirements: the most complex use cases are associated with many requirements, whilst the simplest ones are related to fewer numbers of requirements. A use case defines a series of interactions between the system and the actors (humans or external systems) that enables a given result or objective to be achieved; use cases are supplemented with scenarios, which enable description of the sequences of actions performed.

Use case models are represented by use case diagrams consisting of:

1. Use cases (represented by ellipses): The use cases of a system constitute a functional decomposition of the behavior of that system, without imposing any internal structure on it. A use case diagram shows the functionalities of the system, without imposing any restrictions on the sequentialization of those functionalities. The use case constitutes an important model, since it embodies the user requirements captured directly from the stakeholders. UML gives great importance to use case diagrams because they form the basis for the subsequent development cycle of the whole system.

A scenario is an instance of a use case, in the same way that an object represents an instance of a given class. In UML, a scenario refers to a give pathway inside a use case, given by a specific combination of conditions; scenarios can be modeled through sequence or collaboration diagrams.

2. Actors (represented by stylized human figures): An actor represents a role that the users can have when interacting with the system. A use case can be initiated by the system or by the actors. While the same actor can be involved in many use cases, a single use case may also entail multiple actors. The total functionality of the system is the sum-total of all use cases that individually represent particular ways of interacting with the system.

 When one defines the actors and the use cases that are part of the system, one is defining the scope of the system that is to be developed that is effectively delimiting the system.

6.3.3 Class Models

Class models are an essential part of the object-oriented paradigm; class models are necessary to indicate the existing classes and their relations.

1. Each class is divided into three parts:

   - The top part is used to indicate the class name
   - The central part indicates the class attributes
   - The bottom part lists the class operations

   The name is mandatory, but the other parts can be omitted.

2. The message is the fundamental unit of communication among objects. If two objects communicate, then there is a connection or link between them. UML basically considers four types of relations between objects that can be shown between the classes in the respective diagrams:

   - Association represents a relation between objects that manifests itself at execution time through the exchange of messages. When a class of objects depends on the services of another class, they should be connected by an association. The associations are represented in UML by lines and, by default, they are bidirectional.

   - Aggregation represents the so-called part-of-relationship that occurs when an object is contained within another, either physically or logically. The included class is called a component or a part and the wider class (the one that includes the component) is called an aggregate or a composite. In UML, an aggregation is represented by a line with an unfilled diamond near the aggregate. It is possible that the components can be shared among various aggregates, if deemed adequate.

   - Composition constitutes a more restricted form of aggregation, in which the components are shown by graphical inclusion in the aggregate; alternatively, a filled diamond can be used. The components of an aggregate-by-composition cannot be shared with other aggregates. The aggregate is responsible for creating and destroying its components.

- Generalization is used when a class is a specialization of another class. The subclass inherits all the characteristics of the superclass and can add new attributes or operations. In UML, this relation between classes is represented by an arrow that begins at the subclass and ends at the superclass.

3. The numbers or symbols at the end of the relations, designated as multiplicity, indicate the number of objects of the respective class that participate in the relation. The multiplicity indicates the upper and lower limits for the number of objects that participate in the relation.

6.3.4 Interaction Models

An interaction model is used for representing an instance of a use case. Interaction models describe how a group of objects communicate amongst them. Normally, an interaction model captures the behavior of a scenario of a given use case, showing the objects and the messages that are exchanged among them. In UML (version 2.2), there are four different types of diagrams that allow interaction models to be represented; since, in their essence, all of these types address the same modeling purposes and are equivalent in terms of what can be modeled, this book presents only sequence diagrams. Sequence models are used to describe the behavior of the system. They can also be used during the system testing for comparing the real behavior of the system (prototype or executable model) with the one that was specified.

 Interaction models address dynamic aspects related to the exchange of messages between the objects. State models, which are also associated with classes, are unsuitable for this purpose because they just describe the internal state changes of the instances of a given class and not what happens among a set of objects (including those from different classes).

The principal elements of sequence diagrams are:

1. As indicated by the temporal axis, the diagram is read from top to bottom; the temporal axis is not associated with any scale, showing just the order (before or after) between the events.

2. Textual annotations are located on the left side of the diagram to identify initial conditions, actions, and activities.

3. Event identifiers: Near a message, one can include an event identifier that indicates which event is responsible for sending that message.

4. For real-time systems that are conscious of time restrictions, timing marks can be used, with the available options explained as follows:
   - Using a bar with a time limit, thus defining the time that it takes to go from the events notified on the extremes of the bar
   - Indicating between the brackets relational expressions that specify time restrictions

5. State marks: These can be added to the sequence diagrams. State marks, represented by rounded-corner rectangles (the same symbol for states in state machines),

are put in the lifeline of a given object, allowing one to identify the various states in which that object can be found. It is a form of relating, more easily, the sequence diagrams with the state diagrams.

6.3.5 State Models

State diagrams can be used for defining the (dynamic, temporal) behavior of a class (i.e., its instances). They allow us to detail all of the states in which each one of those objects can be found and the transitions between states triggered by conditions to which those objects are responsive. In a conventional state diagram, one and only one state is active in each instant. A system state is represented by a set of variables, whose values contain all of the information necessary about the past of the system and that simultaneously restrict the future system behavior. A state represents a period of time during which the system exhibits a specific type of behavior.

A state is an ontological condition that persists for a significant period of time that is distinguishable and disjointed from other similar conditions. A state differs from other states in the following:

- The events it accepts
- The transitions it takes as a result of the accepted events
- The actions it performs

A transition is a response to an event that causes a state change. State machines are used when a transition between states occurs, mainly as an answer to significant events. State machines extend the most conventional diagrams along three axes related to hierarchy, concurrency, and communication. Figure 6.3 shows an example of a state machine, which is composed of two main elements, the *states* and the *transitions*, represented respectively by rounded-corner rectangles and arrows. The diagram shows also superstates Stt1 and Stt3. A superstate represents a state that contains other states inside its contour, reflecting the mechanism to hierarchically structure a state machine. This abstraction mechanism permits a state machine to be constructed and seen at the desired level of detail.

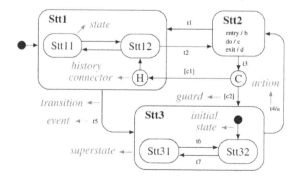

FIGURE 6.3
A state machine.

6.3.6 Activity Models

Activity models are useful to relate the control flow among the activities of a given business process. These models address behavioral aspects of the systems or entities under consideration. These models are appropriate when the behavior change occurs, mainly due to the end of the action/activity executed and not to the occurrence of events, as is the case with state models.

 The choice between a state model and an activity model is not always easy to make. State models are normally used for entities that go through different states. The transition of states is made based on events that occur in the context of the entity under consideration. Activity models are relevant for illustrating the relations among the various tasks or activities that constitute a given process. A transition from an activity to another one frequently occurs only when the first activity ends.

6.4 Enterprise Modeling

Enterprise modeling is the process of creating an integrated enterprise model that captures the aspects of the enterprise required for the modeling purpose at hand. An enterprise model consists of a number of related submodels, each focusing on a particular aspect of the enterprise, for example, processes, business rules, concepts/information, vision/goals, or actors. An enterprise model describes the current or future state of an enterprise and contains the commonly shared enterprise knowledge of the stakeholders involved in the modeling process. The role of an enterprise model is to achieve model-driven enterprise design, analysis, and operation.

Enterprise modeling can be represented by

1. Textual representation: Structured text descriptions using natural language are the simplest means of documentation and are also highly flexible, as there are no restrictions as to what terminology and formulations may be used. However, complex facts quickly become confusing with this approach, and the individuality of description shows the greatest variation between authors. Furthermore, neither automated processing nor analysis of the descriptions is possible.

2. Spreadsheet representation: This provides basic options for comparing and analyzing tables. When tabular representations are highly formalized and use particular predetermined terms, for example, it is possible for the information they contain to be processed automatically. However, there also are problems with using spreadsheet representations to describe complex facts, as in the case of multinested structures or iterations on different levels.

3. Graphic representation without the use of a specific notation: Graphic representation uses graphic elements arranged or connected together to convey certain semantic meanings. These descriptions are easy to create and are a good documentation method for creative modeling workshops in particular. The high level of clarity can be further improved with the help of graphics applications such as mind map programs, but the inconsistent representation and the depiction of complex facts are again problematic, for example, when comparing and evaluating the descriptions.

4. Graphic representation with the use of a specific notation: The fourth representation type is graphic representation with a more formal definition of the language and notation.

   a. Models can be used for communication among stakeholders and developers.
   b. The models can be checked to ensure that the language and notation are correct, which helps to avoid errors in the models.
   c. Computer-aided comparison of different models is possible, e.g., between models of the current situation and the target situation, or between different enterprises or divisions.
   d. The information contained in the model can be reused, for instance, in computer-based information systems and to develop software solutions.
   e. Depending on the model purpose as well as the language and notation, it is also possible to simulate the sequences recorded in the model or to manage workflows.

F. B. Vernadat (1996) provides several principles applicable to enterprise models:

1. Range or scope: the functionalities and processes to be included in the model
2. Viewpoint: aspects of business activity to be covered by or to be left out of the model
3. Separation of concerns: decomposition of enterprise activity into separate functional or process domains
4. Functional decomposition: structuring of a model into a hierarchy of functions and subfunctions as well as processes and subprocesses
5. Genericity: distinguishing between functions and processes, which may be common to business in general (Section 6.6), or to the industrial sector with which the enterprise is associated as well as those specific to the enterprise itself
6. Reusability: the use of existing enterprise models and processes as far as possible and minimization of the need to customize functions or processes
7. Decoupling: separate consideration of things to be done (i.e., processes) and the agents performing them (i.e., resources) in order to preserve operational flexibility
8. Separation of data and control: separate consideration of the data needed by a process from the control or business rules that actually make a process operate
9. Visualization: nonambiguous and simple tabular graphical formalism to easily communicate the model

6.4.1 Enterprise Model Components

A visual model consists of symbols in the form of geometric shapes such as rectangles and ellipses and the lines connecting them (e.g., arrows). The symbols are referred to as model components and the connections as relationships. Together, model components and relationships are known as model elements. Depending on the types provided in the modeling language that is used, model elements are distinguished by model component type or relationship type furnished by the language. Every model component has a specific model component type and every relationship has a specific relationship type. Together, model component types and relationship types are referred to as elements of the modeling language. The association of model component type with a corresponding relationship type is defined by the modeling language via rules and integrity/consistency conditions.

Many modeling languages support views and levels to enable reduction of the complexity of the representation.

1. Stakeholders: The critical factor for the success of enterprise modeling and the resulting change initiatives is to involve all relevant stakeholders in the project. There are many different actors involved in the modeling process. All those who have direct or indirect interest in modeling or the results are regarded as stakeholders. Stakeholders also include those who have no decision-making role in the course of a modeling activity or who do not have relevant information, but who may still contribute to the project result, for example, with experience in similar projects.

     Stakeholders can be divided into two main groups as follows:
     - External stakeholders include customers, partners, subcontractors, legislators, and shareholders of the enterprise
     - Internal stakeholders include the employees, project team, the departments concerned, managers, and executives

   Stakeholder relation to a project or its outcome is not always overt. There can also be so-called indirect or hidden stakeholders. They may, for instance, be members of the management hierarchy with some interest in the project outcome and who could be positively or negatively affected by it.

2. Modeling activities: By modeling activities, we mean all activities involved in the construction or development of models, such as moderated modeling sessions, workshops, and creating models based on data by analysis activities (e.g., interviews, document analysis).

3. Views: A view is defined by the component types and relationship types constituting the view. For instance, the "process view" for an enterprise model contains only the model's processes and their relationships, the roles responsible for them, and the information technology systems used; then, the component types "process," "role," and "information technology system" and the relationship types allocated to "process" are a part of this view.

4. Levels: Levels are used to allow model components to be refined. This means that if the parts or decomposition structure of a model component need to be refined for modeling purposes, then the model component can be refined on the subjacent refinement level. The model component and refinement are clearly associated with each other, for example, by an identifier. The existence of a refinement is generally recognizable from the representation of the model component in the upper level, such as the symbol labeling. All relationships to the model component in the upper level must also exist in the refinement level and be clearly related to the model components in the refinement level. Refinements of model components are often presented as submodels.

6.4.2 Enterprise Knowledge Development

An enterprise model consists of a number of related "submodels," each describing the enterprise from a particular perspective—for example, the purpose of the organization, business processes, entities, and structure. Enterprise knowledge development is an example of a typical enterprise modeling that includes an overall model composed of inter-related submodels for integrating different views of the organization (Bubenko Jr. et al. 1997).

Enterprise knowledge development is composed of six integrated submodels focusing on a different aspect of the enterprise. For example, the Goals model contains business goals and business problems, divided into threats and weaknesses, causes, business opportunities, and constraints. The modeling components of the submodels are related between themselves within a submodel (intra-model relationships) as well as with components of other submodels (inter-model relationships).

Figure 6.4 shows inter-model relationships. The ability to trace decisions, components, and other aspects throughout the enterprise is dependent on the use and understanding of

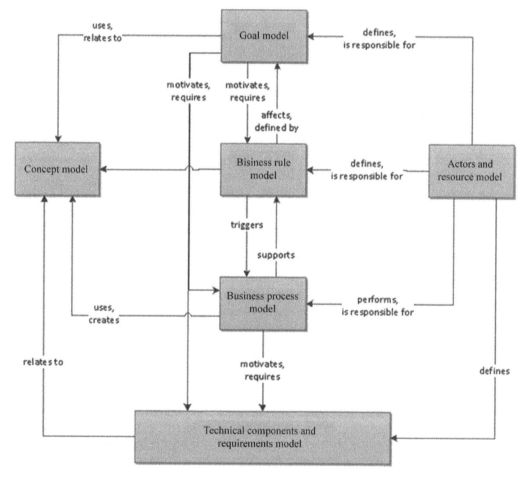

FIGURE 6.4
Relationship between enterprise knowledge development submodels.

these relationships. When developing a full enterprise model, these relationships between components of the different submodels play an essential role. For instance, statements in the Goals model allow for different concepts to be defined more clearly in the Concepts model. A link is then specified between the corresponding Goals model component and the concepts in the Concepts model. In the same way, goals in the Goals model motivate particular processes in the Business Process model. The processes are needed to achieve the goals stated. A link therefore is defined between a goal and the process. Links between models make the model traceable. They show, for instance, why certain processes and information system requirements have been introduced.

There are limitations in the way submodels and their relationships may be populated. These are controlled by a number of static as well as dynamic consistency rules, which control their permissible state transitions. These are necessary because they allow for analysis and comparison.

The six interrelated submodules are also explained in Zikra et al. (2011).

1. Concepts model: This is related to the business ontology and vocabulary; it addresses questions related to the things and "phenomena" covered in other submodels.

   It is used to strictly define the "things" and "phenomena" one is talking about in the other models. We represent enterprise concepts, attributes, and relationships. Concepts are used to define more strictly expressions in the Goals model as well as the content of information sets in the Business Process model.

   A Concepts model usually clarifies questions, such as what concepts are recognized in the enterprise (including their relationships to goals, activities and processes, and actors); how are they defined; and what business rules and constraints monitor these objects and concepts.

   Concepts that are necessary to describe the static aspects of enterprises and information systems are modeled in the Concepts model. They include resources and information objects that are used, processed, exchanged, produced, and stored in the organization, together with their relationships and attributes.

   A concept represents entities about which the enterprise stores or processes information. Concepts represent resources, information objects, or other things that are of interest to the enterprise. They are described by attributes that declare properties for the concepts. Concepts can be related to each other using a concept relationship, which can be of three kinds:
   - Binary relationship, which is a general kind of relationship
   - Generalization relationship, which relates a general concept to a more specific one
   - Aggregation relationship, which is used to indicate that a concept is composed of other concepts

2. Goals model: This is related to the organization's vision and strategy; it addresses questions related to what the organization wants to achieve or to avoid as well as why and when.

   Goals models usually clarify questions, such as where should the organization be moving; what are the goals of the organization; what are the importance, criticality, and priorities of these goals; how are goals related to each other; and which problems are hindering the achievement of goals.

Organizational business goals are recorded and represented in the Goals model. A business goal is a future state-of-affairs that the enterprise aims to attain, and through which it can grow and generate profit. An enterprise can identify potential desirable situations as opportunities, which highlight new possibilities or capabilities that can be transformed into actual business goals. Both opportunities and business goals are defined as types of intentional components because they share many properties. Intentional components can support (or conflict) each other, indicating that achieving one contributes to (or detracts from) achieving the other. Moreover, modeling opportunities as intentional components allows the identification of concepts, roles, processes, and requirements; otherwise, associated only with business goals.

Figure 6.5 shows the Goals model.

The operationalization relationship provides additional structure to the Goals model by allowing business goals to be decomposed into smaller, more concrete subgoals. Operationalization enables organizing the intentional components as a hierarchy.

Decomposition can occur in one of three types, or modes:

- AND operationalization, which indicates that the fulfillment of all subgoals is necessary to fulfill the goal
- OR operationalization, which is when the fulfillment of at least one subgoal is enough to fulfill the goal
- XOR operationalization, which is when subgoals are exclusive alternatives for the goal

Goals have roles that are responsible for them, they track the progress of their fulfillment and make sure the necessary resources are allocated for the relevant purposes.

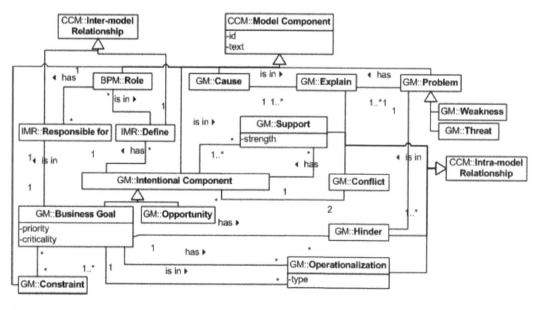

FIGURE 6.5
The Goal model.

Achieving the business goals is usually hindered by various obstacles, and it pays to include those obstacles in the model to provide a clearer view of the organizational landscape. Problems that hinder business goals can be either internal to the enterprise, in which case they are considered weaknesses, or external, in which case they are modeled as threats. The cause that explains a problem is a useful insight when identified explicitly and can contribute to finding suitable measures and solutions. In addition, a business goal is bound by constraints, which represent rules and regulations that affect how the organization operates. Constraints are always external to the organization; internal rules and regulations are described using the business rules model.

3. Business Process model: This is related to the procedural aspects of business operations; it addresses questions related to business processes and how they handle information and material.

The Business Process model is used to define enterprise processes, the way they interact, and the way they handle information as well as material. A business process is assumed to consume input in terms of information and/or material and produce output(s) of information and/or material. In general, the Business Process model is similar to what is used in traditional dataflow diagram models.

The Business Process model usually clarifies questions, such as which business activities and processes are recognized in the organization, or should be there, to manage the organization in agreement with its goals; how should the business processes, tasks, etc. be performed (e.g., via workflows, state transitions, or process models); and which are their information needs.

Business goals identified in the Goals model give rise to, or motivate, the design of business processes that describe activities in the enterprise needed to realize the goals. The Business Process model provides a view over the processes and their composition and structure. A process model component stands for different sizes of processes at both the business- and information systems-levels, thus providing a unified dynamic view of the enterprise and its information systems. The relationship between a process and its subprocesses is captured as a composition relationship, indicating that the subprocesses work together to accomplish the top process. The metamodel includes no limit to the number of decomposition levels, a decision which is left to the specific needs of projects.

Figure 6.6 shows the Process model.

The flow between processes is described using the process flow relationship, which connects processes in one execution flow. The type of the relationship indicates whether the processes are performed in a specific manner as follows:

- Parallel (AND connection)
- Optional (OR connection)
- Conditional (XOR connection)

Processes are affected by events, which are external occurrences that influence the execution of the process and cause it to deviate into certain paths, for example, at the decision points.

Concepts that are consumed and produced are included in the Business Process model using inter-model relationships, denoting the inputs that guide the process execution and outputs that result from the execution.

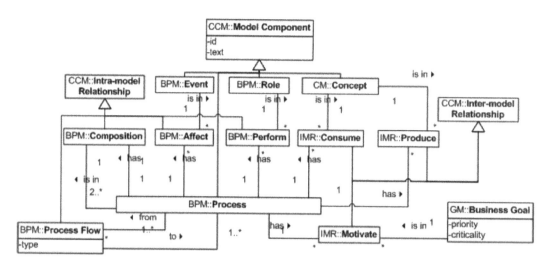

FIGURE 6.6
The Process model.

4. Business Rules model: This is related to the business policies and rules; it addresses questions related to business rules and how they support the organization's goals.

The Business Rules model is used to define and maintain explicitly formulated business rules, consistent with the Goals model. Business rules may be seen as operationalization or limits of goals.

The Business Rule model usually clarifies questions, such as which rules affect the organization's goals, are there any policies stated, how is a business rule related to a goal, and how can the goals be supported by rules.

Internal rules and regulations that govern the enterprise provide boundaries for the concepts and business processes. Business rules are often formulated together with the business goals to specify how the goals will be achieved. Concepts and business processes that are motivated by the business goals are governed by the defined business rule, and this is captured in the Business Rules model.

Figure 6.7 shows the Business Rule model.

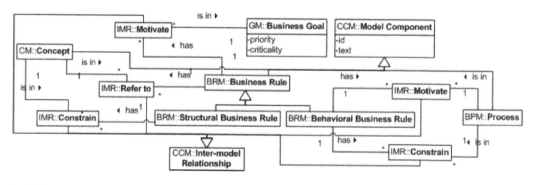

FIGURE 6.7
The Business Rule model.

Business rules are represented in the metamodel as model components that are motivated by business goals. In other words, the business rules affect the fulfillment of business goals. A business rule refers to one or more concepts that are constrained by it. When a rule defines a necessity that needs to be guaranteed at all times by the involved concepts, it is called a structural business rule. When a rule addresses derived or dynamic properties that must be checked at certain points in time or when certain events occur, it is called a behavioral business rule. This type of business rule constraints the enterprise in terms of the change of its state and can lead to different results depending on the triggering events.

Breaking a structural business rule produces an invalid state for the enterprise and hence must be prevented. However, it is possible to break behavioral rules, and such breaches entail corrective action that returns the enterprise to a valid state. While structural rules constrain concepts, behavioral rules constrain processes and can motivate the design of additional processes that are needed to enforce the rules.

5. Actors and Resources model: This is related to the organizational structure; it addresses questions related to the responsibilities for goals and processes as well as how the actors are interrelated.

   The Actors and Resources model is used to describe how different actors and resources are related to one another and how they are related to components of the Goals model and of the Business Process model. For instance, an actor may be the responsible for a particular process in the Business Process model or the actor may pursue a particular goal in the Goals model.

   The Actors and Resources model usually clarifies questions, such as who is/should be performing which processes and tasks and how is the reporting and responsibility structure between actors defined.

   Actors that perform processes in the enterprise are modeled as roles, which can also provide and be responsible for goals and can be related to requirements. A role stands for a general position that is independent of the actual persons filling it and it can represent physical persons, virtual persons, or automated systems.

6. Technical Components and Requirements model: This is related to the information systems needs; it addresses questions related to the business requirements for the information systems and how they are related to other submodels of the enterprise model.

The Technical Components and Requirements model becomes relevant when the purpose of enterprise modeling is to aid in defining requirements for the development of an information system. Attention is focused on the technical system that is needed to support the goals, processes, and actors of the enterprise. Initially, one needs to develop a set of high-level requirements or goals for the information system as a whole. Based on these, one can attempt to structure the information system in a number of subsystems, or technical components. The Technical Components and Requirements model is an initial attempt to define the overall structure and properties of the information system to support the business activities, as defined in the Business Process model. Furthermore, the Technical Components and Requirements model can be used to document the existing information system and information technology landscape in an enterprise.

The Technical Components and Requirements model usually clarifies questions, such as what are the requirements for the information system to be developed, which requirements are generated by the business processes, which information systems and information technology components are used in the enterprise in what business process by what actor, and which potential has emerging information and communication technology for process improvement.

The Common Components model is a conceptual abstraction that spans all other models. The model component is the topmost concept in the metamodel. Each model component has a unique identifier and a text field that allows the component to be labeled with a single name, a sentence, or a long phrase depending on the modeling needs. A modeling component has a description, which is a portion of text that provides additional clarification for the component.

The relationship concept is a model component that connects other model components with each other. Two distinct types of relationships are defined in the metamodel: (1) intra-model relationships that link components within the same model and (2) inter-model relationships that enable components from different models to be related with each other. The inter-model relationships facilitate traceability among the models and provide mechanisms to design intersecting models.

High-level requirements, also called business requirements, express the stakeholders' desires for a future information system. Business requirements are refined into more concrete information systems requirements that are better understood by system designers. The line separating business requirements and system requirements is vague and hard to identify, but the decomposition is always necessary. Therefore, the metamodel for the RM (Figure 6.7) includes a single requirement component that serves as a high-level as well as a concrete system requirement. Decomposition of a requirement occurs on any level and continues depending on the judgment of the modeler and the specific needs of the project. The decomposition relationship is used to connect a parent requirement with its child requirements, which can be all necessary (AND decomposition), alternatives (OR decomposition), or exclusive alternatives (XOR decomposition). Requirements that negatively affect the realization of each other are connected using the conflict relationship. Also, requirements that positively affect the realization of each other are connected using the dependency relationship.

Requirements at different levels of decomposition are motivated by business goals. However, some requirements address system-related issues that are not relevant to the high-level organizational goals. When those requirements are elicited, information systems constraints that motivate or hinder them must be identified and assessed.

6.5 Process Modeling

A business process model is the result of mapping a business process. This business process can be either a real-world business process as perceived by a modeler or a conceptualized business process. Business process modeling is the human activity of creating a business process model. Business process modeling involves an abstraction from the real-world business process because it serves a certain modeling purpose. Therefore, only those aspects relevant to the modeling purpose are included in the process model. Business process modeling languages guide the procedure of business process modeling by offering a predefined set of elements and relationships for business processes. A business process modeling language can be specified using a metamodel. In conjunction with a respective method, it establishes a business process modeling technique.

The presentation and approach in this subsection is adapted from Russell et al. (2016).

6.5.1 Semiotic Ladder

Process models are assembled from signs and, like in the case of any other signs, the modeling efforts are guided by the theories from semiotics. The study of signs spans across the semiotic ladder, as follows:

1. Social: Communities of users; the norms governing use for different purposes; and the organizational framework for using the model.
2. Pragmatic: Roles played by models—hypothesis, directive, description, and expectation; responsibility for making and using the model; and conversations needed to develop and use the model.
3. Semantic: Interpretation of the elements of the model in terms of the real world; ontological assumptions; operations for arriving at values of elements; and justification of external validity.
4. Syntactic: Languages—natural, constrained, or formal—and logical and mathematical methods for modeling.
5. Empirical: A variety of elements distinguished; error frequencies when being written and read by different users; coding (shapes of boxes); and ergonomics of human–computer interaction for documentation and modeling tools.
6. Physical: Use of various media for modeling—documents, wall charts, computer-based modeling tools, and so on; physical size and amount and effort to manipulate them.

The SQUEAL framework has been used for the evaluation of modeling and modeling languages of a large number of perspectives, including data, object, process, enterprise, and goal-oriented modeling on the corresponding dimensions:

1. Social quality: The goal defined for social quality is agreement among social actor's interpretations. Prior to evaluating social quality, perceived semantic quality should be addressed.
2. Pragmatic quality is the correspondence between the model M and the actor interpretation (I and T), and the application of it. One differentiates between social pragmatic quality (to what extent people understand the models) and technical pragmatic quality (to what extent tools can be made that can interpret the model). Before evaluating pragmatic quality, empirical quality should be addressed.
3. Semantic quality is the correspondence between the model M and the domain D. This includes both validity and completeness. Before evaluating semantic quality, syntactic quality should be addressed.
4. Syntactic quality is the correspondence between the model M and the language extension L. Before evaluating syntactic quality, physical quality should be addressed.
5. Empirical quality deals with comprehension and predictable error frequencies when a model M is read or written by different social actors. Before evaluating empirical quality, physical quality should be addressed.
6. Physical quality: The basic quality goal is that the externalized model M is available to the relevant social and technical actors.

These statements are true where quality has been defined referring to the correspondence between statements belonging to the following sets:

G, the set of goals of the modeling task.

L, the language extension—that is, the set of all statements that are possible to make according to the rules of the modeling languages used.

D, the domain—that is, the set of all statements that can be stated about the situation.

M, the externalized model itself.

K, the explicit knowledge relevant to the domain of the audience.

I, the social actor interpretation—that is, the set of all statements that the audience interprets that an externalized model consists of.

T, the technical actor interpretation—that is, the statements in the model as 'interpreted' by modeling tools.

1. The study of semantic modeling has led to the identification of the following four standard hierarchical relations:

   • Classification: Specific instances are considered as a higher-level object type (a class) via the is-instance-of relationship

   • Aggregation: An object is related to the components that compose it via the is-part-of relationship (e.g., a bicycle has wheels, a seat, a frame, handlebars)

   • Generalization: Similar object types are abstracted into a higher-level object type via the is-a relationship (e.g., an employee is a person, a male singer is a singer, and a conference is an event)

   • Association: Several object types are considered as a higher-level object type via the is-a-member-of relationship

   Depending on need, there have been approaches to support the development of new modeling languages (the so-called metamodeling) rather than the use of existing, defined languages. In particular, this is exploited in domain-specific modeling and domain-specific languages. The term "meta" indicates that something is after something; that is, a metamodel is a model after (of) a model. In principle, it is possible to apply an infinite number of meta-levels.

2. The generally accepted conceptual framework for metamodeling explains the relationships between "user data," model, metamodel, and meta-metamodel (Figure 6.8):

   a. M0: The user object layer that comprises the information that we wish to describe.

   b. M1: The model layer that comprises the metadata that describe information. Metadata are informally aggregated as models.

   c. M2: The metamodel layer that comprises the descriptions (i.e., meta-metadata) that define the structure and semantics of metadata. Meta-metadata are informally aggregated as metamodels. A metamodel can also be considered as a "language" for describing different kinds of data.

   d. M3: The meta-metamodel layer that comprises the description of the structure and semantics of meta-metadata. In other words, it is the "language" for defining different kinds of metadata (modeling languages) in simple cases consisting of "nodes" and "edges" between "nodes."

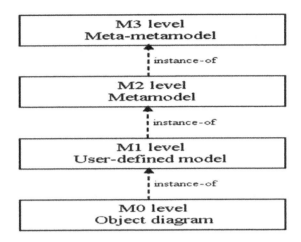

FIGURE 6.8
Meta-levels as defined in the Object Management Group's MOF.

3. There are a number of basic principles of modeling addressing syntactic, semantic, and pragmatic demands on the proper creation of process models. They are also applicable to enterprise models. The principles are:

a. The principle of accuracy: The model complies with the corresponding excerpt of the real world.

b. The principle of relevance: Modeling constructs should be included in the model with a purpose—not all reality should be represented in the model. Which information is relevant for a model depends on the intended use of the model.

c. The principle of economical efficiency: The costs of modeling should not exceed the intended benefit; that is, enterprise modeling should not be used for addressing trivial problems that can be resolved otherwise.

d. The principle of clarity: Models should be presented legibly and clearly, without more constructs than necessary.

e. The principle of comparison: Models created with different modeling techniques should be comparable at least to some extent.

f. The principle of systematic structure: If several models are created, they should be connected together in some structure in order to show how they contribute to the overall purpose of modeling.

6.5.2 Process Modeling Languages

6.5.2.1 Petri Nets

C. A. Petri proposed Petri nets as a means of describing the operation of discrete distributed systems. Petri nets (which are also known as place/transition nets nets) are a particularly useful means of describing the dynamics of processes. One of their attractions is that they have a simple graphical format in conjunction with precise operational semantics that provide an intuitive way of modeling both the static and dynamic aspects of processes.

A Petri net takes the form of a directed bipartite graph wherein the nodes are either transitions or places. Transitions correspond to the activities or events of which the process is made up and places represent intermediate stages that exist during the operation of a process. Arcs connect places and transitions in such a way that places can only be connected to transitions and vice versa—that is, places and transitions alternate along any path in the graph. A directed arc from a place to a transition indicates an input place to a transition, while a directed arc from a transition to a place indicates an output place from a transition. These places play an important role in the overall operational semantics of Petri nets.

The operational semantics of a Petri net are described in terms of tokens, which signify a thread of control flowing through a process. Places in a Petri net can contain any number of tokens. The distribution of tokens across all of the places in a net is called a marking and signifies the overall state of the Petri net. A transition in a Petri net can "fire" whenever there is one or more tokens in each of its input places; assuming that the firing of a transition is an atomic action that occurs instantaneously and cannot be interrupted; and, when a token fires, it consumes a token from each input place and adds a token to each output place.

 Petri nets execute nondeterministically; since firing is atomic, when multiple transitions in a Petri net are enabled, only one transition can fire at a time. Thus, an enabled transition fires at a time of its choosing. These features make Petri nets particularly suitable for modeling concurrent process executions such as those that occur in business processes.

Petri nets are often used not only for the modeling of business processes and workflows but also for the verification of desirable behavior. The so-called soundness property defined for workflow nets is of pivotal importance in this context. It demands that a process should have:

1. The option to complete
2. Proper completion guaranteed
3. No dead tasks that will never be executed

Based on a Petri net and an initial marking, one can check soundness by calculating the so-called reachability graph. The reachability graph represents all states that can be reached in a Petri net as nodes and all permitted state changes as directed arcs between these nodes. If the net is large and there is a high degree of parallelism, such a verification approach might suffer from the state explosion problem. This problem can be partially solved by applying reduction rules. Deadlocks are a prominent type of error that results in a net being unsound.

6.5.2.2 *Event-Driven Process Chains*

Event-driven process chains (EPCs) were developed by August-Wilhelm Scheer as part of the Architecture of Integrated Information Systems framework at the University of Saarland in Germany in the early 1990s. Essentially, an EPC model describes a business process in terms of a series of function-based transformations between a set of input events and a set of output events. The EPC is a business process modeling language for the representation of temporal and logical dependencies of activities in a business process. It is utilized in the Architecture of Integrated Information Systems framework as the central method for the conceptual integration of the functional, organizational, data, and output perspectives in information systems design.

An EPC model takes the form of a directed graph, which always starts and ends with events. The EPC syntax offers function type elements to capture the activities of a process and event type elements describing preconditions and postconditions of functions. For the definition of complex routing rules, there are three kinds of connector types:

- AND (symbol ∧)
- OR (symbol ∨)
- XOR (symbol ×)

The AND, OR, and XOR constructs can be utilized as either join or split operators. Connectors have either multiple incoming and one outgoing arc (join connectors) or one incoming and multiple outgoing arcs (split connectors). As a syntax rule, functions and events have to alternate, either directly or indirectly, when they are linked via one or more connectors. Furthermore, OR- and XOR-splits after events are not allowed, since events cannot make decisions. Control-flow arcs are used instead to link these elements. The EPC notation represents functions as rounded rectangles, events as hexagons, and connectors as circles with the respective symbol in it.

Within the model, events correspond to potential states that may exist within a process, and functions essentially describe actions that are undertaken to transform one state (or set of states) to another. Hence, a function is always preceded and followed by an event. It is not permissible for an event to be linked either directly (or indirectly through a join or split construct) to another event, nor for a function to be linked to another function (i.e., events and functions alternate along any path in the graph). Where several events precede or follow a function (i.e., events and functions alternate along any path in a model), one of the AND, OR, or XOR constructs can be used to define the intended split or join behavior between the event and function nodes.

6.5.2.3 Yet Another Workflow Language

Yet Another Workflow Language (YAWL) can be considered a superset of both Petri nets and EPCs in terms of modeling elements. The analysis of both Petri nets and EPCs revealed that these languages have problems with representing certain behavior. While EPCs are not able to express state-based patterns properly, Petri nets do not support advanced synchronization semantics such as defined by the OR-join. Furthermore, both languages do not provide a mechanism to express multiple instantiation and cancellation. Triggered by their analysis of control-flow modeling support by existing workflow systems, van der Aalst et al. (2003) identified a set of 20 so-called workflow patterns. These patterns cover different behavioral properties of a process that one might want to express by the help of a modeling language. YAWL was defined to directly support the specification of all patterns.

The YAWL syntax includes conditions and tasks that match Petri net places and Petri net transitions, respectively. Similar to Petri nets, conditions and tasks have to alternate; however, single conditions between two tasks can be omitted. YAWL tasks optionally include a split and a join condition of type AND, XOR, or OR with basically the same semantics as the respective EPC connectors.

A multiple instance task might be executed several times in parallel until a condition is fulfilled. Such multiple instance tasks specify four parameters:

- The minimum
- The maximum number of instances
- A threshold for continuation
- Whether new instances may be created dynamically or not

Also, after a task is completed, a specified set of other tasks in a cancellation area may be cancelled. Using this mechanism, it is easy to express exceptional behavior when a process must be terminated abnormally.

6.5.2.4 Unified Modeling Language Activity Diagrams

UML activity diagrams are part of the UML modeling framework and provide a means of describing the operation of a process. Although originally intended for describing software processes, they have also shown themselves to be useful for describing business processes. Like Business Process Modeling and Notation (BPMN), UML is managed under the auspices of the Object Management Group. The current version of the UML standard (version 2.5) was finalized by the Object Management Group in 2015.

The main UML constructs are divided into four groups:

1. Actions: An Action corresponds to a single step within an activity in a business process. It can be either atomic and self-contained in terms of its definition or, in the case of a Call Behavior Action, it may involve a call to another activity. An Action can have preconditions and postconditions associated with its execution, which can be graphically depicted. The AcceptEventAction waits for the occurrence of an event meeting a specified condition. This event may be triggered from within the process instance via a SendSignalAction or it may be a time-based event (in which case the receiving AcceptEventAction is denoted by a different symbol).

2. Nodes: Nodes are constructs that interlink actions in a process and further clarify the specific details associated with control and data flow.
   a. An InitialNode marks the starting point for a process. A process may be terminated by the following:
      - ActivityFinal node, which immediately causes the process instance to terminate when the first execution thread reaches it
      - FlowFinal node, which simply consumes execution threads but allows the process instance to continue until all active execution threads have reached an end node
   b. A DecisionNode allows the thread of control in the incoming branch to be split into one or more outgoing branches on a conditional basis, while the corresponding MergeNode allows threads of control in multiple incoming branches to be merged into a single outgoing branch on an unconditional basis.
   c. The ForkNode provides the ability to split the thread of control in an incoming branch into several outgoing branches, while the corresponding JoinNode supports the synchronization of the execution threads in multiple incoming branches, only allowing the outgoing branch to be triggered when all incoming branches have been triggered.
   d. The DataStore node denotes a persistent store of data within a process. Three types of ObjectNode identify abstract activity nodes that are part of the object flow in an activity. These may correspond to data elements and signals used within a process and may include Pins, which denote input and output data values.

3. Paths: There are two types of paths identifying flows within a UML 2.5 activity diagram:

- ControlFlow identifies how the thread of control is passed between nodes in a process
- ObjectFlow signifies the flow of objects, data elements, tokens, and signals in a process

4. Containment elements: These provide various mechanisms for grouping nodes within a process model for specific purposes.

6.5.3 Business Process Modeling Notation

BPMN is an Extensible Markup Language-based language for defining business processes with a formal metamodel and an associated graphical notation. The initial version of BPMN was proposed by the Business Process Modeling Institute, an industry consortium, in 2002 as a graphical modeling language. It was informally defined and intended primarily for high-level modeling of business processes.

Since 2005, it has been under the auspices of the Object Management Group following a merger with the Business Process Modeling Institute. Its focus has now broadened from business process modeling to offering a range of techniques supporting all aspects of business process capture—from high-level, abstract modeling through to detailed business process definitions capable of direct execution. All of these techniques coexist within the same metamodel, thus ensuring that the semantics of the various levels are consistent.

BPMN version 2.0.2 is designed to be utilized as:

1. High-level, graphical business modeling language (with a limited range of modelling constructs).
2. Detailed graphical modeling language (with a comprehensive range of modelling constructs).
3. Executable business process language, capturing sufficient details about the control-flow, data, and resource aspects of a business process so that it can be directly executed by a business process engine.

We discuss BPMN in more detail in Chapter 11.

6.6 Process Description for Storing Business Process Models

Modeling of processes is a complex and time-consuming task that can be simplified by the reuse of process models. A repository is, therefore, necessary to store and manage process models. However, the mass of process models available in repositories cannot be reused because process models are either domain-specific processes or the repositories are not publically open for change and growth. Furthermore, most repositories are proprietary and not extensible. Hence, the conception of a Universal Process Repository, whose component process description database and entailed data model is capable of storing fundamental information of processes independent of any language, was realized (Shahzad et al. 2009).

In the Universal Process Repository, process definitions exist at two levels: the user level and the repository level. The user level is a higher level at which a business process is viewed as a process model. At this level, a business process is modeled by using graphical constructs of a process modeling language such as BPMN, EPC, or YAWL. However, the process model is not directly stored in the repository. The repository level is a lower level at which a business process is stored as a process description. The process description is not directly accessible to users of the repository, but it can be modified by changing its respective process model at the user level because a process description in the repository is derived from a process model.

As discussed in the last section, there are several process modeling languages (e.g., EPC, YAWL, BPMN) that can be used for modeling business processes. These process modeling languages have different elements and control structures so that the specification of a business process varies from one language to another. In order to provide support for different modeling languages in the Universal Process Repository, a common format for storing and sharing process models is needed, wherein the common format only stores fundamental elements of process models.

Since (1) a process model is defined as a graphical depiction of a business process detailing the arrangement of task interdependency, controls, and allocated resources and (2) a business process is a collection of related, structured activities or tasks that produce a specific service or product (serve a particular goal) for a particular customer or customers, then the specification of process description can be defined as:

$$PD = \{elements, control\text{-}flow, process\ logic\} \tag{6.1}$$

where:

Elements of a process model are the fundamental units of a process model, i.e., the activities, resources, and agents

Control flows are the possible structures (control structures) between multiple elements in a process model, e.g., sequence, AND, OR, etc.

Process logic is a logical association/binding between elements of a process model and is defined between two elements of a process model, e.g., a sequence between two activities or resource allocation to an activity

The corresponding generic metamodel for business processes is shown in Figure 6.9.
The concrete elements are obtained by employing the following four perspectives:

1. Functional perspective: The functional perspective defines the elements that are being performed. This perspective represents "what" elements (activities) of a process model are performed.

   It is established that a process consists of a set of activities and that a process may consist of subprocesses that also consist of activities. The execution of a business process is initiated by an event called a start event and terminated by an event called an end event. A subprocess is a part of a process that can exist independently, whereas an activity is a concrete instance of a task that is obtained while executing a particular case of a business process.

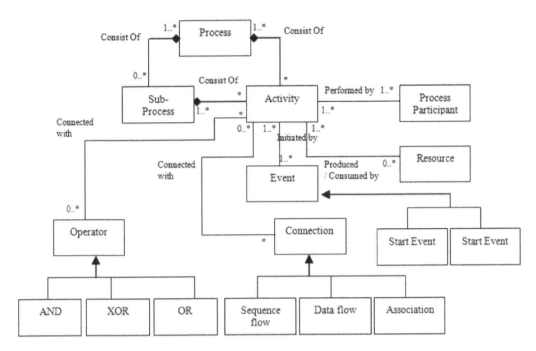

FIGURE 6.9
Generic metamodel for business processes.

2. Behavioral perspective: This perspective defines the order in which activities are executed and the point(s) where they are be executed. The behavioral perspective represents "when" and "how" activities of a process model are performed. It gives dependencies between activities and how they are to be executed. These dependencies are called control flows.

   A control flow is a relationship between two or more activities and it can be of two types, either operator or connection. Operator is a node that is used to split or join more than two elements and can either be an XOR, OR, or AND. Connection is an edge that connects two activities, an activity with a participant, an activity with an events, or an activity with a resource. There are three types of connections: sequence flow, data flow, and association.

3. Organizational perspective: This perspective defines the organizational units wherein business activities are performed and the involved agent. The organizational perspective represents "where" and "by whom" business activities are realized. It is established that an activity can consume, produce, or transfer a resource between participants. Participants are the entities that can execute a task to take/ transfer control of a resource and they could be an organizational unit or agent. Organizational units may have predefined duty-descriptions called roles, which are assigned to agents. An agent can be a person, software, machine, or a service.

4. Informational perspective: This perspective defines resources that are consumed or produced during the execution of a business activity. The resources are the information elements and the documents in which these elements are stored. Information elements are the messages or data about the activity, e.g., messages about the output(s) of an activity that can affect execution of the following activity.

The resulting concrete elements are used for extending Equation 6.1 to form the generic process description:

$$PD = \{\text{elements, control-flow, process logic}\} \qquad (6.2)$$

where:

Elements = {start-event, activity, participant, resource, end-event}

Control flow = {operator, connection}; connection = sequence flow,
　　　　　　dataflow, association

Process logic = {(start-event, activity, connection)
　　　　　　(activity, activity, connection), (participant, activity, connection)
　　　　　　(task, operator, connection) (operator, activity, connection)
　　　　　　(task, stop event, connection) (resource, activity, connection)
　　　　　　(activity, resource, connection) (operator, operator, connection)}

and,

connection is a combination of the type and label of the connection

By using the matching (from Table 6.1) and process description (from Equation 6.2), language-specific process description can be produced. The language-specific process description for BPMN is as follows.

TABLE 6.1

Matching Concepts of Generic Metamodel and Process Modeling Languages

Generic Metamodel	Activity Diagram	BPMN	EPC	YAWL
Subprocess activity	Activity	Subprocess task	Subprocess function	Task
Event				
Start event	Initial node	Start event	Preactivity event	Input condition on activity
End event	Final node (process)	End event	Postactivity event	Output condition on activity
Control flow				
Operator	Fork node, join, decision, merge	AND/OR/XOR	XOR, AND, OR connector	AND, XOR, OR split and join
Connection	Control flow, object flow	Complex sequence flow, association, message flow	Control flow	No formal name of the construct
Participant		Pool	Org. unit, org. role	
Resource Informational resource	Object node	Data objects	Information objects	

BPMN: Business Process Modeling and Notation; EPC: Event-driven Process Chain; YAWL: Yet Another Workflow Language.

Elements = {start event, tasks, pools, dataobject, end event}

Operators = {AND, OR, XOR}

Connection = {sequence flow-ID, message flow-ID, association-ID}; ID is unique identifier

Process logic = {(start-event, task, connection) (task, task, connection),

(pool, task, connection) (task, operator, connection)

(operator, task, connection) (dataobject, task, connection)

(task, dataobject, connection) (task, stop event, connection)

(operator, operator, connection)}

6.7 Summary

This chapter began with an introduction to the concept of a model: a model represents in a simplified way the reality for a given purpose, emphasizing some elements and ignoring others. Models can be characterized according to three dimensions: representativeness (e.g., prescriptive, descriptive); perspective (e.g., behavioral, structural); and form (e.g., symbolic, physical). The chapter presents an ontology that introduces relevant concepts related to modeling and permits one to distinguish and associate concepts like model, specification, description, diagram, language, and notation. It discusses some structural and behavioral models that are routinely used in the context of software modeling. In the latter part, the chapter presented several frequently-used business process modeling languages including Petri nets, EPCs, YAWL, UML activity diagrams, and BPMN.

7

Distributed Systems

The origins of big data technologies come from database systems and distributed systems as well as data mining and machine learning algorithms that can process these vast amounts of data to extract the necessary knowledge. Several distributed database prototype systems were developed in the 1980s and 1990s to address the issues of data distribution, data replication, distributed query and transaction processing, distributed database metadata management, and other topics. More recently, many new technologies have emerged that combine database and distributed technologies. These technologies and systems are being developed for dealing with the storage, analysis, and mining of the vast amounts of data that are being produced and collected and are referred to generally as big data technologies (see Chapter 9).

The centralized approach to processing data, in which users access a central database on a central computer through personal computers and workstations, dominated organizations from the late 1960s through the mid-1980s because there was no alternative approach to compete with it. The introduction of reasonably priced personal computers during the 1980s, however, facilitated the placement of computers at various locations within an organization; users could access a database directly at those locations. Networks connected these computers, so users could access not only data located on their local computers but also data located anywhere across the entire network.

This chapter addresses issues involved in distributed databases wherein a database is stored on more than one computer.

7.1 Distributed Systems

Distributed systems consist of a collection of heterogeneous but fully autonomous components that can execute on different computers. Whilst each of these components has full control over its constituent subparts, there is no master component that possesses control over all of the components of a distributed system. Thus, for each of these systems to appear as a single and integrated whole, the various components need to be able to interact with each other via predefined interfaces through a computer network.

The characteristic global features of a successful distributed system are as follows.

- Distributed systems are heterogeneous, arising from the need to (say) integrate components on a legacy IBM mainframe, with the components newly created to operate on a UNIX workstation or Windows NT machine.

- Distributed systems are scalable, in that, when a component becomes overloaded with too many requests or users, another replica of the same component can be instantiated and added to the distributed system to share the load amongst them. Moreover, these instantiated components can be located closer to the local users and other interacting components to improve the performance of the overall distributed system.

- Distributed systems execute components concurrently in a multi-threaded mode via multiply invoked components corresponding to the number of simultaneously invoked processes.

- Distributed systems are fault-tolerant in that they duplicate components on different computers, so that, if one computer fails, another can take over without affecting the availability of the overall system.

- Distributed systems are more resilient, in that, whereas distributed systems have multiple points of failure, the unaffected components are fully operational even though some of the components are not functional or are malfunctioning. Moreover, the distributed system could invoke another instance of the failed components along with the corresponding state of the process (characterized by the program counter, the register variable contents, and the state of the virtual memory used by the process) to continue with the process.

- Distributed systems demonstrate invariance or transparency, with reference to characteristics such as:
  - Accessibility, either locally or across networks to the components
  - Physical location of the components
  - Migration of components from one host to another
  - Replication of components including their states
  - Concurrency of components requesting services from shared components
  - Scalability in terms of the actual number of requests or users at any instance
  - Performance in terms of the number and type of available resources
  - Points of failure, be it a failure of the component, network, or response

The terms *parallel systems* and *distributed* are often used interchangeably; however, the term *distributed* refers to a wider class of systems, while the term *parallel* implies a subclass of tightly coupled systems. Distributed systems include any architecture or system that allows the computation to be broken down into units and executed concurrently on different computing elements, whether these are processors on different nodes, processors on the same computer, or cores within the same processor. Distributed often implies that the locations of all of the constituting computing elements are not the same and that such elements might be heterogeneous in terms of hardware and software features. Classic examples of distributed computing systems include computing grids or Internet computing systems, which combine together the biggest variety of architectures, systems, and applications in the world.

A parallel system refers to a model in which the computation is divided among several processors sharing the same memory. The architecture of a parallel computing system is often characterized by the homogeneity of components: each processor is of the same type and has the same capability as the others. The shared memory has a single address space, which is accessible to all of the processors. Parallel programs are then broken down into several units of execution that can be allocated to different processors and can communicate with each other by means of the shared memory.

> Originally, parallel systems used to include only those architectures that featured multiple processors sharing the same physical memory and computer. However, parallel systems are now considered to include all those architectures that are based on the concept of shared memory, regardless of whether this is physically collocated or created with the support of libraries, specific hardware, and a highly efficient networking infrastructure. For example, a cluster that the nodes are connected through an InfiniBand network and configured with a distributed shared memory system can also be considered a parallel system.

7.1.1 Distributed Computing

Distributed computing studies the models, architectures, and algorithms used for building and managing distributed systems. A distributed system is a collection of independent computers that appears to its users as a single coherent system. Distributed systems are primarily focused on the aggregation of distributed resources and unified usage. This is accomplished by communicating with other computers only by exchanging messages.

A distributed system is the result of the interaction of several components across the entire computing stack from hardware to software. The hardware and operating system layers make up the bare-bones infrastructure of one or more data centers, where racks of servers are deployed and connected together through high-speed connectivity. This infrastructure is managed by the operating system, which provides the basic capabilities of machine and network management. The core logic is then implemented in the middleware, which manages the virtualization layer and is deployed on the physical infrastructure in order to maximize its utilization and provide a customizable runtime environment for applications. The middleware provides different facilities and functionalities per the requirement of the end customers and users. These facilities range from virtual infrastructure building and deployment to application development and runtime environments.

The different layers constituting the distributed system stack are as follows:

1. Hardware layer: At the very bottom layer, computer and network hardware constitute the physical infrastructure; these components are directly managed by the operating system, which provides the basic services for interprocess communication (IPC), process scheduling and management, and resource management in terms of file systems and local devices. Taken together, these two layers become the platform on top of which specialized software is deployed to turn a set of networked computers into a distributed system.

2. Operating system layer: The use of well-known standards at the operating system level and even more at the hardware and network levels allows for easy harnessing of heterogeneous components and their organizational structure into a coherent and uniform system. For example, network connectivity between different devices is controlled by standards, which allow them to interact seamlessly. At the operating system level, IPC services are implemented on top of standardized communication protocols such as Transmission Control Protocol/Internet Protocol, User Datagram Protocol, or others.

3. Middleware layer: The middleware layer leverages such services to build a uniform environment for the development and deployment of distributed applications.

This layer supports the programming paradigms for distributed systems, which we will discuss in Chapters 5 through 7 of this book. By relying on the services offered by the operating system, the middleware develops its own protocols, data formats, and programming language or frameworks for the development of distributed applications. All of them constitute a uniform interface to distributed application developers that is completely independent from the underlying operating system and hides all of the heterogeneities of the bottom layers.

4. Application layer: The topmost layer is represented by the applications and services designed and developed to use the middleware. These can serve several purposes and often expose their features in the form of graphical user interfaces accessible locally or through the Internet via a Web browser.

Architectural styles for distributed systems are helpful in understanding the different roles of components in the system and how they are distributed across multiple computers.
Architectural styles are of two types:

- System architectural style
- Software architectural style

7.1.1.1 System Architectural Styles

System architectural styles cover the physical organization of components and processes over a distributed infrastructure. They provide a set of reference models for the deployment of such systems and help engineers not only maintain a common vocabulary in describing the physical layout of systems but also quickly identify the major advantages and drawbacks of a given deployment and whether it is applicable for a specific class of applications.
These reference models can be further enhanced or diversified according to the specific needs of the application to be designed and implemented.

1. N-Tier architecture: In the 1980s, the prior monolithic architecture began to be replaced by the client/server architecture, which split applications into two pieces in an attempt to leverage new inexpensive desktop machines. Distributing the processing loads across many inexpensive clients allowed client/server applications to scale more linearly than single host/single process applications could, while the use of off-the-shelf software like relational database management systems greatly reduced application development time. While the client could handle the user interface and data display tasks of the application and the server could handle all of the data management tasks, respectively there was no clear solution for storing the logic corresponding to the business processes being automated. Consequently, the business logic tended to split between the client and the server; typically, the rules for displaying data became embedded inside the user interface, while the rules for integrating several different data sources became stored procedures inside the database. Whereas this division of logic made it difficult to reuse the user interface code with a different data source, it also made it equally difficult to use the logic stored in the database with a different front-end user interface (e.g., automated teller machine, mobile) without being required to redevelop the logic implemented in the earlier interface. Thus, a customer service system

developed for a particular client system (e.g., a 3270 terminal, a personal computer, or a workstation) would have great difficulty in providing telephony and Internet interfaces with the same business functionality.

The client/server architecture failed to recognize the importance of managing the business rules applicable to an enterprise independent of both the user interface and the storage and management of enterprise data. The three-tiered application architecture of the 1990s resolved this problem by subdividing the application into three distinct layers, as follows:

a. Data management, which stores and manages data independent of how they are processed and displayed by the other layers

b. Business logic, which implements the business logic to process data independent of how they are stored or displayed by the other two layers

c. Presentation, which formats and displays the data independent of the way they are interpreted/processed and stored by the other two layers

With the advent of the Internet in the past few years, the three tiers were split even further to accommodate the heterogeneity in terms of the user interfaces, processing systems, or databases existing in various parts of an enterprise.

 The power of the n-tier architecture is derived from the fact that, instead of treating components as integral parts of systems, components are treated as stand-alone entities capable of providing services for applications. Applications exist only as cooperating constellation of components, and each component in turn can simultaneously be part of many different applications.

2. Peer-to-peer: The peer-to-peer model introduces a symmetric architecture in which all the components, called peers, play the same role and incorporate both client and server capabilities of the client/server model. More precisely, each peer acts as a server when it processes requests from other peers and as a client when it issues requests to other peers. With respect to the client/server model that partitions the responsibilities of the IPC between server and clients, the peer-to-peer model attributes the same responsibilities to each component. Therefore, this model is quite suitable for highly decentralized architecture, which can scale better along the dimension of the number of peers. The disadvantage of this approach is that the management of the implementation of algorithms is more complex in this case than in the client/server model.

7.1.1.2 Software Architectural Styles

Software architectural styles are based on the logical arrangement of software components. They are helpful because they provide an intuitive view of the whole system, despite its physical deployment.

1. Data-centered architectures: The repository architectural style is the most relevant reference model in this category. It is characterized by two main components: the central data structure, which represents the current state of the system, and a collection of independent components, which operate on the central data. The ways in which the independent components interact with the central data structure can be very heterogeneous. In particular, repository-based architectures differentiate and specialize further into subcategories according to the choice of control discipline to apply for the shared data structure.

Data-centered architectures are of two types as follows:

a. Database systems: In this case, the dynamics of the system are controlled by the independent components, which, by issuing an operation on the central repository, trigger the selection of specific processes that operate on data.

b. Blackboard systems: In this case, the central data structure itself is the main trigger for selecting the processes to execute; knowledge sources representing the intelligent agents sharing the blackboard react opportunistically to changes in the knowledge base—almost in the same manner in which a group of specialists brainstorm in a room in front of a blackboard.

The blackboard architectural style is characterized by three main components:

- Knowledge sources: These are the entities that update the knowledge base that is maintained in the blackboard.

- Blackboard: This represents the data structure that is shared among the knowledge sources and stores the knowledge base of the application.

- Control: The control is the collection of triggers and procedures that govern the interaction with the blackboard and update the status of the knowledge base.

Blackboard models have become popular and widely used for artificial intelligent applications in which the blackboard maintains the knowledge about a domain in the form of assertions and rules, which are entered by domain experts. These operate through a control shell that controls the problem-solving activity of the system. Particular and successful applications of this model can be found in the domains of speech recognition and signal processing.

2. Data flow architectures: In the case of data-flow architectures, it is the availability of data that controls the computation. With respect to the data-centered styles, in which the access to data is the core feature, dataflow styles explicitly incorporate the pattern of data flow, since their design is determined by an orderly motion of data from component to component, which is the form of communication between them. Styles within this category differ in one of the following ways: how the control is exerted, the degree of concurrency among components, and/or the topology that describes the flow of data.

Dataflow architectures are optimal when the system to be designed embodies a multistage process, which can be clearly identified into a collection of separate components that need to be orchestrated together. Within this reference scenario, components have well-defined interfaces exposing input and output ports, and the connectors are represented by the data streams between these ports.

a. Batch sequential style: The batch sequential style is characterized by an ordered sequence of separate programs executing one after the other. These programs are chained together by providing as input for the next program the output generated by the last program after its completion, which is most likely in the form of a file. This design was very popular in the mainframe era of computing and still finds applications today. For example, many distributed applications for scientific computing are defined by jobs expressed as sequences of programs that, for example, prefilter, analyze, and postprocess data. It is very common to compose these phases using the batch sequential style.

b. Pipe-and-filter style: The pipe-and-filter style is a variation of the previous
    style for expressing the activity of a software system as a sequence of data
    transformations. Each component of the processing chain is called a filter, and
    the connection between one filter and the next is represented by a data stream.
    With respect to the batch sequential style, data is processed incrementally and
    each filter processes the data as soon as they are available on the input stream.
    As soon as one filter produces a consumable amount of data, the next filter can
    start its processing. Filters generally do not have a state, know the identity of
    neither the previous nor the next filter, and are connected with in-memory data
    structures such as first-in/first-out buffers or other structures. This particular
    sequencing is called pipelining and introduces concurrency in the execution
    of the filters.

A classic example of this architecture is the microprocessor pipeline, whereby multiple instructions are executed at the same time by completing a different phase of
each of them. We can identify the phases of the instructions as the filters, whereas the
data streams are represented by the registries that are shared within the processors.
Another example is the Unix shell pipes (i.e., cat <file-name>| grep<pattern>| wc-l),
wherein the filters are the single shell programs composed together and the connections are their input and output streams that are chained together. Applications of this
architecture can also be found in the compiler design (e.g., the lex/yacc model is based
on a pipe of the following phases | scanning | parsing | semantic analysis | code
generation); image and signal processing; and voice and video streaming.

3. Call and return architectures: This category identifies all systems that are orga-
    nized into components mostly connected together by method calls. The activity
    of systems modeled in this manner is characterized by a chain of method calls
    whose overall execution and composition identify the execution of one or more
    operations. The internal organization of components and their connections may
    vary. Nonetheless, it is possible to identify three major subcategories, which are
    differentiated by the way the system is structured and how methods are invoked:
    top-down style, object-oriented style, and layered style.

    a. Top-down style: This architectural style is quite representative of systems
        developed with imperative programming, which leads to a divide-and-conquer
        approach to problem resolution. Systems developed according to this style are
        composed of one large main program that accomplishes its tasks by invok-
        ing subprograms or procedures. The components in this style are procedures
        and subprograms, and connections are method calls or invocation. The calling
        program passes information with parameters and receives data from return
        values or parameters. Method calls can also extend beyond the boundary of a
        single process by leveraging techniques for remote method invocation, such as
        remote procedure call and all its descendants. The overall structure of the pro-
        gram execution at any point in time is characterized by a tree, the root of which
        constitutes the main function of the principal program. This architectural style
        is quite intuitive from a design point of view but hard to maintain and manage
        in large systems.

    b. Layered style: The layered system style allows the design and implementa-
        tion of software systems in terms of layers, which provide a different level
        of abstraction of the system. Each layer generally operates with at most two
        layers: specifically, the one that provides a lower abstraction level and the

one that provides a higher abstraction layer. Specific protocols and interfaces define how adjacent layers interact. It is possible to model such systems as a stack of layers, one for each level of abstraction. Therefore, the components are the layers and the connectors are the interfaces and protocols used between adjacent layers. A user or client generally interacts with the layer at the highest abstraction, which, in order to carry its activity, interacts and uses the services of the lower layer. This process is repeated (if necessary) until the lowest layer is reached. It is also possible to have the opposite behavior occur: events and callbacks from the lower layers can trigger the activity of the higher layer and propagate information up through the stack.

The advantages of the layered style are as follows:

- It supports a modular design of systems and allows users to decompose the system according to different levels of abstractions by encapsulating together all the operations that belong to a specific level.

- It enables layers to be replaced as long as they are compliant with the expected protocols and interfaces, thus making the system flexible.

The main disadvantage is the lack of extensibility, since it is not possible to add layers without changing the protocols and the interfaces between layers. This also makes it complex to add operations. Examples of layered architectures are the modern operating system kernels and the International Standards Organization/Open Systems Interconnection or the Transmission Control Protocol/Internet Protocol stack.

c. Object-oriented style: This architectural style encompasses a wide range of systems that have been designed and implemented by leveraging the abstractions of object-oriented programming. Systems are specified in terms of classes and implemented in terms of objects. Classes define the type of components by specifying the data that represent their state and the operations that can be done over these data. One of the main advantages over the top-down style is that there is a coupling between data and the operations used to manipulate them. Object instances become responsible for hiding their internal state representation and for protecting the integrity while providing operations to other components. This leads to a better decomposition process and more manageable systems. Disadvantages of this style are mainly that (1) each object needs to know the identity of an object if it wants to invoke operations on it and (2) shared objects need to be carefully designed in order to ensure the consistency of their state.

4. Virtual architectures: The virtual machine class of architectural styles is characterized by the presence of an abstract execution environment (generally referred as a virtual machine) that simulates features that are not available in the hardware or software. Applications and systems are implemented on top of this layer and become portable over different hardware and software environments as long as there is an implementation of the virtual machine they interface with. The general interaction flow for systems implementing this pattern is the following: the program (or the application) defines its operations and state in an abstract format, which is interpreted by the virtual machine engine. The interpretation of a program constitutes its execution. It is quite common in this scenario that the engine maintains an internal representation of the

program state. Very popular examples within this category are rule-based systems, interpreters, and command-language processors.

Virtual machine architectural styles are characterized by an indirection layer between applications and the hosting environment. This design has the major advantage of decoupling applications from the underlying hardware and software environment, but, at the same time, it introduces some disadvantages, such as a slowdown in performance. Other issues might be related to the fact that, by providing a virtual execution environment, specific features of the underlying system might not be accessible.

a. Rule-based style: This architecture is characterized by representing the abstract execution environment as an inference engine. Programs are expressed in the form of rules or predicates that hold true. The input data for applications is generally represented by a set of assertions or facts that the inference engine uses to activate rules or to apply predicates, thus transforming data. The output can either be the product of the rule activation or a set of assertions that holds true for the given input data. The set of rules or predicates identifies the knowledge base that can be queried to infer properties about the system. This approach is quite peculiar, since it allows expression of a system or a domain in terms of its behavior rather than in terms of the components. Rule-based systems are very popular in the field of artificial intelligence. Practical applications can be found in the field of process control, where rule-based systems are used to monitor the status of physical devices by being fed from the sensory data collected and processed by programmable logic controllers (PLCs) and by activating alarms when specific conditions on the sensory data apply. Another interesting use of rule-based systems can be found in the networking domain: network intrusion detection systems often rely on a set of rules to identify abnormal behaviors connected to possible intrusions in computing systems.

b. Interpreter style: The core feature of the interpreter style is the presence of an engine that is used to interpret a pseudo-program expressed in a format acceptable for the interpreter. The interpretation of the pseudo-program constitutes the execution of the program itself. Systems modeled according to this style exhibit four main components: the interpretation engine that executes the core activity of this style, an internal memory that contains the pseudo-code to be interpreted, a representation of the current state of the engine, and a representation of the current state of the program being executed. This model is quite useful in designing virtual machines for high-level programming (e.g., Java, C#) and scripting languages (e.g., Awk, PERL, and so on). Within this scenario, the virtual machine closes the gap between the end-user abstractions and the software/hardware environment in which such abstractions are executed.

5. Independent components: This class of architectural style models systems in terms of independent components that have their own life cycles, which interact with each other to perform their activities. There are two major categories within this class—communicating processes and event systems—which differentiate in the way the interaction among components is managed.

a. Communicating processes: In this architectural style, components are represented by independent processes that leverage IPC facilities for coordination management. This is an abstraction that is quite suitable to modeling distributed systems that, being distributed over a network of computing nodes, are necessarily composed of several concurrent processes. Each of the processes provides other processes with services and can leverage the services exposed by the other processes. The conceptual organization of these processes and the way in which the communication happens vary according to the specific model used, either peer-to-peer or client/server. Connectors are identified by IPC facilities used by these processes to communicate.

b. Event systems: In this architectural style, the components of the system are loosely coupled and connected. In addition to exposing operations for data and state manipulation, each component also publishes (or announces) a collection of events with which other components can register. In general, other components provide a callback that will be executed when the event is activated. During the activity of a component, a specific runtime condition can activate one of the exposed events, thus triggering the execution of the callbacks registered with it. Event activation may be accompanied by contextual information that can be used in the callback to handle the event. This information can be passed as an argument to the callback or by using some shared repository between components. Event-based systems have become quite popular, and support for their implementation is provided either at the API level or the programming language level.

The main advantage of such an architectural style is that it fosters the development of open systems: new modules can be added and easily integrated into the system as long as they have compliant interfaces for registering to the events. This architectural style solves some of the limitations observed for the top-down and object-oriented styles:

- The invocation pattern is implicit, and the connection between the caller and the callee is not hard-coded; this gives a lot of flexibility since the addition or removal of a handler to events can be done without changes in the source code of applications.
- The event source does not need to know the identity of the event handler in order to invoke the callback.

The disadvantage of such a style is that it relinquishes control over system computation. When a component triggers an event, it does not know how many event handlers will be invoked and whether or not there are any registered handlers. This information is available only at runtime and, from a static design point of view, becomes more complex to identify the connections among components and to reason about the correctness of the interactions.

7.1.1.3 Technologies for Distributed Computing

Middleware is system services software that executes between the operating system layer and the application layer and provides services. It connects two or more applications, thus providing connectivity and interoperability to the applications. Middleware is not a silver bullet that will solve all integration problems. Due to overhyping in the 1980s and early 1990s, the term "middleware" has lost popularity but is coming back in the last few years. The middleware concept, however, is today even more important for integration, and all integration projects will have to use one or many different middleware solutions. Middleware is mainly used to denote products that provide glue between applications, which is distinct from simple data import and export functions that might be built into the applications themselves.

All forms of middleware are helpful in easing the communication between different software applications. The selection of middleware influences the application architecture, because middleware centralizes the software infrastructure and its deployment. Middleware introduces an abstraction layer in the system architecture and thus reduces the complexity considerably. On the other hand, each middleware product introduces a certain communication overhead into the system, which can influence performance, scalability, throughput, and other efficiency factors. This is important to consider when designing the integration architecture, particularly if our systems are mission-critical and are used by a large number of concurrent clients.

Middleware is connectivity software that is designed to help manage the complexity and heterogeneity inherent in distributed systems by building a bridge between different systems, thereby enabling the communication and transfer of data. Middleware could be defined as a layer of enabling software services that allow application elements to interoperate across network links, despite differences in underlying communications protocols, system architectures, operating systems, databases, and other application services. The role of middleware is to ease the task of designing, programming, and managing distributed applications by providing a simple, consistent, and integrated distributed programming environment. Essentially, middleware is a distributed software layer or platform that lives above the operating system and abstracts over the complexity and heterogeneity of the underlying distributed environment with its multitude of network technologies, machine architectures, operating systems, and programming languages.

The middleware layers are interposed between applications and Internet transport protocols. The middleware abstraction comprises two layers. The bottom layer is concerned with the characteristics of protocols for communicating between processes in a distributed system and how the data objects—for example, a customer order—and data structures used in application programs can be translated into a suitable form for sending messages over a communications network, taking into account that different computers may rely on heterogeneous representations for simple data items. The layer above is concerned with IPC mechanisms, while the layer above that is concerned with non-message- and message-based forms of middleware. Message-based forms of middleware provide asynchronous messaging and event notification mechanisms to exchange messages or react to events over electronic networks. Non-message-based forms of middleware provide synchronous communication mechanisms designed to support client–server communication.

Middleware uses two basic modes of message communication:

1. Synchronous or time-dependent: The defining characteristic of a synchronous form of execution is that message communication is synchronized between two communicating application systems, which must both be up and running, and that execution flow at the client's side is interrupted to execute the call. Both sending and receiving applications must be ready to communicate with each other at all times. A sending application initiates a request (sends a message) to a receiving application. The sending application then blocks its processing until it receives a response from the receiving application. The receiving application continues its processing after it receives the response.

2. Asynchronous or time-independent: With asynchronous communication, an application sends (requestor or sender) a request to another while it continues its own processing activities. The sending application does not have to wait for the receiving application to complete and for its reply to come back. Instead, it can continue processing other requests. Unlike the synchronous mode, both application systems (sender and receiver) do not have to be active at the same time for processing to occur.

The basic messaging processes inherently utilize asynchronous communication. There are several benefits to asynchronous messaging; these include:

1. Asynchronous messaging clients can proceed with application processing independently of other applications. Loose coupling of senders and receivers optimizes system processing by not having to block the sending client processing while waiting for the receiving client to complete the request.

2. Asynchronous messaging allows batch and parallel processing of messages to occur. The sending client can send as many messages to receiving clients without having to wait for the receiving clients to process previously sent messages. On the receiving end, different receiving clients can process the messages at their own speed and timing.

3. There is less demand on the communication network because the messaging clients do not have to be connected to each other or the message-oriented middleware (MOM) while messages are processed. Connections are active only to send messages to the MOM and get messages from the MOM.

4. The network does not have to be available at all times because of the timing independence of client processing. Messages can wait in the queue of the receiving client if the network is not available. MOM implements asynchronous message queues at its core. It can concurrently service many sending and receiving applications.

Despite the performance drawbacks, synchronous messaging has several benefits over asynchronous messaging. The tightly coupled nature of synchronous messaging means that the sending client can better handle application errors in the receiving client. If an error occurs in the receiving client, the sending client can try to compensate for the error. This is especially important when the sending client requests a transaction to be performed in the receiving client. The better error handling ability of synchronous messaging means that it is easier for programmers to develop synchronous messaging solutions. Since both the sending and receiving clients are online and connected, it is easier for programmers to debug errors that might occur during the development stage. Furthermore, since most developers are also more familiar with programming using synchronous processing, this also facilities the development of synchronous messaging solutions over asynchronous messaging solutions.

When speaking of middleware products, we encompass a large variety of technologies. The most common forms of middleware are as follows:

1. Database access technologies
   - Microsoft open database connectivity
   - Java database connectivity
2. Asynchronous middleware
   - Store and forward messaging
   - Publish/subscribe messaging
   - Point-to-point queuing
   - Event-driven processing mechanism

3. Synchronous middleware
   - Remote procedure call
   - Remote method invocation (RMI)
4. MOM (Messaging-Oriented Middleware)
   - Integration brokers
   - Java messaging service
5. Request/reply messaging middleware
6. Transaction processing monitors
7. Object request brokers
   - Object Management Group Common Object Request Broker Architecture object request broker-compliant
   - Java RMI and RMI-Internet Inter-orb Protocol (Internet Inter-ORB Protocol)
   - Microsoft COM/Distributed Component Object Model/COM+/.NET Remoting/WCF
8. Application servers
9. Service-oriented architecture
   - Web services using Web Services Description Language; Universal Description Discovery, and Integration; Simple Object Access Protocol, and Extensible Markup Language
   - Representational state transfer-ful services
10. Enterprise service buses
11. Enterprise systems

For a detailed discussion on the aforementioned technologies, refer to the companion volume "Guide to Cloud Computing for Business and Technology Managers" (Kale 2015).

7.2 Distributed Databases

A distributed database is a logically interrelated collection of shared data (and a description of this data), physically distributed over a computer network. The distributed database management system (DDBMS) is the software that transparently manages the distributed database.

A DDBMS is distinct from distributed processing, wherein a centralized database management system (DBMS) is accessed over a network. It is also distinct from a parallel DBMS, which is a DBMS that runs across multiple processors and disks and which has been designed to evaluate operations in parallel, whenever possible, in order to improve performance. The advantages of a DDBMS are that it is enabled to reflect the organizational structure; it makes remote data more shareable; it improves reliability, availability, and performance; it may be more economical; and it provides for modular growth, facilitates integration, and helps organizations remain competitive. The major disadvantages are cost, complexity, lack of standards, and experience.

A DDBMS may be classified as homogeneous or heterogeneous. In a homogeneous system, all sites use the same DBMS product. In a heterogeneous system, sites may run different DBMS products, which need not be based on the same underlying data model, and so the system may be composed of relational, network, hierarchical, and object-oriented DBMSs. A multidatabase system (MDBS) is a distributed DBMS in which each site maintains complete autonomy. An MDBS resides transparently on top of existing database and file systems and presents a single database to its users. It maintains a global schema against which users issue queries and updates; an MDBS maintains only the global schema, while the local DBMSs themselves maintain all user data.

Communication takes place over a network, which may be a local area network or a wide area network. Local area networks are intended for short distances and provide faster communication than wide area networks. A special case of the wide area network is a metropolitan area network, which generally covers a city or suburb. As well as having the standard functionality expected of a centralized DBMS, a DDBMS needs extended communication services; extended system catalog; distributed query processing; and extended security, concurrency, and recovery services.

 Network design and performance issues are critical for an efficient operation of a DDBMS and are an integral part of the overall solution. The nodes may all be located in the same campus and connected via a local area network, or they may be geographically distributed over large distances and connected via a long-haul or wide-area network. Local area networks typically use wireless hubs or cables, whereas long-haul networks use telephone lines, cables, wireless communication infrastructures, or satellites.

The DDBMS appears like a centralized DBMS by providing a series of transparencies. With distribution transparency, users should not know that the data have been fragmented/replicated. With transaction transparency, the consistency of the global database should be maintained when multiple users are accessing the database concurrently and when failures occur. With performance transparency, the system should be able to efficiently handle queries that reference data at more than one site.

A relation may be divided into a number of subrelations called fragments, which are allocated to one or more sites. Fragments may be replicated to provide improved availability and performance. There are two main types of fragmentation: horizontal and vertical. Horizontal fragments are subsets of tuples and vertical fragments are subsets of attributes. The definition and allocation of fragments are carried out strategically to achieve locality of reference, improved reliability and availability, acceptable performance, balanced storage capacities and costs, and minimal communication costs.

7.2.1 Characteristics of Distributed Databases

7.2.1.1 Transparency

A highly transparent system offers a lot of flexibility to the end user and application developer since it implies being oblivious of the underlying details on their part. The concept of transparency extends the general idea of hiding implementation details from end users. In the case of a traditional centralized database, transparency simply pertains to logical and physical data independence for application developers. However, in a DDB scenario, the data and software are distributed over multiple nodes connected by a computer network, so additional types of transparencies are introduced.

1. Distribution or network transparency: This refers to freedom for the user from the operational details of the network and the placement of the data in the distributed system.

    Distribution transparency can be of two types:

    a. Naming transparency implies that once a name is associated with an object, then the named objects can be accessed unambiguously without additional specification as to where the data are located.

    b. Location transparency refers to the fact that the command used to perform a task is independent of the location of the data and the location of the node where the command was issued.

2. Fragmentation transparency:

    Fragmentation transparency can be of two types:

    a. Horizontal fragmentation distributes a relation (table) into subrelations that are subsets of the tuples (rows) in the original relation, which is also known as sharding in the newer big data and cloud computing systems.

    b. Vertical fragmentation distributes a relation into subrelations wherein each subrelation is defined by a subset of the columns of the original relation. Fragmentation transparency makes the user unaware of the existence of fragments.

3. Replication transparency implies copies of the same data objects may be stored at multiple sites for better availability, performance, and reliability. Replication transparency makes the user unaware of the existence of these copies.

7.2.1.2 Availability and Reliability

Reliability and availability are two of the most common potential advantages cited for distributed databases. Reliability is broadly defined as the probability that a system is running (not down) at a certain time point, whereas availability is the probability that the system is continuously available during a time interval. Reliability and availability of the database are directly related to the faults, errors, and failures associated with it. Fault is the cause of an error. Errors constitute that subset of system states that causes the failure. A failure can be described as a deviation of a system's behavior from that which is specified in order to ensure correct execution of operations.

A reliable DDBMS tolerates failures of underlying components, and it processes user requests as long as database consistency is not violated.

A DDMS system can adopt several strategies to achieve the objective of system reliability, as follows:

1. A cure-oriented fault tolerance strategy recognizes that faults will occur, and it designs mechanisms that can detect and remove faults before they can result in a system failure.

2. A prevention-oriented strategy attempts to ensure that the final system does not contain any faults. This is achieved through an exhaustive design process followed by extensive quality control and testing.

A DDBMS recovery manager deals with failures arising from transactions, hardware, and communication networks. Hardware failures can either be those that result in the loss of main memory contents or of secondary storage contents. Network failures occur due to errors associated with messages and line failures. Message errors can include their loss, corruption, or out-of-order arrival at destination.

7.2.1.3 Scalability and Partition Tolerance

Scalability determines the extent to which the system can expand its capacity while continuing to operate without interruption.
   Scalability can be of two types:

1. Horizontal scalability: This refers to expanding the number of nodes in the distributed system. As nodes are added to the system, some of the data and processing loads are distributed from existing nodes to the new nodes.
2. Vertical scalability: This refers to expanding the capacity of the individual nodes in the system, such as expanding the storage capacity or the processing power of a node.

The concept of partition tolerance states that the system should have the capacity to continue operating while the network is partitioned. As the system expands its number of nodes, it is possible that the network, which connects the nodes, may have faults that cause the nodes to be partitioned into groups of nodes. The nodes within each partition are still connected by a subnet-work, but communication among the partitions is lost.

7.2.1.4 Autonomy

Autonomy determines the extent to which individual nodes or databases in a connected DDB can operate independently. A high degree of autonomy is desirable for increased flexibility and customized maintenance of an individual node.
   Autonomy can be of three types:

1. Design autonomy refers to independence of data model usage and transaction management techniques among nodes
2. Communication autonomy determines the extent to which each node can decide on sharing of information with other nodes
3. Execution autonomy refers to independence of users to act as they please

7.2.2 Advantages and Disadvantages of Distributed Databases

The advantages of distributed databases are as follows:

1. Improved ease and flexibility of application development: Developing and maintaining applications at geographically distributed sites of an organization is facilitated due to transparency of data distribution and control.
2. Increased availability: This is achieved by the isolation of faults to their site of origin without affecting the other database nodes connected to the network.

When the data and DDBMS software are distributed over many sites, one site may fail while other sites continue to operate. Only the data and software that exist at the failed site cannot be accessed. Further improvement is achieved by judiciously replicating data and software at more than one site. In a centralized system, failure at a single site makes the whole system unavailable to all users. In a distributed database, some of the data may be unreachable, but users may still be able to access other parts of the database. If the data in the failed site has been replicated at another site prior to the failure, then the user will not be affected at all. The ability of the system to survive network partitioning also contributes to high availability.

3. Improved performance: A distributed DBMS fragments the database by keeping the data closer to where it is needed most. Data localization reduces the contention for central processing unit and input/output services and simultaneously reduces access delays involved in wide-area networks. When a large database is distributed over multiple sites, smaller databases exist at each site. As a result, local queries and transactions accessing data at a single site have better performance because of the smaller local databases. In addition, each site has a smaller number of transactions executing than if all transactions are submitted to a single centralized database. Moreover, interquery and intraquery parallelism can be achieved by executing multiple queries at different sites, or by breaking up a query into a number of sub-queries that execute in parallel. This contributes to improved performance.

4. Easier expansion via scalability: In a distributed environment, expansion of the system in terms of adding more data, increasing database sizes, or adding more nodes is much easier than in centralized (nondistributed) systems.

The disadvantages of distributed databases are as follows:

1. More complex treatment of concurrent update: Concurrent update in a distributed database is treated basically the same way it is treated in nondistributed databases. A user transaction acquires locks, and the locking is two-phase. (Locks are acquired in a growing phase, during which time no locks are released and the DDBMS applies the updates. All locks are released during the shrinking phase.) The DDBMS detects and breaks deadlocks, and then the DDBMS rolls back interrupted transactions. The primary distinction lies not in the kinds of activities that take place but in the additional level of complexity that gets created by the very nature of a distributed database.

If all of the records to be updated by a particular transaction occur at one site, then the problem is essentially the same as in a nondistributed database. However, the records in a distributed database might be stored at many different sites. Furthermore, if the data is replicated, each occurrence might be stored at several sites, with each requiring the same update to be performed. Assuming each record occurrence has replicas at three different sites, an update that would affect five record occurrences in a nondistributed system might affect 20 different record occurrences in a distributed system (i.e., each record occurrence together with its three replica occurrences).

Having more record occurrences to update is only part of the problem. Assuming each site keeps its own locks, the DDBMS must send many messages for each record to be updated: a request for a lock; a message indicating that the record is already locked by another user or that the lock has been granted; a message directing that the update be performed; an acknowledgment of the update; and, finally, a message indicating that the record is to be unlocked. Because all those messages must be sent for each record and its occurrences, the total time for an update can be substantially longer in a distributed database.

A partial solution to minimize the number of messages involves the use of the primary copy mentioned earlier. Recall that one of the replicas of a given record occurrence is designated as the primary copy. Locking the primary copy, rather than all copies, is sufficient and will reduce the number of messages required to lock and unlock records. The number of messages might still be large, however, and the unavailability of the primary copy can cause an entire transaction to fail. Thus, even this partial solution presents problems.

Just as in a nondistributed database, deadlock is a possibility in a distributed database. In a distributed database, however, deadlock is more complicated because two types of deadlock are possible:

a. Local deadlock is deadlock that occurs at a single site in a distributed database. If each of two transactions is waiting for a record held by the other at the same site, the local DBMS can detect and resolve the deadlock with a minimum number of messages needed to communicate the situation to the other DBMSs in the distributed system.

b. Global deadlock involves one transaction that requires a record held by a second transaction at one site, while the second transaction requires a record held by the first transaction at a different site. In this case, neither site has information individually to allow this deadlock to be detected; this is a global deadlock, and it can be detected and resolved only by sending a large number of messages between the DBMSs at the two sites.

2. Update of replicated data: Replicating data can improve processing speed and ensure that the overall system remains available, even when the database at one site is unavailable. However, replication can cause update problems, most obviously in terms of the extra time needed to update all of the copies. Instead of updating a single copy of the data, the DBMS must update several copies. Because most of these copies are at sites other than the site initiating the update, each update transaction requires extra time to update each copy and extra time to communicate all of the update messages over the network.

Often, a DDBMS designates one copy of the data to be the primary copy. As long as the primary copy is updated, the DDBMS considers the update to be complete. The primary site and the DDBMS must ensure that all the other copies are in sync. The primary site sends update transactions to the other sites and notes whether any sites are currently unavailable. If a site is unavailable, the primary site must try to send the update again at some later time and continue trying until it succeeds. This strategy overcomes the basic problem, but it obviously uses more time. Further, if the primary site is unavailable, the problem would remain unresolved.

3. More complex query processing: Processing queries is more complex in a distributed database. The complexity occurs because of the difference in the time it takes to send messages between sites and the time it takes to access a disk.

Systems that are record-at-a-time-oriented can create severe performance problems in distributed systems. If the only choice is to transmit every record from one site to another site as a message and then examine it at the other site, the communication time required can become unacceptably high. DDBMSs that permit a request for a set of records, as opposed to an individual record, outperform record-at-a-time systems.

4. More complex recovery measures: Although the basic recovery process for a distributed data-base is the same as for centralized database, there is an additional potential problem. To make sure that the database remains consistent, each database update should be made permanent or aborted and undone, in which case, none of its changes will be made. In a distributed database, with an individual transaction updating several local databases, it is possible—because of problems affecting individual sites—for local DBMSs to commit the updates at some sites and undo the updates at other sites, thereby creating an inconsistent state in the distributed database. The DDBMS must not allow this inconsistency to occur.

A DDBMS usually prevents this potential inconsistency through the use of two-phase commit. The basic idea of two-phase commit is that one site, often the site initiating the update, acts as coordinator. In the first phase, the coordinator sends messages to all other sites requesting that they prepare to update the database; in other words, each site acquires all necessary locks. The sites do not update at this point, however, but they do send messages to the coordinator stating that they are ready to update.

If, for any reason, any site cannot secure the necessary locks or if any site must abort its updates, the site sends a message to the coordinator that all sites must abort the transaction. The coordinator waits for replies from all sites involved before determining whether to commit the update, according to the following:

a. If all replies are positive, the coordinator sends a message to each site to commit the update. At this point, each site must proceed with the commit process.

b. If any reply is negative, the coordinator sends a message to each site to abort the update, and each site must follow this instruction. In this way, the DDBMS guarantees consistency.

While a process similar to two-phase commit is essential to the consistency of the database, two problems are associated with it. For one thing, many messages are sent during the process. For another, during the second phase, each site must follow the instructions from the coordinator; otherwise, the process will not accomplish its intended result. This process means that the sites are not as independent as you would like them to be.

5. More complicated security and backup requirements: With a single central database, there is a need to secure the central physical site, the central database, and the network connecting users to the database at the central site. The security requirements for a distributed database are more demanding, requiring the securement of every physical site and every database, in addition to securing the network. Backing up a distributed database is also more complicated and is best initiated and controlled from a single site.

6. More difficult management of the data dictionary: A distributed database introduces further complexity to the management of the data dictionary or catalog. The choice of storing the data dictionary can have three options:

   a. Choose one site and store the complete data dictionary at this site and this site alone

   b. Store a complete copy of the data dictionary at each site

   c. Distribute, possibly with replication, the data dictionary entries among the various sites

   Although storing the complete data dictionary at a single site is a relatively simple approach to administer, retrieving information in the data dictionary from any other site is more time-consuming because of the communication involved. Storing a complete copy of the data dictionary at every site solves the retrieval problem because a local DBMS can handle any retrieval locally. Because this second approach involves total replication (every data dictionary occurrence is replicated at every site), updates to the data dictionary are more time-consuming. If the data dictionary is updated with any frequency, the extra time needed to update all copies of the data dictionary might be unacceptable.

   One intermediate strategy is to partition the data by storing data dictionary entries at the site at which the data they describe are located. Interestingly, this approach also suffers from a problem. If a user queries the data dictionary to access an entry not stored at the user's site, the system has no way of knowing the entry's location. Satisfying this user's query might involve sending a message to every other site, which involves a considerable amount of network and DDBMS overhead.

7. More complex database design: A distributed database adds another level of complexity to database design. Distributing data does not affect the information-level design. During the physical-level design in a nondistributed database, disk activity—both the number of disk accesses and the volumes of data to be transported—is one of the principal concerns. Although disk activity is also a factor in a distributed database, communication activity becomes another concern during the physical-level design. Because transmitting data from one site to another is much slower than transferring data to and from the disk, in many situations, communication activity is the most important physical-level design factor. In addition, you must consider possible fragmentation and replication during the physical-level design.

7.2.3 Data Replication and Allocation

Replication is useful in improving the availability of data. The most extreme case is replication of the whole database at every site in the distributed system, thus creating a fully replicated distributed database. This can improve availability remarkably because the system can continue to operate as long as at least one site is up. It also improves the performance of retrieval (read performance) for global queries because the results of such queries can be obtained locally from any one site; hence, a retrieval query can be processed at the local site where it is submitted, if that site includes a server module. The disadvantage of full replication is that it can slow down update operations (write performance) drastically, since a single logical update must be performed on every copy of the database to keep the copies consistent. This is especially true if many copies of the database exist. Full replication makes the concurrency control and recovery techniques more expensive than they would be if there was no replication.

The other extreme from full replication involves having no replication—that is, each fragment is stored at exactly one site. In this case, all fragments must be disjointed, except for the repetition of primary keys among vertical (or mixed) fragments. This is also called nonredundant allocation.

Between these two extremes, we have a wide spectrum of partial replication of the data—that is, some fragments of the database may be replicated, whereas others may not be. The number of copies of each fragment can range from one up to the total number of sites in the distributed system. A special case of partial replication is occurring heavily in applications where mobile workers—such as sales forces, financial planners, and claims adjustors—carry partially replicated databases with them on laptops and personal digital assistants and synchronize them periodically with the server database. A description of the replication of fragments is sometimes called a replication schema.

Each fragment—or each copy of a fragment—must be assigned to a particular site in the distributed system. This process is called data distribution (or data allocation). The choice of sites and the degree of replication depend on the performance and availability goals of the system and on the types and frequencies of transactions submitted at each site. For example, if high availability is required, transactions can be submitted at any site and, when most transactions are retrieval-only, a fully replicated database is a good choice. However, if certain transactions that access particular parts of the database are mostly submitted at a particular site, the corresponding set of fragments can be allocated at that site only. Data that are accessed at multiple sites can be replicated at those sites. If many updates are performed, it may be useful to limit replication. Finding an optimal or even a good solution to distributed data allocation is a complex optimization problem.

7.2.4 Concurrency Control and Recovery in Distributed Databases

For concurrency control and recovery purposes, numerous problems arise in a distributed DBMS environment that are not encountered in a centralized DBMS environment. These include the following:

- Dealing with multiple copies of the data items: The concurrency control method is responsible for maintaining consistency among these copies. The recovery method is responsible for making a copy consistent with other copies if the site on which the copy is stored fails and recovers later.

- Failure of individual sites: The DDBMS should continue to operate with its running sites, if possible, when one or more individual sites fail. When a site recovers, its local database must be brought up-to-date with the rest of the sites before it rejoins the system.

- Failure of communication links: The system must be able to deal with the failure of one or more of the communication links that connect the sites. An extreme case of this problem is that network partitioning may occur. This breaks up the sites into two or more partitions, wherein the sites within each partition can communicate only with one another and not with sites in other partitions.

- Distributed commit: Problems can arise with committing a transaction that is accessing databases stored on multiple sites if some sites fail during the commit process. The two-phase commit protocol is often used to deal with this problem.

- Distributed deadlock: Deadlock may occur among several sites, so techniques for dealing with deadlocks must be extended to take this into account.

Distributed concurrency control and recovery techniques must deal with these and other problems. In the following subsections, we review some of the techniques that have been suggested to deal with recovery and concurrency control in DDBMSs.

To deal with replicated data items in a distributed database, a number of concurrency control methods have been proposed that extend the concurrency control techniques that are used in centralized databases. We discuss these techniques in the context of extending centralized locking. Similar extensions apply to other concurrency control techniques. The idea is to designate a particular copy of each data item as a distinguished copy. The locks for this data item are associated with the distinguished copy, and all locking and unlocking requests are sent to the site that contains that copy.

A number of different methods are based on this idea, but they differ in their method of choosing the distinguished copies. In the primary site technique, all distinguished copies are kept at the same site. A modification of this approach is the primary site with a backup site. Another approach is the primary copy method, wherein the distinguished copies of the various data items can be stored in different sites. A site that includes a distinguished copy of a data item basically acts as the coordinator site for concurrency control on that item. We discuss these techniques next.

7.2.4.1 Distributed Recovery

The recovery process in distributed databases is quite involved. We give only a very brief idea of some of the issues here. In some cases, it is difficult even to determine whether a site is down without exchanging numerous messages with other sites. For example, suppose that site X sends a message to site Y and expects a response from Y but does not receive it. There are several possible explanations:

- The message was not delivered to Y because of communication failure
- Site Y is down and could not respond
- Site Y is running and sent a response, but the response was not delivered

Without additional information or the sending of additional messages, it is difficult to determine what actually happened.

Another problem with distributed recovery is distributed commit. When a transaction is updating data at several sites, it cannot commit until it is sure that the effects of the transaction on every site cannot be lost. This means that every site must first have recorded the local effects of the transactions permanently in the local site log on disk. The two-phase commit protocol is often used to ensure the correctness of distributed commit.

7.2.5 Rules for Distributed Databases

C.J. Date (Date, C.J. "Twelve Rules for a Distributed Database." *ComputerWorld* 21.23, June 8, 1987) formulated 12 rules that distributed databases should follow. The basic goal is that a distributed database should feel like a nondistributed database to users; that is, users should not be aware that the database is distributed. The 12 rules serve as a benchmark against which you can measure DDBMSs. The 12 rules are as follows:

1. Local autonomy: No site should depend on another site to perform its database functions.

2. No reliance on a central site: The DDBMS should not rely on a single central site to control specific types of operations. These operations include data dictionary management, query processing, update management, database recovery, and concurrent update.

3. Continuous operation: Performing functions such as adding sites, changing versions of DBMSs, creating backups, and modifying hardware should not require planned shutdowns of the entire distributed database.

4. Location transparency: Users should not be concerned with the location of any specific data in the database. Users should feel as if the entire database is stored at their location.

5. Fragmentation transparency: Users should not be aware of any data fragmentation that has occurred in the database. Users should feel as if they are using a single central database.

6. Replication transparency: Users should not be aware of any data replication. The DDBMS should perform all of the work required to keep the replicas consistent; users should be unaware of the data synchronization work carried out by the DDBMS.

7. Distributed query processing: Readers already learned about the complexities of query processing in a distributed database. The DDBMS must process queries as rapidly as possible.

8. Distributed transaction management: Readers already learned about the complexities of update management in a distributed database and the need for the two-phase commit strategy. The DDBMS must effectively manage transaction updates at multiple sites.

9. Hardware independence: Organizations usually have many different types of hardware, and a DDBMS must be able to run on this hardware. Without this capability, users are restricted to accessing data stored only on similar computers, disks, and so on.

10. Operating system independence: Even if an organization uses similar hardware, different operating systems might be used within the organization. For the same reason that it is desirable for a DDBMS to support different types of hardware, a DDBMS must be able to run on different operating systems.

11. Network independence: Because different sites within an organization might use different communications networks, a DDBMS must run on different types of networks and not be restricted to a single type of network.

12. DBMS independence: Another way of stating this requirement is that a DDBMS should be heterogeneous; that is, a DDBMS should support different local DBMSs. Supporting heterogeneous DBMSs is a difficult task. In practice, each local DBMS must "speak" a common language; this common language most likely is Structured Query Language.

7.3 Summary

In this chapter, we provided an introduction to distributed computing as a foundation for better understanding of cloud-enabled business processes. Distributed systems constitute a large umbrella under which several different software systems are classified. Unification of parallel and distributed computing allows one to harness a set of networked and heterogeneous computers and present them as a unified resource. Architectural styles help to categorize and provide reference models for distributed systems. More precisely, system architectural styles are more concerned with the physical deployment of such systems, whereas software architectural styles define logical organizations of components and their roles. These two styles are the fundamental deployment blocks of any distributed system. Message-based communication is the most relevant abstraction for IPC and forms the basis for several techniques of IPC, which is a fundamental element in distributed systems; it is the element that ties together separate processes and allows them to be seen as a unified whole.

The latter half of the chapter introduced the concepts, characteristics, and issues related to distributed databases. As part of the discussion, the chapter covered the use of data replication (to improve system reliability and availability), concurrency control, and recovery techniques. The chapter ends with Codd's 12 rules for distributed databases, which were devised based on his rules for relational database systems.

8

Service-Oriented Architecture

A service-oriented architecture (SOA) maps information technology (IT) systems easily and directly to a business's operational processes and supports a better division of labor between the business and technical staff. One of the great potential advantages of solutions created using an SOA with Simple Object Access Protocol (SOAP) or representational state transfer (REST) Web services is that they can help resolve this perennial problem by providing better separation of concerns between business analysts and service developers. Analysts can take responsibility for defining how services fit together to implement business processes, while the service developers can take responsibility for implementing services that meet business requirements. This will ensure that the business issues are understood well enough to be implemented in technology and that the technology issues are understood well enough to meet the business requirements.

Integrating existing and new applications using an SOA involves defining the basic Web service interoperability layer to bridge features and functions used in current applications such as security, reliability, transactions, metadata management, and orchestration; it also involves the ability to define automated business process execution flows across the Web services after an SOA is in place. An SOA with Web services enables the development of services that encapsulate business functions and that are easily accessible from any other service; composite services allow a wide range of options for combining Web services and creating new business process and, hence, application functionality.

8.1 Service-Oriented Architecture

Integration seems to be one of the most important strategic priorities, mainly because new innovative business solutions demand integration of different business units, business systems, enterprise data, and applications. Integrated information systems improve the competitive advantage with unified and efficient access to the information. Integrated applications make it much easier to access relevant, coordinated information from a variety of sources. It is clear that replacing existing systems with new solutions will often not be a viable proposition. Companies soon realize that the replacement is more complicated, more complex, more time-consuming, and more costly than even their worst-case scenarios could have predicted: often, too much time and money have been invested and too much knowledge has been incorporated. Therefore, standard ways to reuse existing systems and integrate them into the global, enterprise-wide information system must be defined.

The modern answer to application integration is an SOA with Web services; SOA is a style of organizing (services), and Web services are its realization. An SOA with Web services is a combination of architecture and technology for consistently delivering robust, reusable services that support today's business needs and which can be easily adapted to satisfy changing business requirements. An SOA enables easy integration of IT systems, provides multichannel access to systems, and automates business processes. When an SOA with its corresponding services is in place, developers can easily reuse existing services in developing new applications and business processes.

A service differs from an object or a procedure because it is defined by the messages that it exchanges with other services. A service's loose coupling to the applications that host it gives it the ability to more easily share data across the department, enterprise, or Internet. An SOA defines the way in which services are deployed and managed. Companies need IT systems with the flexibility to implement specialized operations, to change quickly with the changes in business operations, and to respond quickly to internal as well as external changes in conditions in order to consequently gain a competitive edge. Using an SOA increases reuse, lowers overall costs, and improves the ability to rapidly change and evolve IT systems, whether old or new.

 As a prerequisite, one will have to deal with a plethora of legacy technologies in order to service-enable them. However, the beauty of services and SOA is that the services are developed to achieve interoperability and to hide the details of the execution environments behind them. In particular, for Web services, this means the ability to emit and consume data is represented as Extensible Markup Language (XML), regardless of development platform, middleware, operating system, or hardware type. Thus, an SOA is a way to define and provision an IT infrastructure to allow different applications to exchange data and participate in business processes, regardless of the operating systems or programming languages underlying these applications.

8.1.1 Defining Service-Oriented Architecture

SOA provides an agile technical architecture that can be quickly and easily reconfigured as business requirements change. The promise of SOA is that it will break down the barriers in IT to implement business process flows in a cost-effective and agile manner that would combine the best of custom solutions as well as packaged applications while simultaneously reducing lock-in to any single IT vendor.

An SOA is a style of organization that guides all aspects of creating and using business services throughout their life cycle (from conception to retirement), as well as defining and provisioning the IT infrastructure that allows different applications to exchange data and participate in business processes regardless of the operating systems or programming languages underlying these applications. The key organizing concept of an SOA itself is a service. The processes, principles, and methods defined by SOA are oriented toward services; the development tools selected by an SOA are oriented toward creating and deploying services; and the runtime infrastructure provided by an SOA is oriented to executing and managing services.

A service is a sum of constituting parts including a description, the implementation, and the mapping layer (termed as transformation layer) between the two. The service implementation, termed as the executable agent, can be any environment for which Web service support is available. The description is separated from its executable agent; one description might have multiple different executable agents associated with it and vice versa. The executable agent is responsible for implementing the Web service processing model as per the various Web service specifications and runs within the execution environment, which is typically a software system or programming language environment. The description is separated from the execution environment using a mapping or transformation layer often implemented using proxies and stubs. The mapping layer is responsible for accepting the message, transforming the XML data to be native format, and dispatching the data to the executable agent.

Web service roles include requester and provider; of these, a requester can be a provider and vice versa. The service requester initiates the execution of a service by sending a message to a service provider, which executes the service and returns the results, if any are specified, to the requester.

8.1.1.1 Services

Services are coarse-grained, reusable IT assets that have well-defined interfaces (or service contracts) that clearly separate the service accessible interface from the service technical implementation. This separation of interface and implementation serves to decouple the service requesters from the service providers so that both can evolve independently for as long as the service contract remains unchanged.

A service is a location on the network that has a machine-readable description of the messages it receives and optionally returns. A service is therefore defined in terms of the message exchange patterns it supports. A schema for the data contained in the message is used as the main part of the contract between a service requester and a service provider. Other items of metadata describe the network address for the service; the operations it supports; and its requirements for reliability, security, and transactional integrity. However, developing a service is quite different from developing an object because a service is defined by the message it exchanges with other services, rather than a method signature. A service usually defines a coarse-grained interface that accepts more data in a single invocation than an object because of the need to map to an execution environment, process the XML, and often access it remotely. Services are executed by exchanging messages according to one or more supported message exchange patterns, such as request/response, one-way asynchronous, or publish/subscribe. Services are meant to solve interoperability problems between applications and for use in composing new applications or application systems, but are not meant as objects are to create the detailed business logic for the applications.

From a business perspective, services are IT assets that correspond to real-world business activities or identifiable business functions that can be accessed according to the service policies related to the following:

- Who is authorized to access the service
- When can the service be accessed
- What is the cost of using the service
- What are the reliability levels of using the service
- What are the performance levels for the service

A service is normally defined at a higher level of abstraction than an object because it is possible to map a service definition to a procedure-oriented language, such as Common Business-oriented Language or Programming Language One, or to a message queuing system such as Java Message Service or Microsoft Message Queuing, as well as to an object-oriented system such as Java Platform, Enterprise Edition (J2EE) or the .NET Framework. Whether the service's execution environment is a stored procedure or a message queue, or the object does not matter, the data are seen through the filter of a Web service, which includes a layer that maps the Web service to whatever execution environment is implementing the service. The use of XML in Web services provides a clear separation between the definition of a service and its execution, so that Web services can work with any software system. The XML representation of the data types and structures of a service via the XML schema allows for the developer to think solely in terms of the data being passed between the services without having to consider the details of the service's implementation. This is quite in contrast to the traditional nature of the integration problem that involves figuring out the implementation of the service in order to be able to talk to it.

One of the greatest benefits of service abstraction is its ability to easily access a variety of service types, including newly developed services, wrapped legacy applications, and applications composed of other newer and legacy services.

8.2 Service-Oriented Architecture Benefits

SOA delivers the following business benefits:

1. Increased business agility: SOA improves throughput by dramatically reducing the amount of time required to assemble new business applications from existing services and IT assets. SOA also makes it significantly easier and less expensive to reconfigure IT and adapt services and IT assets to meet new and unanticipated requirements. Thus, the business adapts quickly to new opportunities and competitive threats, while IT quickly changes existing systems.

2. Better business alignment: As SOA services directly support the services that the enterprise provides to customers, this tends to occur.

3. Improved customer satisfaction: As SOA services are independent of specific technology, they can readily work with an array of customer-facing systems across all customer touch points that effectively reduce development time; increase customer engagement time; and, hence, increase customer solutions, enabling enhanced customer satisfaction.

4. Improved the return on investment of existing assets: SOA dramatically improves the return on investment of existing IT assets by reusing them as services in the SOA by identifying the key business capabilities of existing systems and using them as the basis for new services as part of the SOA.

5. Reduced vendor lock-in and switching costs: As SOA is based on loosely coupled services with well-defined, platform-neutral service contracts, it avoids vendor and technology lock-in at all levels—namely, application platforms and middleware platforms.

6. Reduced integration costs: SOA projects can focus on composing, publishing, and developing Web services independently of their execution environments, thus obviating the need to deal with avoidable complexity. Web services and XML simplify integration because they focus on the data being exchanged instead of the underlying programs and execution environments.

Technical benefits of SOA include the following:

1. More reuse: Service reuse lowers development costs and speed.

2. Efficient development: As services are loosely coupled, SOA promotes modularity that enables easier and faster development of composite applications. Once service contracts have been defined, developers can separately and independently design and implement each of the various services. Similarly, service requestors too can be designed and implemented based solely with reference to the published service

contracts without any need to contact the concerned developers or without any access to the developers of the service providers.

3. Simplified maintenance: As services are modular and loosely coupled, they simplify maintenance and reduce maintenance costs.

4. Incremental adoption: As services are modular and loosely coupled, they can be developed and deployed in incremental steps.

8.3 Characteristics of Service-Oriented Architecture

1. Dynamic, discoverable, and metadata-driven: Services should be published in a manner by which they can be discovered and consumed without intervention of the provider. Service contracts should use metadata to define service capabilities and constraints and should be machine-readable so that they can be registered and discovered dynamically to lower the cost of locating and using services, reduce corresponding errors, and improve management of services.

2. Designed for multiple invocation styles: It is important to design and implement service operations that implement business logic that supports multiple invocation styles, including asynchronous queuing, request/response, request/callback, request/polling, batch processing, and event-driven publish/subscribe.

3. Loosely coupled: This implies loose coupling of the interface and technology; interface coupling implies that the interface should encapsulate all implementation details and make them nontransparent to service requesters, while technology coupling measures the extent to which a service depends on a particular technology, product, or development platform (e.g., operating systems, application servers, packaged applications, and middleware).

4. Well-defined service contracts: Service contracts are more important than the service implementations because they define the service capabilities and how to invoke the service in an interoperable manner. A service contract clearly separates the service's externally accessible interface from the service's technical implementation; consequently, the service contract is independent of any single service implementation. The service contract is defined based on the knowledge of the business domain and not so much on the service implementation. It is defined and managed as a separate artifact, is the basis for sharing and reuse, and is the primary mechanism for reducing interface coupling.

   Changing a service contract is generally more expensive than modifying the implementation of a service because, while changing a service implementation is relatively a localized effort, changing a service contract may entail changing hundreds or thousands of service requesters.

5. Standards-based: Services should be based on open standards as much as possible to achieve the following benefits:

   - Minimizing vendor lock-in by isolating from proprietary, vendor-specific technologies and interfaces
   - Increasing the choice of service requesters for alternate service providers and vice versa

It is important to base the service-level data and process models on mature business domain standards as and when they become available. This is in addition to complying with technology standards like SOAP; Web Services Description Language (WSDL); Universal Description, Discovery, and Integration (UDDI); and the WS* specification.

6. Granularity of services and service contracts: Services and service contracts must be defined at a level of abstraction that makes sense to service requesters as well as service providers. To achieve this, services should perform discrete tasks and provide simple interfaces to encourage reuse of and loose coupling.

   An abstract interface at the appropriate level of granularity promotes ready substitutability, which enables any of the existing service providers to be replaced by a new service provider without affecting any of the service requesters.

7. Stateless: Services should be stateless because they scale more efficiently in this form, since any service request can be routed to any service instance. In contrast, stateful interactions do not scale efficiently because the server needs to track which service is serving which client and cannot reuse a service until the conversation is finished or a time-out has occurred.

   Thus, services should be implemented so that each invocation is independent and does not depend on the service maintaining client-specific conversations in the memory or in a persistent state between the invocations.

8. Predictable service-level agreements (SLAs): A service delivery platform must provide service-level management capabilities for the defining, monitoring, incident-logging, and metering of SLAs for service usage. SLAs should be established early on because they affect service design, implementation, and management. There should also be provisions for fine-tuning of SLAs based on the feedback of ongoing operations.

   Typically, SLAs define metrics for services such as response time, throughput, availability, and meantime between failures. Above all, SLAs are usually tied up to a business model whereby service requesters pay more for higher or more stringent SLAs but charge a penalty when service providers default on their SLA commitments.

9. Design services with performance in mind: Service invocation should not be modeled on local function calls, since local transparency may result in a service that is on another machine on the same local-area network or another local-area network or wide-area network.

8.4 Service-Oriented Architecture Applications

An SOA can be thought of as an approach to building IT systems, in which business services are the key organizing principle to align IT systems with the needs of the business. Any business that can implement an IT infrastructure that allows it to change more rapidly than its competitors has an advantage over them. The use of an SOA for integration, business process management, and multichannel access allows any enterprise to create a more strategic environment, one that more closely aligns with the operational characteristics of the business. Earlier approaches to building IT systems resulted in systems that were tied to the features and functions of a particular environment technology (such as Common Object Request Broker Architecture, J2EE, and Component Object Model/Distribute Component Object Model), since they employed environment-specific characteristics like procedure or object or message orientation to provide solutions to business problems. The way in which services are developed now aligns them better with the needs of the business than was the case with previous generations of technology. What is new in the concept of SOA is the clear separation of the service interface from execution technology, enabling the choice of the best execution environment to be made for any job and tying all of these executional agents together using a consistent architectural approach.

8.4.1 Rapid Application Integration

The combination of Web services and SOA provides a rapid integration solution that readily aligns IT investments and corporate strategies by focusing on shared data and reusable services rather than on proprietary integration products. These enterprise application integration (EAI) products proved to be expensive, consumed considerable time and effort, and were prone to higher rates of failure. Applications can more easily exchange data by using a Web service defined at the business logic layer than by using a different integration technology, because Web services represent a common standard across all types of software. XML can be used to independently define the data types and structures. Creating a common Web service layer or an overlay of services into the business logic tiers of application also allows one to use a common service repository in which to store and retrieve service descriptions. If a new application seeks to apply an existing service into one of these applications, it can query the repository to obtain the service description to quickly generate (say) SOAP messages to interact with it. Finally, the development of service-oriented entry points at the business logic tier allows for a business process management engine to drive an automatic flow of execution across the multiple services.

8.4.2 Multichannel Access

Enterprises often use many channels to ensure good service and maintain customer loyalty; therefore, they benefit from being able to deliver customer services over a mixture of access channels. In the past, enterprises often developed monolithic applications that were tied to a single-access channel, such as a 3270 terminal, a personal computer interface, or a Web browser. The proliferation of access channels represented a significant challenge to IT departments to convert monolithic applications to allow multichannel access. The basic solution is to service-enable these using an SOA with Web services that are good for enabling multichannel access because they are accessible from a broad range of clients, including the Web, Java, C#, and mobile devices. In general, business services change much less frequently than do the delivery channels through which they are accessed. Business services refer to operational functions such as vendor management, purchase order management, and billing, which do not vary very often, whereas client devices and access channels are based on new technologies, which tend to change.

8.4.3 Business Process Management

A business process is a real-world activity that consists of a set of logically related tasks that, when performed in an appropriate sequence and in conformity with applicable rules, produce a business outcome. Business process management (BPM) is the name for a set of software systems, tools, and methodologies that enable enterprises to identify, model, develop, deploy, and manage such business processes. BPM systems are designed to help align business processes with desirable business outcomes and ensure that the IT systems support those business processes. BPM systems let business users model their business processes graphically in a way that the IT department can implement; the graphical depiction of a business process can be used to generate an executable specification of the process. Unlike traditional forms of system development wherein the process logic is deeply embedded in the application code, BPM explicitly separates the business process logic from other application code. Separating business process logic from other application code leads to increased productivity, reduced operational costs, and improved agility. When implemented correctly, enterprises can thus quickly respond to changing market conditions and seize opportunities for gaining competitive advantage.

SOA with Web services can better automate business processes because Web services help with achieving the goals of BPM more quickly and easily.

8.5 Service-Oriented Architecture Ingredients

Web services are new standards for creating and delivering cooperative applications over the Internet. Web services allow applications to communicate irrespective of the platform or the operating system.

8.5.1 Objects, Services, and Resources

Any distributed system involves sending messages to some remote entity. Underlying the differences between many systems are the abstractions used to model these entities; they define the architectural qualities of the system. Three abstractions—in particular, object, resource, and service—are commonly used to describe remote entities; their definitions, however, are not always clearly distinguished. Yet, the nature of these abstractions has a profound effect on the distributed communication paradigms that result from their use. One approach to identifying the similarities and differences between them is to understand them in terms of their relationship to two properties: state and behavior.

8.5.1.1 Objects

Objects have both state and behavior. The state is maintained through the internal data, while the behavior of the object is defined through the public operations on that data. A primary issue in these systems is the management of object identifiers, which are global pointers to instances of objects. It has been argued that architectures based on global pointers lead to brittle systems if they are scaled to Internet size because of the proliferation of references and the need to maintain the integrity of the pointers. As a result, these systems are considered to be best-suited to medium-sized networks within a single domain, with known latencies and static addressing and intimate knowledge of the middleware models used.

8.5.1.2 Services

A service is a view of some resource, usually a software asset. Implementation detail is hidden behind the service interface. The interface has well-defined boundaries, providing encapsulation of the resource behind it. Services communicate using messages. The structure of the message and the schema, or form, of its contents are defined by the interface. Services are stateless. This means that all the information needed by a service to perform its function is contained in the messages used to communicate with it.

The service abstraction shares commonalities with the object abstraction but displays crucial differences as follows:

- Like an object, a service can have an arbitrary interface.
- Like distributed object systems that use an IDL, services usually describe this interface in a description language.
- Unlike objects, services use a message-oriented model for communication. This has quite different semantics and implications regarding invoking a procedure on a remote object. In the latter, what the remote entity is plays a part. In the case of objects, the class of an object must be known. Once this class is known, behavior based on the class can be inferred by the consumer. Services, however, do not share class. Instead, they share contracts and schema. Therefore, what an entity is has no bearing on communication, and nothing is inferred. Furthermore, communication with an object involves addressing an instance. This is not the case with services, as is discussed in the next item.
- Unlike objects, services do not have state. Object orientation teaches us that data and the logic that acts on those data should be combined, while service orientation suggests that these two things should be separate. Therefore, a service acts upon state but does not expose its own state. Put another way, services do not have instances. You cannot create and destroy a service in the way in which you can do to an object.

8.5.1.3 Resources

The term resource is used here to specifically refer to the abstraction used by the Web and related initiative such as the Semantic Web. Such a resource is different from a distributed object in a number of ways, as follows:

The resource state is not hidden from a client as it is in object systems. Instead, standard representations of state are exposed. In object systems, the public interface of an object gives access to a hidden state.

- Unlike distributed objects, resources do not have operations associated with them. Instead, manipulation and retrieval of resource representations rely on the transfer protocol used to dereference the uniform resource identifier.
- As a consequence, a resource can be viewed as an entity that has a state but does not have the logic to manipulate that state—that is, it has no behavior.

Because resources have no behavior, they do not define how their state can be manipulated. While this could be viewed as limiting and potentially leading to ad hoc, underspecified interactions, in the case of the Web, the opposite is actually true. While an object-oriented system defines proprietary behavioral interfaces for every object, leading to a proliferation of means of manipulating objects, the Web uses a single, shared interface: Hypertext Transfer Protocol (HTTP). The few methods defined by HTTP allow arbitrary resources to be exchanged and manipulated, making interactions between entities far simpler and, hence, scalable. Imagine, for example, that every Web server limited its own interface to accessing the resources in its charge. This would require a browser to digest a new service interface and generate client-side code every time you clicked on a link, a process that would severely influence the scalability of the system as a whole.

8.5.2 Service-Oriented Architecture and Web Services

Web services are new standards for creating and delivering cooperative applications over the Internet. They allow applications to communicate irrespective of the platform or the operating system. By using Web services, developers can eliminate major porting and quality testing efforts, potentially saving millions of dollars. They will radically change the way that applications are built and deployed in future.

A developer can create an application out of reusable components. However, one question to consider is what good is it to have a large library of reusable components if nobody knows that they exist, where they are located, or how to link to and communicate with them? Web services are standards for finding and integrating object components over the Internet. They enable a development environment wherein it is no longer necessary to build complete and monolithic applications for every project. Instead, the core components can be combined from other standard components available on the Web to build the complete applications that run as services to the core applications.

Some of the past approaches for enabling program-to-program communications included combinations of program-to-program protocols such as Remote Procedure Call and application programming interfaces (APIs) coupled with architectures such as Common Object Model, Distributed Common Object Model, and Common Object Request Broker Architecture. However, without a common underlying network, common protocols for program-to-program communication, and a common architecture to help applications to declare their availability and services, it has proven difficult to implement cross-platform program-to-program communication between application modules. These previous attempts to set up standards for accomplishing these objectives were not very successful because of the following:

- They were not functionally rich enough and are difficult to maintain as the best of the breed
- They were vendor-specific, as opposed to using open and cross vendor standards
- They were too complex to deploy and use

The use of Web service standards holds the potential for correcting each of these deficiencies. This new approach presents applications as services to each other and enables applications to be rapidly assembled by linking application objects together.

With the advent of the Internet and its protocols, most vendors and enterprises have graduated to a common communication and network protocol—the Internet's Transmission Control Protocol/Internet Protocol. Additionally with the availability of Web standards such as XML, SOAP, UDDI, and WSDL, vendors enable customers to:

1. Publish specifications about application modules via WSDL
2. Find those modules (either on the internal intranet or on the Internet) via UDDI

3. Bind the applications together to work seamlessly and cooperatively and deliver the holistic functionality of composite application via SOAP and XML

The significance of Web services for the future is by reason of the following:

- Web services will enable enterprises to reduce development costs and expand application functionality at a fraction of the cost per traditional application development and deployment methods.
- Web services will enable independent software vendors to bring products to market more quickly and to respond to competitive threats with more flexibility.
- Web services will enable enterprises to reuse existing legacy application functionality with the latest applications and technologies.
- Web services will obviate the need of porting applications to different hardware platforms and operating systems at great expense.
- Web services enable applications to communicate irrespective of platform or operating system.
- Web services will have the effect of leveling the playing field because it will enable even specialized boutique application firms to compete easily with well-established and resourceful original equipment manufacturers.
- Web Services will enable only those original equipment manufacturers that focus on providing comprehensive implementations and highly productive application development environments for Web services to flourish.
- Web services will enable applications to be packaged not only as licenses but also as services; this will give a big fillip to ASP (Application Service Provider) services and will consequently expand the overall market size tremendously.
- Web services will enable value-added resellers to rapidly add new functionality to current product offerings or to customize the existing applications of customers.
- Web services will enable enterprises to adapt better to changing market conditions or competitive threats.

Figure 8.1 shows the Web services usage model.

1. Describing Web services: WSDL

WSDL is an XML-based language used to describe the goods and services that an organization offers and provides a way to access those services electronically.

WSDL is an XML vocabulary that provides a standard way of describing service IDLs. WSDL is the resulting artifact of a convergence of activities between NASSL (IBM Corp., Armonk, NY) and SDL (Microsoft Corp., Redmond, WA). It provides a simple way for service providers to describe the format of requests and response messages for Remote Method Invocations (RMIs). WSDL addresses this topic of service IDLs independent of the underlying protocol and encoding requirements. In general, WSDL provides an abstract language for defining the published operations of a service with their respective parameters and data types. The language also addresses the definition of the locations and binding details of the service.

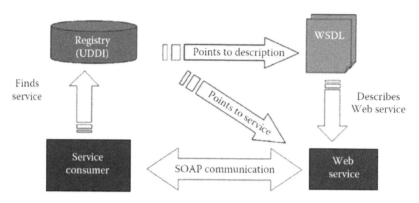

FIGURE 8.1
Web services usage model.

2. Accessing Web services: SOAP

SOAP is an XML-based lightweight protocol for the exchange of information in a decentralized distributed environment. SOAP is a means by which different systems can communicate, based on the HTTP Web standard. It specifies how to encode an HTTP header and XML file so that different applications, running on different systems, can share data. SOAP defines a messaging protocol between requestor and provider objects, such that the requesting objects can perform a remote method invocation on the providing objects in an object-oriented programming fashion. The SOAP specification was coauthored by Microsoft Corporation (Redmond, WA); IBM Corporation (Armonk, NY); Lotus Software (Cambridge, MA); UserLand Software (Los Altos, CA); and DevelopMentor (Torrance, CA). The specification subsequently spawned the creation of the W3C XML Protocol Workgroup, which includes more than 30 participating companies.

In most vendor implementations of SOA, SOAP forms the basis for distributed object communication. Although SOA does not define a messaging protocol, SOAP has recently been referred to as the SOA protocol due to its common use in SOA implementations. The beauty of SOAP is that it is completely vendor-neutral, allowing for independent implementations relative to platform, operating system, object model, and programming language. Additionally, transport and language bindings as well as data-encoding preferences are all implementation-dependent.

3. Finding Web services: UDDI

UDDI is an XML-based registry that enables organizations in a global business-to-business environment to locate each other. The UDDI specification provides a common set of SOAP APIs that enable the implementation of a service broker. The UDDI specification was outlined by IBM Corporation (Armonk, NY); Microsoft Corporation (Redmond, WA); and Ariba (Palo Alto, CA) to help facilitate the creation, description, discovery, and integration of Web-based services.

UDDI is like a telephone directory that additionally also does the following:

• Indicates the suitability of a potential partner
• Describes the access mechanism by which an enterprise can be interfaced with

The motivation behind UDDI.org, a partnership and cooperation between more than 70 industry and business leaders, is to define a standard for business-to-business interoperability.

8.5.3 Service-Oriented Architecture and Representational State Transfer-Ful Services

REST is a style of software architecture for distributed hypermedia systems such as the Web. As such, it is not strictly a method for building Web services. The terms "representational state transfer" and "REST" were introduced in 2000 in the doctoral dissertation of Roy Fielding, one of the principal authors of the HTTP specifications 1.0 and 1.1.

REST refers to a collection of network architecture principles that outline how resources are defined and addressed. The term is often used in a looser sense to describe any simple interface that transmits domain-specific data over HTTP without an additional messaging layer such as SOAP or session tracking via HTTP cookies. These two meanings can conflict as well as overlap. It is possible to design a software system in accordance with Fielding's REST architectural style without using HTTP and without interacting with the Web. It is also possible to design simple XML + HTTP interfaces that do not conform to REST principles but instead follow a model of Remote Procedure Call. Systems that follow Fielding's REST principles are often referred to as RESTful.

Proponents of REST argue that the Web's scalability and growth are a direct result of a few key design principles. Application state and functionality are abstracted into resources. Every resource is uniquely addressable using a universal syntax for employment in hypermedia links, and all resources share a uniform interface for the transfer of state between client and resource. This transfer state consists of a constrained set of well-defined operations and a constrained set of content types, optionally supporting code on demand. State transfer uses a protocol that is client–server-based, stateless and cacheable, and layered.

An important concept in REST is the existence of resources, each of which is referenced with a global identifier (e.g., a uniform resource identifier in HTTP). In order to manipulate these resources, components of the network (user agents and origin servers) communicate via a standardized interface (e.g., HTTP) and exchange representations of these resources (i.e., the actual documents conveying the information). For example, a resource, which is a circle, may accept and return a representation that specifies a center point and radius, formatted in Scalable Vector Graphics, but may also accept and return a representation that specifies any three distinct points along the curve as a comma-separated list.

Any number of connectors (e.g., clients, servers, caches, tunnels) can mediate the request, but each does so without seeing past its own request (referred to as layering, another constraint of REST and a common principle in many other parts of information and networking architecture). Thus, an application can interact with a resource by knowing two things: the identifier of the resource and the action required—it does not need to know whether there are caches, proxies, gateways, firewalls, tunnels, or anything else between it and the server actually holding the information. The application does, however, need to understand the format of the information (representation) returned, which is typically an Hypertext Markup Language, XML, or JavaScript Object Notification document of some kind, although it may instead be an image, plain text, or any other content.

RESTful Web services rely on HTTP as a sufficiently rich protocol to completely meet the needs of Web service applications. In the REST model, the HTTP GET, POST, PUT, and DELETE verbs are used to transfer data (often in the form of XML documents) between client and services. These documents are representations of resources that are identified by normal Web uniform resource identifiers. This use of standard HTTP and Web technologies means that RESTful Web services can leverage the full Web infrastructure, such as caching and indexing. The transactional and database integrity requirements of Create, Retrieve, Update, and Delete correspond to HTTP's POST, GET, PUT, and DELETE.

One benefit that should be obvious with regard to web-based applications is that a RESTful implementation allows a user to bookmark specific queries (or requests) and enables those to be conveyed to others across email and instant messages or to be injected into wikis. Thus, this representation of a path or entry point into an application state becomes highly portable. A RESTful Web service is a simple Web service implemented using HTTP and the principles of REST. Such a Web service can be thought of as a collection of resources comprising three aspects, as follows:

1. The uniform resource identifier for the Web service

2. The Multipurpose Internet Mail Extension type of the data supported by the Web service (it is often JavaScript Object Notification, XML, or YAML, but it can be anything)

3. The set of operations supported by the Web service using HTTP methods, including but not limited to POST, GET, PUT, and DELETE

REST provides improved response time and reduced server load due to its support for the caching of representations. REST improves server scalability by reducing the need to maintain session state. This means that different servers can be used to handle different requests in a session.

REST requires less client-side software to be written versus other approaches, because a single browser can access any application and any resource. REST depends less on vendor software and mechanisms, which layer additional messaging frameworks on top of HTTP. It provides equivalent functionality when compared with alternative approaches to communication, and it does not require a separate resource discovery mechanism, because of the use of hyperlinks in representations. REST also provides better long-term compatibility because of the capability of document types such as HTML to evolve without breaking backward or forward compatibility and the ability of resources to add support for new content types as they are defined without dropping or reducing support for older content types.

SOAs can be built using REST services—an approach sometimes referred to as REST-oriented architecture. The main advantage of REST-oriented architecture is ease of implementation, agility of the design, and the lightweight approach. The latest version of WSDL now contains HTTP verbs and is considered to be an acceptable method of documenting REST services. There is also an alternative known as Web Application Description Language.

8.6 Enterprise Service Bus

An enterprise service bus (ESB) is an open standard-based message backbone designed to enable the implementation, deployment, and management of SOA-based solutions, with a focus on assembling, deploying, and managing distributed SOAs. An ESB is a set of infrastructure capabilities implemented by middleware technology that enable an SOA and alleviate disparity problems between applications running on heterogeneous platforms and using diverse data formats. The ESB supports service invocations as well as message and event-based interactions with appropriate service levels and manageability. The ESB is designed to provide interoperability between larger-grained applications and other components via standard-based adapters and interfaces. The bus functions as both a transport and transformation facilitator to allow for the distribution of these services over disparate systems and computing environments.

Conceptually, the ESB has evolved from the store and forward mechanism found in middleware products and now is a combination of EAI, Web services, Extensible Stylesheet Language Transformation, and orchestration technologies such as Business Process Execution Language. To achieve its operational objectives, the ESB draws from traditional EAI broker functionality, in that it provides integration services such as connectivity and routing of messages based on business rules, data transformation, and adapters to applications. These capabilities are themselves SOA-based, in that they are spread out across the bus in a highly distributed fashion and hosted in separately deployable service containers. This is a crucial difference from traditional integration brokers, which are usually heavyweight, highly centralized, and monolithic in nature. The ESB approach allows for the selective deployment of integration broker functionality exactly where it is needed with no additional overbloating where it is not required.

To surmount problems of system heterogeneity and information model mismatches in an SOA implementation, an EAI middleware supporting hub-and-spoke integration patterns could be used. The hub-and-spoke approach introduces an integration layer between the client and server modules that must support interoperability among and coexist with deployed infrastructure and applications, and not attempt to replace them. However, this approach has its own drawbacks, as a hub can be a central point of failure and can quickly become a bottleneck.

Communication through a bus connection reduces complexity, which is considered a common problem within an enterprise. Integration through point-to-point connections can often become very complex when a company grows. As a result, they often acquire more software. The applications are all directly connected with each other, which result in a "spider web-like" image. Applications are, therefore, more difficult to manage (Figure 8.2).

Using an ESB, the software components are integrated by only connecting to the bus. The bus will then establish further links between the components.

A scalable distributed architecture such as an SOA needs to employ a constellation of hubs. The requirements to provide an appropriately capable and manageable integration

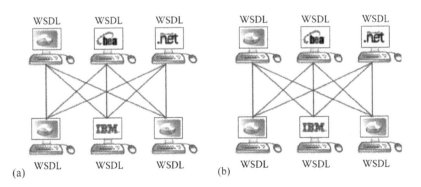

FIGURE 8.2
ESB reducing connection complexity.

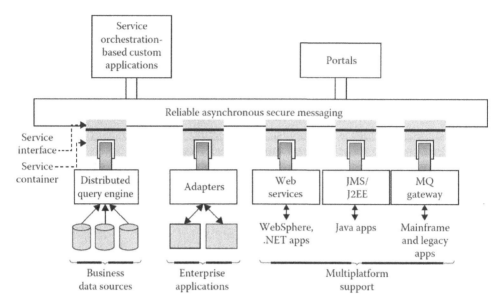

FIGURE 8.3
ESB linking disparate systems and computing environments.

infrastructure for Web services and SOA are coalescing into the concept of the ESB, which will be the subject of this section. The two key ideas behind this approach are to loosely couple the systems taking part in the integration and to break up the integration logic into distinct, easily manageable pieces.

Figure 8.3 shows a simplified view of an ESB that integrates a J2EE application using JMS, an .NET application using a C# client, an MQ application that interfaces with legacy applications, and external applications and data sources using Web services. In an ESB application, development tools allow new or existing distributed applications to be exposed as Web services and be accessed via a portal. In general, resources in the ESB are modeled as services that offer one or more business operations. Technologies like J2EE Connector Architecture (JCA) may also be used to create services by integrating packaged applications (e.g., enterprise resource planning systems), which would then be exposed as Web services.

The ESB distributed processing infrastructure is aware of applications and services and uses content-based routing facilities to make informed decisions about how to communicate with them. In essence, the ESB provides docking stations for hosting services that can be assembled and orchestrated and are available for use to any other service on the bus. Once a service is deployed into a service container, it becomes an integral part of the ESB and can be used by any application or service connected to it. The service container hosts, manages, and dynamically deploys services and binds them to external resources, such as data sources, enterprise, and multiplatform applications (Figure 8.3).

The distributed nature of the ESB container model allows individual event-driven services to be plugged into the ESB backbone on an as-needed basis. It allows them to be highly decentralized and to work together in a highly distributed fashion, while they are scaled independently from one another. Applications running on different platforms are abstractly decoupled from each other and can be connected together through the bus as logical endpoints that are exposed as event-driven services.

Endpoints in the ESB depicted in Figure 8.3 provide abstraction of physical destination and connection information (like Transmission Control Protocol/Internet Protocol host name and port number). In addition, they facilitate asynchronous and highly reliable communication between service containers using reliable messaging conventions. Endpoints allow services to communicate using logical connection names, which an ESB will map to actual physical network destinations at runtime. This destination independence gives the services that are part of the ESB the ability to be upgraded, moved, or replaced without having to modify code and disrupt existing ESB applications. For instance, an existing ESB invoicing service could be easily upgraded or replaced with a new service without disrupting other applications. Additionally, duplicate processes can be set up to handle failover if a service is not available. The endpoints can be configured to use several levels of quality of service (QOS), which guarantee communication despite network failures and outages.

8.6.1 Characteristics of an Enterprise Service Bus Solution

There are alternative ways to implement an ESB. The ESB itself can be a single centralized service or even a distributed system consisting of peer and subpeer ESBs—in the form of an ESB federation—all working in tandem to keep the SOA system operational. In small-scale implementations of integration solutions, the physical ESB infrastructure is likely to be a centralized ESB topology. A centralized ESB topology is concentrated on a single cluster, or hub, of servers. This solution is reminiscent of hub-and-spoke middleware topologies, which employ a central node that manages all interactions between applications and prevents an application having to integrate multiple times with several other applications (Kale 2015). The hub-and-spoke approach simply carries out one integration process on the central node, which is a central point of control responsible for integration/translation activities, maintaining routing information, service naming, and so forth. The most popular hub-and-spoke EAI solution for the interenterprise arena is integration brokering.

Even though a hub-and-spoke solution is capable of being stretched out across organizational boundaries, it still does not allow the local autonomy that individual business units require to operate semi-independently of each other. This is usually caused by the integration broker's inability to easily span firewalls and network domains. However, as explained earlier in this chapter, the most serious drawback of this approach is that hub-and-spoke solutions can quickly become a point of contention for large-scale implementations. In an environment of loosely coupled units, it does not make sense for business process flow between localized applications or security domains to be managed by a single centralized authority like an integration broker.

In circumstances wherein organizational or geographically dispersed units need to act independently from one another, the infrastructure may become more physically distributed while retaining at least logically the central control over configuration. This calls for a federated hub solution. A federated ESB allows different enterprises such as manufacturers, suppliers, and customers to plug together their integration domains into a larger federated integration network. This topology allows for local message traffic, integration components, and adapters to be locally installed, configured, secured, and managed, while also allowing for a single integrated transaction and security model. A federated ESB solution is used to form a virtual network of trading partners across industries and services able to take advantage of the wider range of options and partnering models.

The physical deployment of the ESB depends on candidate ESB technologies such as specialized MOM, integration brokers, and application servers. The use and combination of different candidate ESB technologies result in a variety of ESB patterns, each having its own requirements and constraints in connection with its physical deployment. Some ESB configurations might be suited to very widespread distribution to support integration over large geographical areas, while others might be more suited to deployment in local-ized clusters to support high availability and scalability. Matching the requirements for physical distribution to the capabilities of candidate technologies is an important aspect of ESB design. Also important is the ability to incrementally extend the initial deployment to reflect evolving requirements to integrate additional systems, or to extend the geographi-cal reach of the ESB infrastructure.

Irrespective of its implementation topology, the main aim of the ESB is to provide vir-tualization of the enterprise resources, allowing the business logic of the enterprise to be developed and managed independently of the infrastructure, network, and provisions of those business services. Implementing an ESB requires an integrated set of middleware facilities that support the following interrelated architectural styles:

- SOAs, wherein distributed applications are composed of granular reusable ser-vices with well-defined, published, and standard-compliant interfaces
- Message-driven architectures, wherein applications send messages through the ESB to receiving applications
- Event-driven architectures, wherein applications generate and consume messages independently of one another

The ESB supports these architectural styles and service interaction capabilities and pro-vides the integrated communication, messaging, and event infrastructure to enable them, as explained in the previous section. To achieve its stated objectives, the ESB amalgamates functional capabilities of application servers, integration brokers, business process man-agement technologies, and product sets into a single integrated infrastructure.

8.6.1.1 Key Capabilities of an Enterprise Service Bus

In order to implement an SOA, both applications and infrastructure must support SOA principles. Enabling an application for SOA involves the creation of service interfaces to existing or new functions, either directly or through the use of adapters. Enabling the infrastructure, at the most basic level, involves the provision of the capabilities to route and deliver secure service requests to the correct service provider. However, it is also vital that the infrastructure supports the substitution of one service implementation by another with no effect on the clients of that service. This requires not only that the service interfaces be specified according to SOA principles but also that the infrastructure allow client code to invoke services irrespective of the service location and the communication protocol involved. Such service routing and substitution are among the many capabilities of the ESB. Additional capabilities can be found in the following list, which describes detailed functional requirements of an ESB. It should be noted that not all of the capabilities described in the following are offered by current commercial ESB systems:

1. Dynamic connectivity capabilities: Dynamic connectivity is the ability to connect to Web services dynamically without using a separate static API or proxy for each service. Most enterprise applications today operate on a static connectivity mode, requiring some static piece of code for each service. Dynamic service connectivity is a key capability for a successful ESB implementation. The dynamic connectiv-ity API is the same regardless of the service implementation protocol (e.g., Web services, JMS, EJB/RMI).

2. Reliable messaging capabilities: Reliable messaging can be primarily used to ensure guaranteed delivery of these messages to their destination and for handling events. This capability is crucial for responding to clients in an asynchronous manner and for a successful ESB implementation.

3. Topic- and content-based routing capabilities: The ESB should be equipped with routing mechanisms to facilitate not only topic-based routing but also more sophisticated content-based routing. Topic-based routing assumes that messages can be grouped into fixed, topical classes so that subscribers can explicate interest in a topic and, as a consequence, receive messages associated with that topic. Content-based routing, on the other hand, allows for subscriptions on the constraints of actual properties (attributes) of business events. Content-based routing forwards messages to their destination based on the context or content of the service. Content-based routing is usually implemented using techniques that can examine the content of a message and apply a set of rules to its content to determine which endpoints in the ESB infrastructure it may need to be routed to next.

4. Transformation capabilities: A critical ability of the ESB is the ability to route service interactions through a variety of transport protocols and to transform from one protocol to another where necessary. Another important aspect of an ESB implementation is the ability to support service messaging models and data formats consistent with the SOA interfaces. A major source of value in an ESB is that it shields any individual component from any knowledge of the implementation details of any other component. The ESB transformation services make it possible to ensure that messages and data received by any component are in the format it expects, thereby removing the need to make changes. The ESB plays a major role in transforming between differing data formats and messaging models, whether between basic XML formats and Web service messages or between different XML formats (e.g., transforming an industry-standard XML message to a proprietary or custom XML format).

5. Service enablement capabilities: Service enablement includes the ability to access already existing resources such as legacy systems—technically obsolete mission-critical elements of an organization's infrastructure—and includes them in an SOA implementation. Tactically, legacy assets must be leveraged, service-enabled, and integrated with modern service technologies and applications.

6. Endpoint discovery with multiple QOS capabilities: The ESB should support the basic SOA need to discover, locate, and bind to services. As many network endpoints can implement the same service contract, the ESB should make it possible for the client to select the best endpoint at runtime, rather than hard-coding endpoints at build time. The ESB should therefore be capable of supporting various QOSs and should allow clients to discover the best service instance with which to interact based on QOS properties. Such capabilities should be controlled by declarative policies associated with the services involved using a policy standard such as the WS-Policy framework.

7. Long-running process and transaction capabilities: Service orientation, as opposed to distributed object architectures such as .NET or J2EE, more closely reflects real-world processes and relationships. Hence, SOA represents a much more natural way to model and build software that solves real-world business processing needs.

Accordingly, the ESB should provide the ability to support business processes and long-running services—services that tend to run for long duration, exchanging messages (conversation) as they progress. Typical examples are an online reservation system, which interacts with the user as well as various service providers (e.g., airline ticketing, insurance claims, mortgage and credit product applications). In addition, in order to be successful in business environments, it is extremely important that the ESB provides certain transactional guarantees. More specifically, the ESB needs to be able to ensure that complex transactions are handled in a highly reliable manner; furthermore, if failure should occur, transactions should be capable of rolling back processing to the original, prerequest state. Long-duration transactional conversations could be made possible if implemented on the basis of messaging patterns using asynchrony, store and forward, and itinerary-based routing techniques.

8. Security capabilities: Generically handling and enforcing security is a key success factor for ESB implementations. The ESB needs both to provide a security model to service consumers and to integrate with the (potentially varied) security models of service providers. Both point-to-point (e.g., Secure Sockets Layer encryption) and end-to-end security capabilities will be required. These end-to-end security capabilities include federated authentication, which intercepts service requests and adds the appropriate user name and credentials; performs validation of each service request and authorization to make sure that the sender has the appropriate privilege to access the service; and, lastly, completes encryption/decryption of XML content at the element level for both message requests and responses. To address these intricate security requirements, the ESB must rely on WS-Security and other security-related standards for Web services that have been developed.

9. Integration capabilities: To support SOA in a heterogeneous environment, the ESB needs to integrate with a variety of systems that do not directly support service-style interactions. These may include legacy systems, packaged applications, or other EAI technologies. When assessing the integration requirements for ESB, several types or styles of integration must be considered, for example, process versus data integration.

10. Management and monitoring capabilities: In an SOA environment, applications cross system (and even organizational) boundaries, overlap, and can change over time. Managing these applications is a serious challenge. Examples include dynamic load-balancing, failover when primary systems go down, and achieving topological or geographic affinity between the client and the service instance. Effective systems and application management in an ESB requires a management framework that is consistent across an increasingly heterogeneous set of participating component systems, while supporting complex aggregate (cross-component) management use cases, such as dynamic resource provisioning and demand-based routing, as well as SLA enforcement in conjunction with policy-based behavior (e.g., the ability to select service providers dynamically based on the QOS they offer compared to the business value of individual transactions).

11. Scalability capabilities: With a widely distributed SOA, there will be the need to scale some of the services or possibly even the entire infrastructure to meet integration demands. For example, transformation services are typically very resource-intensive and may require multiple instances across two or more computing nodes. At the same time, it is necessary to create an infrastructure that can support the large nodes present in a global service network. The loose-coupled

nature of an SOA requires that the ESB use a decentralized model to provide a cost-effective solution that promotes flexibility in scaling any aspect of the integration network. A decentralized architecture enables the independent scalability of individual services as well as the communications infrastructure itself.

8.6.1.2 Enterprise Service Bus Scalability

Scalability is a particularly important issue for any automated business integration solution. Scalability is concerned in the case of ESB translation as to how well the particular ESB implementation has been designed. The use of asynchronous communications, message itineraries, and message and process definitions allows for different parts of the ESB to operate independently of one another. This results in a decentralized model that provides complete flexibility in scaling any aspect of the integration network. Such a decentralized architecture enables independent scalability of individual services as well as the communications infrastructure itself. For instance, parallel execution of business operations and itinerary-based routing significantly contribute to the highly distributed nature of the ESB, as there is no centralized rule engine to refer back to for each step in the process.

Typical integration broker technologies handle scalability using a centralized hub-and-spoke model; that is, they handle changes in load and configuration by increasing broker capacity or by adding brokers in a centralized location. A centralized rule engine for the routing of messages can quickly become a bottleneck and also a single point of failure. In contrast, ESB allows capacity to be added where it is most needed—at the service itself.

When the capacity of a single broker is reached, brokers can be combined into clusters. These may act as a single virtual broker to handle increased demand from users and applications. The ESB's use of integration brokers and broker clusters increases scalability by allowing brokers to communicate and dynamically distribute load on the bus. For example, in the event that an increase in the use of the inventory services has overloaded the capacity of their host machine(s), new machines and new brokers can be added to handle the load without the need to change any of the services themselves and without requiring any additional development or administration changes to the messaging system. The notion of a separately deployable, separately scalable messaging topology in combination with a separately deployable, separately scalable ESB service container model is what uniquely distinguishes this architectural configuration. The distributed functional pieces are able to work together as one logical piece with a single, globally accessible namespace for locating and invoking services.

8.6.1.3 Event-Driven Nature of Enterprise Service Buses

In an ESB-enabled, event-driven SOA, applications and services are treated as abstract service endpoints, which can readily respond to asynchronous events. Applications and event-driven services are tied together in an ESB-enabled, event-driven SOA in a loosely coupled fashion, which allows for them to operate independently from each other while still providing value to a broader business function. An event source typically sends messages through the ESB, which publishes the messages to the objects that have subscribed to the events. The event itself encapsulates an activity and is a complete description of a specific action. To achieve its functionality, the ESB must support both the established Web service technologies such as SOAP, WSDL, and Business Process Execution Language, as well as emerging standards like WS-ReliableMessaging and WS-Notification.

An SOA requires an additional fundamental technology beyond the service aspect to realize its full potential: event-driven computing. Ultimately, the primary objective of most SOA implementations is to automate as much processing as necessary and to provide critical and actionable information to human users when they are required to interact with a business process. This requires that the ESB infrastructure itself recognize meaningful events and respond to them appropriately. The response could be either by automatically initiating new services and business processes or by notifying users of business events of interest; putting the events into topical context; and, often, suggesting the best courses of action. In the enterprise context business events, such as a customer order, the arrival of a shipment at a loading dock, the payment of a bill, and so forth affect the normal course of a business process and can occur in any order at any point in time. Consequently, applications that use orchestrated processes that exchange messages need to communicate with each other using a broad capability known as an event-driven SOA.

An event-driven SOA is an architectural approach to distributed computing wherein events trigger asynchronous messages that are then sent between independent software components that need not have any information about each other by abstracting away from the details of underlying service connectivity and protocols. An event-driven SOA provides a more lightweight, straightforward set of technologies to use in building and maintaining the service abstraction for client applications.

8.7 Summary

Services and SOAs are pragmatic responses to the complexity and interoperability problems encountered by the builders of previous generations of large-scale integrated applications. Although it is possible to design and build service-oriented systems using any distributed computing or integration middleware, only Web services technologies can today meet the critical requirement for seamless interoperability that is such an important part of the service-oriented vision. This chapter presented the definition and characteristics of SOAs as well as approaches to realizing the vision of service-oriented systems with Web services and RESTful services, respectively. The last part of the chapter shows how, with an ESB SOA implementation, previously isolated enterprise resource planning, Customer Relationship Management (CRM), supply chain management, and financial and other legacy systems can become SOA-enabled and integrated more effectively than when relying on custom, point-to-point coding or proprietary EAI technology. An ESB supporting Web services with more established application integration techniques enables an enterprise-wide solution that combines the best of both of these worlds.

9

Cloud Computing

Many motivating factors have led to the emergence of cloud computing. Businesses require services that include both infrastructure and application workload requests, while meeting defined service levels for capacity, resource tiering, and availability. Information technology (IT) delivery often necessitates costs and efficiencies that create a perception that IT is a hindrance, not a strategic partner. Issues include underutilized resources, overprovisioning or underprovisioning of resources, lengthy deployment times, and lack of cost visibility. Virtualization is the first step toward addressing some of these challenges by enabling improved utilization through server consolidation, workload mobility through hardware independence, and efficient management of hardware resources.

The virtualization system is a key foundation for the cloud computing system. Using this, we can stitch together computing resources so as to make it appear that there is one large computer behind which the complexity is hidden. By coordinating, managing, and scheduling resources such as central processing units, network, storage, and firewalls in a consistent way across internal and external premises, we create a flexible cloud infrastructure platform. This platform includes security, automation and management, interoperability and openness, self-service, pooling, and dynamic resource allocation. In the view of cloud computing we are advocating for, applications can run within an external provider, in internal IT premises, or in combination as a hybrid system—what matters is how they are run, not where they are run.

Cloud computing builds on virtualization to create a service-oriented computing model. This is done through the addition of resource abstractions and controls to create dynamic pools of resources that can be consumed through the network. Benefits include economies of scale, elastic resources, self-service provisioning, and cost transparency. Consumption of cloud resources is enforced through resource metering and pricing models that shape user behavior. Consumers benefit through leveraging allocation models such as pay-as-you-go to gain greater cost efficiency, lower barrier to entry, and immediate access to infrastructure resources.

9.1 Cloud Definition

The following is the National Institute of Standards and Technology (NIST) working definition for cloud computing:

> "Cloud computing is a model for enabling convenient, on-demand network access to a shared pool of configurable computing resources (e.g., networks, servers, storage, applications, and services) that can be rapidly provisioned and released with minimal management effort or service provider interaction."

This cloud model promotes availability and is composed of five essential characteristics, three delivery models, and four deployment models.

The five essential characteristics are:

- On-demand self-service
- Broad network access
- Resource pooling
- Rapid elasticity
- Measured service

The three delivery models are:

1. Infrastructure as a service (IaaS)
2. Platform as a service (PaaS)
3. Software as a service (SaaS)

The four deployment models are:

1. Public cloud
2. Private cloud
3. Hybrid cloud
4. Community cloud

Cloud computing is the IT foundation for cloud services and it consists of technologies that enable cloud services. The key attributes of cloud computing are shown in Table 9.1. Key attributes of cloud services are described in Table 9.2.

TABLE 9.1

Key Attributes of Cloud Computing

Attributes	Description
Off site, third-party provider	In the cloud execution, it is assumed that a third party provides services. There is also a possibility of in-house cloud service delivery.
Accessed via the Internet	Services are accessed via standard-based, universal network access. It can also include security and quality-of-service options.
Minimal or no IT skill required	There is a simplified specification of requirements.
Provisioning	Includes self-service requesting, near real-time deployment, and dynamic and fine-grained scaling.
Pricing	Pricing is based on usage-based capability and is fine-grained.
User interface	User interface includes browsers for a variety of devices and with rich capabilities.
System interface	System interfaces are based on Web services application programming interface providing a standard framework for accessing and integrating among cloud services.
Shared resources	Resources are shared among cloud services users; however, via configuration options with the service, there is the ability to customize.

TABLE 9.2

Key Attributes of Cloud Services

Attributes	Description
Infrastructure systems	Includes servers, storage, and networks that can scale as per user demand.
Application software	Provides web-based user interface, Web services application programming interfaces, and a rich variety of configurations.
Application development and deployment software	Supports the development and integration of cloud application software.
System and application management software	Supports rapid self-service provisioning and configuration and usage monitoring.
Internet Protocol networks	Connect end users to the cloud and the infrastructure components.

9.2 Cloud Characteristics

Large organizations such as IBM Corporation (Armonk, NY); Dell (Round Rock, TX); Microsoft Corporation (Redmond, WA); Google (Mountain View, CA); Amazon (Seattle, WA); and Sun Microsystems (Santa Clara, CA) have already started to take strong positions with respect to cloud computing. They are so much behind this latest paradigm that the success is virtually guaranteed. The essential characteristics of the cloud environment include:

1. On-demand self-service that enables users to consume computing capabilities (e.g., applications, server time, network storage) as and when required

2. Rapid elasticity and scalability that enables functionalities and resources to be rapidly, elastically, and automatically scaled out or in as demand rises or drops

   According to the current demand requirements, automatic services are provided. This is done using software automation, enabling the expansion and contraction of service capability, as needed. This dynamic scaling must be performed while maintaining high levels of reliability and security.

   These characteristics show the following features:

   a. An economical model of cloud computing that enables consumers to order required services (e.g., computing machines and/or storage devices). The requested service could scale rapidly upward or downward on demand.

   b. It is a machine responsibility that does not require any human to control the requested services. The cloud architecture manages on-demand requests (e.g., increase or decrease in service requests), availability, allocation, subscription, and the customer's bill.

3. Broad network access: Capabilities are available over the network and accessed through standard mechanisms that promote use by heterogeneous thin or thick client platforms (e.g., mobile phones, tablets, laptops, and workstations).

   Capabilities are available over the network and a continuous Internet connection is required for a broad range of devices such as personal computers, laptops, and mobile devices, using standards-based application programming interfaces (for example, ones based on Hypertext Transfer Protocol). The deployment of services in the cloud includes everything from using business applications to the latest applications on the newest smartphones.

4. Multitenancy and resource pooling that enables the combination of heterogeneous computing resources (e.g., hardware, software, processing, servers, network bandwidth) to serve multiple consumers; these resources are dynamically assigned.

A virtualized software model is used, which enables the sharing of physical services, storage, and networking capabilities. Regardless of the deployment model—whether it is a public cloud or private cloud—the cloud infrastructure is shared across a number of users.

A cloud vendor provides a pool of resources (e.g., computing machines, storage devices, and networks) to customers. The cloud architecture manages all available resources via global and local managers for different sites and local sites, respectively.

This feature allows big data to be distributed on different servers, which is not possible using traditional models such as supercomputing systems.

5. Measured provision to automatically control and optimize resource allocation and to provide a metering capability to determine the usage for billing purpose, allowing easy monitoring, controlling, and reporting.

Resource usage can be monitored, controlled, and reported, providing transparency for both the provider and the consumer of the utilized service. This concept uses metering for managing and optimizing the service and to provide reporting and billing information. In this way, consumers are billed for services according to how much they have actually used during the billing period. In short, cloud computing allows for the sharing and scalable deployment of services, as needed, from almost any location and for which the customer can be billed based on actual usage.

9.2.1 Cloud Storage Infrastructure Requirements

Data are growing at an immense rate and, with the combination of technology trends such as virtualization with the increased economic pressures and exploding growth of unstructured data and regulatory environments that are requiring enterprises to keep data for longer periods of time, it is easy to see the need for a trustworthy and appropriate storage infrastructure. Storage infrastructure is the backbone of every business. Whether a cloud is public or private, the key to success is creating a storage infrastructure in which all resources can be efficiently utilized and shared. Because all data resides on the storage systems, data storage becomes even more crucial in a shared infrastructure model.

The most important cloud infrastructure requirements are as follows:

1. Elasticity: Cloud storage must be elastic so that it can quickly adjust with underlying infrastructure according to changing requirement of the customer demands and comply with service level agreements.

2. Automatic: Cloud storage must have the ability to be automated so that policies can be leveraged to make underlying infrastructure changes such as placing user and content management in different storage tiers and geographic locations quickly and without human intervention.

3. Scalability: Cloud storage needs to scale quickly up and down according to the requirements of customer. This is one of the most important requirements that make the cloud so popular.

4. Recovery performance: Cloud storage infrastructure must provide fast and robust data recovery as an essential element of a cloud service.

5. Reliability: As more and more users are depending on the services offered by a cloud, reliability becomes increasingly important. Various users of the cloud storage want to make sure that their data are reliably backed up for disaster recovery purposes, and the cloud should be able to continue to run in the presence of hardware and software failures.

6. Operational efficiency: Operational efficiency is a key to a successful business enterprise that can be ensured by better management of storage capacities and cost benefits. Both of these features should be an integral part of the cloud storage.

7. Latency: Cloud storage models are not suitable for all applications, especially for real-time applications. It is important to measure and test network latency prior to committing to a migration. Virtual machines can introduce additional latency through the time-sharing nature of the underlying hardware and unanticipated sharing and reallocation of machines can significantly affect run times.

8. Data retrieval: Once the data are stored on the cloud, they can be easily accessed from anywhere at any time as long as a network connection is available. Ease of access to data in the cloud is critical in enabling seamless integration of cloud storage into existing enterprise workflows and to minimize the learning curve for cloud storage adoption.

9. Data security: Security is one of the major concerns of cloud users. As different users store more of their own data in a cloud, they want to ensure that their private data are not accessible to other users who are not authorized to see them. If this is the case, than the user can use a private cloud, because security is assumed to be tightly controlled in the case of a private cloud. However, in case of public clouds, data should either be stored on a partition of a shared storage system, or cloud storage providers must establish multitenancy policies to allow multiple business units or separate companies to securely share the same storage hardware.

Storage is the most important component of IT infrastructure. Unfortunately, it is almost always managed as a scarce resource because it is relatively expensive and the consequences of running out of storage capacity can be severe. Nobody wants to take the responsibility of being the storage manager; thus, the storage management suffers from slow provisioning practices.

9.3 Cloud Delivery Models

Cloud computing is not a completely new concept for the development and operation of Web applications. It allows for the most cost-effective development of scalable Web portals on highly available and fail-safe infrastructures. In the cloud computing system, we must address different fundamentals such as virtualization, scalability, interoperability, quality of service, failover mechanism, and the cloud deployment models (e.g., private, public, hybrid) within the context of the taxonomy. The taxonomy of the cloud includes the different participants involved in the cloud along with the attributes and technologies that are coupled to address their needs and the different types of services, such as "X as a service" offerings wherein X is software, hardware, platform, infrastructure, data, or business.

9.3.1 Infrastructure as a Service

Infrastructure as a Service (IaaS) model is about providing compute and storage resources as a service. According to the NIST, IaaS is defined as follows:

> "The capability provided to the consumer is to provision processing, storage, networks, and other fundamental computing resources where the consumer is able to deploy and run arbitrary software, which can include operating systems and applications. The consumer does not manage or control the underlying cloud infrastructure but has control over operating systems, storage, deployed applications, and possibly limited control of select networking components (e.g., host firewalls)."

The user of IaaS has single ownership of the hardware infrastructure allotted to him or her (may be a virtual machine) and can use it as if it is his or her own machine on a remote network, having total control over the operating system and software on it. IaaS is illustrated in Figure 9.1. The IaaS provider has control over the actual hardware and the cloud user can request the allocation of virtual resources, which are then allocated by the IaaS provider on the hardware (generally without any manual intervention). The cloud user can manage the virtual resources as desired, including installing any desired operating system, software, and applications. Therefore, IaaS is well-suited for users who want complete control over the software stack that they run; for example, the user may be using heterogeneous software platforms from different vendors, and they may not desire to switch to a PaaS platform wherein only selected middleware is available. Well-known IaaS platforms include Amazon Elastic Compute Cloud (Amazon, Seattle, WA); Rackspace (Rackspace Inc., Wincrest, TX);

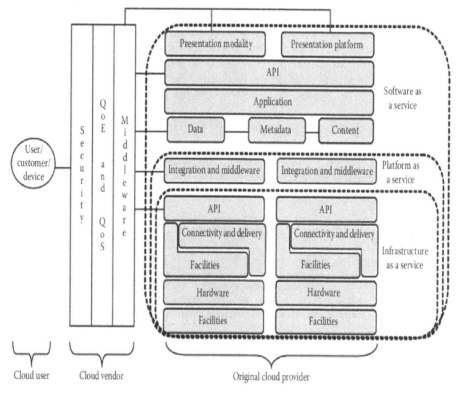

FIGURE 9.1
The cloud reference model.

and RightScale (RightScale, Santa Barbara, CA). Additionally, traditional vendors such as Hewlett-Packard (Palo Alto, CA); IBM Corporation (Armonk, NY); and Microsoft Corporation (Redmond, WA) offer solutions that can be used to build private IaaSs.

9.3.2 Platform as a Service

Platform as a Service (PaaS) model is designed to provide a system stack or platform for application deployment as a service. NIST defines PaaS as follows:

"The capability provided to the consumer is to deploy onto the cloud infrastructure consumer-created or acquired applications created using programming languages and tools supported by the provider. The consumer does not manage or control the underlying cloud infrastructure including network, servers, operating systems, or storage, but has control over the deployed applications and possibly application hosting environment configurations."

Figure 9.2 shows a PaaS model diagrammatically. The hardware, as well as any mapping of the hardware to virtual resources such as virtual servers, is controlled by the PaaS provider. Additionally, the PaaS provider supports selected middleware, such

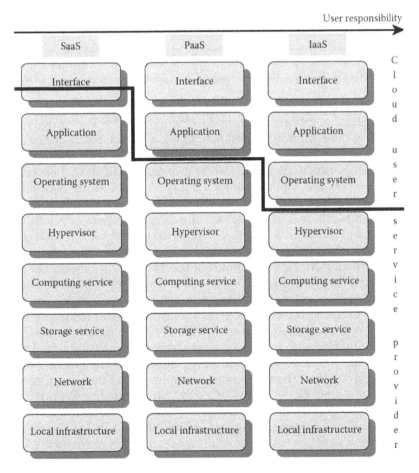

FIGURE 9.2
Portfolio of services for the three cloud delivery models.

as a database, Web application server, and so on. The cloud user can configure and build on top of this middleware, such as by defining a new database table in a database. The PaaS provider maps this new table onto their cloud infrastructure. Subsequently, the cloud user can manage the database as needed and develop applications on top of this database. PaaS platforms are well-suited to those cloud users who find that the middleware they are using matches the middleware provided by one of the PaaS vendors. This enables them to focus on the application. Windows Azure (Microsoft Corporation, Redmond, WA); Google App Engine (Google, Mountain View, CA); and Apache Hadoop (Apache Software Foundation, Forest Hill, MD) are some well-known PaaS platforms. As in the case of IaaS, traditional vendors such as Hewlett-Packard (Palo Alto, CA); IBM Corporation (Armonk, NY); and Microsoft Corporation (Redmond, WA) offer solutions that can be used to build private PaaSs.

9.3.3 Software as a Service

Software as a Service (SaaS) is about providing the complete application as a service. SaaS has been defined by the NIST as follows:

> "The capability provided to the consumer is to use the provider's applications running on a cloud infrastructure. The applications are accessible from various client devices through a thin client interface such as a web browser (e.g., web-based email). The consumer does not manage or control the underlying cloud infrastructure including network, servers, operating systems, storage, or even individual application capabilities, with the possible exception of limited user-specific application configuration settings."

Any application that can be accessed using a Web browser can be considered as an example of SaaS. These points are illustrated in Figure 9.2. The SaaS provider controls all the layers apart from the application. Users who log in to the SaaS service can both use the application as well as configure the application for their use. For example, users can use Salesforce.com (Salesforce.com, Inc., San Francisco, CA) to store their customer data. They can also configure the application, for example, by requesting additional space for storage or adding additional fields to the customer data that are already being used. When configuration settings are changed, the SaaS infrastructure performs any management tasks required (e.g., allocation of additional storage) to support the changed configuration. SaaS platforms are targeted towards users who want to use the application without any software installation [in fact, the motto of Salesforce.com (Salesforce.com, Inc., San Francisco, CA), one of the prominent SaaS vendors, is "no software"]. However, for advanced usage, some small amount of programming or scripting may be necessary to customize the application for usage by the business (e.g., adding additional fields to customer data). In fact, SaaS platforms like Salesforce.com (Salesforce.com, Inc., San Francisco, CA) allow many of these customizations to be performed without programming, albeit by specifying business rules that are simple enough for nonprogrammers to implement. Prominent SaaS applications include Salesforce.com (Salesforce.com, Inc., San Francisco, CA) for customer relationship management; Google Docs (Google, Mountain View, CA) for document sharing; and web email systems such as Gmail (Google, Mountain View, CA), Hotmail (Microsoft Corporation, Redmond, WA), and Yahoo! Mail (Oath Inc., Sunnyvale, CA). IT vendors such as Hewlett-Packard (Palo Alto, CA) and IBM Corporation (Armonk, NY) also sell systems that can be configured to set up SaaSs in a private cloud; SAP (SAP SE, Walldorf, Germany), for example, can be used as a SaaS offering inside an enterprise.

Table 9.3 presents a comparison of the three cloud delivery models.

TABLE 9.3

Comparison of Cloud Delivery Models

Service Type	IaaS	PaaS	SaaS
Service category	VM rental; online storage	Online operating environment, online database, online message queue	Application and software rental
Service customization	Server template	Logic resource template	Application template
Service provisioning	Automation	Automation	Automation
Service accessing and using	Remote console, Web 2.0	Online development and debugging, integration of offline development tools and cloud	Web 2.0
Service monitoring	Physical resource monitoring	Logic resource monitoring	Application monitoring
Service level management	Dynamic orchestration of physical resources	Dynamic orchestration of logic resources	Dynamic orchestration of application
Service resource optimization	Network visualization, server visualization, storage visualization	Large-scale distributed file system. Database, middleware, etc.	Multitenancy
Service measurement	Physical resource metering	Logic resource usage metering	Business resource usage metering
Service integration and combination	Load balance	SOA	SOA, mashup
Service security	Storage encryption and isolation, VM isolation, VLAN; SSL/SSH	Data isolation, operating environment isolation, SSL	Data isolation, operating environment isolation, SSL; Web authentication and authorization

9.4 Cloud Deployment Models

9.4.1 Private Clouds

A private cloud has an exclusive purpose for a particular organization. The cloud resources may be located on or off the premises and could be owned and managed by either the consuming organization or a third party. This may be an example of an organization that has decided to adopt the infrastructure cost-saving potential of a virtualized architecture on top of existing hardware. In effect, the organization feels unable to remotely host its data, so it looks to the cloud to improve resource utilization and automate the management of such resources. Alternatively, an organization may wish to extend its current IT capability by using an exclusive, private cloud that is remotely accessible and provisioned by a third party. Such an organization may feel uncomfortable with its data being held alongside a potential competitor's data in the multitenancy model.

9.4.2 Public Clouds

A public cloud, as its name implies, is available to the general public and is managed by an organization. The organization may be a business [such as Google (Mountain View, CA)], academic, or a governmental department. The cloud computing provider owns and manages the cloud infrastructure. The existence of many different consumers within one cloud architecture is referred to as a multitenancy model.

9.4.3 Hybrid Clouds

Hybrid clouds are formed when more than one type of cloud infrastructure is utilized for a particular situation. For instance, an organization may rely on a public cloud for some aspect of its business, yet also have a private cloud on the premises for data that are sensitive. As organizations start to exploit cloud service models, it is increasingly likely that a hybrid model will most commonly be adopted, as the specific characteristics of each of the different service models are harnessed in this approach. The key enabler here is the open standards by which data and applications are implemented, since, if portability does not exist, then vendor lock-in to a particular cloud computing provider becomes likely. Lack of data and application portability has been a major hindrance for the widespread uptake of grid computing, and this is one aspect of cloud computing that can facilitate much more flexible, abstract architectures.

9.4.4 Community Clouds

Community clouds are a model of cloud computing wherein the resources exist for a number of parties who have a shared interest or cause. This model is very similar to the single-purpose grids that collaborating research and academic organizations have created to conduct large-scale scientific experiments. The cloud is owned and managed by one or more of the collaborators in the community and it may exist either on or off the premises.

9.5 Cloud Benefits

Cloud computing is an attractive paradigm that promises numerous benefits, inherent in the characteristics, as mentioned earlier. These include:

- Optimization of a company's capital investment by reducing costs of purchasing hardware and software, resulting in a much lower total cost of ownership and, ultimately, a whole new way of looking at the economics of scale and operational IT
- Simplicity and agility of operations and use, requiring minimal time and effort to provision additional resources
- Enables an enterprise to tap into a talent pool, as and when needed, for a fraction of the cost of hiring staff or retaining the existing staff and, thus, enabling the key personnel in the organizations to focus more on producing value and innovation for the business
- Allows small organizations to access IT services and resources that would otherwise be out of their reach, thus placing large organizations and small businesses on a more level playing field
- Provides novel and complex computing architectures and innovation potential
- Furnishes a mechanism for disaster recovery and business continuity through a variety of fully outsourced ICT services and resources

Cloud computing can be massively scalable, and there are built-in benefits of efficiency, availability, and high utilization that, in turn, result in reduced capital expenditure and reduced operational costs. It permits seamless sharing and collaboration through virtualization. In general, cloud computing promises cost savings, agility, innovation, flexibility, and simplicity. The offerings from vendors, in terms of services of the application, platform, and infrastructure, are continuing to mature and the cost savings are becoming particularly attractive in the current competitive economic climate. Another broader aim of cloud technology is to make supercomputing available to the enterprises, in particular, and the public, in general.

The major benefits of the cloud paradigm can be distilled to its inherent flexibility and resiliency, the potential for reducing costs, the availability of very large amounts of centralized data storage, the existence of the means to rapidly deploy computing resources, and its scalability.

1. Flexibility and resiliency: A major benefit of cloud computing is the flexibility, though cloud providers cannot provide infinite configuration and provisioning flexibility and will seek to offer structured alternatives. They might offer a choice among a number of computing and storage resource configurations at different capabilities and costs, and the cloud customer will have to adjust his or her requirements to fit one of those models.

   The flexibility offered by cloud computing can be in terms of:

   • Automated provisioning of new services and technologies
   • Acquiring increased resources on an as-needed basis
   • Ability to focus on innovation instead of maintenance details
   • Device independence
   • Freedom from having to install software patches
   • Freedom from concerns about updating servers

   Resiliency is achieved through the availability of multiple redundant resources and locations. As autonomic computing becomes more mature, self-management and self-healing mechanisms can ensure the increased reliability and robustness of cloud resources. Also, disaster recovery and business continuity planning are inherent in using the provider's cloud computing platforms.

2. Reduced costs: Cloud computing offers reductions in system administration, provisioning expenses, energy costs, software licensing fees, and hardware costs. The cloud paradigm, in general, is a basis for cost savings because capability and resources can be paid for incrementally without the need for large investments in computing infrastructure. This model is especially true for adding storage costs for large database applications. Therefore, capital costs are reduced and replaced by manageable, scalable operating expenses.

   There might be some instances, particularly for long-term, stable computing configuration usage, wherein cloud computation might not have a cost advantage over using one's internal resources or directly leasing equipment.

   For example, if the volume of data storage and computational resources required are essentially constant and there is no need for rapid provisioning and flexibility, an organization's local computational capabilities might be more cost-effective to employ than using a cloud.

Resources are used more efficiently in cloud computing, resulting in substantial support and energy cost savings. The need for highly trained and expensive IT personnel is also reduced; client organizational support and maintenance costs are reduced dramatically because these expenses are transferred to the cloud provider, including 24/7 support that in turn is spread onto a much larger base of multiple tenants or clients.

Another reason for migrating to the cloud is the drastic reduction in the cost of power and energy consumption.

3. Centralized data storage: Many data centers are an ensemble of legacy applications, operating systems, hardware, and software and are a support and maintenance nightmare. This situation requires more specialized maintenance personnel, increased costs because of lack of standardization, and a higher risk of crashes. The cloud not only offers a larger amounts of data storage resources than are normally available in local, corporate computing systems but also enables a decrease or increase in the resources used per requirements, with the corresponding adjustments in operating cost. This centralization of storage infrastructure results in cost efficiencies in utilities, real estate, and trained personnel. Also, data protection mechanisms are much easier to implement and monitor in a centralized system than on large numbers of computing platforms that might be widely distributed geographically in different parts of an organization.

4. Reduced time to deployment: In a competitive environment where rapid evaluation, development, and deployment of new approaches, processes, solutions, or offerings is critical, the cloud offers the means to use powerful computational or large storage resources on short notice within a small period of time, without requiring sizeable initial investments of money, efforts, or time (in hardware, software, and personnel). Thus, this rapid provisioning of the latest technologically upgraded and enhanced resources can be accomplished at a relatively small cost (with minimal costs associated with replacing discontinued resources) and offers the client access to advanced technologies that are constantly being acquired by the cloud provider. Improved delivery of services obtained by rapid cloud provisioning improves time to market and, hence, market growth.

5. Scalability: Cloud computing provides the means, within limits, for a client to rapidly provision computational resources to meet increases or decreases in demand. Cloud scalability provides for optimal resources so that computing resources are provisioned per requirements seamlessly, ensuring maximum cost-benefit to the clients. Since the cloud provider operates on a multitenancy utility model, the client organization has to pay only for the resources it is using at any particular time.

9.6 Cloud Technologies

Virtualization is widely incorporated to deliver customizable computing environments on demand. Virtualization technology is one of the fundamental components of cloud computing. Virtualization allows for the creation of a secure, customizable, and isolated execution environment for running applications without affecting other users' applications. The basis of this technology is the ability of a computer program—or a combination of software and hardware—to emulate an executing environment separate from the one that hosts such programs. For instance, we can run a Windows operating system (Microsoft Corporation, Redmond, WA) on top of a virtual machine, which itself is running on the Linux operating system. Virtualization provides a great opportunity to build elastically scalable systems that can provision additional capability with minimum costs.

9.6.1 Virtualization

Resource virtualization is at the heart of most cloud architectures. The concept of virtualization allows for an abstract, logical view of the physical resources to be realized and includes servers, data stores, networks, and software. The basic idea is to pool physical resources and manage them as a whole. Individual requests can then be served as required from these resource pools. For instance, it is possible to dynamically generate a certain platform for a specific application at the very moment when it is needed—that is, instead of a real machine, a virtual machine is instituted.

Resource management grows increasingly complex as the scale of a system as well as the number of users and the diversity of applications using the system increase. Resource management for a community of users with a wide range of applications running under different operating systems is a very difficult problem. Resource management becomes even more complex when resources are oversubscribed and users are uncooperative. In addition to external factors, resource management is affected by internal factors, such as the heterogeneity of the hardware and software systems, the ability to approximate the global state of the system and to redistribute the load, and the failure rates of different components. The traditional solution for these problems in a data center is to install standard operating systems on individual systems and rely on conventional operating system techniques to ensure resource sharing, application protection, and performance isolation. System administration, accounting, security, and resource management are very challenging for the providers of service in this setup; application development and performance optimization are equally challenging for the users.

The alternative is resource virtualization, a technique analyzed in this chapter. Virtualization is a basic tenet of cloud computing—which simplifies some of the resource management tasks. For instance, the state of a virtual machine (VM) running under a VM monitor (VMM) can be saved and migrated to another server to balance the load. At the same time, virtualization allows users to operate in environments with which they are familiar, rather than forcing them to work in idiosyncratic environments. Resource sharing in a virtual machine environment requires not only ample hardware support and, in particular, powerful processors but also architectural support for multilevel control. Indeed, resources such as central processing unit cycles, memory, secondary storage, and input/output and communication bandwidth are shared among several virtual machines; for each VM, resources must be shared among multiple instances of an application. There are two distinct approaches for virtualization:

- Full virtualization: This is feasible when the hardware abstraction provided by the VMM is an exact replica of the physical hardware. In this case, any operating system running on the hardware will run without modifications under the VMM.
- Paravirtualization: This requires some modifications of the guest operating systems because the hardware abstraction provided by the VMM does not support all of the functions the hardware performs.

One of the primary reasons that companies have implemented virtualization is to improve the performance and efficiency of processing of a diverse mix of workloads. Rather than assigning a dedicated set of physical resources to each set of tasks, a pooled set of virtual resources can quickly be allocated as needed across all workloads. Reliance on a pool of virtual resources allows companies to improve latency. This increase in service delivery speed and efficiency is a function of the distributed nature of virtualized environments and helps to improve overall time-to-realize value. Using a distributed set of physical resources, such as servers, in a more flexible and efficient way delivers significant benefits in terms of cost savings and improvements in productivity:

1. Virtualization of physical resources (e.g., servers, storage, and networks) enables substantial improvement in the utilization of these resources.
2. Virtualization enables improved control over the usage and performance of IT resources.
3. Virtualization provides a level of automation and standardization to optimize the computing environment.
4. Virtualization provides a foundation for cloud computing.

Virtualization increases the efficiency of the cloud that makes many complex systems easier to optimize. As a result, organizations have been able to achieve the performance and optimization to be able to access data that were previously either unavailable or very hard to collect. Big data platforms are increasingly used as sources of enormous amounts of data about customer preferences, sentiment, and behaviors (see Section 8.1.1). Companies can integrate this information with internal sales and product data to gain insight into customer preferences to make more targeted and personalized offers.

9.6.1.1 Characteristics of a Virtualized Environment

In a virtualized environment, there are three major components: guest, host, and virtualization layer. The guest represents the system component that interacts with the virtualization layer rather than with the host, as would normally happen. The host represents the original environment where the guest is supposed to be managed. The virtualization layer is responsible for recreating the same or a different environment where the guest will operate.

Virtualization has three characteristics that support the scalability and operating efficiency required for big data environments:

1. Partitioning: In virtualization, many applications and operating systems are supported in a single physical system by partitioning (separating) the available resources.
2. Isolation: Each virtual machine is isolated from its host physical system and other virtualized machines. Because of this isolation, if one virtual instance crashes, the other virtual machines and the host system are not affected. In addition, data are not shared between one virtual instance and another.
3. Encapsulation: A virtual machine can be represented (and even stored) as a single file, so it can be identified easily based on the services it provides. For example, the file containing the encapsulated process could be a complete business service.

This encapsulated virtual machine could be presented to an application as a complete entity. Thus, encapsulation could protect each application so that it does not interfere with another application.

Virtualization abstracts the underlying resources and simplifies their use; isolates users from one another; and supports replication, which, in turn, increases the elasticity of the system. Virtualization is a critical aspect of cloud computing, equally important to the providers and consumers of cloud services, and plays an important role in the following:

- System security because it allows for the isolation of services running on the same hardware
- Portable performance and reliability because it allows for applications to migrate from one platform to another
- Development and management of services offered by a provider
- Performance isolation

1. Virtualization advantages: The process of using computer resources to imitate other resources is valued for its capability to increase IT resource utilization, efficiency, and scalability. One obvious application of virtualization is server virtualization, which helps organizations to increase the utilization of physical servers and potentially save on infrastructure costs; companies are increasingly finding that virtualization is not limited only to servers but is also valid and applicable across the entire IT infrastructure, including networks, storage, and software. For instance, one of the most important requirements for success with big data is having the right level of performance to support the analysis of large volumes and varied types of data. If a company only virtualizes the servers, they may experience bottlenecks from other infrastructure elements such as storage and networks; furthermore, they are less likely to achieve the latency and efficiency that they need and are more likely to expose the company to higher costs and increased security risks. As a result, a company's entire IT environment needs to be optimized at every layer from the network to the databases, storage, and servers—virtualization adds efficiency at every layer of the IT infrastructure.

   For a provider of IT services, the use of virtualization techniques has a number of advantages, as follows:
   a. Resource usage: Physical servers rarely work to capacity because their operators usually allow for sufficient computing resources to cover peak usage. If virtual machines are used, any load requirement can be satisfied from the resource pool. In case the demand increases, it is possible to delay or even avoid the purchase of new capacities.
   b. Management: It is possible to automate resource pool management. Virtual machines can be created and configured automatically as required.
   c. Consolidation: Different application classes can be consolidated to run on a smaller number of physical components. Besides server or storage consolidation, it is also possible to include entire system landscapes, data and databases, networks, and desktops. Consolidation leads to increased efficiency and thus to cost reduction.

d. Energy consumption: Supplying large data centers with electric power has become increasingly difficult and, over its lifetime, the cost of energy required to operate a server is higher than its purchase price. Consolidation reduces the number of physical components. This, in turn, reduces the expenses for energy supply.

e. Less space required: Each and every square yard of data center space is scarce and expensive. With consolidation, the same performance can be obtained on a smaller footprint and the costly expansion of an existing data center might possibly be avoided.

f. Emergency planning: It is possible to move virtual machines from one resource pool to another. This ensures better availability of the services and makes it easier to comply with service-level agreements. Hardware maintenance windows are inherently no longer required.

2. Virtualization benefits: Since the providers of cloud services tend to build very large resource centers, virtualization leads not only to a size advantage but also to a more favorable cost situation. This results in the following benefits for the customer:

a. Dynamic behavior: Any request can be satisfied just in time and without any delays. In case of bottlenecks, a virtual machine can draw on additional resources (such as storage space and input/output capabilities).

b. Availability: Services are highly available and can be used day and night without stop. In the event of technology upgrades, it is possible to hot-migrate applications because virtual machines can easily be moved to an up-to-date system.

c. Access: The virtualization layer isolates each virtual machine from the others and from the physical infrastructure. This way, virtual systems feature multitenant capabilities and, using a roles concept, it is possible to safely delegate management functionality to the customer. Customers can purchase IT capabilities from a self-service portal (customer emancipation).

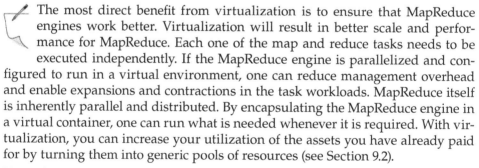 The most direct benefit from virtualization is to ensure that MapReduce engines work better. Virtualization will result in better scale and performance for MapReduce. Each one of the map and reduce tasks needs to be executed independently. If the MapReduce engine is parallelized and configured to run in a virtual environment, one can reduce management overhead and enable expansions and contractions in the task workloads. MapReduce itself is inherently parallel and distributed. By encapsulating the MapReduce engine in a virtual container, one can run what is needed whenever it is required. With virtualization, you can increase your utilization of the assets you have already paid for by turning them into generic pools of resources (see Section 9.2).

3. Virtualization challenges: There are side effects of virtualization, notably the performance penalty and the hardware costs. All privileged operations of a VM must be trapped and validated by the VMM, which ultimately controls system behavior; the increased overhead has a negative impact on performance. The cost of the hardware for a VM is higher than the cost for a system running a traditional operating system because the physical hardware is shared among a set of guest operating systems and is typically configured with faster and/or multicore processors, more memory, larger disks, and additional network interfaces as compared with a system running a traditional operating system.

A drawback of virtualization is the fact that the operation of the abstraction layer itself requires resources. Modern virtualization techniques, however, are so sophisticated that this overhead is not too significant: due to the particularly effective interaction of current multicore systems with virtualization technology, this performance loss plays only a minor role in today's systems. In view of possible savings and the quality benefits perceived by the customers, the use of virtualization pays off in nearly all cases.

9.6.2 Service-Oriented Computing

Service-oriented architecture (SOA) introduces a flexible architectural style that provides an integration framework through which software architects can build applications using a collection of reusable functional units (services) with well-defined interfaces, which it combines in a logical flow. Applications are integrated at the interface (contract) and not at the implementation level. This allows for greater flexibility, since applications are built to work with any implementation of a contract, rather than to take advantage of a feature or idiosyncrasy of a particular system or implementation. For example, different service providers (of the same interface) can be dynamically chosen based on policies, such as price, performance, or other quality of system guarantees, current transaction volume, and so on.

Another important characteristic of an SOA is that it allows many-to-many integration; that is, a variety of consumers across an enterprise can use and reuse applications in a variety of ways. This ability can dramatically reduce the cost/complexity of integrating incompatible applications and increase the ability of developers to quickly create, reconfigure, and repurpose applications as business needs arise. Benefits include reduced IT administration costs, ease of business process integration across organizational departments and with trading partners, and increased business adaptability.

SOA is a logical way of designing a software system to provide services to either end-user applications or to other services distributed in a network, via published and discoverable interfaces. To achieve this, SOA reorganizes a portfolio of previously siloed software applications and support infrastructure in an organization into an interconnected collection of services, each of which is discoverable and accessible through standard interfaces and messaging protocols. Once all of the elements of an SOA are in place, existing and future applications can access the SOA-based services as necessary. This architectural approach is particularly applicable when multiple applications running on varied technologies and platforms need to communicate with one another.

The essential goal of an SOA is to enable general-purpose interoperability among existing technologies and extensibility to future purposes and architectures. SOA lowers interoperability hurdles by converting monolithic and static systems into modular and flexible components, which it represents as services that can be requested through an industry standard protocol. Much of SOA's power and flexibility derives from its ability to leverage standards-based functional services, calling them when needed on an individual basis or aggregating them to create composite applications or multistage business processes. The building-block services might employ preexisting components that are reused and can also be updated or replaced without affecting the functionality or integrity of other independent services. In this latter regard, the services model offers numerous advantages over large monolithic applications, in which modifications to some portions of the code can have unintended and unpredictable effects on the rest of the code to which it is tightly bundled. Simply put, an SOA is an architectural style, inspired by the service-oriented approach to computing and designed for enabling extensible interoperability.

SOA as a design philosophy is independent of any specific technology, for example, Web services or Java Platform, Enterprise Edition. Although the concept of SOA is often discussed in conjunction with Web services, the two are not synonymous. In fact, SOA can be implemented without the use of Web services, for example, using Java, C#, or Java Platform, Enterprise Edition. However, Web services should be seen as a primary example of a message delivery model that makes it much easier to deploy an SOA. Web services standards are key to enabling interoperability as well as important issues including quality of system, system semantics, security, management, and reliable messaging.

9.6.2.1 Advantages of Service-Oriented Architecture

Enterprises may use SOA for the following:

> Implementing end-to-end collaborative business processes: The term end-to-end business process signifies that a succession of automated business processes and information systems in different enterprises (which are typically involved in inter-company business transactions) are successfully integrated. The aim is to provide seamless interoperation and interactive links between all the relevant members in an extended enterprise—ranging from product designers, suppliers, trading partners, and logistics providers to end customers. At this stage, an organization moves into the highest strategic level of SOA implementation. Deployment of services becomes ubiquitous, and federated services collaborate across enterprise boundaries to create complex products and services. Individual services in this extended enterprise may originate from many providers, irrespective of company-specific systems or applications.

> Implementing enterprise service orchestrations: This basic SOA entry point focuses on a typical implementation within a department or between a small number of departments and enterprise assets and includes two steps. The first step is transforming enterprise assets and applications into an SOA implementation. This can start by service-enabling existing individual applications or by creating new applications using Web services technology. This can begin by specifying a Web service interface into an individual application or application element (including legacy systems). The next step after this basic Web service implementation is executing service orchestrations out of the service-enabled assets or newly created service applications.

> Service enabling the entire enterprise: The next stage in the SOA entry point hierarchy is when an enterprise seeks to provide a set of common services based on SOA components that can be used across the entire organization. Enterprise-wide service integration is achieved on the basis of commonly accepted standards. This results in achieving service consistency across departmental boundaries and is a precursor to integrating an organization with its partners and suppliers. Consistency is an important factor for this configuration, as it provides both a uniform view to the enterprise and its customers as well as helps to ensure compliance with statutory or business policy requirements.

 One problem that arises when implementing an SOA at the enterprise level or when implementing a cross-enterprise collaborative SOA is how to manage the SOA model, how to categorize the elements in this model, and how to organize them in such a way that the different stakeholders reviewing the model can understand it. Toward this end, it is often convenient to think of the SOA as comprising a number of distinct layers of abstraction that emphasize service interfaces, service realizations, and compositions of services into higher-level business processes. Each of these describes a logical separation of concerns by defining a set of common enterprise elements; each layer uses the functionality of the layer below it, adding new functionality, to accomplish its objective. The logical flow employed in the layered SOA development model may focus on a top-down development approach, which emphasizes how business processes are decomposed into a collection of business services and how these services are implemented in terms of preexisting enterprise assets.

9.6.2.2 Layers in Service-Oriented Architecture

SOA can considered to include the following six distinct layers:

1. Domains: A business domain is a functional domain composed of a set of current and future business processes that share common capabilities and functionality and which can collaborate with each other to accomplish a higher-level business objective, such as loans, insurance, banking, finance, manufacturing, marketing, and human resources.

2. Business processes: This layer is formed by subdividing a business domain, such as distribution, into a small number of core business processes, such as purchasing, order management, and inventory, which are made entirely standard for use throughout the enterprise; having a large number of fine-grained processes leads to tremendous overhead and inefficiency and, hence, having a small collection of coarser-grained processes that are usable in multiple scenarios is a better option.

3. Business services: For any process, the right business services is to subdivide it into increasingly smaller subprocesses until the process cannot be divided any further. The resulting subprocesses then become candidate-indivisible (singular) business services for implementation. Business services automate generic business tasks that provide value to an enterprise and are part of standard business process. The more processes that an enterprise decomposes in this way, the more commonality across these subprocesses can be achieved. In this way, an enterprise has the chance of building an appropriate set of reusable business services.

   This layer relies on the orchestration interface of a collection of business-aligned services to realize reconfigurable end-to-end business processes. Individual services or collections of services that exhibit various levels of granularity are combined and orchestrated to produce new composite services that not only introduce new levels of reuse but also allow the reconfiguration of business processes.

   The interfaces get exported as service descriptions in this layer using a service description language, such as Web Services Description Language. The service description can be implemented by a number of service providers, each offering various choices of qualities of service based on technical requirements in the areas of availability, performance, scalability, and security.

   During the exercise of defining business services, it is also important to take existing utility logic, ingrained in code, and expose it as services, which themselves become candidate services that specify not the overall business process but rather the mechanism for implementing the process. This exercise should thus yield two categories of services: business functionality services that are reusable across multiple processes and a collection of fine-grained utility (or commodity) services, which provide value to and are shared by business services across the organization. Examples of utility services include services implementing calculations, algorithms, and directory management services.

4. Infrastructure services: Infrastructure services are subdivided into technical utility services, access services, management and monitoring services, and interaction services; these are not specific to any single line of business but rather are reusable across multiple lines of business. They also include mechanisms that seamlessly interlink services that span enterprises. This can, for example, include the policies, constraints, and specific industry messages and interchange standards (such as the need to conform to specific industry message as well as interchange standards like Electronic Data Interchange for Administration, Commerce, and Transport; SWIFT; xCBL; eBusiness Extensible Markup Language Business Process Specification Schema; or RosettaNet) that an enterprise, say within a particular vertical marketplace, must conform to in order to work with other similar processes. Access services are dedicated to transforming data and integrating legacy applications and functions into the SOA environment. This includes the wrapping and service enablement of legacy functions.

5. Service realizations: This layer is the component realization layer that uses components for implementing services out of preexisting applications and systems found in the operational systems layer. Components comprise autonomous units of software that may provide a useful service or a set of functionality to a client (business service) and have meaning in isolation from other components with which they interoperate.

6. Operational systems: This layer is used by components to implement business services and processes. This layer contains existing enterprise systems or applications, including customer relationship management and enterprise resource planning systems, as well as applications, legacy applications, database systems and applications, and other packaged applications. These systems are usually known as enterprise information systems.

9.7 Business Processes with Service-Oriented Architecture

Every enterprise has unique characteristics that are embedded in its business processes. Most enterprises perform a similar set of repeatable routine activities that may include the development of manufacturing products and services, bringing these products and services to market and satisfying the customers who purchase them. Automated business processes can perform such activities. We may view an automated business process as a precisely choreographed sequence of activities systematically directed toward performing a certain business task and bringing it to completion. Examples of typical processes in manufacturing firms include, among other things, new product development (which cuts across research and development, marketing, and manufacturing); customer order fulfillment (which combines sales, manufacturing, warehousing, transportation, and billing); and financial asset management. The possibility to design, structure, and measure processes as well as determine their contribution to customer value makes them an important starting point for business improvement and innovation initiatives.

The largest possible process in an organization is the value chain. The value chain is decomposed into a set of core business processes and support processes that are necessary to produce a product or product line. These core business processes are subdivided into activities. An activity is an element that performs a specific function within a process. Activities can be as simple as sending or receiving a message or as complex as coordinating the execution of other processes and activities. A business process may encompass complex activities, some of which run on back-end systems, such as a credit check, automated billing, a purchase order, stock updates and shipping, or even such frivolous activities as sending a document or filling out a form. A business process activity may invoke another business process in the same or a different business system domain. Activities will inevitably vary greatly from one company to another and from one business analysis effort to another.

At runtime, a business process definition may have multiple instantiations, each operating independently of the other, and each instantiation may have multiple activities that are concurrently active. A process instance is a defined thread of activity that is being enacted (managed) by a workflow engine. In general, instances of a process, its current state, and the history of its actions will be visible at runtime and expressed in terms of the business process definition so that the following can occur:

- Users can determine the status of business activities and business
- Specialists can monitor the activity and identify potential improvements to the business process definition

9.7.1 Process

A process is an ordering of activities with a beginning and an end; it has inputs (in terms of resources, materials, and information) and a specified output (the results it produces). We may thus define a process as any sequence of steps that is initiated by an event; transforms information, materials, or commitments; and produces an output. A business process is typically associated with operational objectives and business relationships, for example, an insurance claims process or an engineering development process. A process may be wholly contained within a single organizational unit or may span different enterprises, such as in a customer–supplier relationship. Typical examples of processes that cross organizational boundaries are purchasing and sales processes jointly set up by buying and selling organizations, supported by EDI and value-added networks. The Internet is now a trigger for the design of new business processes and the redesign of existing ones.

A business process is a set of logically related tasks performed to achieve a well-defined business outcome. A (business) process view implies a horizontal view of a business organization and looks at processes as sets of interdependent activities designed and structured to produce a specific output for a customer or a market. A business process defines the results to be achieved, the context of the activities, the relationships between the activities, and the interactions with other processes and resources. A business process may receive events that alter the state of the process and the sequence of activities. A business process may produce events for input to other applications or processes. It may also invoke applications to perform computational functions as well as post assignments to human work lists to request actions by human actors. Business processes can be measured, and different performance measures apply, such as cost, quality, time, and customer satisfaction.

A business process has the following behaviors:

- It may contain defined conditions triggering its initiation in each new instance (e.g., the arrival of a claim) and defined outputs at its completion.
- It may involve formal or relatively informal interactions between participants.
- It has a duration that may vary widely.
- It may contain a series of automated activities and/or manual activities. Activities may be large and complex, involving the flow of materials, information, and business commitments.
- It exhibits a very dynamic nature, so it can respond to demands from customers and to changing market conditions.
- It is widely distributed and customized across boundaries within and between enterprises, often spanning multiple applications with very different technology platforms.
- It is usually long-running—a single instance of a process such as order to cash may run for months or even years.

Every business process implies processing: a series of activities (processing steps) leading to some form of transformation of data or products for which the process exists. Transformations may be executed manually or in an automated way. A transformation will encompass multiple processing steps. Finally, every process delivers a product, such as a mortgage or an authorized invoice. The extent to which the end product of a process can be specified in advance and can be standardized impacts the way that processes and their workflows can be structured and automated.

Processes have decision points. Decisions have to be made with regard to routing and allocation of processing capacity. In a highly predictable and standardized environment, the trajectory in the process of a customer order will be established in advance in a standard way. Only if the process is complex and if the conditions of the process are not predictable will routing decisions have to be made on the spot. In general, the customer orders will be split into a category that is highly proceduralized (and thus automated) and a category that is complex and uncertain. Here, human experts will be needed, and manual processing is a key element of the process.

9.7.2 Workflow

A workflow system automates a business process, in whole or in part, during which documents, information, or tasks are passed from one participant to another for action, according to a set of procedural rules. Workflows are based on document life cycles and form-based information processing, so, generally, they support well-defined, static, clerical processes. They also provide transparency, since business processes are clearly articulated in the software, and are agile because they produce definitions that are fast to deploy and change.

A workflow can be defined as the sequence of processing steps (execution of business operations, tasks, and transactions), during which information and physical objects are passed from one processing step to another. Workflow is a concept that links together technologies and tools able to automatically route events and tasks with programs or users.

Process-oriented workflows are used to automate processes whose structure is well-defined and stable over time, which often coordinate subprocesses executed by machines and which only require minor user involvement (often only in specific cases). An order management process or a loan request is an example of a well-defined process. Certain process-oriented workflows may have transactional properties. The process-oriented workflow is made up of tasks that follow routes, with checkpoints represented by business rules—for example, a pause for a credit approval. Such business process rules govern the overall processing of activities, including the routing of requests, the assignment or distribution of requests to designated roles, the passing of workflow data from activity to activity, and the dependencies and relationships between business process activities.

A workflow involves activities, decision points, rules, routes, and roles. These are briefly described later. Just like a process, a workflow normally comprises a number of logical steps, each of which is known as an activity. An activity is a set of actions that are guided by the workflow. An activity may involve manual interaction with a user or workflow participant or may be executed using diverse resources such as application programs or databases. A work item or dataset is created and is processed and changed in stages at a number of processing or decision points to meet specific business goals. Most workflow engines can handle very complex series of processes.

A workflow can depict various aspects of a business process including automated and manual activities, decision points and business rules, parallel and sequential work routes, and how to manage exceptions to the normal business process. A workflow can have logical decision points that determine which branch of the flow a work item may take in the event of alternative paths. Every alternate path within the flow is identified and controlled through a bounded set of logical decision points. An instantiation of a workflow to support a work item includes all possible paths from beginning to end.

Within a workflow, business rules at each decision point determine how workflow-related data are to be processed, routed, tracked, and controlled. Business rules are core business policies that capture the nature of an enterprise's business model and define the conditions that must be met in order to move to the next stage of the workflow. Business rules are represented as compact statements about an aspect of the business that can be expressed within an application and, as such, determine the route to be followed. For instance, for a health care application, business rules may include policies on how new claims validation, referral requirements, or special procedure approvals are implemented. Business rules can represent among other things typical business situations such as escalation (e.g., "send this document to a supervisor for approval") and managing exceptions (e.g., "this loan is more than $50,000; send it to the MD").

9.7.3 Business Process Management

Business process management (BPM) is a commitment to expressing, understanding, representing, and managing a business (or the portion of business to which it is applied) in terms of a collection of business processes that are responsive to a business environment of internal or external events. The phrase *management of business processes* includes process analysis, process definition and redefinition, resource allocation, scheduling, measurement of process quality and efficiency, and process optimization. Process optimization includes collection and analysis of both real-time measures (monitoring) and strategic measures (performance management) as well as their correlation as the basis for process improvement and innovation. A BPM solution is a graphical productivity tool for modeling, integrating, monitoring, and optimizing process flows of all sizes, crossing any application, company boundary, or human interaction. BPM codifies value-driven processes and institutionalizes their execution within the enterprise. This implies that BPM tools can help to analyze, define, and enforce process standardization. BPM provides a modeling tool to visually construct, analyze, and execute cross-functional business processes.

BPM is more than process automation or traditional workflow. BPM within the context of enterprise application integration and e-business integration provides the flexibility necessary to automate cross-functional processes. It adds conceptual innovations and technology from enterprise application integration and e-business integration and reimplements it on an e-business infrastructure based on Web and XML standards. Conventional applications provide traditional workflow features that work well only within their local environment. However, integrated process management is then required for processes spanning enterprises. Automating cross-functional activities, such as checking or confirming inventory between an enterprise and its distribution partners, enables corporations to manage processes by exception based on real-time events driven from the integrated environment. Process execution then becomes automated, requiring human intervention only in situations where exceptions occur; for example, inventory level has fallen below a critical threshold or manual tasks and approvals are required.

The distinction between BPM and workflow is mainly based on the management aspect of BPM systems: BPM tools place considerable emphasis on management and business functions. Although BPM technology covers the same space as workflow, its focus is on the business user and provides more sophisticated management and analysis capabilities. With a BPM tool, the business user is able to manage all the processes of a certain type, for example, claim processes, and should be able to study them from historical or current data and produce costs or other business measurements. In addition, the business user should also be able to analyze and compare the data or business measurements based on the different types of claims. This type of functionality is typically not provided by modern workflow systems.

9.7.4 Business Processes via Web Services

Business processes management and workflow systems today support the definition, execution, and monitoring of long-running processes that coordinate the activities of multiple business applications. However, because these systems are activity-oriented and not communication (message)-oriented, they do not separate internal implementation from external protocol description. When processes span business boundaries, loose coupling based on precise external protocols is required because the parties involved do not share application and workflow implementation technologies and will not allow external control over the use of their backend applications. Such business interaction protocols are by necessity message-centric; they specify the flow of messages representing business actions among trading partners, without requiring any specific implementation mechanism. With such applications, the loosely coupled, distributed nature of the Web enables exhaustive and full orchestration, choreography, and monitoring of the enterprise applications that expose the Web services participating in the message exchanges.

Web services provide a standard and interoperable means of integrating loosely coupled Web-based components that expose well-defined interfaces, while abstracting the implementation- and platform-specific details. Core Web service standards such as Simple Object Access Protocol; Web Services Description Language; and Universal Description,

Discovery, and Integration provide a solid foundation to accomplish this. However, these specifications primarily enable the development of simple Web service applications that can conduct simple interactions. The ultimate goal of Web services, though, is to facilitate and automate business process collaborations both inside and outside of the enterprise's boundaries. Useful business applications of Web services in enterprise application integration and business-to-business environments require the ability to compose complex and distributed Web service integrations and the ability to describe the relationships between the constituent low-level services. In this way, collaborative business processes can be realized as Web service integrations.

A business process specifies the potential execution order of operations originating from a logically interrelated collection of Web services, each of which performs a well-defined activity within the process. A business process also specifies the shared data passed between these services, the external partners' roles with respect to the process, joint exception handling conditions for the collection of Web services, and other factors that may influence how Web services or organizations participate in a process. This would enable long-running transactions between Web services in order to increase the consistency and reliability of business processes that are composed out of these Web services.

The orchestration and choreography of Web services are enabled under three specification standards, namely, the Business Process Execution Language (BPEL) for Web Services, WS-Coordination, and WS-Transaction. These three specifications work together to form the bedrock for reliably choreographing Web service-based applications, providing BPM, transactional integrity, and generic coordination facilities. BPEL is a workflow-like definition language that describes sophisticated business processes that can orchestrate Web services. WS-Coordination and WS-Transaction complement BPEL to provide mechanisms for defining specific standard protocols for use by transaction processing systems, workflow systems, or other applications that wish to coordinate multiple Web services.

9.7.4.1 Service Composition

The platform-neutral nature of services creates the opportunity for building composite services by combining existing elementary or complex services (the component services) from different enterprises and in turn offering them as high-level services or processes. Composite services (and, thus, processes) integrate multiple services—and put together new business functions—by combining new and existing application assets in a logical flow.

The definition of composite services requires coordinating the flow of control and data between the constituent services. Business logic can be seen as the ingredient that sequences, coordinates, and manages interactions among Web services. By programming a complex, cross-enterprise workflow task or business transaction, it is possible to logically chain discrete Web services activities into cross-enterprise business processes. This is enabled through orchestration and choreography (because Web services technologies support coordination and offer an asynchronous and message-oriented way to communicate and interact with application logic).

1. Orchestration: This describes how Web services can interact with each other at the message level, including the business logic and execution order of the interactions from the perspective and under the control of a single endpoint. This is, for

instance, demonstrated in the case of a process flow wherein the business process flow is seen from the vantage point of a single supplier. Orchestration refers to an executable business process that may result in a long-lived, transactional, multi-step process model. With orchestration, business process interactions are always controlled from the (private) perspective of one of the business parties involved in the process.

2. Choreography: This is typically associated with the public (globally visible) message exchanges, rules of interaction, and agreements that occur between multiple business process endpoints, rather than a specific business process that is executed by a single party. Choreography tracks the sequence of messages that may involve multiple parties and multiple sources, including customers, suppliers, and partners, where each party involved in the process describes the part it plays in the interaction and no party owns the conversation. Choreography is more collaborative in nature than orchestration. It is described from the perspectives of all parties (common view) and, in essence, defines the shared state of the interactions between business entities. This common view can be used to determine specific deployment implementations for each individual entity. Choreography offers a means by which the rules of participation for collaboration can be clearly defined and agreed to in a joint manner. Each entity may then implement its portion of the choreography as determined by their common view.

9.8 Summary

This chapter introduces the concept of cloud computing. It describes its definition, presents the cloud delivery and deployment models, and highlights its benefits for enterprises. In part of the chapter, we discussed the primary challenges faced during provisioning of cloud services, namely, scalability, multitenancy, and availability. The later part of the chapter describes virtualization technology, which is one of the fundamental components of cloud computing, Virtualization allows for the creation of a secure, customizable, and isolated execution environment for running applications without affecting other users' applications. One of the primary reasons companies implement virtualization is to improve the performance and efficiency of processing of a diverse mix of workloads. Rather than assigning a dedicated set of physical resources to each set of tasks, a pooled set of virtual resources can be quickly allocated as needed across all workloads. Virtualization provides a great opportunity to build elastically scalable systems that can provision additional capability with minimum costs. Finally, the chapter leverages SOA to explain the cloud-based realization of business processes in terms of Web services.

Section III

Enterprise Process Management Systems

As stated in the prologue, what is unique in this book is the process-centric paradigm being proposed to replace the traditional data-centric paradigm for enterprise systems. The traditional paradigm is covered in several publications including M. Weske (2012); A.H.M. ter Hofstede, W.M.P. van der Aalst, M. Adams, and N. Russell (Eds.) (2010); Jan vom Brocke and M. Rosemann (Eds.) (2014); W. M. P. van der Aalst (2002); M. Reichert and B. Weber (2012); and M. Dumas, M. La Rosa, J. Mendling, and H. Reijers (2013). Though there may seem to be a lot of apparent commonality between these and the present book, the context is quite different. This book primarily focuses on exploring various aspects of the process-oriented paradigm as an alternative to the traditional data-oriented paradigm.

Chapter 10 first introduces the concept of business process management and its characteristics. It then explains the concept of business process management systems and its variation of enterprise process management systems being brought to focus in this book.

Chapter 11 describes Business Process Modeling and Notation 2.0 (BPMN), which is a graphical notation for modeling business processes and standardizes the notation used by business experts on the one hand and information technology specialists on the other, thus finally bridging the gap between them. Using BPMN, business analysts can describe organizational processes in a way that can be understood by developers and system integrators and that can serve as a blueprint for implementing the services and orchestrations required to support those processes.

Chapter 12 describes a development methodology that would smoothly transition from requirements to implementation.

Chapter 13 discusses how BPMN 2.0 can not only capture business requirements but also provide the backbone of the actual solution implementation. The chapter also describes the use of SAP Process Orchestration to give a practical context to the discussion presented in this chapter. This overview includes descriptions of SAP Business Process Management for addressing business process management, SAP Business Rules Management to address business rules management, and SAP Process Integration for addressing the process integration management.

10

Business Process Management Systems

The advantages of a functional organization are that it is easier to adhere to standards because different groups specialize in a function or task, it expedites function-specific or vertical information flow, it achieves scale economies because each functional group is dedicated to just that function, and there is clarity in roles. On the other hand, a functional organization is typically much slower to respond to an external need because it has to coordinate action or response across multiple functions, lacks flexibility at a process level, and does not provide adequate visibility or information flow across a business process that spans multiple functions. A functional organization has been found to lead to significant coordination and control issues and to be unresponsive to customer or market needs.

A process-centric organization, in contrast, revolves around end-to-end business processes. While a function-centric organization has enabled enterprises to increase scale in the post-Industrial Revolution era, dramatic increases in scale, along with specialization, have led to organizational silos and have made them less responsive to the market, changes in customer expectations fueled by the Internet, and mobile communications. This weakness of the function-centric organization has become more apparent in today's highly dynamic world in which it is a critical competitive necessity for businesses to adapt and innovate their processes end-to-end.

Information technology can fulfill its role as a strategic differentiator only if it can provide enterprises with a mechanism to enable sustainable competitive advantage—the ability to change business processes in sync with changes in the business environment and at optimum costs. This is achievable on the foundation of service-oriented architecture (SOA), which exposes the fundamental business capabilities as flexible, reusable services; SOA along with the constituting services is the foundation of a modern business process management system (BPMS). The services support a layer of agile and flexible business processes that can be easily changed to provide new products and services to keep ahead of the competition. The most important value of SOA is that it provides an opportunity for information technology (IT) and the business to communicate and interact with one another at a highly efficient and equally understood level. That common, equally understood language is the language of business process or enterprise processes in Business Process Modeling and Notation (BPMN).

10.1 Process-Oriented Enterprise

Enterprise systems (ES) enable an organization to truly function as an integrated enterprise, with integration occurring across all functions or segments of the traditional value chain, for example sales, production, inventory, purchasing, finance and accounting, personnel and administration, and so on. They do this by modeling primarily the business processes as the basic business entities of the enterprise rather than by modeling data handled by the enterprise (as done by the traditional IT systems). However, every ES might not be completely successful in doing this. In a break with the legacy enterprise-wide solutions, modern ES treats business processes as more fundamental than data items.

Collaborations or relationships manifest themselves through the various organizational and interorganizational processes. A process may be generally defined as the set of resources and activities necessary and sufficient to convert some form of input into some form of output. Processes are internal, external, or a combination of both; they cross functional boundaries; they have starting and ending points; and they exist at all levels within the enterprise.

The significance of a process to the success of the enterprise's business is dependent on the value, with reference to the customer, of the collaboration that it addresses and represents. In other words, the nature and extent of the value addition by a process to a product or service delivered to a customer is the best index of the contribution of that process to the company's overall customer satisfaction or customer collaboration. Customer knowledge by itself is not adequate; it is only when the enterprise has effective processes for sharing this information and integrating the activities of frontline workers and displays the ability to coordinate the assignment and track the work that enterprises can become effective.

Thus, this approach not only recognizes inherently the significance of various process-related techniques and methodologies such as process innovation, business process improvement, business process redesign, business process reengineering (BPR), and business process management (BPM) but also treats them as fundamental, continuous, and integral functions of the management of a company itself. A collaborative enterprise enabled by the implementation of an ES is inherently amenable to business process involvement, which is also the essence of any total quality management-oriented effort undertaken within an enterprise.

10.1.1 Value-Added Driven Enterprise

Business processes can be seen as the very basis of the value addition within an enterprise that was traditionally attributed to various functions or divisions in an enterprise. As organizational and environmental conditions become more complex, global, and competitive, processes provide a framework for dealing effectively with the issues of performance improvement, capability development, and adaptation to the changing environment.

Along a value stream (i.e., a business process), the analysis of the absence or creation of added value or (worse) destruction of value critically determines the necessity and effectiveness of a process step. The understanding of value-adding and non-value-adding processes (or process steps) is a significant factor in the analysis, design, benchmarking, and optimization of business processes leading to BPM in the companies. BPM provides an environment for analyzing and optimizing business processes.

Values are characterized by value determinants, for example:

- Time (cycle time and so on)
- Flexibility (options, customization, composition, and so on)
- Responsiveness (lead time, number of hand-offs, and so on)
- Quality (rework, rejects, yield, and so on)
- Price (discounts, rebates, coupons, incentives, and so on)

We must hasten to add that we are not disregarding cost (i.e., materials, labor, overhead, and so forth) as a value determinant. However, the effect of cost is truly a result of a host of value determinants such as time, flexibility, and responsiveness.

The nature and extent of a value addition to a product or service is the best measure of that addition's contribution to the company's overall goal for competitiveness. Such value expectations are dependent on the following:

- The customer's experience of similar product(s) and/or service(s)
- The value delivered by the competitors
- The capabilities and limitations of locking into the base technological platform

However, value as originally defined by Michael Porter in the context of introducing the concept of the value chain is meant to be more in the nature of the cost at various stages. Rather than a value chain, it is more of a cost chain! Porter's value chain is also a structure-oriented concept and, hence, a static concept. Here, we mean value as the satisfaction of not only external but also internal customers' requirements, as defined and continuously redefined as the least total cost of acquisition, ownership, and use.

Consequently, in this formulation, one can understand the company's competitive gap in the market in terms of such process-based, customer-expected levels of value and the value delivered by the company's process for the concerned products or services. Customer responsiveness focuses on costs in terms of the yield. Therefore, we can perform market segmentation for a particular product or services in terms of the most significant customer values and the corresponding value determinants or what we term as critical value determinants.

Strategic planning exercises can then be understood readily in terms of devising strategies for improving on these process-based critical value determinants based on the competitive benchmarking of these collaborative values and processes between the enterprise and customers. These strategies and the tactics resulting from analysis, design, and optimization of the process will in turn focus on the restrategizing of all relevant business process at all levels. This can result in the modification or deletion of the process or the creation of a new one.

10.2 History of Business Process Management

10.2.1 First-Wave Business Process Management—Process Improvement (1970s–1980s)

The concept of the first wave was dominated by Fredrick Taylor's theory of scientific management, also known as Taylorism. He was able to prove that it was more efficient to standardize processes rather than look for a men with extraordinary abilities. He observed how activities were performed and measured them in terms of time and quantity. This enabled him to find the best way to perform the activity. Taylor introduced standardization around the same time as Ford introduced the assembly line.

Taylorism is fundamentally a theory that laid down the fundamental principles of large-scale manufacturing through assembly-line factories. The theory focuses on production efficiency by breaking every action, job, or task into small and simple segments that can be easily analyzed and taught. The factory workers were trained at that time to follow specific steps that required narrowly focused skills and endurance. The goal was to gain a high degree of efficiency from both machine and worker and to achieve the maximization of profit for the benefit of both workers and management.

Standardization had led to a drastic improvement in product quality and productivity. Taylor's scientific management also applied to management ranks. In his opinion, managers were responsible for motivating and monitoring their employees. In order to do this effectively, specialization in management was required. This view had led to the introduction of functional managerial departments like accounting, recruitment, production, and so on. The supervisor of a department became responsible for the available resources and had to report to a chief executive officer, who in turn was responsible for the business goals and the organization's vision.

IT emerged during the first wave. It was used to automate business activities in order to reduce labor costs, improve consistency, or increase volumes. The initiative to invest in IT was made by the individual departments, which resulted in a lack of alignment with other departments. Organizations were building a fragmented infrastructure with many standalone applications and a large overhead in functionalities and data.

The first kind of information systems for process management were the industrial computer-aided manufacturing systems. They revolutionized a large number of factories in the 1970s. The roots of modern BPM systems are fundamentally in these systems as the latter evolved gradually into a more generic type of system that could be applied also to nonindustrial processes. The earliest commercial BPM systems or actual workflow management systems were introduced in the 1980s. The earliest workflow management systems were built around document management. They were fundamentally considered employee productivity tools that enabled the routing of office documents between employees in offices.

10.2.2 Second-Wave Business Process Management—Process Redesign and Reengineering (1990s)

The second wave of BPM was heralded with the publication of an article arguing that business processes could be improved by redesigning them and combining them with the usage of IT (Chang, 2006; Davenport and Short, 1990). They defined business process redesign in the following five steps:

- Setting business objectives
- Identifying the processes that have to be redesigned
- Measuring the existing process
- Identifying the possible contribution of the introduction of IT to the process
- Making a prototype of the new designed process

The revolutionary aspect from their approach was that they perceived that IT should not only support a single business activity but also the whole process. Applications had to be responsible for the process flow, meaning that applications could also initialize business activities present at other applications.

In a remarkable departure from this stance, Hammer (1990) claimed that the automation efforts of the past did not improve productivity significantly. The first wave of BPR entailed improving the process incrementally, but Hammer's prescription was to build it afresh. The benefits of this approach can be explained by a local optimization problem: fine-tuning a process resembled looking for a local optimum, whilst rebuilding it enabled exploring other local optima that are also available—the other local optima could yield higher revenues than the initial local optimum. Thus, the only way to ensure the best possible implementation of a process was via starting with a clean sheet.

Some of the principals advocated by Hammer are as follows:

- Organize around outputs, not tasks.
- Put the decisions and control, and hence all relevant information, into the hands of the performer.
- Have those who use the outputs of a process perform the process, including the creation and processing of the relevant information.
- The location of user, data, and process information should be immaterial; it should function as if all were in a centralized place.

The approach to BPR promoted by Hammer (1990) was more popular. The increased demand for system integration led the IT industry to build huge but modular enterprise resource planning (ERP) packages, which were implemented throughout the organization. The advantage of ERP was that it regulated the internal process flows.

BPR was fundamentally a management approach in which technology (IT) was not considered as a major issue but instead displaying more of a supportive role. The idea of new BPR efforts was that processes should be manually reengineered through a one-time activity to achieve a radical improvement in business performance.

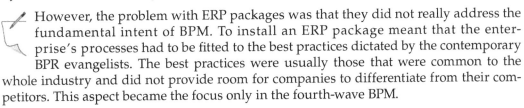 However, the problem with ERP packages was that they did not really address the fundamental intent of BPM. To install an ERP package meant that the enterprise's processes had to be fitted to the best practices dictated by the contemporary BPR evangelists. The best practices were usually those that were common to the whole industry and did not provide room for companies to differentiate from their competitors. This aspect became the focus only in the fourth-wave BPM.

10.2.3 Third-Wave Business Process Management—Processes in Constant Change (2000s)

This wave is characterized by the realization that business processes require constant improvement, also known as agility. Organizations need to have agile processes to be able to adapt to their changing environment. During the second wave, many business processes were been reengineered to make them fit an upcoming implementation of ERP. However, the lack of agility of ERP prevents companies from being able to have a constant reengineering approach. The reason for why it is so hard to change ERP is the complexity of the related processes. Changing a simple activity at the delivery department could successively have great consequences for its ledgers, the ordering process of raw materials, and production planning, among others.

In the third wave, the primary goal of BPM was to enable the enterprise to respond to constant change via the processes. Accordingly, they are made the central focus in all of an enterprise's integration efforts whilst simultaneously freeing them from their concrete castings in technology. This was made possible by agile and flexible business processes that are like first-class citizens of all enterprise assets. Continuous process improvement and value chain monitoring also play a very important role.

A BPMS is used to separate the process flow from the execution. Existing applications perform business activities like they have always been doing right from the first wave, while a new application, the BPMS' orchestration module, coordinates and controls the process flow based upon a set of business rules.

BPMS correspond to this wave.

10.2.4 Fourth-Wave Business Process Management—Process-Based Competitive Advantage (2010s)

The fourth wave is where process performance was integrated into enterprise performance. This means not only identifying the process weaknesses that have the most strategic significance and fixing them but also understanding how process strengths can be better leveraged for enhanced enterprise performance.

Enterprise process management systems (EPMS) correspond to this wave.

10.2.5 Fifth-Wave Business Process Management—Process-Driven Strategy (2020s)

The fifth wave is where processes will be integrated into the enterprise strategy. This means not only identifying the process weaknesses that have the most business significance and fixing them but also understanding how processes can be better leveraged for enhanced business strategy.

Strategic process management systems (SPMS) will correspond to this wave.

10.3 Business Process Life Cycle

Figure 10.1 shows the life cycle of a business process.

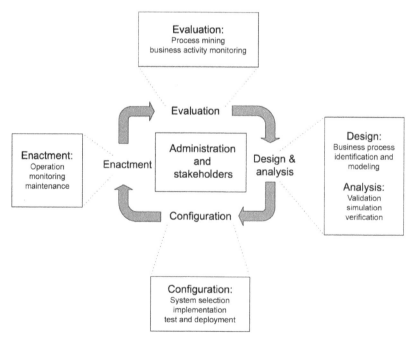

FIGURE 10.1
Business process life cycle.

1. Design: This phase typically involves capturing the operational details of the process using some form of modeling notation. Ideally, sufficient details of the process are recorded to facilitate its direct enactment; however, this relies on the use of an executable modeling formalism, such as that provided by a workflow offering. Generally, the design is captured using notations such as BPMN, event-driven process chains, or Unified Modeling Language activity diagrams, and it takes the form of a conceptual process model.

The business process life cycle commences with the Design phase, in which surveys on the business processes and their organizational and technical environments are conducted. Based on these surveys, business processes are identified, reviewed, validated, and represented by business process models. Business process modeling has an evolutionary character in the sense that the process model is analyzed and improved so that it actually represents the desired business process and that it does not contain any undesired properties.

Business process modeling techniques as well as validation, simulation, and verification techniques are used during this phase. Business process modeling is the core technical subphase during process design. Based on the survey and the findings of the business process improvement activities, the informal business process description is formalized using a particular business process modeling notation. Once an initial design of a business process is developed, it needs to be validated with all of the stakeholders. Explicit business process models expressed in a graphical notation facilitate communication about these processes, so that different stakeholders can communicate efficiently and refine and improve them as needed.

Most BPMS provide a simulation environment that can be used in this phase. Simulation techniques can be used to support validation, because certain undesired execution sequences might be simulated that show deficits in the process model. Simulation of business processes also allows stakeholders to walk through the process in a step-by-step manner and to check whether the process actually exposes the desired behavior. Business processes involving multiple participants play an increasing role to foster the collaboration between enterprises.

2. Configuration: Once the business process model is designed and verified, the business process needs to be implemented. For this, the system needs to be configured according to the organizational environment of the enterprise and the business processes whose enactment it should control. This configuration includes the interactions of the employees with the system as well as the integration of the existing software systems with the BPMS. The latter is important, since, in today's business organizations, most business processes are supported by existing software systems. Depending on the information technology infrastructure, the process configuration phase might also include implementation work, for instance, attaching legacy software systems to the BPMS.

The business process can be implemented via:

- A set of policies and procedures that the employees of the enterprise need to comply with. In this case, a business process can be realized without any support by a dedicated BPMS.
- A dedicated software system. The business process model is enhanced with technical information that facilitates the enactment of the process by the BPMS.

The configuration of a BPMS might also involve transactional aspects. While, in business process management, database applications with transactional properties play an important role in realizing process activities, transactional properties can also be defined at the business process level; a subset of the process activities form one business transaction, so that either all activities in this set are performed successfully or none are executed, realizing the atomicity property. Unfortunately, the techniques that guarantee transactional behavior in database systems cannot be used for business process transactions, since they are based on preventing access to data objects by locking, and locking data objects during process instances is not a valid option. Business transactions are currently at the research stage; therefore, this book does not investigate them further.

Typically, the configuration process is done using facilities provided by the BPMS tool and involves activities such as importing or creating the candidate process model using some form of a graphical editor, defining data objects and their interrelationship with the control-flow aspects of the process model as well as defining resources and the distribution of work within the process to those resources. Figure 10.2 outlines the standard architecture for a BPMS. It consists of two main parts:

- A *BPMS engine*, which handles the execution of a business process on a centralized basis and manages the current process state, working data, work distribution, and so on for each process instance that is initiated

- A *worklist handler* for each user who is involved in a process, which advises them of the work that needs to be undertaken and provides them with the opportunity to interact with the BPMS engine for advisement of their work preferences and management of the scheduling and completion of work to which they have committed

Once the system is configured, the implementation of the business process needs to be tested. Traditional testing techniques from the software engineering area are used at the level of process activities to check, for instance, whether a software

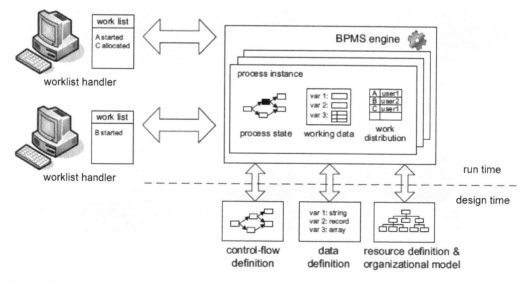

FIGURE 10.2
Schematic of a BPMS.

system exposes the expected behavior. At the process level, integration and performance tests are important for detecting potential run-time problems during the configuration phase.

Once the test subphase is complete, the system is deployed in its target environment. Depending on the particular setting, additional activities might be required, for instance, the training of personnel and migration of application data to the new realization platform.

 Process design and system configuration are *design-time* activities that involve the development of a process model that has sufficient detail to allow it to be directly executed. In contrast, the next two stages in the life cycle are runtime activities, which occur once the model of the business process that has been developed is actually under execution. Traditionally, in many systems, there has been a distinction between the design-time and runtime process models, and they were handled by distinct components of the BPMS software. The design-time process model was used to facilitate the overall definition and capture of the business process and was often undertaken using a graphical design tool or editor. Once finalized, the model was converted to a runtime process model that was used as the basis of process execution by the BPMS. With the increased use of executable process models such as BPMN 2.0, the design time and runtime models are effectively now one and the same.

3. Enactment: Once the system configuration phase is completed, business process instances are ready to be enacted. Business process instances are initiated to fulfill the business goals of a company and typically follow a defined event—for instance, the receipt of an order sent by a customer.

   The process enactment phase encompasses the actual runtime of the business process. The BPMS actively controls the execution of business process instances as defined in the business process model. Process enactment needs to cater to a correct process orchestration, guaranteeing that the process activities are performed according to the execution constraints specified in the process model.

   Process monitoring is an important mechanism for providing accurate information on the status of business process instances. A monitoring component of a BPMS visualizes the status of business process instances. Detailed information on the current state of process instances is available in a BPMS—the state information can be used to visualize and monitor process instances. During business process enactment, valuable execution data is gathered, typically in some form of a log file. These log files consist of ordered sets of log entries, indicating events that have occurred during business processes. Start of activity and end of activity entries are typical information stored in execution logs. The log information forms the basis for the evaluation of processes in the next phase of the business process life cycle.

4. Monitoring and evaluation: This phase uses the information available to monitor, evaluate, and improve business process models and their implementation. Execution logs are evaluated using business activity monitoring and process mining techniques. These techniques aim at identifying the quality of business process models and the adequacy of the execution environment. For instance, business activity monitoring might identify that a certain activity takes too long due to a shortage of resources required to conduct it. Since this information is useful also for business process simulation, these phases are strongly related.

10.4 Concept of Business Process Management

BPM addresses the following two important issues for an enterprise:

1. The strategic long-term positioning of the business with respect to both current and envisaged customers, which will ensure that the enterprise will be competitively and financially successful both locally and globally
2. The enterprise's capability/capacity, which is the totality of all of the internal processes that dynamically realize this positioning of the business

Traditionally, positioning has been considered as an independent set of functional tasks split within the marketing, finance, and strategic planning functions. Similarly, capability/capacity has usually been considered the preserve of the individual operational departments that may have mutually conflicting priorities and measures of performances (see Section 1.4.3).

The problem for many enterprises lies in the fact that there is a fundamental flaw in the organizational structure—organizational structures are hierarchical, while the transactions and workflows that deliver the solutions (i.e., the products and services) to the customers are horizontal. Quite simply, the structure determines who the customer really is. The traditional management structures condition managers to put functional needs above those of the multifunctional processes to which their functions contribute. This results in the following:

- Various departments competing for resources
- Collective failure in meeting or exceeding customers' expectations
- An inability to coordinate and collaborate on multifunctional, customer-centric processes that would truly provide competitive differentiation in future markets

The traditional mass-marketing type of organization works well for researching market opportunities, planning the offering(s), and scheduling all of the steps required to produce and distribute the offering(s) to the marketplace (where it is either selected or rejected by the customer). It takes a very different kind of organization—namely, a customized-marketing type organization—to build long-term relationships with customers so that they call such organizations first when they have a need because they trust that such enterprises will be able to respond with an effective solution. This is customer-responsive management, which we will discuss in the section that follows.

BPM is the process that manages and optimizes the inextricable linkages between the positioning and the capability/capacity of an enterprise. A company cannot position the enterprise to meet a customer need that it cannot fulfill without an unprofitable level of resources, nor can it allocate enhanced resources to provide a cost-effective service that no customer wants.

Positioning leads to higher levels of revenue through increasing the size of the market, retaining first-time customers, increasing the size of the wallet share, and so on. Positioning has to do with factors such as:

- Comprehending customer needs
- Understanding competitor initiatives
- Determining the business' financial needs

- Conforming with legal and regulatory requirements
- Heeding environmental constraints

The capability/capacity has to be aligned with the positioning or else it has to be changed to deliver the positioning. Capability/capacity has to do with internal factors, including:

- Key business processes
- Procedures and systems
- Competencies, skills, training, and education

The key is to have a perceived differentiation of being better than the competition in whatever terms the customers choose to evaluate or measure and to deliver this at the lowest unit cost.

In practice, BPM has developed a focus on changing capability/capacity in the short-term to address current issues. This short-term change in capability/capacity is usually driven by the need to:

- Reduce the cycle time to process customer orders
- Improve quotation times
- Lower variable overhead costs
- Increase product range to meet an immediate competitor threat
- Rebalance resources to meet current market needs
- Reduce work-in-progress stocks
- Meet changed legislation requirements
- Introduce short-term measures to increase market share (e.g., increased credit limit from customers hit by recessionary trends)

10.4.1 Business Process

A business process is typically a coordinated and logically sequenced set of work activities and associated resources that produce something of value to a customer. A business process can be simply defined as a collection of activities that create value by transforming inputs into more valuable outputs. These activities consist of a series of steps performed by actors to produce a product or service for the customer. Each process has an identified customer; it is initiated by a process trigger or a business event (usually a request for a product or service arriving from the process customer); and it produces a process outcome (the specific product or a service requested by the customer) as its deliverable.

A business process is a set of logically related tasks performed to achieve a well-defined business outcome. A (business) process view implies a horizontal view of a business organization and looks at processes as sets of interdependent activities designed and structured to produce a specific output for a customer or a market. A business process defines the results to be achieved, the context of the activities, the relationships between the activities, and the interactions with other processes and resources. A business process may receive events that alter the state of the process and the sequence of activities. A business process may produce events for input into other applications or processes. It may also invoke applications to perform computational functions as well as post assignments to human work lists to request actions by human actors. Business processes can be measured, and different performance measures apply, such as cost, quality, time, and customer satisfaction.

There is a substantial difference between the concept of BPM and BPMS. BPM is a concept of a much broader scope than the BPMS that implement a subset of the tenets of BPM. The last part of this chapter explains the concept of BPMS and their variation of EPMS. In contrast to BPMS that reflect the "data item"-focused, bottom-up stance of the traditional IT view of the enterprise, EPMS embody a "business process"-focused, top-down stance of the information systems view of the enterprise. The traditional paradigm is covered in several publications like M. Weske (2012), A.H.M. ter Hofstede, W.M.P. van der Aalst, M. Adams, and N. Russell (Eds.) (2010), Jan vom Brocke and M. Rosemann (Eds.) (2014), W. M. P. van der Aalst (2002), M. Reichert and B. Weber (2012) and M. Dumas, M. La Rosa, J. Mendling, and H. Reijers (2013).

10.5 Business Process Management

BPM refers to activities performed by enterprises to design (capture processes and document their design in terms of process maps); model (define business processes in a computer language); execute (develop software that enables the process); monitor (track individual processes for performance measurement); and optimize (retrieve process performance for improvement) operational business processes by using a combination of models, methods, techniques, and tools. BPM approaches based on IT enable support or automate business processes, in whole or in part, by providing computer-based systems support. These technology-based systems help coordinate and streamline business transactions, reduce operational costs, and promote real-time visibility in business performance.

BPM can be defined as *managing the achievement of an organization's objectives through the improvement, management, and control of essential business process.* BPM is focused on improving corporate performance by managing a company's business processes.

BPM is a commitment to expressing, understanding, representing, and managing a business (or the portion of business to which it is applied) in terms of a collection of business processes that are responsive to a business environment of internal or external events. The phrase "management of business processes" includes process analysis, process definition and redefinition, resource allocation, scheduling, measurement of process quality and efficiency, and process optimization. Process optimization includes the collection and analysis of both real-time measures (monitoring) and strategic measures (performance management) and their correlation as the basis for process improvement and innovation. A BPM solution is a graphical productivity tool for modeling, integrating, monitoring, and optimizing process flows of all sizes that cross any application, company boundary, or human interaction. BPM codifies value-driven processes and institutionalizes their execution within the enterprise. This implies that BPM tools can help to analyze, define, and enforce process standardization. BPM provides a modeling tool to visually construct, analyze, and execute cross-functional business processes.

Scenarios suitable for considering the application of BPM within various areas include the following:

1. Management
   - Problem: Lack of reliable or conflicting management information
   - Consider: The need to provide managers with more control over their processes
   - Consider: The need for the introduction of a sustainable performance environment

- Consider: The need to create a culture of high performance
- Consider: The need to gain the maximum return on investment from the existing legacy systems
- Consider: Budget cuts

2. Customers/suppliers/partners
    - Problem: An unexpected increase in number of customers, suppliers, or partners
    - Problem: Long lead times to meet customer/supplier/partners requests
    - Problem: Dissatisfaction with service, which could be due to high churn rates of staff or the staff being unable to answer questions adequately within the required time frames (responsiveness)
    - Consider: The establishment of an organizational desire to focus upon customer intimacy
    - Consider: Customer segmentation or tiered service requirements
    - Consider: The introduction and strict enforcement of service levels
    - Consider: The possibility of major customers, suppliers, and/or partners requiring unique (different) processes
    - Consider: The need for a true end-to-end perspective to provide visibility or integration

3. Product and services
    - Problem: The existence of an unacceptably long lead time to market (lack of business agility)
    - Problem: Products or services are complex
    - Consider: The establishment of product-specific services like quality, compliance, etc
    - Consider: New products or services comprise existing product/service elements

4. Organization
    - Problem: The need to provide the business with more control of its own processes
    - Problem: Organization objectives or goals are not being met
    - Consider: The introduction of process management, linked to organizational strategy, performance measurement, and management of people
    - Problem: Compliance or regulation—for example, organizations currently have to comply with pollution, environment, and forest cover violation norms
    - Consider: The initiation of process projects that will provide the platform to launch process improvement or BPM projects
    - Problem: The need for business agility to enable the enterprise to respond to opportunities as they arise
    - Problem: Difficulty coping with high growth
    - Consider: Proactively planning for high growth
    - Consider: Change in strategy—deciding to change direction or pace of operational excellence, product leadership, or customer intimacy
    - Consider: Reorganization or restructuring—changing roles and responsibilities

- Problem: Mergers and acquisitions—these cause the organization to "acquire" additional complexity or necessitate rationalization of processes; the need to retire acquired legacy systems could also contribute
- Consider: BPM projects enable a process layer to be "placed" across these legacy systems, providing time to consider appropriate conversion strategies

 Existing functioning processes also are prone to progressive degradation, loss of efficiencies because of altered circumstances, changes in products or services, etc. Business processes may become candidates for BPM because of the following:

- The need for provision of visibility of processes from an end-to-end perspective
- Lack of communications and understanding of the end-to-end process by the parties performing parts of the process
- Unclear roles and responsibilities from a process perspective
- Lack of process standardization
- Quality is poor and the volume of rework is substantial
- Lack of clear process goals or objectives
- Too many hand-offs or gaps in a process, or no clear process at all
- Processes change too often or not at all

10.6 Management by Collaboration

The business environment witnessed tremendous and rapid changes beginning the 1990s. There is now an increasing emphasis on being customer-focused and on leveraging and strengthening the company's core competencies. This has forced enterprises to learn and develop abilities to change and respond rapidly to the competitive dynamics of the global market.

Companies have learned to effectively reengineer themselves into flatter organizations, with closer integration across the traditional functional boundaries of the enterprise. There is an increasing focus on employee empowerment and cross-functional teams. In this book, we are proposing that what we are witnessing is a fundamental transformation in the manner that businesses have been operating in for the last century.

This change, which is primarily driven by the information revolution of the past few decades, is characterized by the dominant tendency to integrate across transaction boundaries, both internally and externally. The dominant theme of this new system of management with significant implications on organizational development is *collaboration*. We will refer to this emerging and maturing constellation of concepts and practices as management by collaboration (MBC). ES, especially BPM systems, are major instruments for realizing MBC-driven enterprises.

MBC is an approach to management primarily focused on relationships. Relationships by their very nature are not static and are constantly in evolution. As organizational and environmental conditions become more complex, globalized, and thus competitive, MBC provides a framework for dealing effectively with the issues of performance improvement, capability development, and adaptation to the changing environment. MBC, as embodied by ES packages such as BPM, has had a major impact on the strategy, structure, and culture of the customer-centric enterprise.

The beauty and essence of MBC are that it incorporates in its very fabric the basic urge of humans for a purpose in life; for mutually beneficial relationships; for mutual commitment; and for being helpful to other beings—that is, for collaborating. These relationships could be at the level of individual, division, enterprise, or even between enterprises. Every relationship has a purpose, and manifests itself through various processes as embodied mainly in the form of teams; thus, the relationships are geared towards attainment of these purposes through the concerned processes.

Because of the enhanced role played by the individual members of an enterprise in any relationship or process, MBC promotes not only their motivation and competence but also develops the competitiveness and capability of the enterprises as a whole. MBC emphasizes the roles of both the top management and the individual members. Thus, the MBC approach covers the whole organization through the means of basic binding concepts such as relationships, processes, and teams. MBC addresses readily all issues of management, including organization development. The issues range from organizational design and structure, role definition and job design, output quality and productivity, interaction and communication channels, and company culture as well as employee issues such as attitudes, perception, values, and motivation.

The basic idea of collaboration has been gaining tremendous ground with the increasing importance of business processes and dynamically constituted teams in the operations of companies. The traditional bureaucratic structures, which are highly formalized, centralized, and functionally specialized, have proven largely to be too slow, too expensive, and too unresponsive to be competitive. These structures are based on the basic assumption that all of the individual activities and task elements in a job are independent and separable. Organizations were structured hierarchically in a "command and control" structure, and it was taken as an accepted fact that the output of the enterprise as a whole could be maximized by maximizing the output of each constituent organizational unit.

On the other hand, by their very nature, teams are flexible, adaptable, dynamic, and collaborative. They encourage flexibility, innovation, entrepreneurship, and responsiveness. For the last few decades, even in traditionally bureaucratic-oriented manufacturing companies, teams have manifested themselves and flourished successfully in various forms as super-teams, self-directed work teams, quality circles, and so on. The dynamic changes in the market and global competition being confronted by companies necessarily lead to flatter and more flexible organizations with a dominance of more dynamic structures like teams.

People in teams, representing different functional units, are motivated to work within the constraints of time and resources to achieve a defined goal. The goals might range from incremental improvements in responsiveness, efficiency, quality, and productivity to quantum leaps in new-product development. Even in traditional businesses, the number and variety of teams instituted for various functions, projects, tasks, and activities has been on the rise.

Increasingly, companies are populated with worker-teams that have special skills, operate semiautonomously, and are answerable directly to peers and to the end customers. Members must both have higher levels of skills than before and also be more flexible and capable of doing more jobs. The empowered workforce with considerably enhanced managerial responsibilities (pertaining to information, resources, authority, and accountability) has resulted in an increase in worker commitment and flexibility. Whereas workers have witnessed gains in the quality of their work life, corporations have obtained returns in terms of increased interactivity, responsiveness, quality, productivity, and cost improvements.

Consequently, in the past few years, a new type of nonhierarchical network organization with distributed intelligence and decentralized decision-making powers has been evolving. This entails a demand for constant and frequent communication and feedback among the various teams or functional groups. ES packages like BPM essentially provides such an enabling environment through modules including business intelligence, Product Lifecycle Management (PLM), and so on.

10.7 Business Process Maturity Model

In modern enterprises, the implementation of process management involves the description, regulation, updating, and improvement of business process systems and the organizational structure in order to ensure the stability and reproducibility of the results. Business process maturity in any organization shows its ability to perform. Maturity assessments measure the degree to which an organization utilizes its processes, people, tools, products, and management efficiently, effectively, and optimally.

Assessments depict how the organization compares itself to its competitors or other organizations; such also helps to manage an organization and evolve it towards higher competence.

Almost all maturity models define five levels of increasing maturity, as follows:

Level 1: Initial Organizations
   The following are the characteristics seen at level 1:
   • Undisciplined: Few repeatable processes, often sacrificed under pressure
   • Individualistic: People rely on personal methods for accomplishing work
   • Inconsistent: Little preparation for managing a work unit
   • Inefficient: Few measures for analyzing effectiveness of practices
   • Stagnant: No foundation or commitment for improvement
Level 2: Managed Organizations
   The following are the characteristics seen at level 2:
   • Committed: Executives commit organization to improving operations
   • Proactive: Managers take responsibility for work unit operations and performance
   • Managed: Commitments are balanced with resources
   • Repeatable: Work units use local procedures that have proven effective
   • Responsible: Work units are capable of meeting their commitments
Level 3: Standardized Organizations
   The following are the characteristics seen at level 3:
   • Organizational: End-to-end business processes are integrated across functions; perform in silos
   • Established: Standard processes are established from best practices in work units

- Adaptable: Standard processes are tailored for best use in different circumstances
- Leveraged: Common measures and processes promote organizational learning
- Professional: Organizational culture emerges from common practices

Level 4: Predictable Organizations

The following are the characteristics seen at level 4:

- Quantitative: Process variation, performance, and capability are understood quantitatively
- Stable: Variation is reduced through reuse, mentoring, and statistical management
- Empowered: Process data empowers staff to manage their own work
- Multifunctional: Functional processes are reengineered as roles in business processes
- Predictable: Outcomes are predictable from subprocess capability and performance

Level 5: Optimizing Organizations

The following are the characteristics seen at level 5:

- Proactive: Improvements are planned to achieve business strategies and objectives
- Systematic: Improvements are evaluated and deployed using orderly methods
- Continual: Individuals and workgroups continuously improve capability
- Aligned: Performance is aligned across the organization
- Preventive: Defects and causes of problems are systematically eliminated

Figure 10.3 Business Process Maturity Model, shows the five levels of business process and, hence, organizational maturity.

FIGURE 10.3
Levels of process maturity.

10.8 Business Process Management Systems

BPMS technology allows the business analyst to collaborate more closely with IT people in implementing projects. The various tools BPMS offer provide a new paradigm for how solutions can be implemented. Organizations are no longer tied to the business processes ingrained in their business applications. With automatic workflow generation and web portal capabilities, workflow can be easily deployed across multiple applications, thus integrating people into the business processes. These technological innovations enable technology to better fulfill the ideals of BPM and the principles of business process analysis (BPA) (i.e., fact-based management). Processes can be managed in a process framework and decisions can be based on quantitative analysis. This framework allows organizations to design, execute, monitor, measure, and enhance their processes.

One of the major advantages of BPMS over traditional IT-enabled business process improvement efforts is that BPMS brings IT closer to the business process owners. IT solutions are typically conceived from a collection of functional specifications. A gap between what the business wants and what IT implements is created when the specifications do not capture the business requirements appropriately. BPMS is able to bridge the gap by allowing business process owners to be directly involved in designing the IT solution. BPMS typically include a graphical process designer tool that enables the design of processes by process owners and business analysts. The tool automatically generates computer code that sometimes can be deployed without IT development help.

To help the business process owners and business analysts in the process design, BPMS include process simulation and modeling functionality. This means that business process owners or analysts can design business processes and run the process designs in simulation mode. BMPS enable the application of predictive and prescriptive analytics. Simulation plays a large role as the supervisory systems that oversee the business processes once they have been implemented. The supervisory aspect of BPMS provides the abilities to monitor, control, and improve business processes. Because BPMS oversee all the steps, whether manual or automated in the business process, they can provide valuable process information and, in that role, serve as the performance monitor for the processes. Process owners can obtain statistics such as average cycle time per transaction, the wait time before a process task that is performed by human participants, and cost data. This is the BMPS-provided support for implementing descriptive analytics.

BPMS give organizations the ability to implement real-time process improvement without the extensive process conversion effort. The original business processes already exist in the business process designer. This eliminates the need to gather current process information. When process deficiencies have been identified (for instance, a bottleneck), business process owners or analysts are able to incorporate improvements into the process using the business process designer. After the improved business process solution is implemented, BPMS allow any work that was started on the original process to finish using the original process and any new work to be performed using the improved process. In essence, the system allows both the original and the improved processes to coexist until all work correlated with the original process is finished. Using BPMS, process improvements can be made without disruption to process output. This is an important facility that is an essential prerequisite for enabling continuous process improvement.

10.8.1 BPMS Products

This subsection provides an overview of commercial BPMS products. Figure 10.4 provides a representative radar chart with the evaluation results of three BPM suites.

1. Cordys BPMS: Cordys BPMS was developed by Cordys, which was a Dutch vendor who specialized in BPM. Cordys BPMS was taken over by OpenText (Waterloo, Canada) and is now called OpenText Process suite.

   Process Suite provides the power and flexibility to digitize, automate, and unify processes across functions, systems, applications, and clouds. The OpenText Process Suite platform easily supports rules-based automation, adaptive process orchestration, dynamic case management, Internet of Things-driven processes, and contextual integrations across enterprise systems and diverse content sources.

   Cordys BPMS supports the definition of key performance indicators (KPIs) with the KPIComposer. In order to calculate KPIs, the required information has to be stored in a database and retrieved from this database by using user-defined methods. These methods are called in the KPIComposer and the KPIs are built based on the information that these methods retrieve. The definition of KPIs in Cordys is therefore not really user-friendly, since the user is forced to write these methods.

2. Oracle BPM Suite: Oracle BPM Suite is developed by Oracle (Redwood City, CA, USA), who was originally a databases developer. Oracle entered the BPM market after the acquisition of BEA.

   The Oracle BPM Suite provides an integrated environment for developing, administering, and using business applications centered around business processes. The Oracle BPM Suite provides the following:

   - Enables the user to create process models based on standards with user-friendly applications. It allows collaboration between process analysts and

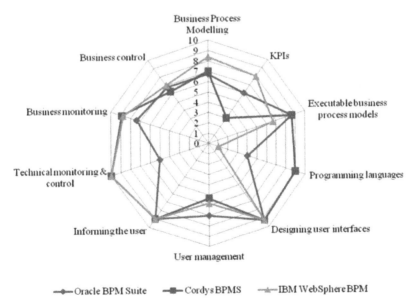

FIGURE 10.4
Radar chart with the evaluation results of the three BPM suites.

process developers. Oracle BPM supports BPMN 2.0 and Business Process Execution Language from modeling and implementation to runtime and monitoring.

- Enables process analysts and process owners to customize business processes and Oracle Business Rules.

- Provides a web-based application for creating business processes, editing Oracle Business Rules, and customizing tasks using predefined components.

- Expands business process management to include flexible, unstructured processes and adds dynamic tasks and supports approval routing using declarative patterns and rules-driven flow determination.

- Enables collaboration by providing integration with Oracle Process Spaces, which drives productivity and innovation.

- Unifies different stages of the application development life cycle by addressing end-to-end requirements for developing process-based applications. Specifically, Oracle BPM unifies the design, implementation, runtime, and monitoring stages. Oracle BPM also enables different personas to participate through all stages of the application life cycle.

Oracle BPM Suite components and subcomponents include:

1. Process Modeling and Implementation
- Oracle BPM Studio
- Oracle Business Process Composer
- Oracle Metadata Service Repository
- Oracle BPM Projects
2. Oracle BPM Runtime Components
- Oracle BPM Engine
- Oracle Human Workflow
- Oracle Business Rules
- Oracle WebLogic Application Server
- Oracle Enterprise Manager

Figure 10.5 shows Oracle BPM components and the application development life cycle.

The Oracle BPA Suite is a separate Oracle product suite based on the Aris platform from IDS Scheer. The Oracle BPA Suite provides comprehensive modeling, analysis, and simulation capabilities for enterprise-wide business processes. Oracle BPA supports capturing business architecture artifacts such as strategic objectives, goals, higher-level KPIs, risks and controls, and conceptual models including value chain diagrams.

The Oracle BPM Suite supports the definition of KPIs with the Oracle BPM Studio, which allows the use of widgets to define graphs on activity workload, activity performance, and process performance. These widgets can be considered as templates with limited options and underlying code. They can be used on a business activity monitoring dashboard that can be shown in the Oracle BPM workspace.

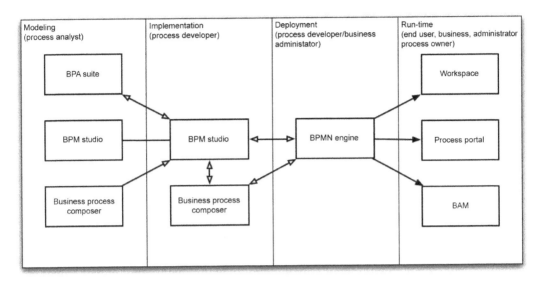

FIGURE 10.5
Oracle BPM components and application development life cycle.

3. IBM WebSphere BPM Suite: The IBM WebSphere BPM suite is developed by IBM Corporation (Armonk, NY, USA), which is originally a computer manufacturer with a long tradition in the servers market.

IBM® Business Process Manager is a comprehensive business process management platform. It provides a robust set of tools to author, test, and deploy business processes, in addition to full visibility and insight for managing the aforementioned business processes. The components of IBM® Business Process Manager provide a unified BPM repository to manage the business processes and their associated artifacts; tools for authors, administrators, and users; and a runtime platform.

The three editions of the product to support various levels of complexity and involvement with business process management are:

1. IBM BPM Express, which is an affordable entry point for initiating BPM. It provides an easy-to-use interface with a process execution, monitoring, and optimization engine, allowing participants to engage in process improvement activities. Ideal for medium-sized businesses, IBM Process Manager Express delivers the same capabilities as the standard edition of IBM® Business Process Manager.

2. IBM BPM Standard, which is a comprehensive BPM platform that provides full visibility and insight to managing business processes. It offers tooling and runtimes for process design, execution, monitoring, and optimization, along with basic system integration support. IBM® Business Process Manager Standard is ideal for multiproject improvement programs that focus on workflow and productivity, scaling easily from initial project to enterprise-wide programs.

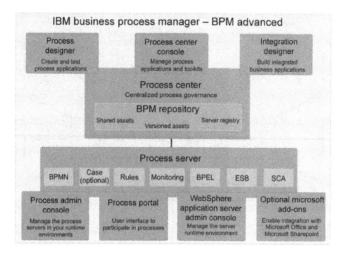

FIGURE 10.6
IBM® business process manager.

3. IBM BPM Advanced, which supports enterprise integration and transaction process management as part of an overall SOA. This software includes the same features as the standard version of the BPM offering, albeit with more advanced integration and connectivity capabilities. It combines simplicity with ease-of-use for task management, as well as extended support for high-volume automation.

Figure 10.6 shows a schematic of IBM® Business Process Manager.

Additionally, IBM WebSphere BPM supports the definition of KPIs with the Integration Developer tool. This feature allows its user to define a monitor model in which a certain event, for example, the start or end of an activity, fires a trigger, which updates some metrics. These metrics are updated at the process instance level so that KPIs can be calculated based on the metrics of multiple process instances.

10.9 Enterprise Process Management Systems

In contrast to BPMS, which reflect the "data item"-driven, reusability-focused, bottom-up stance of the traditional IT view of the enterprise, EPMS embody the "business process"-driven, requirements-focused, top-down stance of the information systems view of the enterprise. EPMS promote a world-view of process-driven or process-centric systems supported by a portfolio of systems like process bases, process warehouses, process intelligence, and process analytics.

This book proposes that instead of the customary *data item* in the traditional IT systems, the business process should become the smallest identifiable and addressable entity within any enterprise system. In other words, it should not be isolated data items or attributes of the entities of the traditional IT systems but rather the processes that access, create, or modify the data item(s) or attribute(s) that should become the focus of enterprise systems.

Thus, instead of the functional-oriented modules of the traditional IT systems, the enterprise systems (discussed in Chapter 1) should be replaced with information system process bases (PBMS) that manage business processes by enabling, like as follows:

Create (sub-)process

Query (sub-)process

Update (sub-)process

Delete (sub-)process

This is not as far-fetched as it may seem at the first sight. SAP's (Walldorf, Germany) move to introduce SAP S/4HANA can be read as a step back from the *data item* world view. This can be repurposed to enable SAP Process Orchestration (SAP PO) (along with the Eclipse-based Developer Studio) to become the development workbench for S/4HANA to reengineer the functionality populating the traditional modules of FI-CO, SD, MM, PP, QM, and so on to processes.

Consequently, there is a need for a development methodology that would smoothly transition from requirements to implementation. Chapter 12 presents the "business process"-driven (or process-centric), requirements-focused, top-down-stanced, spreadsheet-driven spreadsheet application development (SAD) methodology for the development of process-centric application systems.

The various phases of the SAD methodology are:

1. The first phase of the SAD methodology deals with the problem of identifying enterprise business processes that are essential for the functioning of the organization.

2. The second phase of the SAD methodology deals with developing a process model for the business processes identified in the previous phase, which involves completing parts I and II of the activity spreadsheet.

3. The third phase of the SAD methodology deals with four subphases, which are "as-is" process model analysis, "to-be" process model creation, "to-be" process model analysis, and process simulation. The first subphase performs an analysis of the process performance of the "as-is" process model and calculates process performance parameters, such as process flow, cycle time efficiency, and process capacity, with the purpose of gaining essential information about what kind of a process we are dealing with. The calculated process performance enables management to make a decision about the necessity for process improvement or innovation. On the other hand, the fourth subphase uses the simulation technique to imitate the functioning of the "to-be" process model in order to study the reality of the process behavior and the possibility of making further improvements.

4. The fourth phase of the SAD methodology deals with the development of a process management system that implements the "to-be" process model, including the class model and the design of the system based on the activity spreadsheet parts I and II.

5. The fifth phase of the SAD methodology deals with controlling the functioning of the improved business process and the process management system.

10.10 Summary

The chapter started with recapitulating the concept of process-oriented enterprise and introduced a snapshot of the history of BPM. It then discussed the business process life cycle constituting of design, configuration, enactment and monitoring, and evaluation. Distinguishing between BPM as a business program and BPMS as its subset realization into a software application, the chapter introduces the concept of BPM and its characteristics. BPMS enable the reconciled i.e., collaborative working of different cross-company stakeholders of any business process, activity, or decision in compliance with its strategy, policy, and procedures. After introducing the concept of BPM, the chapter described the BPM methodology in detail. The chapter looked at MBC as a unifying framework in the context of the customer-centric and customer-responsive enterprise. After presenting the Process Maturity Model, it then explains the concept of BPMS and their variation, EPMS.

11

Business Process Modeling and Notation

Business Process Modeling and Notation (BPMN version 1.0) was proposed in May 2004 and adopted by the Object Management Group (Needham, MA) for ratification in February 2006. The current version is BPMN 2.0. BPMN is based on the revision of other notations and methodologies, especially Unified Modeling Language (UML) Activity Diagram, UML EDOC Business Process, IDEF, ebXML BPSS, Activity-Decision Flow Diagram, RosettaNet, LOVeM, and Eventdriven Process Chains. A key goal in the development of BPMN was to create a bridge from notation to execution languages; executability has become an important part of version 2.0 of the BPMN specification. The primary goal of BPMN was to provide a notation that is readily understandable by all business users, from the business analysts who create the initial draft of the processes to the technical developers responsible for implementing the technology that will support the execution and performance of those processes and, finally, to the business people who will manage and monitor those processes. Above all, BPMN standardizes the notation used by business experts on the one hand and information technology specialists on the other, thus finally bridging the gap between them.

11.1 Business Process Modeling and Notation Core Elements

Process diagrams, also called business process diagrams, are at the core of BPMN modeling. They are a graphical representation of what needs to be executed, in what sequence, when, and under what specific conditions; they must also include mention of particular exception situations and how they are to be handled.

BPMN has five core element categories for implementing the properties of business process diagrams; these are:

1. Flow objects, which are the main graphical elements of BPMN and define the behavior of a process. There are three separate types of flow objects:
   - Event (displayed as a circle)
   - Activity (displayed as a rectangle with rounded corners), which can be further subdivided into tasks and subprocesses
   - Gateway (displayed as a diamond)

Table 11.1 shows notation for flow objects.

TABLE 11.1

Flow Objects

Flow Object Type	Description	Symbol
Events	Events come in three basic forms, start intermediate and end. A start-event indicates where a particular starts, while an end-event indicates where the process ends. An intermediate-event occurs between a start-event and an end-vent and is used to respond to a trigger in order to trigger another element.	Start Intermediate End
Activities	An activity is a step in a process that performs work. There are three types of activities: process, sub process and task. A task is an atomic activity (i.e., cannot be broken down into smaller parts). Processes and sub-processes are non-atomic entities (i.e., they can be divided into smaller parts).	
Gateways	A gateway can be used for splitting and joining flows. Typically gateways are used for if-then-else decisions, while only in special situations there is a need for using it for joining.	

2. Data, or information that is either processed within a process or exchanged between different processes. This comprises the following five BPMN elements:
   - Data object
   - Data input
   - Data output
   - Data store
   - Message

3. Connecting objects, which allow an individual to connect flow objects to one another or to connect to supplementary information. There are three different types of connecting objects:
   - Sequence flow
   - Message flow
   - Association

4. Swim lanes, which are used to group the primary modeling elements mentioned earlier. There are two types of grouping in BPMN:
   - Pools
   - (Swim) lanes

5. Artifacts, which are used to provide additional information about the process. There are two types of artifacts:
   - Group
   - Text annotation

Table 11.2 shows notations for connecting object types, swim-lane object types, and artifact types.

TABLE 11.2

Connecting Objects: (a) Basic Types, (b) Swim-Lane Object Types, and (c) Artefact Types

(a)

Connecting Object Type	Description	Symbol
Sequence Flow	Sequence flows define the sequence of the activities to be performed in a process.	
Message Flow	Message flows show the flows of messages between two participants. A message flow connects two separate pools or objects within the separate pools, but never two objects within the same pool.	
Association	Associations associate data, text, and other artifacts with flow objects. Associations show the inputs and output of activities. The arrow head can be used to show sequences of association.	

(b)

Swim Lane Type	Description	Symbol
Pool	The pool symbol is used to represent a participant in a process. Thus, it can partition a set of activities from others, e.g., activities in different companies. Different pools can be connected by message flows.	
Lane	A lane is used for sub-partitions within a pool. Lanes can divide activities, e.g., according to executing department.	

(c)

Artifact	Description	Symbol
Data object	Data objects show the way in which data are required or produced by activities. Associations connect data object to activities and flows. A data object can have a state which can change during a process.	Name [State]
Group	Groups are used for documentation or analysis purposes, and they do not affect sequence flows.	
Annotation	Annotations are used for providing additional text information to the reader of a BPD.	Text Annotation allows a Modeler to provide additional Information

11.1.1 Events

The most common types of events are start and end events, which are used in top-level processes.

1. Start events: There are several start event types dependent on how such events can be triggered. The start event with a message trigger is probably the most common way of marking the beginning of a BPMN process.

   The various types of triggers are:

   - A message trigger, which is used for processes that begin when a certain message is received.

   - A timer trigger, which is used for processes that begin at a certain specified date and time (or after a certain period of time). The timer event can also be used for processes that need to be triggered periodically, after a certain amount of time has elapsed.

   - A condition trigger, which is used for processes that begin when a certain condition becomes true, such as, for example, the "temperature is below 0°." The condition is usually an expression based on some data that are accessible to the process.

   - A signal trigger is similar to a message trigger, but it works in broadcast mode; that is, it does not have a particular recipient associated with it. Rather, when a signal is thrown, every process with a start event enabled for this signal will begin to run.

   Multiple and parallel multiple triggers represent a combination of any of the previous event types. For example, a process that is triggered either when a message is received or when a condition is true has a start event with multiple triggers. If the occurrence of any of such events is enough to start the process, then the multiple trigger should be used. On the other hand, if the occurrence of all such events is required in order to start the process, then the parallel multiple trigger should be used. In this case, the process will start only after all of the required events have occurred.

2. End events: End events represent the different results that a process may produce. Typically, the type of end event is the logical counterpart of the corresponding type of start event. For example, the end event with a message result means that the process ends by sending a message, whereas the start event with a message trigger means that the process begins by receiving a message. However, as an exception, the concept of a "terminate event" means that, if the process flow comes to this event, then the process instance will terminate immediately. In particular, all branches that may be running in parallel will also be terminated. Also, if there are loops or multiple-instance activities, these will be terminated as well.

   The various types of results are:

   - Message result, or when the process will end by sending a message to some recipient.

   - Signal result, or when the process will end by broadcasting a signal.

- Multiple results (e.g., a message and a signal, or multiple messages, or multiple signals), or when the process will end by producing a collection of all of these results. Here, there is no need to distinguish between multiple and parallel multiple, since an end event with multiple results has, in effect, multiple "parallel" results.

11.1.2 Activities

A process is comprised of several subprocesses and activities.
BPMN 2.0 defines several kinds of activities:

- Service task is an automated activity that consists of the invocation of some service or application.
- Send task is an activity that consists of sending a message to an external participant.
- Receive task is the counterpart of the send task. Basically, it represents an activity whose main purpose is to receive a message. The activity is completed only when the message has been received.
- Instantiating receive task means that, upon the arrival of a message, a new process instance will be created. Instantiating receive, if used, must be the first activity in the process and it must have no incoming sequence flows—its icon (an envelope enclosed in a circle) is intended to resemble a start event that is triggered by a message. In fact, the instantiating receive can be used to replace the start event in a process.
- Manual task is intended to represent an activity that is to be performed without information technology support. This could be any action in the physical world that is not monitored or supported by an information technology system.
- User task represents an activity that is assigned to some user. Typically, this task will be sent as a work item to the user's work list, and the execution engine will be waiting for an output or completion message before resuming the process.
- Script task contains a series of instructions that are to be carried out by the engine that will be executing the process. When the engine reaches the script task, it will execute the code contained therein. For this purpose, the script must be written in a language that the engine is able to interpret and execute.
- Business rule task is used to invoke business rules, which can be relevant to perform calculations or make decisions based on user-defined parameters. The business rule task is a means to invoke an external business rules engine that will evaluate the rules and return the results back to the process. The process can then use these results to decide how it should proceed. The reason for why these rules are not embedded in the process is so that they can be changed at any time according to business requirements.

11.1.3 Subprocesses

Another interesting possibility is to define an activity as a subprocess. This means that an activity becomes a placeholder for some process logic that one may want to insert at that point in the process.

Subprocesses are of two forms:

- If collapsed, the subprocess looks like a regular activity except for the plus sign (i.e., "C") indicating that it contains additional process logic.
- If expanded, the subprocess shows the logic that is contained inside it. Such logic must follow the same design principles as a top-level process, so, usually, it contains a start event, a sequence of activities, and an end event. It is only when the subprocess reaches its end event that the parent process can proceed to the next activity.

A particular type of subprocess that has a much different behavior from the rest is the ad-hoc subprocess. This is a kind of subprocess that is not bound to the typical, well-structured behavior of a sequence flow. Basically, an ad-hoc subprocess contains a set of activities that can be executed in any order. In particular, there is no restriction on when each activity can begin and end, so the ad-hoc subprocess can also be regarded as a block where everything can run in any order, including in parallel. However, rather than using an ad-hoc subprocess, the best way to represent parallelism in BPMN is through the use of a parallel gateway.

11.1.4 Gateways

Gateways are used to represent decisions. Gateways are of several types; however, regardless of the type of gateway that is being used, each gateway that splits the flow in multiple paths is matched by another gateway of the same type that merges those paths back into the main flow.

BPMN 2.0 defines several kinds of gateways:

- In an exclusive gateway, one and only one branch must be chosen. To make things clearer, the exclusive gateway can also be drawn with a symbol (an "X" that stands for XOR, i.e., exclusive-OR). A gateway without a symbol is assumed to be an exclusive gateway. In the case of the exclusive gateway, the process moves on to the next activity as soon as one branch is complete—all other branches are simply skipped.
- In a parallel gateway, all branches are followed in parallel. In the case of the parallel gateway, the merging gateway is especially significant in that it works as a synchronizing merge; that is, the process will not move on to the next activity until all parallel branches coming into the merging gateway have been completed.
- The inclusive gateway is an unusual type of gateway in the sense that it allows an arbitrary number of branches to be followed. If only one branch is followed, then it is equivalent to an exclusive gateway. If all paths are followed, then it is equivalent to a parallel gateway. Finally, if any number of branches between one and all of them is activated, then these exact same branches will be synchronized at the end.
- A complex gateway is used when the splitting and/or merging condition(s) cannot be appropriately described by any of the previous gateways. It is included in BPMN for completeness, but its use can hardly be recommended, since it does not convey a precise idea of the execution semantics.

TABLE 11.3

Looping

Loop	Description	Symbol
Activity looping	The loop is repeated as many times as indicated in the attributes of the task or sub-processes it is placed in.	
Sequence looping	Loops can be made by the use of gateways which connect to an upstream object by a sequence flow	

11.1.5 Looping

A process represents a sequence of activities where each activity is executed before moving on to the next one. In particular, each activity is executed at most once. However, in practice, there may be scenarios where a single activity has to be run multiple times. BPMN enables a user to specify if an activity is to be executed multiple times. In some cases, the activity will be executed a number of times until a certain condition is true. The loop activity, on the other hand, is a means to keep an activity running until some condition is true. This may not necessarily involve a different object in each iteration. In fact, the loop may be run over the same object until either the state of that object changes or some other condition becomes true.

In other cases, the number of times that an activity is to be run is known in advance, and all those runs can be triggered at once, either sequentially or in parallel. This concept is referred to as multi-instance in BPMN. Usually, the multiple-instance activity, either in parallel or sequential form, is used when there is a collection of objects to be processed independently of one another. In this case, each instance of the activity is intended to handle a different object.

Table 11.3 shows notation for looping.

11.1.6 Intermediate Events

Intermediate events are events that occur somewhere along the flow of the process. These events can be used either to wait for some input or to produce some output. In BPMN, an intermediate event that waits for some input is said to be "catching," while an intermediate event that produces some output is said to be "throwing." There are several types of both catching and throwing events, and all of these events have a similar rationale to the start and end events discussed earlier.

BPMN 2.0 defines several kinds of intermediate events, as follows:

- A timer event is an intermediate event that waits until a certain deadline has been reached or until a certain amount of time has passed.
- A condition event waits until a certain condition is true.

- A signal event waits for a certain signal.
- A multiple event can wait for multiple things to happen (e.g., a message and a condition, a message and a timer, etc.).

As with the start events discussed earlier, there are two variants for an intermediate event with multiple triggers: the simple multiple will allow the process to proceed after any of those triggers has occurred, whereas the parallel multiple requires all triggers to occur before the process can proceed.

11.1.7 Event-Based Gateway

The event-based gateway is similar to an intermediate event with multiple triggers. In fact, each branch coming out of this gateway has an intermediate (catching) event, which means that every branch will wait for some event to occur. The event that occurs first will determine the branch to be followed, and the remaining branches will be skipped.

BPMN 2.0 enables either exclusive or parallel versions of an event-based gateway being the first element in a process (or subprocess). In the former case, the process will begin in one of the possible ways shown in the diagram; that is, either by a message, a condition, or a timer. The first event to occur instantiates the process, determines the branch to be executed, and ensures all other branches are skipped. In the latter case, the first event to occur instantiates the process, but the remaining branches will be kept alive and listening for their respective events; in this case, the process will be complete when all branches have been executed. Naturally, only the first event instantiates the process—the remaining events will just trigger additional branches within the same process instance.

11.2 Exception Handling

In BPMN, there are several different ways to represent exceptions and to include behavior that is specifically targeted at handling those exceptions.

BPMN 2.0 language provides several constructs to represent exception handling in business processes:

- Error events are the traditional solution to the problem of representing exceptions in BPMN. This is a special type of event that can be either thrown or caught and therefore easily enables one to map these error events to the exception-handling mechanisms of an execution language such as Business Process Execution Language.

  The error event is a special kind of event that can take the form of an intermediate event (if the error is being caught) or an end event (if the error is being thrown). In the former case, the error event acts as an intermediate (catching) event attached to the boundary of an activity—in the case of occurrence of an error during execution, the event interrupts the activity and takes the process through an exception flow. In the latter case, the activity throws an error by means of an end event; since the activities that come after the error-throwing event cannot really be executed, it cannot be used as an intermediate event but rather only as an end event.

- Intermediate events attached to the boundary of activities are the most commonly used constructs to represent exceptions. Typically, if such an event occurs, the activity is interrupted and the process follows a different path. These attached events are very useful when modeling business processes, but it is not always easy to map them to an execution language like Business Process Execution Language, since the flow that is associated with attached events may not follow a nested block structure. In particular, the trigger may be a message, a timer, a condition, or a signal. An event can be specified with multiple triggers (i.e., any combination of messages, timers, conditions, and signals): either any of the triggers will fire the event, or all triggers are required to occur in order to fire the event (i.e., parallel multiple).

  The attached events are interrupting events in the sense that their occurrence interrupts the execution of the activity they are attached to. However, BPMN also enables noninterrupting attached events; for instance, when someone sends an inquiry while the activity is running, the use of a noninterrupting message event allows the inquiry to be handled and a response to be returned without interrupting the activity.

- Escalation events are a variation on the error events, with the main purpose of alerting someone else—particularly, someone who is above in the hierarchical structure of the organization—of some problematic situation that occurs in the business process. In fact, they do not represent an error in the sense of a system error but rather a condition (i.e., a business problem) that occurs during the execution of a business process and which requires some special handling. In particular, an escalation event means that someone with higher responsibility (e.g., a supervisor) will be called to intervene, or at least will be notified. This is quite useful when modeling business processes in organizations with some form of hierarchical structure. However, the semantics associated with escalation events are not impactful from an execution point of view.

  A significant difference between error events and escalation events is that escalation events may be thrown by intermediate events and may also be caught by noninterrupting attached events.

- Event subprocesses can be triggered by an event occurring in parallel with the main process flow. This event may occur at any point during the process, and the subprocess will be run immediately as a reaction to that event. Because an event subprocess is able to keep listening for events during the entire duration of a process, it has some advantages when compared with the intermediate events that cease to listen for the event trigger once the activity or subprocess is completed.

  The error event as an intermediate (catching) event and as an end (throwing) event can actually be used as start event in an event subprocess. However, for this kind of start event, there is only the interrupting version; this makes an event subprocess with an error event (as a start event) a true exception handler in the sense that it listens for errors and, in the case of an error occurring, it interrupts the parent process and handles the error.

11.3 Transactions

In business processes, transactions work in a different way from the traditional transactions in database systems. In particular, in a business process, there are long-running transactions, where work is committed in a stepwise fashion instead of being held until the very end of the transaction. Consequently, in the case of a rollback, an activity or subprocess cannot be rolled back since it has already been committed, but will instead have to be compensated to effectively roll back an activity or subprocess. The BPMN language provides several constructs to represent transactions and compensation in business processes. Compensation may appear in a process model without an explicit reference to an enclosing transaction; the use of compensation implies that the activity or subprocess where compensation is being used is transactional.

The BPMN language provides several constructs to represent transactions and compensation in business processes, as follows:

- Compensation handlers: There is an association between task A and task B and, in particular, this association means that task B is the compensation handler for task A. The fact that task B is a compensation handler is indicated by the compensation marker inside it. Such a marker effectively precludes task B from being used in the normal flow of the process. It can only be used as a compensation handler that is connected to the boundary of some other activity through an association. The association is represented as an arrow with a dotted line, as opposed to an arrow with a solid line that represents a sequence flow. Thus, task B may never end up being executed; however, it will be executed if the need arises to compensate task A. Naturally, such need may only arise after task A has been successfully executed.

  Another way to specify a compensation handler is through the use of an event subprocess. In the previous section, we have seen that a subprocess may have a number of event subprocesses and that each event subprocess has a start event with a specific trigger. For the purpose of compensation handling, it is possible to use an event subprocess with a start event that has a compensation trigger. The event subprocess will be triggered if there is a need to compensate for the enclosing subprocess. Again, such need may arise only after the enclosing subprocess has completed successfully.

- Transactional subprocesses: The transactional subprocess can be regarded as a transactional concept that serves as a container for other activities or subprocesses. The transactional subprocess has the distinctive feature in that it can be canceled, meaning that its inner activities will have to be compensated. The fact that the subprocess is transactional is indicated by the double-line border. Cancel events can only be used in transactional subprocesses, and they have special semantics in the sense that the occurrence of a cancel event automatically triggers the compensation of all activities contained in the transactional subprocess. The cancel event is a special type of event that can take the form of an end event or an intermediate event attached to the boundary of the transactional subprocess.

  These events work in a similar way to the attached intermediate event, which catches an error, and to the end event, which throws an error.

- Compensation events: Compensation handlers can also be triggered explicitly through the use of compensation events. These events can take the form either of an intermediate (throwing) event or an end event. Each of these events may specify a particular activity that is to be compensated or may not specify any activity to be compensated, in which case, such means that all activities in the enclosing process or subprocess should be compensated.

11.4 Sample Purchasing Scenario Represented in Business Process Modeling and Notation

The basic structure and elements in a BPMN process model can be illustrated by using a purchasing scenario as an example. The example purchasing scenario can be described as follows:

1. In a company, an employee needs a certain commodity (e.g., a printer cartridge). In order to get that product, a requisition form must be filled out and submitted to the warehouse.
2. The warehouse will check whether the product is available in stock. If it is available, then the warehouse dispatches the product to the employee.
3. Otherwise, the product must be purchased from an external supplier. In this case, the item is not available in-house, so the purchasing department prepares a purchase order and sends it to a supplier.
4. The supplier confirms the order and delivers the product directly to the warehouse.
5. The warehouse receives the product, which includes updating the stock, and dispatches the product to the employee who originally submitted the request.

Figure 11.1 shows the corresponding process model using BPMN. It consist of two entities—the company and the supplier—represented by:

- A "purchase process" pool, which is subdivided into three organizational units represented by
  - An employee swim lane corresponding to the employee who requests the product
  - A warehouse swim lane corresponding to the warehouse that stores the product
  - A purchase department swim lane corresponding to the department that processes the purchase of the product
- A "supplier" pool, which is left blank because nothing is known about the internal behavior of the supplier other than the fact that it receives the purchase order and returns an order confirmation

The swim lane is a placeholder for BPMN flow constructs, such as the activities, gateways, and events described earlier. The swim lane is a means to assign responsibility for certain tasks to a given organizational unit; whatever is placed inside a swim lane is assumed to happen within the context of that organizational unit.

The process begins in the "employee" swim lane with a start event. The first activity that appears after the start event is "fill in requisition." This activity is then followed by "check product availability," which is performed by the warehouse, on a different swim lane. The warehouse checks the inventory and determines the quantity available for the requested product.

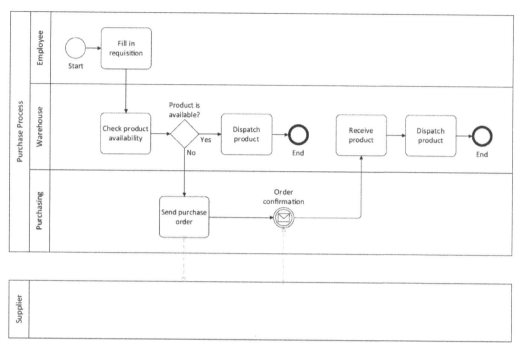

FIGURE 11.1
Sample purchase scenario model using BPMN.

As a result of this step, it may happen that the product is either available (if quantity > 0) or not available (if quantity = 0). Therefore, at this point, the process must contain a decision. This decision is represented by a gateway, which in this case is an exclusive-OR gateway (i.e., either one or the other of the following, but not both, can occur):

- If the product is available, then the warehouse dispatches it to the employee and the process ends, as indicated by an end event.
- If, the product is not available from the warehouse, the purchasing department prepares and sends a purchase order to an external supplier in form of a message.

In general, sequence flows (represented by solid arrows) can only take place within the boundaries of a pool; that is, sequence flows are applicable only to the internal processes within an organization unit. Between organizations, the interaction is represented by message flows (represented by dashed arrows). It is assumed that, regardless of the way the supplier designs its own internal processes, these will be compatible with those message exchanges.

After the company sends the purchase order, the process will wait for the order confirmation to arrive, represented as an intermediate event named as "order confirmation." The sequence flow will proceed to the next activity only when the order confirmation has been received.

Whether the product is available in the warehouse or is received upon purchase from the supplier, the "dispatch product" process dispatches the product to the employee who submitted the original request. The activity "dispatch product" appears twice in the swim lane for the warehouse and it would appear that such an activity has been duplicated unnecessarily. For example, by drawing an arrow from "receive product" to the first

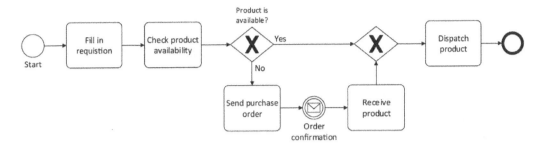

FIGURE 11.2
Modified sample purchase scenario model using BPMN.

"dispatch product" on the left, it appears that the process would be able to accomplish the same thing without the need for the second "dispatch product" activity on the right. However, this is contrary to the principle of nested block structure, which states that it is much easier to ensure the correct behavior of a process that follows a nested block structure, as opposed to one with arbitrary connections between any pair of nodes.

In Figure 11.1, there is a splitting exclusive gateway, but there is no matching merge. This is possible because both paths eventually lead to an end event, so there is no need to merge them back to a common flow. However, if the dispatch activity is seen as being exactly the same in both paths, then the process can be redesigned as shown in Figure 11.2. Here, if the product is available in the warehouse then the process proceeds immediately to "dispatch product"; otherwise, the product must be ordered first and only then dispatched to the employee.

 This process follows a nested block structure because the splitting gateway initiates a block that is closed by the merging gateway. The same principle must be obeyed for other types of gateways, including those of a parallel, inclusive, or complex nature, where the merging also plays a synchronization role.

11.5 Characteristics of Business Process Modeling and Notation for Modeling Software Engineering Processes

With the increasing demands regarding flexibility and adaptability of development processes, the constant evolution of development methods and tools, and the trend toward continuous product deployment, better support for process engineers in terms of universally applicable modeling notations as well as simulation and enactment mechanisms has become more desirable than ever. The discipline of business process modeling has attained a greater level of consensus and standardization, leading most notably to the BPMN idea. The success of BPMN as a standard business process modeling notation concept has prompted the question of whether BPMN could also be used for modeling software engineering processes.

BPMN relies on the following three fundamental assumptions that affect its scope of applicability:

1. A process consists of a set of isolated process instances (also called cases) that interact with each other in very limited ways.

2. An instance is a sequence of activities that transform objects associated with the instance along the way from a start state to an end state (possibly among multiple possible end states).

3. Each atomic activity task is an atomic unit of work performed by a single actor.

11.5.1 Business Process Modeling and Notation Strengths

In general, BPMN is suitable to capture sequential relations between activities, whereby the completion of an activity enables commencement of other activities.

1. Modeling control flows: BPMN is armed with special types of gateways that allow one to capture complex synchronization conditions; for example, the OR-join (inclusive) synchronization gateway allows for the capture of points in a process wherein the execution must wait for all "active" incoming threads to complete before proceeding.

2. Modeling events and messages: another distinguishing feature of BPMN is its richness of event types, which range from the timer and message events to conditional events, escalation events, compensation events, and error events. Given the wide range of events produced, and consumed by modern software development environments, the richness of the event type spectrum supported by BPMN is an attractive feature vis-a-vis of other software process modeling notations.

3. Modeling executable process: BPMN is designed to also support the enactment of business processes via so-called executable BPMN models. The executable subset of BPMN defines a number of properties that can be associated to processes, tasks, events, and flows in order to specify the execution behavior to the level of detail required by a business process management system (BPMS). For example, in an executable BPMN, one can associate rules to the flows coming out of the XOR-split or OR-split gateways, which can be interpreted by a BPMS. It is also possible to bind a task in a process to an external (Internet) service (so-called service tasks) or to a script in a programming language (so-called script tasks). BPMN also enables to define the schema of objects manipulated by a process as well as mapping rules to link the data objects manipulated by the process to the data required as input or provided as output by each individual task in the process.

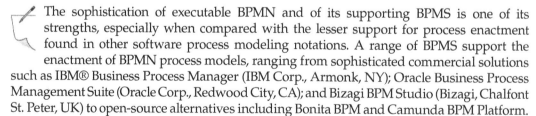 The sophistication of executable BPMN and of its supporting BPMS is one of its strengths, especially when compared with the lesser support for process enactment found in other software process modeling notations. A range of BPMS support the enactment of BPMN process models, ranging from sophisticated commercial solutions such as IBM® Business Process Manager (IBM Corp., Armonk, NY); Oracle Business Process Management Suite (Oracle Corp., Redwood City, CA); and Bizagi BPM Studio (Bizagi, Chalfont St. Peter, UK) to open-source alternatives including Bonita BPM and Camunda BPM Platform.

11.5.2 Business Process Modeling and Notation Weaknesses

The following are some of the inherent limitations of BPMN that hinder capturing software processes:

1. Modeling resources: BPMN is rather limited in the resource perspective. BPMN enables the allocation of tasks to roles via lanes. It is also possible to capture

business processes that involve multiple independent entities, such as, for example, multiple companies in a business-to-business process (e.g., a contractor and a subcontractor) via so-called pools that communicate via message flows. However, one clear limitation of BPMN along the resource perspective is its inability to capture the fact that a given task is performed jointly by multiple resources (e.g., human actors) with different roles (e.g., analyst and developer). Indeed, a task in BPMN must belong to exactly one lane.

 UML activity diagrams provide the ability to designate that a given activity in a process involves multiple performers with different roles. It also supports the ability to designate the state in which a data object should be when it is consumed or produced by an activity in a process.

2. Modeling data: BPMN is also somewhat limited along the data perspective. In the data perspective, BPMN primarily relies on the concept of a data object, meaning a logical unit of data that can be read by or created or modified by a task or an event. It also supports a concept of a data store that can be used for capture purposes, for example, a database or document management system that is read by or modified by a task or event. However, data objects in BPMN do not have a notion of state.

3. Modeling "in totality": A more fundamental limitation of BPMN that hampers its use for software process modeling is its inherent focus on business processes consisting of isolated instances. These cases are executed independently without any interaction between them other than the fact that they may share the same resources. The isolated case assumption is generally a convenient abstraction. The modeler can focus on describing one case of the process in isolation, without worrying about possible interactions. On the other hand, this assumption hampers the inability for modelers to capture intercase dependencies, which occur in software processes.

   While it is possible in BPMN to model the fact that a process spawns multiple instances of a subprocess and waits for some or all of them to complete, but it is not possible to model the fact that an instance of a process must wait for a collection of instances of the same process (or of another process) to reach a certain state before continuing.

11.5.3 Business Process Modeling and Notation Drawbacks

BPMN does not provide a mechanism that would allow one to link the completion of one task to a condition on the data objects manipulated by the process. It is not possible to express in BPMN that the normal completion of a task is determined by a given condition becoming true. In other words, the completion of a task in a BPMN process has to be explicitly signaled by the resource performing the task and cannot be automatically determined based on the current state of the data objects in the process.

11.6 Spreadsheet-Based Process Modeling

Graphical process model notations such as the BPMN provide established and successful ways for the specification or documentation of intended or existing processes. However, these notations tend to be rather unintuitive for people who do not know them. Even worse, software tools that can be used for the creation and maintenance of such graphical models are complex and require special user skills in most cases. In order to close the gap between BPM method experts and domain experts, other representations of a process model that are simpler, such as spreadsheets, can be helpful. Spreadsheets offer a simple and (especially in business) well-known way to organize data in rows and columns. A spreadsheet-based process model could be easy to understand and use for most people who operate computers for work.

The main idea is to export graphical models into easier spreadsheets that can be subsequently modified by domain experts and imported back into the process modeling tool: generally, a process can be represented synchronously in a spreadsheet-based model as well as in a graphical model. Transformations between graphical notation and spreadsheets have to be defined. In order to really close the gap between process and domain experts, the transformation algorithms will have to be used in a synchronization mechanism that enables a model to roundtrip between both of the worlds.

11.6.1 Process Model Transformations into Spreadsheets

There are different approaches to modeling processes using spreadsheets that depend on the envisaged degree of fidelity (Krumnow and Decker 2010). Some examples include:

1. The simple sequence approach. As the existing tools are mostly for business process method experts as users, this first approach tries to be as simple as possible: only the modeling of sequences of activities is supported. Activities have a number of property types that can be assigned once or several times per activity. These multiple assignments of properties are necessary, e.g., for activities that have two input data objects.

   A difficulty of this approach exists in the realization of multiple properties in a spreadsheet. If an customized spreadsheet editor is used, the cells can be enabled to contain lists of values. If Excel (Microsoft Corp., Redmond, WA) is used, the problem is much harder. Here, comma-separated strings could be used. Alternatively, a line-break-separated string could be used, which leads to a list layout for multiple properties.

2. The branching approach. This approach adds some new elements and, more importantly, a successor property to each element to address process models that contain not only sequences but also complex control flow structures. In order to support branching and joining within one model, gateways and events are necessary. As in BPMN, the basic three gateway types (parallel, exclusive, and inclusive) have different execution semantics. Events can be used to express reached states in a process model. More important in our case, they can be used to model different conditions after branching gateways. Finally, subprocesses are activities that have their own process model(s) describing their internal behavior.

   The difficulty with this approach is the identification of the element type for a certain row. This could be obtained by introducing a new property to each row that holds the type of the represented activity. As this entails the user to have a preunderstanding of the differences between the types, a work-around for this can be: depending on the given name, the position within the process' flow, and the used properties, the type of an element can be deduced automatically by humans or by the computer.

3. The additional properties approach. The earlier approach still has no support to specify properties, for example of an input document or an assigned role. As mentioned before, this is due to the fact that all of those elements are just represented by simple strings. This can be mended by enabling elements like data objects to be represented by rows that are linked to activities in a manner similar to the control flow, which links two control flow elements.

The difficulty with this approach is that, although this results in enhanced expressiveness with regards to the behavior and structure of the attached elements, the spreadsheets effectively have gotten more complex: even if, for the attached element, only the name is modeled, there are a lot of associating links connecting an activity row to attached element rows.

11.6.2 Process Model Transformations

In order to benefit from the established techniques for graphical models as well as from the easiness of spreadsheets, both worlds have to be transformable into each other. Therefore, this section will show how a spreadsheet-based model can be transformed from and into BPMN.

For a natural ordering of elements within the produced spreadsheet, first, the nodes have to be sequentialized. Thereby, pairs of two nodes that are connected by control flow, whereby the source has only one outgoing flow and the target has only one incoming flow, are placed next to each other in a list. By iterating over this list, the spreadsheet can be created. Here, four functions have be implemented. The first two functions check whether an element or an element's relation is valid, the third creates rows, and the fourth adds connections between rows (or data values to rows).

In order to transform a graphical model into a spreadsheet, we need a transformation T. The following algorithm shows how T can be implemented:

```
nodeArray = getNodesInSequentialOrder(model) for each node in
nodeArray:
 if isSupportedElement(node):
  createRow(node)
for each node in nodeArray:
 if isSupportedElement(node):
  for each connectedNode of node:
   if isSupportedRelation(node, connectedNode):
    addRelation(node, connectedNode)
```

Similarly, in order to transform a valid spreadsheet into a graphical notation, a transformation T^{-1} is needed. Here, a similar algorithm can be used:

```
for each row of spreadsheet:
 if isSupportedRow(node):
  createElement(row)
for each row of spreadsheet:
 if isSupportedRow(node):
  for each property of row:
   // this includes the implicit order of rows
   if isLink(property) && isSupported(node, property):
    addRelation(row, property)
```

11.6.3 Business Process Modeling and Notation Transformations

It can now be inspected which parts of the BPMN 2.0 can be transformed into spreadsheets and vice versa.

In the transformation of BPMN to spreadsheet, there exists a lot of BPMN elements that cannot be transformed into either one of the approaches, for example subprocesses and collapsed (black-box) pools but also descriptive element groups and annotations. More importantly, message flows cannot be transformed into spreadsheets at all. Since message flows are used to model the interaction of different processes, they are a pretty complicated construct and can therefore not be pressed into a spreadsheet-based model that aims for simplicity. Moreover, attached boundary events cannot be transformed and there exist restrictions for containment in pools and lanes as well as for associations.

Table 11.4 shows the transformability of BPMN elements and relations.

In the transformation of spreadsheet to BPMN, all elements of the three approaches can be transformed into BPMN elements. Thereby, every row of a spreadsheet is interpreted as an activity, except if one of the following criteria is met:

- In II and III: If the name starts with AND, XOR, or OR, the element is a gateway.
- In II and III: If the element has no predecessor/successor, it is a start event/end event.
- In II and III: If the ref property is set, then the element is a collapsed subprocess.
- In III: If the element is connected through a typed relation (e.g., input), then the element's type can be deducted from the relation.

TABLE 11.4

Transformability of BPMN Elements and Relations

	Approach I	Approach II	Approach III
Task	↰	↰	↰
All events, collapsed subprocess	⊘	↰	↰
Parallel-, data-based and event-based exclusive- and inclusive gateways	⊘	↰	↰
Collapsed subprocess	⊘	↰	↰
Pool, lane	⊘	↵[5] + ↰	↵[5] + ↰
Data object	⊘	↵ + ↰[6]	↰
Subprocess, collapsed pool, complex gateway, group, annotation	⊘	⊘	⊘
Sequence flow	↵ + ↰[4]	↰	↰
Message flow	⊘	⊘	⊘
Associations (directed and undirected) with data	⊘	↵ + ↰[7]	↵ + ↰[7]
Containment in pool and lane	⊘	↰	↵[8] + ↰
Attachment of boundary events	⊘	⊘	⊘

11.7 Summary

BPMN is a graphical notation for modeling business processes. This chapter explored the wide range of elements that BPMN provides to create business process models. The notation of BPMN is sufficiently clear so as to describe process behavior in a way that can be translated into an executable form. Using BPMN, business analysts can describe organizational processes in a way that can be understood by developers and system integrators and that can serve as a blueprint for implementing the services and orchestrations required to support those processes. Chapter 12 presents the spreadsheet application development methodology for the development of process-centric applications, while engineering and implementation of process-centric applications is the focus of Chapter 13.

12

Development of Process-Centric Application Systems

This chapter presents the spreadsheet-driven spreadsheeter application development (SAD) methodology for the development of process-centric application systems. The first phase of SAD methodology deals with the problem of identifying enterprise business processes that are essential for the functioning of the organization. The second phase of SAD methodology deals with developing a process model for the business processes identified in the previous phase and involves completing parts I and II of the activity spreadsheet.

The third phase of SAD methodology deals with four subphases, which are "as-is" process model analysis, "to-be" process model creation, "to-be" process model analysis, and process simulation. The first subphase performs an analysis of the process performance of the "as-is" process model and calculates process performance parameters, such as process flow, cycle time efficiency, and process capacity, with the purpose of gaining essential information about what kind of a process we are dealing with. The calculated process performance enables management to make a decision about the necessity for process improvement or innovation. On the other hand, the fourth subphase uses the simulation technique to imitate the functioning of the "to-be" process model in order to study the reality of the process behavior and the possibility of making further improvements. The fourth phase of SAD methodology deals with the development of a process management system that implements the "to-be" process model including the class model and the design of the system based on the activity spreadsheet parts I and II. The fifth phase of the SAD methodology deals with controlling the functioning of the improved business process and the process management system.

However, before diving into the details of SAD methodology, the chapter visits the concepts of deductive database (DB) and deductive spreadsheet as a preparatory step. Deductive DBs are an attempt to overcome the limitations of traditional DB systems by incorporating the characteristics features of expert systems. A deductive spreadsheet is a tool that enables users to define logic statements and inference rules for symbolic reasoning in the same way that current spreadsheets allow users to define mathematical formulae for numerical calculations.

12.1 Deductive Databases

Deductive DBs were proposed as an attempt to overcome the limitations of traditional DB systems by incorporating the characteristics features of expert systems. DBs are characterized by their ability to manage large volumes of data, although they usually perform simple operations to manipulate the data. The main feature of expert systems is to provide reasoning capabilities to help decision-making, but they usually are not able to manage large volumes of data; expert systems were developed to support the process of decision-making within narrow domains in particular contexts.

Deductive DBs could be seen as an integration of data (as in a DB management system) and knowledge (as in an expert system). Data are represented by means of extensions of DB predicates (i.e., facts), while knowledge is represented by the intension of DB predicates. Knowledge, or intensional information, is defined by means of rules that allow us to deduce new information from that explicitly stored in the DB; rules are of two types:

- Deductive rules, which allow us to define new facts (view or derive facts) from stored facts
- Integrity constraints, which state conditions to be satisfied by the DB

A deductive DB consists of three finite sets:

1. A set of facts: Facts state basic information that is known to be true in the DB.
2. A set of deductive rules: Deductive rules allow for the derivation of new facts from other facts stored in the DB.
3. A set of integrity constraints: Integrity constraints correspond to conditions that each state of the DB should satisfy.

A deductive DB D is a triple D = (F, DR, IC)

where:
F is a finite set of ground facts
DR is a finite set of deductive rules
IC is a finite set of integrity constraints

The set F of facts is called the extensional part of the DB (EDB), while the sets DR and IC together form the so-called intensional part of the DB (IDB).

DB predicates are traditionally partitioned into:

1. A base predicate that appears in the EDB and, possibly, in the body of deductive rules and integrity constraints
2. A derived (or view) predicate that appears only in the IDB and is defined by means of some deductive rule; that is, facts about derived predicates that are not explicitly stored in the DB and can only be derived by means of deductive rules

 Base predicates in deductive DBs correspond to relations. Therefore, base facts correspond to tuples in relational DBs. In that way, it is not difficult to see the clear correspondence between the EDB of a deductive DB and the logical contents of a relational one.

The concept of *view* is used in DBs to delimit the DB content relevant to each group of users. A view is a virtual data structure, derived from base facts or other views by means of a definition function. Therefore, the extension of a view does not have an independent existence because it is completely defined by the application of the definition function to the extension of the DB.

Views provide the following advantages:

- They simplify the user interface, because users can ignore the data that are not relevant to them.
- They favor logical data independence, because they allow for changing of the logical data structure of the DB without the need to perform corresponding changes to other rules.
- They make certain queries easier or more natural to define, since, by means of them, we can refer directly to the concepts instead of having to provide their definition.
- They provide a protection measure, because they prevent users from accessing data external to their view.

Real DB applications use many views. However, the power of views can be exploited only if a user does not distinguish a view from a base fact. That implies the need to perform query and update operations on the views, in addition to the same operations on the base facts. In deductive DBs, views correspond to derived predicates and are defined by means of deductive rules.

12.1.1 Query Processing

Deductive DB management systems must provide a query-processing system that is able to answer queries specified in terms of views as well as in terms of base predicates. The subject of query processing deals with finding answers to queries requested on a certain DB. A query evaluation procedure finds answers to queries according to the DB semantics.

Two basic approaches compute the answers of a query Q:

1. Bottom-up (forward chaining): The query evaluation procedure starts from the base facts and applies all deductive rules until no new consequences can be deduced. The requested query is then evaluated against the whole set of deduced consequences, which is treated as if it was base information.

2. Top-down (backward chaining): The query evaluation procedure starts from a query Q and applies deductive rules backward by trying to deduce new conditions required to make Q true. The conditions are expressed in terms of predicates that define Q and can be understood as simple subqueries that, appropriately combined, provide the same answers as Q. The process is repeated until conditions only in terms of base facts are achieved.

At first glance, the top-down approach might seem preferable to the bottom-up approach, because it takes into account the constants in the initial query during the evaluation process. For the same reason, the top-down approach does not take into account all possible consequences of the DB but only those that are relevant to perform the computation. However, the top-down approach also presents several inconveniences:

- Top-down methods are usually one tuple at a time. Instead of reasoning on the entire extension of DB predicates, as the bottom-up method does, the top-down approach considers base facts one by one as soon as they appear in the definition of a certain subquery. For that reason, top-down methods traditionally have been less efficient.

- Top-down methods may not terminate. In the presence of recursive rules, a top-down evaluation method could enter an infinite loop and never terminate its execution.

- At definition time, it is not always possible to determine whether a top-down algorithm terminates. Thus, in a top-down approach, we do not know whether the method will finish its execution if it is taking too much time to get the answer.

- Repetitive subqueries: During the process of reducing the original query to simpler subqueries that provide the same result, a certain subquery may be requested several times. In some cases, that may cause reevaluation of the subquery, thus reducing efficiency of the whole evaluation.

12.1.2 Update Processing

Deductive DB management systems must also provide an update processing system able to handle updates specified in terms of base and view predicates. By taking into account the intensional information provided by views and integrity constraints, the objective of update processing is to perform the work required to apply the requested update:

1. Change computation: A deductive DB can be updated through the application of a given transaction—that is, a set of updates of base facts. Due to the presence of deductive rules and integrity constraints, the application of a transaction may also induce several changes on the intensional information (i.e., on views and integrity constraints). Given a transaction, change computation refers to the process of computing the changes on the extension of the derived predicates induced by changes on the base facts specified by that transaction.

2. View updating: As the advantages provided by views can be achieved only if a user does not distinguish at view from a base fact, a deductive update processing system must also provide the ability to request updates on the derived facts, in addition to updates on base facts. Because the view extension is completely defined by the application of the deductive rules to the EDB, changes requested on a view must be translated to changes on the EDB.

3. Integrity constraint enforcement: This refers to the problem of deciding the policy to be applied when some integrity constraint is violated due to the application of a certain transaction. The most conservative policy is that of integrity constraint checking, aimed at rejecting the transactions that violate some constraint.

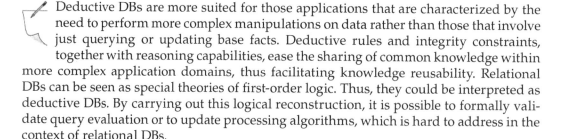 Deductive DBs are more suited for those applications that are characterized by the need to perform more complex manipulations on data rather than those that involve just querying or updating base facts. Deductive rules and integrity constraints, together with reasoning capabilities, ease the sharing of common knowledge within more complex application domains, thus facilitating knowledge reusability. Relational DBs can be seen as special theories of first-order logic. Thus, they could be interpreted as deductive DBs. By carrying out this logical reconstruction, it is possible to formally validate query evaluation or to update processing algorithms, which is hard to address in the context of relational DBs.

12.2 Deductive Spreadsheet

Microsoft Excel (Microsoft Corp., Redmond, WA) and Google (Google, Mountain View, CA) spreadsheets allow users to routinely perform complex custom calculations on numerical data. The typical spreadsheet's clever interface makes it easy to use productively with little or no training and its gentle learning curve enables users to reinforce their skills and acquire new ones in a learning-by-doing fashion. However, spreadsheets do not enable users to perform symbolic reasoning with the same degree of facility and usability. A deductive spreadsheet is a tool that enables users to define logic statements and inference rules for symbolic reasoning in the same way that current spreadsheets allow users to define mathematical formulas for numerical calculations.

Taking inspiration from the automated data inference of the normal spreadsheet, the deductive spreadsheet paradigm enables users to define useful forms of inference among their *symbolic and numerical* data. The key idea underlying the deductive spreadsheet is centered around interpreting a group of columns and rows as a relation and then providing support for manipulating these relations as first-class objects and for extending the core mechanisms of evaluate, update, and explain to these new entities.

12.2.1 Traditional Spreadsheet

The traditional spreadsheet was born as an electronic incarnation of accounting books and, as such, it provides outstanding support for numerical calculation.

A spreadsheet is a collection of cells which can contain either a value (e.g., "42," "12.99," "Total," or the default blank value) or a formula (e.g., "(A3 − 32) * 5/9"). From a programming language point of view, a spreadsheet is just a simple functional language without recursion—its expressive power is very limited.

Spreadsheet applications provide three core functionalities:

1. Evaluation: When loading a spreadsheet file, a spreadsheet application computes the formula contained in the cells and displays the corresponding value. This yields the evaluated spreadsheet displayed on the user's screen.

2. Update: Once a spreadsheet is loaded (and evaluated), every time the user modifies the contents of a cell, changes are propagated to all parts of the spreadsheet that depend on this location and the value of the affected cells is redisplayed.

3. Explanation: The ability to answer questions such as "Why does this cell report this value?" is an essential functionality, as it has been shown that the vast majority of spreadsheets are riddled with errors (e.g., [EB02, Pan98, BG87]). Commercial spreadsheets support explanation by offering tools that visualize dependencies among cells in an evaluated spreadsheet, although new approaches have been proposed (e.g., [CC00]).

The closest a traditional spreadsheet has to offer to logical reasoning are the common Boolean operators AND, OR, and NOT, which are intended to be used in the conditions of IF statements (though, even there, their prenex syntax makes for unnecessarily complex expressions). One can hardly perform any serious reasoning with those. Because its formulas are drawn from a simple functional language without recursion, the traditional spreadsheet does not have the computational power to support the forms of reasoning we are interested in. Note that this limitation is also what makes spreadsheet calculations always terminate. As we extend the traditional spreadsheet with support for symbolic reasoning, we shall strive to maintain this characteristic.

12.2.2 Logic Programming

There are a number of reasons why Prolog is an unlikely foundation for the deductive spreadsheet:

1. Unless carefully coded by an experience programmer, Prolog specifications are extremely prone to nontermination. Sometimes an action as simple as issuing a query with a variable instead of a constant can cause an infinite loop. Writing the conditions of an inference rule in the "wrong" order can have the same effect (this is as if the spreadsheet formula A1CA2 computed 5, but A2CA1 hung the computer).

    This is clearly undesirable in the hands of an end user: absurdly unpredictable behaviors of this kind lead to frustration and the user may give up before they have acquired the skills needed to avoid these pitfalls in the first place.

2. Nontermination and slow-termination would still be an issue, as Prolog has very high computational power. Differently from a spreadsheet, it would be impossible to guarantee that a task written in full Prolog will terminate, or terminate in a timely manner.

3. The operational model of Prolog does not blend well into a spreadsheet-like application. Prolog operates top-down; that is, it starts from a user query and looks at the inference rules that may have entailed it. It then tries to prove each of their conditions by looking at the rules that may have entailed them, and so on until all these subgoals have been satisfactorily proved. The variable instantiation is then reported to the user as a final value. If the user wants another value, they must ask Prolog to search for another proof, and so on until all of the different ways to solve the query have been examined.

Datalog, a language derived from logic programming, is used as a representation language to define the contents and the structure of the information stored in the deductive spreadsheet. Datalog is a declarative, nonprocedural language that is uniform and set-oriented. In contrast to Prolog, the Datalog evaluation strategy is bottom-up: it starts with the true facts of a logical specification and uses them to compute all of their immediate consequences according to the given inference rules. It then uses these derived facts and the inference rules to compute a second round of consequences, then a third, and so on until all of the logical consequences of the specification have been discovered. The syntactic restrictions ensure termination, even in the presence of recursive rules.

Bottom-up evaluation is a good fit for the deductive spreadsheet for the following several reasons:

- Termination is guaranteed. This is a desirable property that blends well into the spreadsheet model.
- It reports all of the solutions to a query, without duplicates. It will be convenient to display them in as many spreadsheet columns as there are variables that participate in the query.

- Because evaluation always starts from the true facts and not from the query, Datalog supports evaluating multiple queries at once. Bottom-up evaluation will compute the answers to all of them simultaneously. This aspect is again reminiscent of a spreadsheet, where, in general, numerous cells contain formulas that will be evaluated simultaneously.
- A change in any part of the specification, either a fact or a rule, will cause immediate reevaluation and updating of all the answers.

For these reasons, a Datalog model with bottom-up evaluation is considered as one of the pillars of the deductive spreadsheet.

12.3 Spreadsheet Application Development Methodology

The presentation and approach in this chapter has been adopted from N. Damij and T. Damij (2014).

12.3.1 Process Identification

The first phase of SAD methodology discusses the problem of identifying the organization's business processes, starting with a set of core processes, which represent the processes that are essential for the functioning of the organization, with the purpose of analyzing and improving them.

Process identification consists of the following two steps:

1. Identification of the business processes of the organization, which is done by organizing interviews with the management at the strategic and business levels and analyzing the organization's documents. The purpose of the interviews with the top level of management is to understand what role the organization plays and where it is heading.
2. Definition of the flow of each of the identified business processes through various functional areas of the organization. This means that, for each listed business process, a group of work processes is identified that are performed within different departments of the organization.

The expected number of core or large business processes that pass through different functional areas of the organization may be between 10 and 20 business processes. The three major processes in an organization are as follows:

- Developing new products
- Delivering products to customers
- Managing customer relationships

There are three types of main processes in the enterprises: core, support, and management processes. The core processes are the operational processes of the business and result in the production of the outputs that are required by the external customer. The support processes are those that enable the core processes to exist. Management processes concern themselves with managing the core processes or the support processes, or they concern themselves with planning at the business level.

Identifying business processes in a company is usually done by organizing interviews with the management at different levels of the organization; these include the strategic, business, and operational levels.

12.3.1.1 Process List

The phase commences by trying to analyze the organization business plans and organizing interviews with people at the top level to elicit important information regarding the organization's mission, vision, strategic plans, and so on.

After accomplishing the plan of interviews at the strategic level, the process of collecting information is continued by conducting interviews with management at the business level in accordance with the plan of interviews created during the previous interviews. The purpose of the interviews with business management is to identify the business processes of the organization or, more precisely, to select which processes are the ones targeted for analysis and improvement.

The results of these interviews are the following:

1. Creation of a list of selected business processes of the organization that are candidate processes for improvement
2. For each of the listed processes, attainment of more detailed information to identify through which of the organization's department(s) or unit(s) the process passes
3. Extension of the plan of interviews to responsible people at the departmental or operational levels in order to plan the interviews in the next step

12.3.1.2 Process Flow Identification

The second step of the first phase deals with defining the flow of each of the listed business processes through the organization's various departments and units.

This information is further reinforced with management at the operational level, which enables acquisition of the information needed to define the process flow using the following procedure:

1. Develop a process spreadsheet that creates a linkage between each of the selected business processes and those work processes executed within the framework of the different constituting departments.

    Figure 12.1 shows the layout of the process spreadsheet.

Functional area	Work process	Business process	
		BP 1	BP 2
FA 1	WP 1	*	*
	WP 2		*
	WP 3	*	
FA 2	WP 4		*
	WP 5		*
	WP 6	*	

FIGURE 12.1
Process spreadsheet.

The process spreadsheet is organized as follows: the first column presents functional areas or departments of the organization; the second column lists work processes grouped by the functional areas in the framework of which they are performed; and, in the following columns of the spreadsheet, the business processes are defined wherein each business process occupies one column of the spreadsheet. An asterisk in any square(i, j) of the process spreadsheet means that the work process defined in row(i) is performed within the framework of the business process defined in column(j), where i ranges from 1 to the number of work processes and j ranges from 1 to the number of business processes.

2. Obtain detailed information about the organizational structure of each department that is involved in performing a certain work process related to the business process discussed, in order to create a plan of interviews with the employees for the next phase.

12.3.2 Process Modeling

The second phase of SAD methodology deals with developing, for the business processes identified in the first phase, a process model consisting of an *activity spreadsheet*. Business process modeling is carried out by organizing interviews with the management at departmental level, followed by conducting detailed interviews with the employees as groups or individuals in the department(s) through which the business process flows. The aim of these interviews is to define and describe in detail each activity performed within the framework of every work process that is related to the business process modeled corresponding to the content of the process spreadsheet developed previously.

A process model is a description and logical presentation of a real process, whose development requires capturing all of the information needed to create a complete understanding of the functioning of the process within the organization, in addition to identifying the process's interactions with its environment. This knowledge represents a precondition for developing a process model that is a true reflection of the original process. SAD methodology carries out business process modeling by developing a spreadsheet called the activity spreadsheet, which represents a model called the "as-is" process model. The model developed describes the behavior of the business process as it exists in reality in the organization.

The activity spreadsheet development consists of two steps:

1. Display of a graphical representation of the process model
2. Description of the process in detail

12.3.2.1 Activity Spreadsheet Development Part I

The development of the activity spreadsheet represents the most important modeling technique used within SAD methodology. This spreadsheet is capable of showing a complex and large business process in a single spreadsheet that is simple and easy to develop, survey, and update.

The activity spreadsheet is usually structured as follows:

1. The first column shows the business process selected.
2. The second column is occupied by subprocesses (if the business process is partitioned into subprocesses).

3. The next column, the "Work Process" column, lists the work processes of the business process.

4. The next column, the "Activity" column, lists the activities grouped by work processes.

5. If there are activities, which are decomposed into tasks, then the next column, the "Task" column, lists tasks grouped by activities.

6. The rest of the spreadsheet is structured as follows:

   • The first row lists the organization's departments and units in which the business process is carried out.

   • The second row lists the resources, grouped by the departments in the first row, that perform the activities defined in the rows of the "Activity" column.

7. The last columns of the first part of the spreadsheet are used to represent outside entities; each entity from the environment occupies one column.

Defining the activity spreadsheet involves defining the constituting business processes, work processes, and activities.

1. Defining business process: The modeling process starts by discovering the behavior of the business processes listed in the process spreadsheet one by one. For each of these business processes, a new activity spreadsheet is created, which represents the "as-is" model of the process discussed. Therefore, the name of the business process selected is written in the first column of the newly created activity spreadsheet.

   If the business process is large and complex, it needs to be partitioned into a set of subprocesses in order to be understood and explained. Accordingly, the subprocesses identified are listed in the second column of the activity spreadsheet.

2. Defining work process: Following the connections indicated in the business process column of the process spreadsheet leads us to identifying its work processes (Figure 11.1). The method continues by listing those work processes in the Work Process column of the activity spreadsheet that are related to the concerned business process. These work processes should be listed in the same sequence order as they are executed in reality.

   Similarly, in accordance with the relations defined in the process spreadsheet between each work process and the department in which it is executed, for each work process listed in the Work Process column, write the name of the department (functional area) in which the work process is performed.

   The process modeling team conducts interviews with the management at the operational level; this means organizing interviews with the management of those departments defined in the first row of the activity spreadsheet. The aim of these interviews is to find answers to the following questions:

   a. In what sequence order should the work processes be listed in the Work Process column of the activity spreadsheet with the purpose of showing the business process discussed as a linkage between the set of work processes defined? This linkage shows that the work processes listed are performed within the framework of different connected departments as in reality.

b. Who are the people responsible for each of the work processes listed in the Work Process column and who are the most experienced and knowledgeable employees regarding their functioning, with whom further interviews should be organized?

3. Defining activities: To identify the work accomplished within each work process, further interviews are conducted with previously identified experienced and knowledgeable employees responsible for the daily performance of the work process's activities. The purpose of these interviews is to identify, list, and gain detailed information about every process's activity. To do this, the following procedure is used:

For each work process defined in the Work Process column:
  For each activity identified within the work process:

1. Write the name of the activity into the Activity (third) column of the activity spreadsheet.
2. Write the name of the resource, which performs the defined activity, into a certain column of the second row of the activity spreadsheet under the first row segment, where the department to which the resource belongs is defined.
3. Determine the inputs or events that enter the activity discussed from other activities or from the environment, and the output(s) that leave the activity to other activities or to the environment.
4. Identify the successor activities of the current activity.
5. If the activity consists of tasks, then list the tasks in the Task (fourth) column of the activity spreadsheet successively as they are performed in reality.
6. Connect the activity by horizontal arrow(s) to the resource(s) that are involved with its execution.
7. Connect the activity by vertical arrow(s) to its successor activity or activities.

An activity is a simple microprocess that consists of one or more tasks that represent a well-defined work initiative performed by one resource. An activity may also be understood as a simple algorithm that consists of a few instructions, such as creating a document or placing an order. The activity starts with an input or event that causes the execution of one or more successive tasks and ends by producing the anticipated output(s).

A task could be understood as an elementary work inititative within an activity, or as a well-defined segment within an algorithm—for example, printing or signing a document.

To make the activity spreadsheet reflect the realty of the business process modeled, we need to link all of the activities horizontally and vertically. This modeling concept is used because each activity in reality is connected to a resource that performs it and to a number of activities from which it gets input(s) and to which it sends an output(s).

The purpose of making horizontal and vertical connections is to transfer the true behavior of the original process into the process model developed, as explained in the following:

- The horizontal linkage means that each activity must be linked to those resources defined in the columns of the second row of the spreadsheet that are needed to perform it. Usually, each activity is linked to two resources; these are the resource that is involved in performing the activity and the resource that provides an input (e.g., a customer), or a resource that receives an output produced by the activity (e.g., a clerk, customer).

- The vertical linkage is used to define the order in which the activities are followed and performed, as in reality. Therefore, each activity is connected with one or more predecessor activities, except the first activity, and is also linked to one or more successor activities, except the last one.

Figure 12.2 shows an example of the activity spreadsheet.

 To carry out process modeling using the activity spreadsheet technique, a small set of flowchart symbols is used inside the cells of the activity spreadsheet, or arrows that connect the symbols into the cells horizontally and vertically are employed:

- Symbol ○ indicates the starting point of a process.

  The symbol ○ in cell(1,11) of Figure 11.2, starts the Surgery business process.

- ◎ Symbol indicates the end point of a process or the end of a certain path of the process.

- For example, symbol in cell(32,11) ends the whole process.

- Symbol □ in cell(i, j) means that resource(j) performs activity(i), where j ranges from 1 to the number of resources and i ranges from 1 to the number of activities.

  For example, symbol □ in cell(1,1) means that resource(1) executes activity(1).

- Symbol ◊ in cell(i, j) means that activity(i) is a decision activity. Such an activity starts different alternative paths and is succeeded by different alternative successor activities.

- For example, symbol ◊ in cell(7,2) means that activity(7) is a decision activity followed by activity(8) or activity(32) as alternative successor activities.

- Horizontal arrows →, ← are used to connect the activity horizontally. A horizontal arrow that is drawn from cell(i, j) to cell(i, k) shows a horizontal linkage from activity(i), which is performed by the resource(j), to resource(k), which is related to the activity's output.

- For example, the existence of an arrow from cell(2,1) to cell(2,2) means that resource(2) receives the output of activity(2), while the placement of an arrow from cell(3,2) to cell(3,1) means that the output of activity(3) is sent to resource(1).

- Vertical arrows ↓, ↑ " are used to link the activities vertically. A vertical arrow that is drawn from cell(i, j) to cell(k, j) shows a vertical linkage from activity(i) to its successor activity(k). For example, an arrow from cell(1,1) to cell(2,1) means that activity(1) is linked vertically to its successor activity(2).

  In our example, a horizontal arrow from cell(2,1) to cell(2,2) continued by a vertical arrow to cell(3,2) means that the output of activity(2) is received by resource(2), which as an input enters activity(3) and triggers its processing. This means in reality that resource "Nurse" executes activity(2); the activity is that she forwards the patient and patient's documents to resource "Doctor". The doctor receives the patient's documents and executes activity(3); that is, he examines the patient.

- Symbol * in cell(i, j) and cell(i, k) means that activity(i) could be performed by resource(j) or resource(k) as alternative resources.

- Symbol | is used to fork outputs of an activity or to merge inputs of different activities.

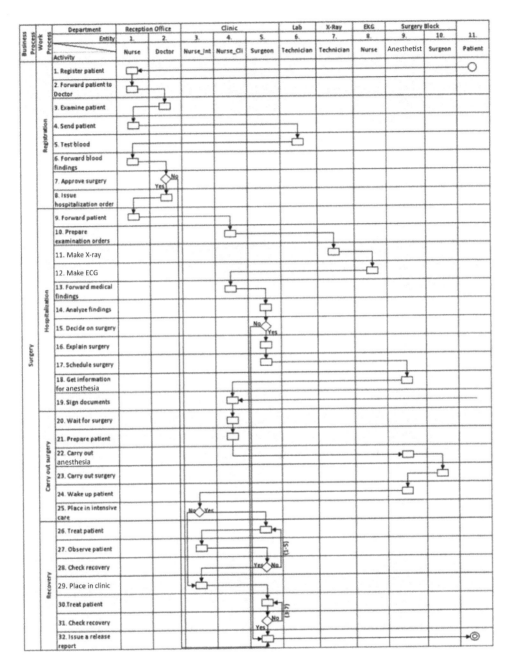

FIGURE 12.2
Activity spreadsheet.

12.3.2.2 Activity Spreadsheet Development Part II

The role of the second part of the spreadsheet is to describe the process behavior and provide detailed information about each activity performed within it. The process description and the process flow presented in the first part of the spreadsheet in the last subsection together create a complete and clear picture of the business process modeled.

The detailed information about the process's behavior is collected during interviews that are organized and conducted with the resources listed in the second row, which are responsible for performing the activities listed in the "Activity" column of the first part of the spreadsheet.

There are a set of parameters that are essential for understanding the functioning of the business process, developing the process model properly, and providing the essential data needed for carrying out the improvement of the process performed in the third phase.

For each activity defined in the "Activity" column, the detailed information required includes:

1. A precise and short description of the activity
2. Input(s) that triggers the processing of the activity
3. Output(s) created by processing the activity
4. Constraints and rules related to the activity's execution
5. Duration of time estimated for performing the activity
6. Resources needed for performing or that are related to the activity

In the columns of the second part of the activity spreadsheet, significant parameters are defined for each activity(i), where i ranges from 1 to the number of activities; these are as follows:

1. Description: This column is used to write a short and precise description of what exactly the work that is carried out by the activity defined in row(i) of the spreadsheet is.
2. Resource: This column is used to define the resource that performs the activity(i).
3. Time: This parameter is used to denote the expected duration needed for activity(i) to be processed and accomplished. The processing time of the activity is a very important factor in carrying out business process improvement and innovation in the third phase.
4. Rule: This characteristic is used to define one or more conditions or rules that must be satisfied in order for the activity(i) to be performed. A rule is a precise statement that defines a constraint, which must be satisfied in order for a certain activity to be executed.
5. Input: This parameter is used to indicate which input(s) are needed to enter activity(i) to trigger its execution.
6. Output: In this column, the output(s) of activity(i) produced as a result of processing the activity are indicated.
7. Cost: This is the sum of the expenses needed to accomplish the activity(i). This parameter is later used to calculate the cost of each work process and consequently the whole business process. Thus, this is an important parameter that needs to be calculated for the purpose of business process improvement and innovation.

Developing the whole activity spreadsheet is an iterative process. Usually, it is necessary for a number of the interviews to be repeated to arrive at a precise understanding of the employees' work. If anything is misunderstood or overlooked, then new interviews should be organized with responsible and knowledgeable employees to clarify it.

12.3.3 Process Improvement and Innovation

The third phase of SAD methodology deals with the changes, improvements, and innovative ideas regarding the business process's functioning and structure in order to optimize it. It also deals with carrying out process improvement and innovation by identifying and implementing changes, searching for better solutions to existing problems, or considering the development of new alternative solutions in order to improve the functioning of the enterprise.

Business process improvement and innovation is connected tightly with customer satisfaction. When the customer is satisfied with the products or services of the organization, the business processes of the organization need to be improved or innovated as soon as possible.

Process improvement and innovation consists of four steps:

1. "As-is" process model analysis: This performs an analysis of the process performance of the "as-is" process model and calculates process performance parameters, such as process flow, cycle time efficiency, and process capacity, with the purpose of identifying existing problems within the "as-is" process model and possibilities available to solve these problems to prompt improvement of the process.

2. "To-be" process model creation: This uses concepts of the knowledge management cycle and ideas gained from process performance analysis to create a "to-be" process model. This subphase consists of two steps: ideas identification and ideas implementation.

3. "To-be" process model analysis: This analyzes the "to-be" process model by calculating the process performance parameters in order to identify the improvement made in comparison with the performance of the "as-is" model.

4. Simulation: This uses the simulation technique to imitate the functioning of the "to-be" process model in order to study the reality of the process behavior and the possibility of making further improvements.

 Process improvement is not a one-time exercise but rather an ongoing one that needs to be done continuously in order to keep the organization's processes effective and competitive.

12.3.3.1 *"As-Is" Process Model Analysis*

The first subphase of the process improvement and innovation phase involves identifying problems discovered within the "as-is" process model developed in the second phase as well as the possible solutions available to address these problems that may lead to the improvement of the process. Process improvement is an ongoing effort that needs to be done on an continuous basis to keep the organization's processes effective and competitive. If it is performed only once or only a few number of times, the process will deteriorate over time and dissipate the value that it had gained across the earlier iterations.

In reality, a number of difficult problems and queue-causing bottlenecks develop over time within each process, leading to ineffectiveness and inefficiency of the process that in turn results in customer dissatisfaction. Similarly, the unavailability of resources

represents another problem that plays an important role in creating queues and consequently in decreasing the effectiveness and the quality of the process.

In order to achieve the organization's goal in making each of its processes more effective, the "as-is" model of each selected process must be analyzed using the process performance measurements described in Chapter 2 in order to assess performance of the
process. These include:

1. Simulation: Simulation is a technique that enables us to imitate the functioning
   of a certain real process by developing a process model whose attributes are the
   same as the attributes of the original one. For this purpose, real-life input data
   is collected and used during experimentation on the behavior of the developed
   model over time, without disturbing the functioning of the original process.
   Additionally, the simulation technique provides the very important possibility
   of carrying out experimentation on the process discussed by generating various
   scenarios and testing different options of "what-if" questions that are based on
   an understanding of the process's functioning and an analysis of the simulation
   output results.

   Thus, the team prepares scenario(s) to run the simulation of this process model.
   Such a simulation enables the improvement team to imitate the behavior of the
   process in an environment similar to reality in order to identify and make changes
   if needed.

   The results of this simulation are later compared with the results from the simulation of the "to-be" process.

   Process simulation is an iterative approach, which may be repeated a number of
   times until the improvement team is satisfied with the solution achieved.

2. Process flow: As explained in Chapter 2, a flow unit (e.g., document, patient, product) enters a process from its environment, proceeds through various activities,
   and exits as an output into the process's environment. A flow unit, job, or transaction on its way through the process may join other flow units at the end of queues
   waiting to be processed by the process' activities.

   The process flow is measured using three key measures: cycle time, flow rate,
   and inventory. This enables the calculation of the following:

   a. The average time that a flow unit needs to pass through the process (average
      cycle time)
   b. The average number of flow units that are inside the process boundaries at any
      point of time (average inventory)
   c. The average number of flow units that pass through the process per unit of
      time (average flow rate)

   The average cycle time of a process is gained from the results of a simulation run
   in the previous step. Information about the average inventory is usually obtained
   from the management during interviews, whereas the average flow rate is calculated using Little's Law.

3. Cycle time efficiency: A flow unit on its way from the start to the end of a process
   goes through a sequence of activities and buffers. Therefore, the cycle time of a
   flow unit within a process consists of the times spent within the process's activities and the waiting times spent in different buffers.

Since theoretical cycle time of a process could be defined as the sum of times of activities needed for processing a flow unit throughout the process; activity time is actually the time needed for an activity to complete the processing of a flow unit; and waiting time is the time spent by a flow unit within a buffer waiting for an activity to start processing it, the cycle-time efficiency can be obtained by dividing the theoretical cycle time by the average cycle time of the process; that is:

Cycle time efficiency = theoretical cycle time/average cycle time

4. Process capacity: The capacity of a process depends on the resources that are needed for performing the activities of the process; different resource pools may have different theoretical capacities and calculating their theoretical capacity leads to the determination of the pool with the minimum theoretical capacity, which represents the bottleneck resource pool of the process and consequently defines the theoretical capacity of the whole process.

The theoretical capacity of the process can be calculated using the following formula:

$$R_p = \frac{c_p}{T_p} * \text{load batch} * \text{scheduled availability}$$

where:

R_p is the theoretical capacity of resource pool p
c_p is the number of resource units in resource pool p
T_p is the unit load of a resource unit resource pool p
Load batch is the ability of a resource unit to perform a number of flow units simultaneously
Scheduled availability is the working time in which a resource unit is scheduled

In addition, capacity utilization is defined as

$$\rho_p = \frac{R}{R_p}$$

where:

ρ_p is the capacity utilization of a resource pool
R is the average flow rate
R_p is the theoretical capacity of the resource pool

12.3.3.2 *"To-Be" Model Creation*

The calculated process performance enables the management to make a decision about the necessity of process improvement or innovation. This information also enables the improvement team to determine which performance parameters are more problematic and must be tackled first in the improvement process.

12.3.3.2.1 Ideation

Notably, the development of a new "to-be" process model that represents the improved behavior of the process discussed requires the improvement team to benefit from the knowledge capture and/or creation concept of the knowledge management cycle.

Business process improvement or innovation should be built on ideas elicited from knowledgeable and experienced people. For this reason, the improvement team should include experienced employees from the organization who could provide such new knowledge.

For this purpose, "knowledge" is of two types:

1. Explicit knowledge concerns the carrying out of an organization's processes and is identified from the organization's documents, which describe in detail different working procedures and also from interviews with employees. This kind of knowledge is usually identified, captured, and used during the first and second phases to develop the process and activity spreadsheets, where the process is identified and modeled.

2. Tacit knowledge is developed by employees through years of experience in performing their daily work activities. Tacit knowledge refers to something that is very difficult to articulate or to put into words or images; it includes highly internalized knowledge such as knowing how to do something or recognizing analogous situations.

Tacit knowledge can be captured by adding an extended spreadsheet to the activity spreadsheet. The aim of these special columns is to obtain and store the tacit knowledge elicited from professional and experienced employees. The knowledge and ideas are obtained first at the activity level about how to do things in more innovative ways in order to accelerate the processing of activities, raise the quality of their outputs, and minimize their cost.

The improvement spreadsheet is structured as follows:

- The first three columns of the spreadsheet are the same as the first three columns of the activity spreadsheet part I.
- The spreadsheet is extended by three new columns that represent the "Lessons Learned" columns group; these are the "Activity," "Work Process," and "Business Process" columns.

12.3.3.2.2 Idea Implementation

The current step implements the knowledge and suggestions stored in the improvement spreadsheet to develop the "to-be" process model. Knowledge sharing and dissemination is done by codification of knowledge, which means translating tacit into explicit knowledge by using it for developing the "to-be" process model.

The development of the "to-be" process model is done by updating:

- The process spreadsheet if the organization of the "to-be" process model differs from the organization of the "as-is" model, which means that the "to-be" process uses different work processes or passes through different functional areas
- The activity spreadsheet corresponding to the ideas and suggestions stored in the improvement spreadsheet

Such a technique of implementing knowledge within the "to-be" process model means that the knowledge is organized in accordance with the context of the working activities performed, within different work processes of the business processes discussed.

12.3.3.3 *"To-Be" Process Model Analysis*

In this subphase, the performance measurements of the "to-be" model of the process developed in the previous subphase are calculated. Such calculation enables us to estimate the improvements made in the process performance of the new "to-be" process as compared with the performance of the existing "as-is" process, which was calculated in the first subphase of the current phase.

This subphase consists of the same four steps as steps 1 to 4 of the first subphase (see Subsection 12.3.3.1); these are:

1. Simulation
2. Process flow
3. Cycle time efficiency
4. Process capacity

Thus, it starts by running a simulation of the "to-be" process and continues by calculating the three process performance measures—namely, process flow, time cycle efficiency, and process capacity—to ascertain the efficacy of the achieved performance improvement.

 This process can be iterated by going back to Subsection 12.3.3.2 until the obtained improvements in the process are to the satisfaction of the improvement team.

12.3.4 System Development

The fourth phase of SAD methodology deals with the development of a process management system that implements the "to-be" process model created in the previous phase. This phase first implements a class model and the design of the system, continues with developing a software system, and finishes by deploying the system in the organizational real environment.

The fourth phase thus consists of three steps:

1. Building a class model of the system using a simple approach
2. Creating the system design according to the structure of the activity spreadsheet developed in the second phase
3. Implementing the class model and design of the system by developing a software application system that is deployed and installed in the organization as so to execute the functionality of the business process discussed

12.3.4.1 *Class Model*

1. Fundamental object-oriented concepts

   This subsection presents an introduction to basic object-oriented concepts.

   a. Object class: An object class symbol consists of three parts. In the first part, the class's name is indicated, the second part lists the attributes of the class, and the third part lists the operations of the objects of the class.

An object is anything identified in the process of information systems development that is recognized by its properties and behavior. An object is anything, real or abstract, about which we store data and those operations that manipulate the data.

An object class describes a group of objects with similar properties (attributes), common behavior (operations), common relationships to other objects, and common semantics. An object class could be understood as an abstraction for representing a number of objects that have similar attributes, behavior, and associations with objects of other classes.

An attribute indicates a determined property of objects in an object class. An attribute is a data value held by the object in a class. Each attribute has a value for each object instance. Different object instances may have the same or different values for a given attribute. An identity attribute is a minimal set of attributes that uniquely identifies and represents an object instance.

The behavior of objects in a class is represented by operations. An operation is a function or transformation that may be applied to or by objects in a class.

b. Association: An association is a relationship between two classes of the class model. The different types of associations are:

one-to-one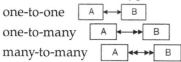

one-to-many

many-to-many

To implement a many-to-many association, that shown earlier is replaced by the following association class shown in the following:

c. Inheritance: Inheritance entails defining a system of hierarchies between classes, where a subclass can inherit attributes and operations from a higher class.

Inheritance can be elaborated in two directions:

i. By the generalization of common aspects of existing classes into a super-class (bottom-up)

- Generalization is the bottom-up analysis of classes of a class model. It means creating a higher superclass for similar attributes and operations of two or more classes of the class model. Generalization represents the best way for sharing similar characteristics (attributes and operations).

- This is achieved by putting these characteristics together in one class from which other classes inherit and use them.

- In addition to the inherited characteristics from the superclass, the classes may have other special characteristics of their own.

ii. By the specialization of existing classes into specialized subclasses (top-down)

- Specialization is the top-down analysis of the classes of a class model. This means refining existing classes into specialized classes.

- This is done by creating subclasses that inherit the characteristics of the refined classes.

- In addition to the characteristics inherited from the existing classes, the created subclasses may have other special characteristics their own.

 Inheritance, discussed above, is one primary reason for conceiving of a spreadsheeter application development (SAD) methodology rather than a tabular application development (TAB) methodology. A multidimensional spreadsheet can be used to specify other dimensions like inheritance, time, security, privacy, trust, analysis, and so on.

2. Modeling approach: The functional dependence concept is an excellent tool for analyzing the relationships existing between the key and nonkey attributes of a relation. It helps in identifying the classes of the class model as well as the relationships that exist between them. Functional dependence is also very useful for analyzing the relationships existing between key attributes of different relations.

   The purpose of this subphase is to introduce an approach towards the creation of an object model of the improved process. The essence of this approach is simplifying the normalization technique by focusing not on the relationships but on the functional dependence between attributes of the user documents.

   a. Identify key attributes: The first step of the approach deals with analyzing the collected user documents one by one to define the key attributes of all objects identified in these documents. The key attribute of an object is a unique property of the object in an object class that represents it and distinguishes it from other objects of the class.

      This involves analyzing each user document carefully in order to identify the following:

      - Key attributes linked to nonkey attributes
      - Key attribute collections related to different repeating groups listed within the document discussed

      Each simple key attribute represents an object class, while a key attribute collection represents an association class that connects two other classes together.

   b. Identify functional dependence: This step involves identifying the functional dependences existing between the attributes of a document, as follows:

      i. For each key attribute defined in step a, identify the functional dependences existing between the key attribute and non-key attributes.

      ii. Identify the functional dependences that exists between the key attribute of the document and other key attributes.

   c. Develop class model: This step deals with building the class model by transforming the results of the analyses accomplished in b into a class model.

12.3.4.2 System Design

This subphase develops the design of the system on the basis of the information collected in the activity spreadsheet of the process.

1. Develop system design: The design of the system is derived from the "to-be" process model; this is from the activity spreadsheet part I of the "to-be" model. The design is actually represented by a spreadsheet that shows the system's design as a hierarchical system, which is structured in accordance with the structural scheme of the improved business process; the design consists of a number

of levels corresponding to the structure of the process shown in the first few columns of the activity spreadsheet part I.

A business process is partitioned into a number of work processes, with each of these work processes possibly consisting of a set of subprocesses, each subprocess possibly consisting of a set of activities, and each activity possibly partitioned into tasks. Therefore:

a. The first level, called the business process level, is derived from the first column of the activity spreadsheet.

b. The second level, called the subprocess level, is created according to the content of the second column of the activity spreadsheet.

c. The third level, called the work process level, is created according to the content of the Work Process column of the activity spreadsheet.

d. The fourth level, called the activity level, is developed from the information comprised in the Activity column of the activity spreadsheet.

e. The fifth level, called the task level, is developed from the information created in the Task column of the activity spreadsheet.

Developing a system design in such a manner means transferring the information collected in the activity spreadsheet into the design model of the system. This fact means that SAD methodology enables the modeler to create a design of the system that is tightly related to the result of the process modeling and improvement, and contributes a great deal to removing and minimizing the gap existing between the systems analysis and systems design.

2. Defining operations and algorithms: The current step deals with completing class model development by identifying and defining operations within the framework of each object class of the class model. These operations actually determine the behavior of the objects of the system, which indicates the behavior of the whole system.

    The input to identify and define operations within the object classes is the activity spreadsheet part II. From each activity or task description within the activity spreadsheet, a number of operations are derived and defined within an object class.

    In addition to the operations indicated within the object classes of the class model, algorithms are also written that show how these operations should be implemented.

 Algorithms connect the lowest level of the design of the system—this is the task or activity level—with object classes of the class model in order to trigger the execution of different operations defined within these classes.

12.3.4.3 System Implementation

This subphase deals with the development of the information system to implement the improved business process as well as the process management system that is essential for supporting the functioning of the improved business process.

Additionally, at the end, the system development team takes care of analyzing and implementing the integration of the system developed within the information system of the organization.

Developing an information system to support the process discussed requires choosing a proper platform for the system, selecting a DB system, and deciding on a programming language.

1. Programming: This step of the system includes creating a DB system, developing a menu system, and implementing a number of programs corresponding to the system design. Usually, this step is started by creating a DB system and transferring the design model into a hierarchical menu system according to the design structural scheme.

   The lowest level of the menu system, which is the activity or task level, is connected to different programs. These programs are developed in correspondence with the algorithms written in the previous subphase, which exactly define the steps needed to execute each activity or task listed in the menu system. As methods specify the way in which operations are encoded in software, a method is an implementation of an operation defined within a class of the class model.

2. Testing: To ensure the quality of the software system developed, the system development team plans for careful testing at different level of the system.

   a. Each program usually implements a certain task of an activity or an activity at the lowest level of the menu system. Therefore, a number of tests should be done in order to assure that the program is free of mistakes and works properly.

   b. A set of tasks may form an activity and a number of activities represent a determined work process. A group of programs that implements the tasks and activities of a certain work process should be tested together to ensure that the work process of concern is performed as it should be.

   c. A major test or tests should be carried out on the whole software system that was developed, first in the laboratory and then in reality.

3. Deporting: The final result of the current phase is a software package, called the process management system, which is deployed by installing it on the computer systems of the organization.

   The development team has to organize presentations and learning courses in order to teach the employees of the organization about the new operation of the process and how to use the newly developed information system.

12.3.5 Maintenance

The fifth phase of SAD methodology deals with controlling the functioning of the improved business processes and the process management system.

12.3.5.1 System Maintenance

This performs the monitoring function in order to uncover problems and deficiencies in the process management system.

To implement the monitoring feature in the process management system, the system should generate a log file that records detailed data about all events happening in each business process instance during its route through the business process activities. In such a way, the software system provides the system developers with all of the data needed for its maintenance. Additionally, the process management system should provide the possibility of visualization of the process. This means that the current state of any process instance flowing through the business process should be capable of visualization at any moment.

If any kind of problem is detected in the functioning of the process management system, then the process management team should analyze the problem identified carefully in order to find a convenient solution.

The system maintenance step is iterative and may be repeated as many times as needed for the purpose of updating the process management system with new suggestions and changes.

12.3.5.2 Process Maintenance

The advantages accruing from the process improvements may start lessening with passage of time because of the changing market environment, competitors, and so on. To address this problem, the company should follow and apply a continuous business process improvement plan to ensure that the organization is always in sync with the changing market conditions and also a step ahead of its competitors.

The process maintenance step is also an iterative approach, which may be repeated many times. The development process restarts from Subsection 12.3.3 in order to update the "to-be" process model with the changes required and solutions found. It then continues with the fourth phase, wherein the new features are implemented within the process management system.

12.4 Summary

As a preparatory step to discussing the SAD methodology, this chapter first introduces the concepts of deductive DB and deductive spreadsheet. Deductive DBs were proposed as an attempt to overcome the limitations of traditional DB systems by incorporating the characteristics features of expert systems. A deductive spreadsheet is a tool that enables users to define logic statements and inference rules for symbolic reasoning in the same way that current spreadsheets allow users to define mathematical formulae for numerical calculations. This chapter then presented the five-phase, spreadsheet-driven SAD methodology for the development of process-centric application systems. The various phases detailed are:

1. An initial phase dealing with the problem of identifying enterprise business processes that are essential for the functioning of the organization

2. A second phase dealing with the development of a process model for the business processes identified in the previous phase involving completing parts I and II of the activity spreadsheet

3. A third phase dealing with four subphases, which are "as-is" process model analysis, "to-be" process model creation, "to-be" process model analysis, and process simulation

4. A fourth phase dealing with the development of a process management system that implements the "to-be" process model including the class model and the design of the system based on the activity spreadsheet parts I and II

5. A fifth phase dealing with controlling the functioning of the improved business process and the process management system

13

Engineering of Process-Centric Application Systems

Business Process Model and Notation (BPMN 2.0) can not only capture business requirements but can also provide the backbone of the actual solution implementation. The same diagram prepared by the business analyst to describe the business's desired "to-be" process can be used to automate the execution of that process on a modern process engine. This is achieved via a new process-centric architecture that preserves simplicity and stability in the business-oriented enterprise process description layer while maximizing flexibility and agility in the underlying service contract implementation layer and vice-a-versa. This is achieved through this service contract implementation layer being interposed between the process-centric application and the system landscape. The process-centric application layer never interacts directly with the underlying system landscape; instead, it always goes through the service contract implementation layer. On the other hand, the process-centric application is also unaffected by changes in the underlying system landscape—what changes is only the logic of the service contract implementation layer. Thus, BPMN is used for both the process-centric application layer and the service contract implementation layer; in particular, to achieve these objectives, the latter is broken out into a stateful integration process and a stateless messaging process.

13.1 Model-Driven Development

The traditional approach to software development involves a modeling process—analysis, requirements specification, design—followed by an implementation process. In the traditional approach, programmers manually write software that conforms (more or less) to specifications described in software models; this process involves transformations that are often incomplete, awkward, and informal. The essence of model-driven software development is the idea that software models can go further than being mere blueprints, and constitute the basis for automatically or semiautomatically generating the software system itself.

Model-driven development proposes to improve the state of the art in software engineering. Software models are intended to improve communication among stakeholders and aid in the overall understanding of both a problem space and a proposed software solution that satisfies given requirements. As with architectural blueprints or miniature three-dimensional models, software models make it possible to explore and test a design and its ramifications before investing in the actual build-out. Model-driven development increases developer productivity, decreases the cost (in time and money) of software construction, improves software reusability, and makes software more maintainable. Likewise, model-driven techniques promise to aid in the early detection of defects such as design flaws, omissions, and misunderstandings between clients and developers.

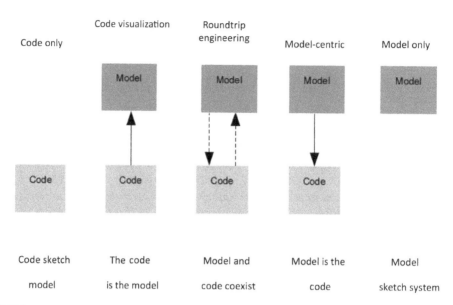

FIGURE 13.1
Spectrum of models.

Figure 13.1 shows a spectrum of modeling ranging from code-only solutions to model-only solutions.

1. In the code-only scenario, even though developers still create mental models and informal models, the system representation is entirely in the code.
2. In the second scenario, the developer uses models primarily as a means for visualizing the code; a reverse-engineering tool reads the code and displays a corresponding model view of what is captured in the code.
3. In the round-trip engineering scenario, a tool maintains tight correspondence between the model and code; changes made to the code are immediately reflected in the model and vice versa. In the model programming scenario, the model is the code and the lower level of code is simply generated and compiled behind the scenes; all changes to the system happen at the model level.
4. The model-only scenario does not interface with the operational system and exist independently for understanding of the system.

The round-trip engineering and model programming scenarios are *model-driven*, while the others are at best model-aware or *model-based*.

13.1.1 Model-Driven Architecture

The Object Management Group (OMG; Needham, MA) is an industry consortium established in 1989 with the goal of defining standards for the interoperability for distributed object systems. OMG adopted the model-driven architecture (MDA) standard in 2001; MDA is aimed at model-driven development or engineering that uses the core OMG standards (e.g., Unified Modeling Language [UML], Meta-Object Facility Specification™ [MOF], XML Metadata Interchange™ [XMI], Common Warehouse Metamodel™ [CWM]).

Based primarily on the principle of architectural separation of concerns, MDA has three objectives:

1. Portability
2. Interoperability
3. Reusability

MDA also has three basic tenets, as follows:

1. Direct representation expresses a desire to shift the focus of software development away from the technology domain and toward the concepts and terminology of the problem domain. The goal is to represent a solution as directly as possible in terms of the problem domain that may result in more accurate designs, improved communication between various participants in the system development process, and overall increased productivity.
2. Automation endorses the concept of using machines to perform rote tasks that require no human ingenuity, freeing software developers to focus on creative problem-solving work. Dealing directly with the underlying implementation is not productive per se—it is the solving of business problems that creates value and qualifies to contribute to the productivity.
3. Building on open standards is important not only because standards promote reuse but also because they cultivate the construction of an ecosystem of tool vendors who address the various needs of MDA.

MDA describes three main layers of architectural abstraction or viewpoints (Figure 13.2):

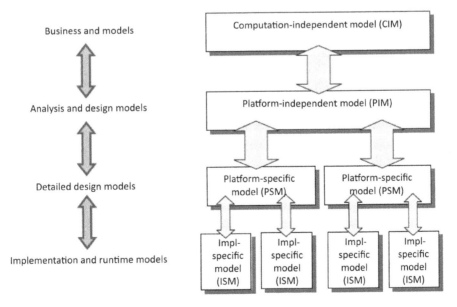

FIGURE 13.2
Layers and implementation of MDA.

1. A computation-independent model (CIM) describes a system environment and its requirements using terminology that is familiar to practitioners in the system domain.

2. A platform-independent model (PIM) describes a system's structure and functions formally, yet without specifying platform-specific implementation details.

3. A platform-specific model (PSM) includes details that are important to the implementation of a system on a given platform. By platform, MDA means a cohesive set of subsystems and technologies on which a system can execute (such as Sun's Java EE or Microsoft's .NET platforms).

One of the main benefits of MDA is that the implementation step, PIM-to-PSM transformation, can presumably be done relatively easily for multiple platforms. Thus, there may be many PSM's corresponding to each of the target platforms. The MDA guide discusses a wide variety of transformation types, techniques, and patterns. As with model-driven development in general, the concept of model transformations is central to the MDA philosophy.

There are mappings between models up and down, as indicated in Figure 13.2. CIM-to-CIM or PIM-to-PIM mappings represent model transformation that occurs when moving from an analysis phase into a design phase:

- PSM-to-PSM transformation is required to configure and package the elements of a PSM for deployment to the desired target environment.

- PSM-to-PIM transformation is required when refactoring or reverse-engineering a system.

MDA has four modeling layers:

M3: The meta-metamodel layer; describes concepts that appear in the metamodel, such as Class. For UML, MOF describes the M3 layer.

M2: The metamodel layer; describes concepts that make up a modeling language; examples include the UML metamodel, the executable UML (xUML; also sometimes labeled xtUML for executable/translatable UML) profile, and a domain-specific metamodel created and customized for a particular company or industry segment.

M1: The user model or model instance layer; class diagrams, statecharts, and other such artifacts are M1-layer elements.

M0: The data instance layer; objects, records, data, and related artifacts exist at this level.

An MDA process may use any of a number of different UML profiles or domain-specific metamodels, rather than using UML exclusively for all modeling activities. While developers usually produce UML diagrams using UML or UML profiles, it is also possible to create an MDA process that uses an MOF-conforming, domain-specific metamodel to then perform domain-specific modeling tasks within the MDA framework.

 One of the most concrete instances of MDA is xUML. The main idea of xUML is to define a UML profile that specifies a well-defined subset of UML that includes a precise action semantics language that can be used in the procedures associated with states in a model's statechart diagrams. When developers use action semantics language to specify the underlying state procedures, we can directly compile and execute the full xUML model.

The agile software development movement advocates making customer satisfaction the highest priority, and agilists see early and continuous delivery of useful software as the path to achieving this goal. They value *individuals and interactions* over processes and tools, working software over comprehensive documentation, customer collaboration over contract negotiation, and responding to change over following a plan. The whole premise of creating complex models and then generating code from those models may seem in contradiction to these generally accepted agile principles; however, there is no apparent contradiction. If models are not executable, then they cannot be agile: if a model is supposed to be a blueprint against which a software system can be built, then it must first go through the effort of creating the blueprint followed by another process of construction—which is essentially nonagile in nature. However, if our models are executable, then we can immediately use them in the way we typically use code (prototyping early and often), and thus the same agile principles that apply to programming can apply equally well to modeling.

13.1.1.1 Model-Driven Architecture Support

OMG elements that support/comprise MDA are described below.

1. MOF (OMG, Needham, MA): In the MDA, models are first-class artifacts, integrated into the development process through the chain of transformations from PIM through PSM to coded application. To enable this, the MDA requires models to be expressed in a MOF-based language. This guarantees that the models can be stored in a MOF-compliant repository, parsed, and transformed by MOF-compliant tools, once rendered into XML Metadata Interchange™ (XMI; OMG, Needham, MA) for transport over a network. Notably, this does not constrain the types of models you can use—MOF-based languages today model application structure, behavior (in many different ways), and data; examples of MOF-based modeling languages include OMG's UML and CWM, while MOF 2.0 is foundation for UML 2.0. Each MDA-based specification has essentially two levels of models: a PIM and one or more PSMs, respectively.

2. UML profiles: UML profiles tailor the language to particular areas of computing (such as enterprise distributed object computing) or particular platforms [such as Enterprise Java Beans (EJB) or Common Object Request Broker Architecture (CORBA)]. In the MDA, both PIMs and PSMs are defined using UML profiles; OMG is well along the way, defining a suite of profiles that span the entire scope of potential MDA applications.

   The current suite of profiles include the following:
   - The UML Profile for CORBA, which defines the mapping from a PIM to a CORBA-specific PSM.
   - The UML Profile for CCM (the CORBA Component Model), OMG's contribution to component-based programming. EJBs are the Java mapping of CCM; an initial take on a profile for EJB appears as an appendix of the UML 2.0 Superstructure specification.
   - The UML Profile for Enterprise Distributed Object Computing is used to build PIMs of enterprise applications. It defines representations for entities, events, process, relationships, patterns, and an enterprise collaboration architecture. As a PIM profile, it needs mappings to platform-specific

profiles. A mapping to Web services is underway; additional mappings will follow.

- The UML Profile for Enterprise Application Integration defines a profile for loosely coupled systems—that is, those that communicate using either asynchronous or messaging-based methods. These modes are typically used in enterprise application integration, but are used elsewhere as well.
- The UML Profile for Quality of Service and Fault Tolerance defines frameworks for real-time and high-assurance environments.
- The UML Testing Profile provides important support for automated testing in MDA-based development environments.

3. XMI (OMG, Needham, MA) defines an Extensible Markup Language (XML)-based interchange format for UML and other MOF-based metamodels and models (because a metamodel is just a special case of a model), by standardizing XML document formats, document type definitions, and schemas. In doing so, it also defines a map from UML to XML. Because one of OMG's XMI updates reflects the incorporation of XML schemas, while MOF point updates were made periodically through OMG's established maintenance process, the numbering of XMI and MOF versions diverged.

4. CWM (OMG, Needham, MA) standardizes a complete, comprehensive metamodel that enables data mining across database boundaries at an enterprise. Similar to a UML profile but in data space instead of application space, it forms the MDA mapping to database schemas. CWM does for data modeling what UML does for application modeling. The CWM is a formal OMG specification. A supplementary specification, CWM Metadata Interchange Patterns, defines patterns that smooth the way to data modeling tool interoperability.

13.1.1.2 Unified Modeling Language

UML helps firms to specify, visualize, and document models of software systems, including their structure and design. Firms can use UML for business modeling and modeling of other nonsoftware systems too. Within UML, one can model most types of applications, running on any type and combination of hardware, operating system, programming language, or network. UML's flexibility allows firms to model distributed applications that use any middleware on the market. Built upon the MOF metamodel, which defines *class* and *operation* as fundamental concepts, UML is a good fit for object-oriented languages and environments such as C++, Java, and C#; one can also use it to model non-object-oriented applications as well in, for example, Fortran, VB, or COBOL. *UML profiles* are subsets of UML tailored to specific environments; they help developers to model transactional, real-time, and fault-tolerant systems in a natural way.

The traditional view of systems modeling distinguishes between static views describing the structures and functional views describing the behavior exposed. These views describe what entities are modeled (as classes describing the types and objects describing the instances of things); how entities react when they receive input (as the state changes, which can be broken down in case the entity is a composite made up of several smaller entities); and how entities interact with each other (in the form of activities in which more than one entity work together and exchange messages with each other).

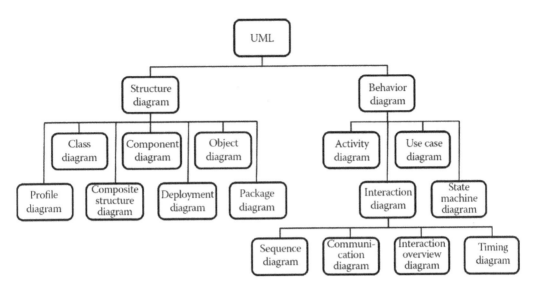

FIGURE 13.3
UML diagram hierarchy.

UML extends these categories for object-oriented software engineering, resulting in the diagrams shown in Figure 13.3.

The diagrams of UML are used to either explain the structure or the behavior of a system by distinguishing between the following:

1. Classes that represent type information (e.g., properties shared by all things of this type)

    The structure diagrams deal with modeling the objects representing the entities that make up the system. The atomic entity is an object that has only attributes and methods assigned. Using such objects, composites can be built that combine atomic objects and potentially already existing composites. More diagrams are used to add more ideas to facilitate the work of object-oriented software engineers, and many of them can be used by systems engineers as well.

    Here is an overview of the structure diagrams:

    a. Class diagrams describe the entity types including their attributes' relationships between the types.

    b. Object diagrams show views of the system with instantiated objects based on their types.

    c. Composite structure diagrams describe the internal structure of composite objects; that is, objects that have at least one object among their attributes. This allows the systems engineer to treat the composite as one structure from the outside and describe how the composite works on the inside.

    d. Component diagrams describe how the system is split up into components. These diagrams show interdependencies and interactions between these components.

e. Package diagrams describe logical groupings and their interdependencies and define software packages.

f. Deployment diagrams describe the allocation of software to hardware components (i.e., what software package is executed on which hardware component).

g. Profile diagrams operate at the meta-model level and show stereotypes. Each object that fulfills the requirements of the stereotype can be used in the operation in a respective role.

2. Objects that represent instance information (e.g., properties exposed by the individual instantiations of a thing of a given type)

The most important three diagrams of the functional view of the systems are activity diagrams (how entities interact); state machine diagrams (how entities react); and use case diagrams (how the overall system behaves). These three core diagrams are supported by more detailed diagrams that often focus on software engineering details.

The behavior diagrams are discussed henceforth:

a. Use case diagrams describe the interactions of actors with the main functionality of the simulation system in terms of the user. These diagrams are often used to communicate what the system does and why it does it with the users.

b. Activity diagrams can be best described as workflows between the entities of the simulation system. They show the overall flow of control, including synchronization between activities, interim results, and so on.

c. State machine diagrams show how the objects or entities react to certain inputs they receive. While activities focus on the entity, external communication state machine diagrams focus on the internal changes.

d. Interaction diagrams use four subtypes to better describe the details of interactions within the system:

   • Interaction overview diagrams provide the big picture and build the frame for the other three diagram types to fill in the details.

   • Sequence diagrams visualize causal orders of an interaction and define the lifespan of a temporary object used within such interactions.

   • Timing diagrams focus on timing constraints of sequences to define the temporal orders.

   • Communication diagrams specify the interactions between entities that are part of the modeled sequence. They are very often used as system internal use cases, as they show several aspects of which entities come together how and when.

The main disadvantage of UML is the focus on object-oriented software systems. Although UML easily can be interpreted to support other systems as well, the software engineering roots are apparent and ubiquitous. This led OMG to the development of the Systems Modeling Language, which is a general modeling language for systems. There is a huge overlap between UML and Systems Modeling Language, but the focus in the latter is on the system rather than on the software.

13.2 Process-Centric Applications

The architecture of a typical composite application is shown in Figure 13.4. Composite applications support end-to-end processes by adding functionality through components or direct synchronous calls via back-end abstraction layers on Web services. Any changes or changed services necessitate changes to the back-end systems. The approach and presentation in this chapter have been adopted from Stiehl (2014).

The characteristics of process-centric applications are listed below:

1. Process-centric applications are by their nature largely user-centric and collaborative.
2. Process-centric applications address the processes that distinguish a company from its competitors.
3. Process-driven applications extend beyond system, application, and company boundaries, which necessitates the involvement of various different systems inside and outside of the company.
4. Process-driven applications are based on the reusability of existing functionality.

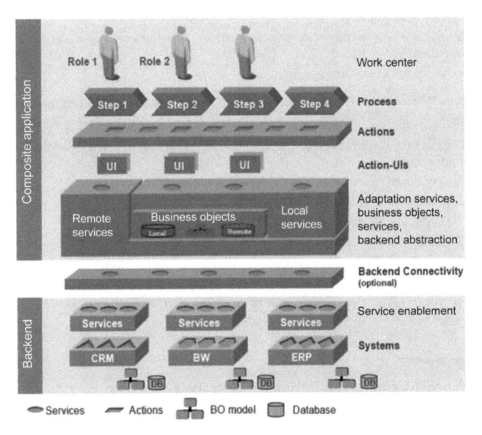

FIGURE 13.4
Architecture of a typical composite application.

Typical scenarios for process-centric applications include:

- Company-specific processes or gaps in processes that are not covered by any existing (standard) applications
- End-to-end scenarios that extend beyond system, application, and company boundaries
- Scenarios that involve a high communication, coordination, and collaboration effort, which to date have been by email, Microsoft Office documents such as Word or Excel files, or on paper
- Solutions with a high demand for reusable and low-maintenance business rules
- Scenarios wherein it is necessary to simplify or recombine separate processes, process steps, transactions, user interfaces, and information technology (IT) technologies
- Processes with both interactive and automated activities
- Scenarios with lightweight business-to-business integrations; that is, scenarios without excessive routing and data mapping or extensive data transformations
- Self-service scenarios such as leave or travel requests (within a company) or public services such as passport applications or damage reports in the public sector (outside the company)
- Processes where frequent changes have already been observed or are expected in the future
- Scenarios with real-time requirements

It is advisable to use process-centric applications in the following cases/for the following reasons:

1. Alignment of business and implementation requirements in a single BPMN model is important
2. Independence from the system landscape is critical
3. More than one system needs to be integrated
4. The system landscape is not stable
5. The solution is complex and justifies the effort involved
6. The solution will provide a competitive advantage
7. The processes in the solution are expected to change frequently
8. The processes in the solution will be used in other organizational units, areas, regions, or other subsidiaries or companies

13.3 Process-Centric Applications Architecture

The EPMS engineering approach presented in this chapter is based on the following basic assumptions:

1. The use of a top-down methodology to determine the main components/ artifacts of the solution. The business processes are undoubtedly the drivers of

the solution; hence the existence of the term "process-centric" in the title of this chapter.

2. A sustainable architecture for process-centric applications that separates the actual business processes at the level of the end application and the technical processes of the so-called service contract implementation layer. The assignment of tasks to the two layers is clearly defined, as is their interaction with each other. The separation by a service contract protects the business processes from the constant changes at the system or technical level.

3. The use of BPMN throughout for modeling as well as for implementing all process components at the business application level and at the level of the service contract implementation layer. This is achieved by differentiation between stateful and stateless processes in the service contract implementation layer.

Figure 13.5 shows the architecture of a process-driven or process-centric application. Process-centric applications have to incorporate intercompany and intracompany relationships and, consequently, reconcile a host of contradictory and vague requirements to come to an optimal solution. This is further exacerbated by the fact that requirements change as markets, organizational structures, and company targets change.

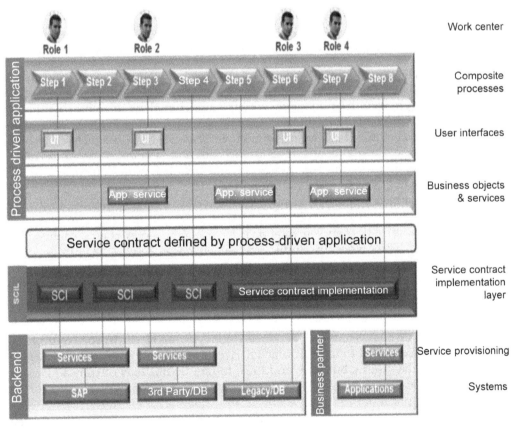

FIGURE 13.5
Architecture of a process-centric application.

As shown in Figure 13.5, process-centric applications follow a layer model comprising a process layer, a user interface layer, and a service or business object layer:

1. End-user perspective is represented by task-oriented user interfaces. They are tailored specifically to the needs of the users in their respective process roles. To realize their tasks, the interfaces and also the process layer avail themselves of the services of the business object and service layer.

2. The business object and service layer provide all of the services that the process and interface layer need to perform the necessary functions. This includes supplying completely new, composite-specific business logic, data persistence for new business objects, and the reuse of existing external services.

3. External services: The corresponding business requirements are defined independently of the IT landscape in the form of a service contract. This service contract is the external representation of the process-driven application and contains not only outgoing calls (from the composite to the service contract implementation layer) but also incoming callback interfaces.

4. Process-centric applications are loosely coupled with the called back-end systems; process-centric applications work with a canonical data type system, which enables a loose coupling with their environment at the data type level. They intentionally abstain from reusing data types and interfaces that may already exist in the back-end systems, since that would compromise their intended independence.

5. Because of this independence, process-centric applications have their own life cycles, which ideally are separate from those of the back-end systems.

All communication between the process-centric application and the back-end systems running in the system landscape passes through the service contract implementation layer. The process-centric application itself provides those business functions that give the company an advantage over its competitors; the service contract implementation layer implements the external services required by the application and contains all of the relevant technical details including the physical connections to the back-end systems, support for various protocols, mapping between different data types, and error handling at the technical level.

This total separation is of fundamental importance to process-centric applications, as it ensures that it is completely decoupled from the back-end: calls are never made directly to an actual system in a process-driven application. Instead, the application communicates exclusively with the service contract implementation layer, using the service contract defined from the perspective of the process-centric application; dependencies between the process-driven application and the back-end system are minimal. The various life cycles of these two worlds are largely independent. The innovative solutions fostered by process-centric applications can be driven forward more quickly and with shorter cycles. The core applications in the older systems, on the other hand, stay stable for a much longer period of time.

 This is welcome news to those responsible for running IT landscapes within companies, whose goal it is to minimize changes to the core processes that bear the load of the day-to-day business and have to handle millions of transactions in a short span of time. This goal is also supported by the noninvasive nature of the process-centric application.

Thanks to the service contract implementation layer, the services provided by the back-end systems are used as originally intended by the provider. The back-end systems are not changed in any way—which is also compatible with the software-as-a-service approach, where standard functions are outsourced to service providers. If, upon closer inspection, any functional disparity is identified between the expectations of the application and the functionality provided by the back-end, this too must be implemented in the service contract implementation layer.

While a process-centric architecture has some disadvantages such as increased complexity, impaired performance, and considerable initial development effort, it also results in numerous advantages including

1. The existence of one single BPMN model for both sides (business and IT)
2. Increased flexibility
3. Alignment of business and implementation requirements in a single BPMN model is important:
   - If business processes need to be adapted
   - If there are changes to the system landscape
4. Quicker and more cost-effective further development of the application
5. Lower maintenance costs
6. Improved portability
7. The ability for business and technical processes to be further developed separately; this is a welcome improvement for many organizations, as it allows them to concentrate on their respective subject areas (separation of concerns)
8. Better overview of end-to-end processes when using enterprise service buses (ESBs), since all communication goes through ESBs
9. Simplified process models for both the business and the technical side, improving the clarity of each individual process

 Only by using process-centric type of architecture can one hope to acquire the flexibility and agility required to adapt to changing business requirements and evolving system landscapes, to implement management strategy quickly and effectively, and to ensure alignment between the business and IT.

13.3.1 Transforming a Process Model into an Executable Process

In the list of priorities, process-centric applications put flexibility and independence from the existing IT landscape far above the reusability of service interfaces. This produces an architecture whose objective is to keep the business process as close as possible to the original model produced by the business department; this architecture benefits from the executability of BPMN, but without any impact on the flexibility of the system as a whole. This approach removes all the technical process details to a separate layer: the service contract implementation layer. Figure 13.6 shows what happens if we apply this principle to the model from Figure 13.7.

Once the business process is implemented, it never communicates directly with other systems; instead, it uses the service contract implementation layer, which decouples the technical details. Vendor companies provide solutions that enable modeling and execution of business processes, business rules, and system/application integrations, which makes tackling the design, development, and operation of distributed scenarios a much less daunting prospect.

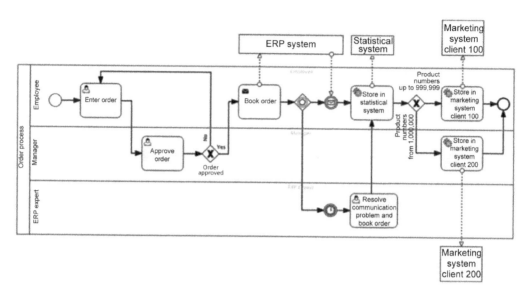

FIGURE 13.6
Order process with separation of layers for a process-centric application.

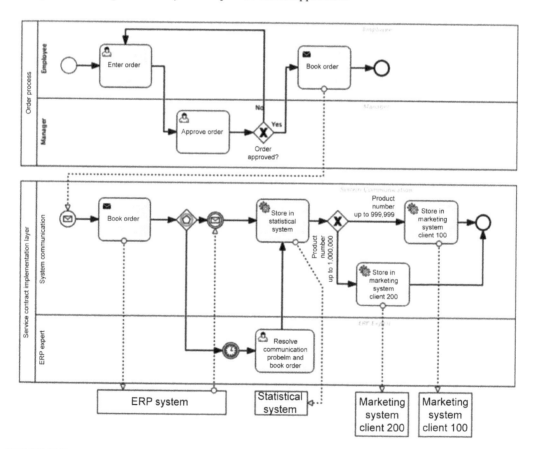

FIGURE 13.7
Order process.

13.3.2 Process-Centric Applications Specifications

 The characteristics of the approach adopted here are of a top-down nature: from the business requirements to the process sequences and processes, the user interfaces, the data to be processed, and, finally, the services to be used.

1. Process information: In process-driven applications especially, the visualization of the process flow is of great importance, as this is the means of communication between the business experts and the architects tasked with implementing the process requirements. Again, we will use BPMN for the process modeling. The process model must show what has to be performed, when, and under what conditions, including:

   a. The sequence flow of the process steps for the happy path, that is, the normal process flow if no errors occur; BPMN achieves this using sequence diagrams.

   b. The typing of activities as either fully automated or requiring end-user interaction; BPMN achieves this using user and service tasks.

   c. The assignment of roles to user tasks; BPMN achieves this using pools and (swim) lanes.

   d. The handling of business exceptions. In BPMN, you have either events or a range of end states at your disposal, which are then evaluated using gateways. Note that the model should only include business exceptions such as delays, quality defects, or cost overruns. Technical exceptions such as connection problems, database failures, or incorrect data formats can be ignored at this stage. This keeps the BPMN model manageable.

2. Exception/event handling: It is crucial to include any business exceptions that may arise during execution of the process. This forces the business departments to also consider potential error scenarios. It is necessary to specify the circumstances in which exceptions may arise during a particular activity as well as the appropriate reaction. In automated steps (service tasks in BPMN), many of the models currently available deal almost exclusively with the "happy path," even though it is usually the errors that occur in process models that generate the most work. The entire process could also terminate, and there must be a solution for this eventuality as well, to determine how to proceed and who to inform.

3. Business objects: In process-centric applications, business objects are seldom used in isolation but rather in relation to other objects; thus, specifying business objects not only requires specifying of the attributes but also the relationships. These details are useful for deciding which technology to use for implementation.

   A detailed description of a business object could contain the following:
   - Meaningful attribute name (e.g., name, postal code)
   - Data type (e.g., string, integer, date, Boolean)
   - Required field (yes/no)
   - Length restrictions (e.g., 15 characters)
   - Value range (e.g., from 0 to 9,999,999)
   - Input masks (e.g., if product numbers follow a particular pattern, predefined symbols are used in the masks to control data entry)

- Storage location of the fields (this is a technical issue and should be defined in cooperation with IT experts)
- Dependencies on and relationships with other fields (e.g., if field xyz contains the value abc, then field uvw must lie within a particular range)

    The type of relationship between the objects depends on whether the child object is deleted if the parent object is deleted. If so, it is a composition (e.g., the child object is an order item and the parent object is the order), while, if not, it is an association (e.g., the child object is a customer and the parent object is the order).

Cardinalities are usually differentiated as follows:

0...1: There can be one relationship to exactly one object.

1...1: There must be one relationship to exactly one object.

0...n: There can be one relationship to several objects

1...n: There must be at least one relationship to an object.

4. User interfaces: User interfaces are very important in process-centric applications because of their collaborative nature and, even at this early phase of development, the input screens must be adapted to the requirements of the end users and their roles. If users are involved during the development of user interface prototypes, their inputs can improve the level of acceptance later on when the interface goes live. It can also reduce costs in the long run, as problems are identified early on and can be remedied without excessive effort or expense.

    Other properties such as visual representations of the data (e.g., charts, bar charts, pie charts, or curves), and interface components such as radio buttons, checkboxes, dropdown lists, calendars, and trees need to be added to individual fields. If there are complex relationships between fields, including input suggestions in the screen can be very useful. Field checks are usually performed using services; a link to the relevant service is sufficient.

5. Services: Process-centric applications do not use existing interfaces of services from application systems such as ERP or SRM solutions (especially for the interfaces of the service contract, which is the external representation of process-centric application), since this would create dependencies. This would effectively isolate what happens in the back-end system to affect the service contract and thus the process-driven application.

13.3.3 Process-Centric Applications Development

The characteristics of the architecture of process-centric applications are as follows:

1. Process-driven applications follow a layer model consisting of the business processes, the user interfaces used in the processes, and the business objects and services relevant for the composite.
2. Process-driven applications work exclusively with a canonical data model, across all layers.

3. Process-driven applications define the external business functions required by means of a service contract (expressed, for example, with Web Services Description Language), which is also based on the canonical data model used and requires a clearly defined business functionality.

4. Processes, user interfaces, and services communicate with back-end systems exclusively through the service contract (by way of the service contract implementation layer). Every single call from a process-driven application goes through this layer.

For a process-driven application, it is advisable to use development environments that enable integrated development of the following:

- Processes
- User interfaces
- Business logic
- Persistence

Highly-integrated development suites enabled for model-driven development have long been used in the Java environment from leading providers like Oracle (Redwood City, CA); IBM Corp., (Armonk, NY); and SAP SE (Walldorf, Germany). Processes are modeled with BPMN, the user interfaces are constructed using What You See Is What You Get editors, and the data displayed on the interfaces are implemented using graphically created class diagrams.

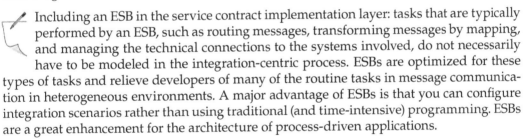 Including an ESB in the service contract implementation layer: tasks that are typically performed by an ESB, such as routing messages, transforming messages by mapping, and managing the technical connections to the systems involved, do not necessarily have to be modeled in the integration-centric process. ESBs are optimized for these types of tasks and relieve developers of many of the routine tasks in message communication in heterogeneous environments. A major advantage of ESBs is that you can configure integration scenarios rather than using traditional (and time-intensive) programming. ESBs are a great enhancement for the architecture of process-driven applications.

13.4 SAP Process Orchestration

Launched in 2012, SAP Process Orchestration (SAP PO; SAP SE, Walldorf, Germany) combined the power of multiple products [such as SAP Business Process Management (BPM), SAP Process Integration (PI), and SAP Business Rules Management (BRM)] into one single product running on the Java stack. SAP PO provides a complete suite of BPM and BRM development and administration tools to help organizations design, model, execute, monitor, manage, and analyze business processes and rules using one platform. This consolidation improves performance, increases efficiency, and reduces total cost of ownership, among other things.

SAP PO is a comprehensive installation package that includes a business process engine, business rules engine, and an ESB in one piece of software, which runs on a Java-only stack. It provides a combination and consolidation package that includes SAP PI and SAP Composition Environment and therefore encapsulates their combined set of features. SAP

PO enables the automation of the organization business processes and rules in a way that facilitates bridging the gap between the business and IT organizations. Both business processes and rules can reuse existing IT assets and thereby reduce total cost of ownership. With SAP PO, organizations can easily deliver reliable messages across the different internal and external systems using a well-established set of integration standards and protocols.

13.4.1 SAP Business Process Management

BPM enables organizations to react and adapt rapidly to changes in their operating environment. BPM enables companies to manage the entire life cycle of their business processes, which involves graphically designing, modeling, executing, monitoring, and continuously improving those business processes. It allows organizations to create new processes based on their existing software and applications, as well as by creating new types of processes that combine different sources of information, technologies, and platforms. Enterprises can improve and enhance existing business processes by reusing existing components or automating certain parts of the process, such as system-to-system and human-to-system information interchange and the execution of complex and general (repetitive) business rules.

SAP BPM introduces a logical level of abstraction for the execution and management of process logic (e.g., service orchestration, task generation, business rules execution, process monitoring) right where it belongs—at the process layer. SAP BPM closes the gap between business and IT by delivering a platform that enables direct interaction among all process stakeholders, including business, IT, partners, and suppliers. Business become aware of how the business processes really look when they are executed; whether that execution is a manual task performed by a customer representative or an automated step executed between two systems. IT can witness see for the first time how their services and mappings are used to create value in real business processes.

 1. SAP Business Workflow is an ABAP-based workflow engine that enables you to design, customize, and execute business processes within SAP back-end systems—that is, inside one SAP system, rather than across SAP systems, as SAP BPM allows. SAP Business Workflow processes are often delivered as a business content functionality part of SAP solutions; SAP Customer Relationship Management, SAP Supplier Relationship Management, and SAP Enterprise Resource Planning customarily use SAP Business Workflow (both out of the box and enhanced) to support approval processes, order processes, processes related to customer interaction, and so on. In contrast, with SAP BPM, most business processes are created either by reusing existing functionality in combination with new process components or by creating new services and process functionality.

   SAP Business Workflow focuses primarily on human-centric processes, in which a substantial number of the tasks are performed in a routine and predictable fashion.

   Another key difference between SAP BPM and SAP Business Workflow is in their underlying technology. As we know, SAP BPM runs on Java, whereas SAP Business Workflow is an ABAP-based workflow engine, which means it can only run on the ABAP stack.

2. SAP BPM is not a reporting tool, and it is not intended as a replacement of SAP Business Intelligence (BI) tools, such as SAP Business Warehouse or SAP BusinessObjects BI. Instead, it is complementary to BI tools, because it leverages new sources of information that can be used in SAP BI or SAP BusinessObjects BI to deliver more accurate and detailed reports and analysis containing different key performance indicators set to business processes. It is good to note that SAP BPM delivers standard out-of-the-box data extractors for SAP Business Warehouse.

SAP BPM applications are by nature process-centric and exist to support and enrich end-to-end business processes, incorporating both manual and automatic tasks, and they can extend beyond enterprise borders.

SAP BPM supports both types of process orchestration; these are:

1. System-centric processes: The main focus of this type of process is on the integration of information sources, generally between two or more services in an orchestrated fashion. Process logic is applied to the service requests or responses in order to coordinate the flow of data from the start to the end of the process.

2. Human-centric processes: Human-centric processes are business processes in which most process activities are predominately performed as manual activities by humans. The process only provides guidance about the steps to follow and gives an overview of the overall process status. An example of a manual process activity part of an human resources recruitment process could be to check the LinkedIn profile of candidates before inviting them in for a job interview.

13.4.1.1 Business Process Modeling and Notation (BPMN 2.0)

SAP BPM (version 7.5) supports roughly 90% of all flow elements declared in the BPMN 2.0 library. SAP NetWeaver Developer Studio is the integrated development environment that incorporates all the tools required to model, develop, and deploy business processes in accordance with the BPMN 2.0 specification. BPMN 2.0 is a generic standard that defines a set of different flow elements to help process owners, business analysts, and IT professionals to understand, analyze, design, and execute business processes in a common way and according to their specific (functional and technical) requirements and at different levels of detail.

 BPMN is an essential enabler of business and IT alignment that provides a common language for all disciplines involved in the modeling, execution, and managing of business processes. SAP provides the facility to convert static BPMN diagrams into executable versions of those BPMN diagrams.

1. Swim lanes are a standard mechanism used in BPMN 2.0 to group process steps into separate visual containers. A swim lane represents a functional entity or responsibility in the process and can be modeled either vertically or horizontally depending on the orientation of the entire BPD.

   There are two types of swim lanes:

   a. Pool: The pool object represents a process participant and serves as the container for a single process. There can be one or more pools per process flow. Pools can also be used to model business-to-business interactions and other similar types of intercompany exchanges of information.

Some important characteristics of a pool include:

- A pool represents a process actor, which can be a person or a system.
- A pool contains a single BPMN process.
- As a best practice, a pool should be used when modeling a process.
- As a best practice, a pool should be labelled with the name of the process it contains.
- A process diagram can contain more than one pool. You can model black-box and white-box pools in your process diagram. A white-box pool is a pool in which the process steps are all known and visible. A black-box is the opposite; that is, it is modeled empty and it normally represents an external entity: a black-box pool is labeled with the name of the process participant it represents.
- You can model a pool and its contents horizontally or vertically.

 A black-box pool (which is a type of process choreography diagram) is BPMN 2.0 compliant, but it is currently not supported by SAP BPM: it can be modeled but not translated into an executable process.

   b. Lane: A lane usually represents user roles, organizational units, or systems that perform activities in the process and is used to arrange and group related process steps within a pool; there can be one or more lanes in one pool.

Some important characteristics of a pool are:

- You can have more than one lane subdivision in one pool.
- A lane represents a process actor, which can be a user role, an organizational unit, or a system.
- Information flow from one lane to another in the same pool is modeled using the sequence flow.
- Information flow from one lane to another in a different pool is done via the message flow.
- You can model a lane and its contents horizontally or vertically.

2. Artifacts are process objects that can be used in a BPD to provide additional information about the process context or its specific activities; they can be linked to other process objects, such as events and tasks, by using associations. Users can also create and import their own set of artifacts.

Artifacts can be of two types:

   a. A data object in BPMN represents the context of a process—that is, the information flowing from start to end through the different steps of a modeled process in SAP BPM. In SAP BPM, data objects have an abstract character because you can use them to define inbound and outbound data structures. A data object can represent an IDoc, a request from a web service of an ABAP proxy, or any other data container interacting with a process. When you create a data object, it needs to be associated with a data type to map its contents with a process activity in your process model.

Some important characteristics of data objects are:

- They represent the context of the business process.

- They feed the process with information produced by its participants.
- They serve as a data container for storing input and output data during process execution or for reporting purposes.
- They link to existing data types (e.g., XML schemas).

  b. Annotation enables providing useful or additional explanatory information about specific parts of the process model. Annotations only provide additional information about individual elements; they do not have an impact on the behavior of the process.

3. Flow objects: When modeling a graphical representation for describing a business process, there are four types of flow objects that can be used:

   a. Events: Running processes are exposed to different types of internal and external events, which might influence the internal behavior and outputs during the course of the process. With events, you specify how a process is started or ended or that the process is temporarily delayed and is waiting for a certain event (time- or message-driven) before proceeding.

      Events can be of four types: Start events, intermediate events, end events, and boundary events.

   b. Activities are the actions performed by the participants of a business process. They are shown in a process flow as rectangles with rounded corners, with their corresponding descriptive icons in the top-left corner and their names describing the actions they represent.

      Activities can be of three types: Automated, human, and subprocess.

   c. Gateways determine the path of the process flow based on predefined conditions set and modeled at design time. A conditional gateway evaluates the parameters provided as input and decides which outgoing sequence flow to follow. A sequence flow can be split, made to run in parallel, or merged; it is also possible to make the process flow dependent on the first event that occurred, applying the event-based choice. Gateways are represented as diamond shapes in a process diagram.

      Gateways can be of six types: exclusive, event-based choice, parallel split, parallel join, uncontrolled merge, and undefined.

4. Connections: Connection objects are the flow elements or connectors that connect the flow objects with each other.

   a. Sequence flow: A sequence flow connects flow objects such as events, activities, and gateways. It defines the order of performance of the flow objects. Each sequence flow connection has only one source and only one target.

      During the performance of the process, a token leaves the source flow object, traverses down the sequence flow, and enters the target flow object. Depending on its source object, a sequence flow can have a conditional expression attribute. The conditions are associated with an exclusive choice gateway. The condition expression must be evaluated before a token can be generated and leave the source object to traverse the flow.

   b. Message flow: A message flow is used to show the flow of messages between two participants that are prepared to send and receive them. The activities and events are connected within a lane and across the lane boundary with a sequence flow.

    c. Data flow defines where data objects are used in one's business process model. The data objects represent the process context. Data mappings show how data used as input and output by the activities and the events in your process are transformed.

    d. The concept of association connects additional information, such as a note, to individual elements in the process model, such as flow objects, swim lanes, and data objects. Such notes are represented by annotations.

13.4.2 SAP Business Rules Management

The business world is constantly changing. These changes can be internally influenced by an organization or externally influenced (e.g., a new employment law to a change in consumer behavior). A typical organization should desire to quickly adapt to such changes in the business environment to keep its competitive advantage. This adaptation might result in a change of existing business rules. Businesses can design and define their decisions and business rules in a BRM system. Given that these rules are subject to constant changes, it makes sense to maintain and keep them separate from the actual business applications. This externalization of business rules creates the flexibility to change such rules without having to change the business applications. Business rules enrich business processes with conditions and constraints that must be met or checked before executing a certain process activity or returning a particular result to a requester. Put another way, a business rule represents constraints that affect the behavior or final result of a business process; for instance, corporate policies are standard business practices that need to be consistently applied across business processes.

SAP BRM is an all-in-one platform that helps the user to automate the execution of business rules and manage their entire life cycle (i.e., model, execute, monitor, and improve in conjunction with the business processes that they are part of). SAP BRM is based on the Java-only stack of SAP PO and supports integration according to service-oriented architecture principles and technologies.

 SAP Business Rules Framework plus (BRFplus) is an ABAP-based, rules-based framework.

    SAP BRM is delivered as part of SAP PO and can be seen as an independent BRMS running in parallel with the SAP BPM and SAP Advanced Adapter Engine Extended (AEX) engines on the SAP Java stack of SAP PO. It consist of three components, namely, Rules Composer, Rules Manager, and Rules Engine.

13.4.2.1 Rules Composer

The Rules Composer represents the design-time of SAP BRM. It is the place wherein the user creates, models, develops, tests, and deploys the business rules. SAP delivers this functionality as part of its Eclipse-based integrated development environment, SAP NetWeaver Developer Studio. SAP NetWeaver Developer Studio offers a rich pallet of business rules perspectives that can be used (depending on the user's role, such as business analyst, business rules developer, or the process owner of the business rule) to model, develop, or maintain business rules.

There are two different approaches for creating business rules, as follows:

    1. A standalone business rule service can be reused by different applications and business processes. You create this type of rule directly from the Rules Composer perspective in SAP NetWeaver Developer Studio. This approach is adopted when

it is determined that a business rule will be generic enough to be used by different processes.

2. Rules can be embedded as part of a business process context and created as part of the Process Composer Development Component. This type of rule is commonly used inside processes that require specific decision logic, and the chance that such a rule will be reused by other applications is very slim.

Subsequently, one needs to determine how to integrate the business rule within your business process. There are different ways of adding the business rules to the process flow in SAP BPM:

- As an automated activity—that is, as a Web service using its Web Services Description Language.
- Inside a gateway condition as a custom-built function—this feature is only supported for a ruleset that has been created inside the same Development Component in which the process flow is maintained.
- Programmatically via Enterprise Java Bean (EJB) custom functions and mappings.

13.4.2.2 Rules Manager

Rules Manager is a rule-centric Web Dynpro application that provides a Web-based environment to administer and monitor previously deployed rules on the rule engine. It allows business managers, IT and functional administrators, and key users to modify business rules and implement changes instantaneously. With Rules Manager, it is possible to create, update, and delete rules, scripts, and decision tables on the fly rather than via time-consuming transport procedures.

There are also different Web-based tools that support the maintenance and management of business rules in SAP PO; these include:

- Business Rules Access Control Management
- Rules Manager Editing Tool for Functional and Business Users
- Business Rules Execution Logs

13.4.2.3 Rules Engine

After modeling, configuring, and locally unit-testing the rules in SAP NetWeaver Developer Studio's Rules Composer, the rules need to be deployed and executed on the Java Web AS. Rules Engine executes the rules on the application server; it achieves this by interpreting and executing the business rules deployed on the application server.

13.4.3 SAP Process Integration

In 2002, SAP Exchange Infrastructure (SAP XI) was launched as part of the SAP NetWeaver suite. SAP XI version 1.0 evolved into SAP XI 2.0 and SAP XI 3.0 in 2004. SAP XI was built on top of a dual-stack architecture, which includes SAP NetWeaver Application Server ABAP (SAP NetWeaver AS ABAP) and SAP NetWeaver Application Server Java (SAP NetWeaver AS Java). After a few improvements and new features, the product was renamed from SAP XI to SAP NetWeaver PI in 2005. In 2010,

SAP PI 7.3 was released with a more productively equipped Java stack: AEX. This is a robust Java-only ESB.

An ESB can enable you to support a service-oriented architecture in your organization's ecosystem. AEX is an ESB and takes care of implementing the communication and interaction between the software applications that are interacting and exchanging data.

Some important characteristics of AEX are:

- Controls the routing of message exchange between applications
- Handles the transformation and mapping of the data and messages transferred from the source to the target system and vice versa (which implies that the message structures of the business applications on both ends of the exchange do not need to be the same)
- Steers the security and conversion of protocol between the service provider and consumer
- Monitors the exchange of messages between the involved systems
- Manages the various versions of the services provided by the ESB

13.5 Summary

This chapter discusses how BPMN 2.0 can not only capture business requirements but also provide the backbone of the actual solution implementation. The same diagram prepared by the business analyst to describe the business's desired "to-be" process can be used to automate the execution of that process on a modern process engine. This is achieved via a new process-centric architecture that preserves simplicity and stability in the business-oriented enterprise process description layer while maximizing flexibility and agility in the underlying service contract implementation layer and vice-a-versa. On the other hand, because of this intervening layer, the process-centric application is also unaffected by changes in the underlying system landscape—what changes is only the logic of the service contract implementation layer. The latter part of the chapter provided an overview of the SAP PO program to give a practical context to the discussion presented in this book. This overview included descriptions of SAP BPM to address business process management, SAP BRM to address business rules management, and SAP PI to address process integration management.

Section IV

Enterprise Process Management Systems Applications

As stated in the Preface, the motivation for this book can be found in the current heightened priority placed on the digital transformation or digitalization of enterprises. A significant part of any digital transformation initiative is a set of process improvement programs with a spectrum of predefined objectives. However, any candidate process improvements would have to be assessed and evaluated for determining which process analysis is critical. For expediting the management and execution of process analyses that are effort- and time-intensive, modeling and simulation are indispensable. In a different context, process simulation can be the primary resource for copious amounts of process data under differing experimental conditions and parameters, which can then be mined and analyzed for characteristics and patterns. Process mining and process analysis are covered in certain publications including W. M. P. van der Aalst (2002); M. Dumas, M. La Rosa, J. Mendling, and H. Reijers (2013); and M. Laguna and J. Marklund (2013).

Chapter 14 explains the rationale for modeling business processes with queuing theory. In business processes, each activity of the process is performed by a resource, specifically, either a human resource or machine resource; thus, if the resource is busy when the job arrives, then the job will wait in a queue until the resource becomes available. The chapter also introduces simulation as a technique that enables defining and experimenting with the imitation of the behavior of a real system in order to analyze its functionality and performance in greater detail.

Chapter 15 focuses on process improvement programs ranging from disruptive to continuous improvement programs—the first corresponds to business process reengineering programs, while the latter corresponds to programs like lean, Six Sigma, and Theory of Constraints. The last part of the chapter focuses on the basic principle of time-based competition by discussing activity-based costing and comparing it with the more advanced time-driven activity-based costing.

Chapter 16 introduces customer conversation systems that can *enable* sales closures through customer interactions rather than merely registering customer orders. It introduces the concept of human interaction management and compares its efficacy with business process management. It also presents the components of an effective customer interaction system, namely, automatic speech recognition, spoken language understanding, dialog management, natural language generation, and text-to-speech synthesis.

14

EPMS for Business Process Analysis

There are three general approaches to process analysis and design: an analytical approach, a computational approach, and a qualitative or knowledge-based approach. First, queueing theory provides a framework to analyze business processes. As an analysis tool, it has a benefit in that an analysis team can quickly build a model and obtain results. The drawbacks are that queueing models can be mathematically complex, are approximate for more complicated systems, and the results are only valid if the actual system being studied matches the underlying assumptions of the queueing model. Second, within computational approaches, there are three main simulation models: continuous simulation, discrete-event simulation, and agent-based simulation. The benefits of simulation are that a system of almost any complexity could, in theory, be modeled accurately. A drawback is that simulation modeling often requires significant expertise and time to both develop a model and to analyze it. Also, to obtain greater accuracy of the results requires the securement of more accurate data than what might be called for in analytical approaches. Third, a knowledge-based approach uses rules or heuristics based on best practices to guide the analysis. There are many heuristics that can be applied; it is through the knowledgeable application of these rules that the process can be improved.

Since a business process is a set of activities, business processes can be modeled with queuing theory. In business processes, a flow or job unit is routed from activity to activity and, at each activity, some transformation is done to the job until the job finally departs the process. Each activity of the process is performed by a resource, either of a human or machine nature. If the resource is busy when the job arrives, then the job must wait in a queue until the resource becomes available. The benefits of applying queueing theory to analyze business processes is that, first, they provide the analyst with insight into the performance of business processes, and, second, the performance analysis can be conducted rapidly, allowing for fast generation of alternative process designs.

Analytical queuing models offer powerful means for understanding and evaluating queuing processes. However, the use of these analytical models is somewhat restricted by their underlying assumptions. The limitations pertain to the structure of the queuing system, the way variability can be incorporated into the models, and the focus on steady-state analysis. Because many business processes are cross-functional and characterized by complex structures and variability patterns, a more flexible modeling tool is needed. Simulation, discussed in the latter half of this chapter, offers this flexibility and represents a powerful approach for analysis and quantitative evaluation of business processes.

Simulation is a technique that enables us to define and launch an imitation of the behavior of a certain real system in order to analyze its functionality and performance in detail. For this purpose, real-life input data is required and collected for use in running, observing the system's behavior over time, and conducting different experiments without disturbing the functioning of the original system. One of the most important properties of the simulation technique is to enable experts to carry out experiments on the behavior of a system by generating various options of "what if" questions. This characteristic of simulation gives a possibility for exploring ideas and creating different scenarios that are based on an understanding of the system's operation and deep analysis of the simulation output results. This actually represents simulation's main advantage, which consequently has led to the widespread use of the technique in various fields for both academic and practical purposes.

 Process simulation can be the primary resource for copious amount of process data under differing experimental conditions and parameters which can then be mined and analyzed for its characteristics and patterns. Process mining and process analysis are covered in several publications like W. M. P. van der Aalst (2002), M. Dumas, M. La Rosa, J. Mendling, and H. Reijers (2013) and M. Laguna and J. Marklund (2013).

14.1 Queuing Systems

We come across people "queuing" for many activities in daily life. It can be the issue of "consulting" in a medical clinic, "rationing" in a ration shop, the issue of cinema tickets, the issue of rail/airline tickets, etc. The arriving people are called "customers," while the person issuing the ticket is referred to as the "server." There can be more than one queue and more than one server in many cases—for example, the outpatient department (OPD), rail tickets, bus tickets, etc. If the server is free at the time of arrival of the customer, he can be serviced immediately. If there are a number of people, a waiting line and consequently waiting time comes into operation. There can also be server idle time.

Queuing theory was originally developed by Agner Krarup Erlang in 1909. Erlang was a Danish engineer who worked in the Copenhagen telephone exchange. While studying the telephone traffic problem, he used a Poisson process as the arrival mechanism and, for the first time, modeled the telephone queues as an M/D/1 queuing system. Ever since the first queuing model, queuing theory has been well-developed and extended to many complex situations, even with complicated queuing networks. These models, together with the advancement of computer technology, have been used widely now in many fields and have shown significant benefits in optimizing behavior within these systems.

The entities that request services are called customers, and the processes that provide services and fulfill customers' needs are called service channels. It is obvious that capacity is the key factor in influencing system behaviors. If the service channels have less capacity and cannot satisfy customer demand, then a waiting line will form and systems may become more and more crowded; thus, the quality of service will be degraded and many customers might choose to leave the system before getting served. From the standpoint of customers, the more service channel capacity, the better; this implies a smaller amount of waiting to be served and a high service quality is present. On the other hand, if the service channels have more capacity than needed, then, from the service provider's perspective, more service channels predominantly mean more investment, capital expenditure, and human labor involved, which increases the operations costs of the service or the manufacturing process.

Thus, one of the most important purposes of studying queuing theory is to find a balance between these two costs, i.e., the waiting cost and the service cost. If the customer waits for too long, he/she may not be happy with the service and thus might not return in the future, causing loss of potential profit; or, conversely, parts may be waiting too long, increasing production cycle time and thus again losing potential sales and profits. These costs are considered to be waiting costs. Service costs are those that increase service capacity such as salary paid to the servers. Queuing theory application balances these two costs by determining the right level of

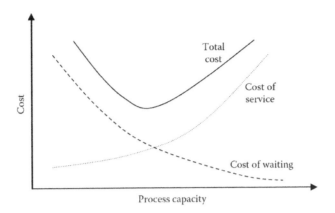

FIGURE 14.1
Total cost of queue operations versus process capacity.

service so that the total cost of the operations (waiting cost + service cost) can be optimized. Figure 14.1 shows the schematic of the total cost of queue operations versus process capacity.

14.1.1 Queuing Process

1. Calling population: This represents a group of flow units, for example customers, some of whom are associated with the queuing system for predetermined purposes. This means that a flow unit joins one or more queues of flow units waiting in different buffers within a certain process.

   The calling population may contain flow units of the same type or flow units of different types. The first is called a homogeneous calling population, whereas the second is called a heterogeneous calling population. Calling populations are usually heterogeneous. For example, patients enter a hospital for different purposes, i.e., different health problems; to this regard, such a calling population consists of different subpopulations.

   The calling population could be understood as an infinite or finite population. The calling population is considered as infinite when a flow unit joins a queue of such a large number of flow units that the queuing system is not affected by the arrival of the new flow unit (for example, a patient joins a waiting list of patients in a long queue that may last months of waiting for the purpose of undergoing an operation). Otherwise, the calling population is considered finite if the criterion for an infinite population is not valid (for example, a patient joins a queue of a number of patients in a waiting room to see a specialist physician).

2. Arrival process: This represents a determined way or path that every flow unit should follow after entering the queuing process. The path for each flow unit is determined depending on the type of flow unit. Such a path consists of a number of activities through which the flow unit passes.

   There are queues, particularly when people (customers) as flow units form the queue, in which the person who joins the queue may make a decision of one of the following three possible actions:

- The person decides to leave and not to join the queue because of the large number of people already in the queue.
- Renege, the person joins the queue, but, after some time, decides to leave the queue.
- The person decides to wait in the queue regardless of the time spent waiting.

3. Queue configuration: This indicates the type of queue that the flow unit joins, which determines the requirements to join a queue and the behavior of a flow unit or customer who joins the queue. There are two types of queues, as follows:
    - Single-line queue configuration requires that a flow unit joins the queue at the end of a single line and the flow unit is served after all the flow units before it are served.
    - The multiple-line queue configuration enables the flow unit to choose one of several queue lines.

4. Queue discipline: Queue discipline represents the rule or discipline used to choose the next flow unit for serving; there are different disciplines used depending on the purpose of the queuing system. The most commonly used rule is known as first-in-first-out. Some queue disciplines also use priority of the flow unit to select the next to be served. This rule is, for example, used in medical institutions, where patients with life-threatening conditions or children have the highest priority to be served first.

5. Service mechanism: This consists of a number of services that perform a set of tasks on the flow unit within a process. The flow unit enters the service facility when the resource is available to provide the flow unit with the service it needs. The time spent by the service in performing the work on the flow unit is called the service time.

14.2 Queuing Models

Whenever an OPD is scheduled, one witnesses large queues at the OPD section prior to the start of the OPD hours to register the patient number tokens. The actors in this situation are the patients arriving to get the tokens for physician's consulting, and the service counter at the hospital or the registration server is providing the service by registering tokens. The arrival process is represented by the interarrival times, while the service process is represented by the service time per patient. The interarrival time is the time between successive patient arrivals. The service time per patient is the time taken to provide the patients the expected service as desired.

 In the earlier OPD clinic example, the interarrival time may be very less during an OPD off day and may be high during an OPD scheduled day. Similarly, the service rate will be high during OPD scheduled days and will be slightly low during the OPD off days. In other words, the interarrival times and service rates are probabilistic.

Queue discipline represents the manner in which the customers waiting in a queue are served. It may be:

- First-come-first-serve
- Service in random order
- Last-come-first-serve

If there are more queues, then the customers often join the queue where the length is small. This is known as *jockeying*. Sometimes, the customers tend to move away from the queue place upon seeing its length. This is known as *balking*. If the customers wait for a long time in the queue, but have not been serviced, then they may move away. This is known as *reneging*.

 The field of queueing theory has developed a taxomomy to describe systems based on their arrival process, service process, and number of servers, written as arrival/service/number servers. The basic notation, widely used in queueing theory, is composed of three symbols separated by forward slashes. The values for the symbols are:

- M for Poisson or exponential distributions
- D for deterministic (constant) distributions
- E for Erlang distributions
- G for general distributions (any arbitrary distribution)
- GI for general independent in the case of arrival rates

There are varieties of queuing models that arise from the elements of a queue that are described next.

14.2.1 Model I: Pure Birth Model

The pure birth model considers only arrivals, and the inter-arrival time in the pure birth model is explained by the exponential distribution. Birth of babies is a classical example for the pure birth model.

Let $P_0(t)$ be the probability of no customer arrivals during a period of time t.

Let $P_n(t)$ be the probability of n arrivals during a period of time t.

As $P_0(t) = e^{-\lambda t}$,

$$P_n(t) = \frac{(\lambda t)^n e^{-\lambda t}}{n!}, n = 0,1,2\ldots$$

This is a Poisson distribution with mean $E\{n/t\} = \lambda t$ arrivals during a period of time t.

14.2.2 Model II: Pure Death Model

The pure death model contradicts the pure birth model, in the sense that only departures are considered in this model. Here, the system starts with N customers at time 0, and no further arrivals are permitted to the system. The departure rate is l customer per unit time. $P_n(t)$ is the probability of n customers in the system after t time units.

So,

$$P_n(t) = \frac{(\mu t)^{N-n} e^{-\mu t}}{(N-n)!}, n = 0,1,2\ldots N$$

and

$$P_0(t) = 1 - \sum_{n=1}^{N} P_0(t)$$

14.2.3 Model III: Generalized Poisson Queuing Model

This model considers both interarrival time and service time, and both these times follow exponential distribution. During the early operation of the system, it will be in the transient state. On the contrary, if the system is in operation for a long time, it attains a steady state. In this model, both the interarrival and the service time exhibit state dependency.

Assuming n as the number of customers in the system ("system" referring to those customers who are waiting for service and who are being serviced), then:

λ_n is the arrival rate where there are n customers in the system already

μ_n is the service rate where there are n customers in the system already

P_n is the steady-state probability of n customers in the system

All of the earlier steady-state probabilities help in determining the different parameters for the model such as average queue length, waiting time in the system, and various measures of system's performance.

Then, with

$$P_n = \left(\frac{\lambda_{n-1}\lambda_{n-2}\ldots\lambda_0}{\mu_n\mu_{n-1}\cdots\mu_1} \right) P_0, \quad n = 1, 2, \ldots$$

we can determine P_0 from the equation $\sum_{n=0}^{\infty} P_0 = 1$.

For n = 0,

$$P_1 = \left(\frac{\lambda_0}{\mu_1} \right) P_0$$

For n = 1,

$$\lambda_0 P_0 + \mu_2 P_2 = (\lambda_1 + \mu_1) P_1$$

Substituting the values of P_1, we get

$$P_2 = \left(\frac{\lambda_1\lambda_0}{\mu_2\mu_1} \right) P_0$$

14.2.4 Single-Server Models

The basic queuing models can be classified into six categories using Kendall notation, which employs six parameters to define a model (P/Q/R): (X/Y/Z).
  The parameters of the notation are as follows:

P is the distribution of the arrival rate.

Q is the distribution of the service rate.

R refers to the number of service channels providing the service.

X is the service discipline; it may be general, first-come-first-serve, service in random order, or last-come-first-serve.

Y is the maximum number of customers allowed to stay in the system at any point in time.

Z is the calling source size.

14.2.4.1 Model IV (M/M/1): (GD/∞/∞)

The features of this model are as follows:

1. There is a single service channel providing the service.
2. Arrival rate or input follows Poisson distribution.
3. The service rate is exponentially distributed.
4. There is no limit on the system's capacity.
5. Customers are served on a first-come-first-served basis.

Assuming,

1. λ: arrival rate of customers (number/hour)
2. μ: service rate (number/hour)
3. T: mean time between arrivals = $1/\lambda$
4. t: average time of servicing = $1/\mu$
5. ρ(rho): utilization factor or traffic intensity = λ/μ
6. ρ_0: idling factor of the facility; that is, the probability of providing the service right away to the customers without them having to wait = $1 - \rho$
7. P_n: probability that there are n customers waiting in the system for service.
8. N: number of customers in the system
9. L_q: length of the queue or average number of customers in the queue waiting for service
10. L_s: average number of customers in the system (both at service counters and in the queue)
11. W_q: average waiting time in the queue
12. W_s: average waiting time in the system
13. W/W > 0: expected waiting time of a customer who has to wait
14. L/L > 0: expected length of a nonempty queue

The formula list for the model $(M/M/1):(GD/\infty/\infty)$ is given in the following:

1. $P_0 = 1 - (\lambda/\mu) = 1 - \rho$

2. $P_n = \left(\dfrac{\lambda}{\mu}\right)\left(1 - \dfrac{\lambda}{\mu}\right) = (\rho)^n \times (1-\rho)$

3. Probability of queue size greater than $n(Q \geq n) = (\rho)^n$

4. $L_s = \left(\dfrac{\lambda}{\mu-\lambda}\right)$

5. $L_q = \left(\dfrac{\lambda}{\mu-\lambda}\right) \times \left(\dfrac{\lambda}{\mu}\right) = \left(\dfrac{\lambda^2}{\mu(\mu-\lambda)}\right)$

6. $W_s = \left(\dfrac{\lambda}{\mu-\lambda}\right) \times \left(\dfrac{\lambda}{\mu}\right) \quad L_s \times \left(\dfrac{1}{\mu}\right) = \left(\dfrac{1}{\mu-\lambda}\right)$

7. $W_q = \left(\dfrac{\lambda}{\mu(\mu-\lambda)}\right)$

8. $L/L > 0 = L_n = \left(\dfrac{\lambda}{\mu-\lambda}\right)$

9. Average waiting time in the nonempty queue $= \left(\dfrac{1}{\mu-\lambda}\right)$

10. Probability of an arrival waiting for t mins or more $= \rho e^{-(\mu-\lambda)t}$

14.2.4.2 Model V (M/M/1): (GD/N/∞)

The features of this model are:

1. A single-service channel to provide the service
2. Both the arrival rate and service rate follow Poisson distribution
3. The number of customers allowed in the system cannot exceed N at any point of time

The formula list is given in the following:

1. (a) $P_N = \dfrac{\left(1 - \dfrac{\lambda}{\mu}\right)}{\left(1 - \dfrac{\lambda}{\mu}\right)} \times \left(\dfrac{\lambda}{\mu}\right)^N , \dfrac{\lambda}{\mu} \neq 1, N = 0,1,2,\ldots N$

$\qquad = \dfrac{(1-\rho)}{(1-\rho)^{N+1}} \times (\rho)^N , \rho \neq 1, N = 0,1,2,\ldots N$

(b) If $\rho = 1$, that is 100% utilization,

$$P_n = \frac{1}{N+1}$$

2. Effective arrival rate of customers (λ_e)

$$\lambda_e = \lambda(1 - P_N) = \mu(L_s - L_q)$$

3. (a) $L_s = \dfrac{\left(\dfrac{\lambda}{\mu}\right)\left[1 - (N+1)(\rho)^N + N(\rho)^{N+1}\right]}{(1-\rho)(1-\rho)^{N+1}}$, if $\rho \neq 1$

$$= \frac{(\rho)\left[1 - (N+1)(\rho)^N + N(\rho)^{N+1}\right]}{(1-\rho)(1-\rho)^{N+1}}, \text{if } \rho \neq 1$$

(b) If $\rho = 1, L_s = N/2$

4. $L_q = L_s - \dfrac{\lambda_e}{\mu} = L_s = \dfrac{\lambda(1-P_N)}{\mu}$

5. $W_s = \dfrac{L_s}{\lambda(1-P_N)}$

6. $W_q = \dfrac{L_q}{\lambda_e} = \dfrac{L_q}{\lambda(1-P_N)} = W_s - \dfrac{1}{\mu}$

14.2.5 Multiple-Server Models

In this case, there will be C counters or servers in parallel to serve the customer. The customer has the option of choosing the server that is free, or that has the least number of people waiting for service. The mean arrival rate (λ) follows Poisson distribution, while the mean service rate (μ) follows exponential distribution.

14.2.5.1 Model VII (M/M/C): (GD/∞/∞)

The features of this model are as follows:

1. Arrival rate and service rate follow Poisson distribution.
2. There are C serving channels.
3. An infinite number of customers is permitted in the system.
4. GD stands for general discipline servicing.

The formula list is given in the following:

1. $\begin{cases} P_{n1} = \dfrac{\rho^n}{n!} & \text{for } 0 \leq n \leq c \\[3mm] P_n = \dfrac{\rho^n}{C^{n-c}C!} P_0 & \text{for } n > c \end{cases}$

2. $P_0 = \left\{ \displaystyle\sum_{n=0}^{C-1} \dfrac{\rho^n}{n!} + \dfrac{\rho^C}{C!\left(1-\dfrac{\rho}{c}\right)} \right\}^{-1}$

3. $L_q = \dfrac{C \cdot \rho}{(C-\rho)^2} P_c$

4. $L_s = L_q + \rho$

5. $W_q = \dfrac{L_q}{\lambda}$

6. $W_s = W_q + \dfrac{1}{\mu}$

Morse (1998) shows that for (M/M/C): (GD/∞/∞)

$$L_q = \frac{\rho}{C-\rho} \text{ as } \frac{\rho}{C} \to 1$$

14.2.5.2 Model VIII (M/M/C): (GD/N/∞)

The features of this model include:

1. The system limit is finite and is equal to N.
2. The arrival rate and service rate follow Poisson distribution.
3. The maximum queue length is $N - C$.
4. There are C service channels.

Here $\lambda_e < \lambda$, because of N

The generalized model can be defined as

$$\lambda_n = \begin{cases} (N-n)\lambda & \text{for } 0 \leq n \leq N \\ 0 & \text{for } n \geq N \end{cases}$$

$$\mu_n = \begin{cases} n\mu & \text{for } 0 \leq n \leq N \\ C\mu & \text{for } C \leq n \leq N \\ 0 & \text{for } n \geq N \end{cases}$$

The formula list is given in the following:

1. $P_n = \begin{cases} N_{Cn}\rho^n \cdot P_0 & \text{for } 0 \leq n \leq C \\ N_{Cn}\dfrac{n!\rho^n}{C!C^{n-C}} \cdot P_0 & \text{for } C \leq n \leq N \end{cases}$

2. $P_0 = \left\{ \displaystyle\sum_{n=0}^{C} N_{Cn}\rho^n + \sum_{n=C+1}^{N} \dfrac{n!\rho^n}{C!C^{n-C}} \right\}^{-1}$

3. $L_q = \displaystyle\sum_{n=c+1}^{N} (n-C)P_n$

4. $L_s = L_q + \dfrac{\lambda_e}{\mu}$

5. $\lambda_e = \mu(C - C_1), C_1 = \displaystyle\sum_{n=0}^{C} (C-n)P_n = \lambda(N - L_s)$

6. $W_s = \dfrac{L_s}{\lambda_e}$

7. $w_q = \dfrac{L_q}{\lambda_e}$

14.3 Simulation

For queuing systems such as the M/M/C queue, the analytical models are well-developed and we can predict their steady-state performance without too much difficulty. We made many assumptions (i.e., Poisson arrival process) about the analytical queuing models in the previous sections so as to simplify the problem so that a mathematical model could be formulated. However, in the real world, the situation becomes more dynamic and complicated than those mathematical models can handle; even though queuing network models are available, many situations are simply beyond the capabilities of the analytical mathematical model.

When modeling these systems, information such as shift patterns, lunch breaks, machine breakdowns, arrival rates, and so forth cannot be ignored, as they will have significant impacts on system performance; also, some systems might never arrive at a steady state and do not operate on a 24/7 basis. So, it is nearly impossible to study these types of systems using queuing theory and models; a theoretical solution for those queuing systems would be difficult to obtain. An alternative to the mathematical model is to use the simulation model instead.

Simulation is the imitation or representation of the behavior of some real thing, state of affairs, or process. The act of simulating something generally entails representing certain key characteristics or behaviors of a selected physical or abstract system. To simulate means to mimic the reality in some way; simulation is a system that represents or emulates the behavior of another system over time. More specifically, a simulation is the imitation of the operation of a real-world process or system over time.

Simulation is a technique that enables us to define and launch an imitation of the behavior of a certain real system in order to analyze its functionality and performance in detail. For this purpose, real-life input data is required and collected for use in running, observing the system's behavior over time, and conducting different experiments without disturbing the functioning of the original system. One of the most important properties of the simulation technique is to enable experts to carry out experiments on the behavior of a system by generating various options of what-if questions. This characteristic of simulation gives a possibility for exploring ideas and creating different scenarios that are based on an understanding of the system's operation and deep analysis of the simulation output results. This actually represents simulation's main advantage, which consequently has led to the widespread use of the technique in various fields for both academic and practical purposes.

Characteristics of simulation:

- Simulation enables the study and experimentation of the internal interactions of a complex system or a subsystem.
- The knowledge gained in designing a simulation model may be of great value toward suggesting improvement in the system under investigation.
- By changing simulation inputs and observing the corresponding outputs, valuable insight may be obtained into which variables are most important and how they influence other variables.
- Simulation can be used to experiment with new designs or policies prior to implementation, so as to prepare for what may happen in real life.
- Simulation can be used to verify analytic solutions.
- Simulation models designed for training allow learning to occur without cost or disruption.
- Animation shows a system in simulated operation so that the plan can be visualized.

The advantages of simulation include:

1. A simulation can help in understanding how the system operates.
2. Bottleneck analysis can be performed, indicating where work-in-process, information, materials, and so on are being excessively delayed.
3. What-if questions can be answered, which is useful in the design of new systems.
4. New policies, operating procedures, decision rules, information flows, organizational procedures and so on can be explored without disrupting the ongoing operations of the real system.
5. Time can be compressed or expanded, allowing for a speed-up or slowdown of the phenomena under investigation.

14.3.1 Simulation Models

The rapid development of computer hardware and software in recent years has made computer simulation an effective tool for process modeling and an attractive technique for predicting the performance of alternative process designs. It also helps in optimizing their efficiency. The main advantage of simulation is that it is a tool that compresses time and space, thus enabling a robust validation of ideas for process design and improvement. Modern simulation software in a sense combines the descriptive strength of the symbolic models with the quantitative strength of the analytical models. It offers graphical representation of the model through graphical interfaces, as well as graphical illustration of the system dynamics through plots of output data and animation of process operations. At the same time, it enables estimation of quantitative performance measures through the statistical analysis of output data. The main disadvantage of simulation is the time spent learning how to use the simulation software and how to interpret the results.

Until recently, simulation software packages could be used only as what-if tools. This means that, given a simulation model, the designer would experiment with alternative designs and operating strategies in order to measure system performance. Consequently, in such an environment, the model becomes an experimental tool that is used to find an effective design. However, modern simulation software packages merge optimization technology with simulation. The optimization consists of an automated search for the best values (nearoptimal values) of input factors (the decision variables). This valuable tool allows designers to identify critical input factors that the optimization engine can manipulate to search for the best values. The best values depend on the measure of performance that is obtained after one or several executions of the simulation model.

 A simulation is a tool for evaluating a given design and an optimization model is a tool used to search for an optimal solution to a decision problem that is a simulation model is, by nature, descriptive, and an optimization model is, by nature, prescriptive.

14.3.1.1 Discrete-Event Simulation

Business processes usually are modeled as computer-based, dynamic, stochastic, and discrete simulation models. The most common way to represent these models in a computer is using discrete-event simulation. In simple terms, discrete-event simulation describes how a system with discrete flow units or jobs evolves over time. Technically, this means that a computer program tracks how and when state variables such as queue lengths and resource availabilities change over time. The state variables change as a result of an event (or discrete event) occurring in the system.

Because the state variables change only when an event occurs, a discrete-event simulation model examines the dynamics of the system from one event to the next. That is, the simulation moves the *simulation clock* from one event to the next and considers that the system does not change in any way between two consecutive events. The simulation keeps track of the time when each event occurs but assumes that nothing happens during the elapsed time between two consecutive events.

 Discreet-event models focus only on the time instances when these discrete events occur. This feature allows for significant time compression because it makes it possible to skip through all of the time segments between events in which the state of the system remains unchanged. Consequently, in a short period of time, a computer can simulate a large number of events corresponding to a lengthy real-time span.

To illustrate the mechanics of a discrete-event simulation model, consider an information desk with a single server. Assume that the objective of the simulation is to estimate the average delay of a customer. The simulation then must have the following state variables:

1. Status of the server (busy or idle)
2. Number of customers in the queue
3. Time of arrival of each person in the queue

As the simulation runs, two events can change the value of these state variables; these are:

- Arrival of a customer, which either changes the status of the server from idle to busy or increases the number of customers in the queue
- Completion of service, which either changes the status of the server from busy to idle or decreases the number of customers in the queue

A single-server queuing process can be represented with a timeline on which the time of each event is marked (Figure 14.2).

Assuming the following notation:

t_j: arrival time of the jth job

$A_j = t_j - t_{j-1}$: time between the arrival of job j – 1 and the arrival of job j

S_j: service time for job j

D_j: delay time for job j

$c_j = t_j + D_j + s_j$: completion time for job j

e_i: time of occurrence of event i

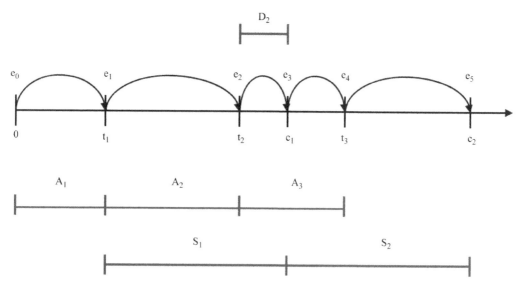

FIGURE 14.2
Events timeline for a single server.

Figure 14.2 shows a graphical representation of the events in a single-server process. This example has six events, starting with event 0 and finishing with event 5. Event 0, e_0, is the initialization of the simulation. Event 1, e_1, is the arrival of the first job, with arrival time equal to t_1. The arrival of the second job occurs at time t_2. Because $c_1 > t_2$, the second job is going to experience a delay. The delay D_2 is equal to the difference between c_1 and t_2 ($D_2 = c_1 - t_2$).

Further in Figure 14.2, the completion time for job 1 is calculated as: $c_1 = t_1 + S_1$, because this jobdoes not experience any delay. The last event in this figure, labeled e_5, is the completion time for job 2. In this case, the calculation of the completion time c_2 includes the waiting time D_2($c_2 = t_2 + D_2 + S_2$).

 There are three main mathematical system formalisms distinguished by how they treat time and data values; they are as follows:

- Continuous systems: These systems are classically modeled by differential equations in linear and nonlinear manners. Values are continuous quantities and are computable for all times.

- Temporally discrete (sampled data) systems: These systems have continuously valued elements measured at discrete time points. Their behavior is described by difference equations. Sampled data systems are increasingly important because they are the basis of most computer simulations and nearly all real-time digital signal processing.

- Discrete-event systems: A discrete-event system is one in which some or all of the quantities take on discrete values at arbitrary points in time. Queuing networks are a classical example. Asynchronous digital logic is a pure example of a discrete-event system. The quantities of interest (say data packets in a communication network) move around the network in discrete units, but they may arrive or leave a node at an arbitrary, continuous time.

Continuous systems have a large and powerful body of theory. Linear systems have comprehensive analytical and numerical solution methods and an extensive theory of estimation and control. Nonlinear systems are still incompletely understood, but many numerical techniques are available, some analytical stability methods are known, and practical control approaches are accessible. The very active field of dynamical systems addresses nonlinear as well as control aspects of systems. Similar results are available for sampled data systems. Computational frameworks exist for discrete-event systems (based on state machines and Petri nets), but are less complete than those for differential or difference equation systems in their ability to determine stability and synthesize control laws. A variety of simulation tools are available for all three types of systems. Some tools attempt to integrate all three types into a single framework, though this is difficult.

Many modern systems are a mixture of all three types. For example, consider a computer-based temperature controller for a chemical process. The complete system may include continuous plant dynamics, a sampled data system for control under normal conditions, and discrete-event controller behavior associated with threshold crossings and mode changes. A comprehensive and practical modern system theory should answer the classic questions about such a mixed system—stability, closed-loop dynamics, and control law synthesis. No such comprehensive theory exists, but constructing one is an objective of current research.

14.3.2 Simulation Procedure

1. Problem formulation: In this step, a problem formulation statement should be prepared, which shows that the problem discussed is understood completely. The problem statement should be signed by the customer or organization that orders the simulation and also by the person or team manager, who is responsible for conducting the system simulation.

2. The setting of objectives and overall project plan: In this step, the simulation team should study if simulation is an appropriate method of solving the problem formulated in the first step. In addition to this, real goals should be defined, which could be expected to be achieved from carrying out the simulation.

    In accordance with the defined goals, the simulation should be considered as an independent project or a subproject within a large project, for example a simulation subproject that deals with the preparation, running, and analysis of results of a simulation of a business process model within a project of business process management.

3. Model conceptualization: This step deals with developing a model of the system that is intended to be simulated. To do this properly, the modeler should use a modeling technique that enables her/him to transfer the behavior of the system into the model developed as closely as possible. The model developed should be shown to the users in order to suggest corrections necessary to make it a true reflection of the original system discussed.

4. Data collection: The simulation of any system requires the collection of detailed data about the system's behavior and each activity performed within the framework of the system. The Collection of data is usually done in connection with system modeling activities; this is when interviews are organized with users.

    Concerning business process management projects, analysts usually collect data about the organization's business processes; their work processes; and each activity within every work process, such as its description, time duration, constraints, resources needed, costs, and other data.

5. Model translation: The model of the system developed in the third step has to be translated into a simulation language program, such as GPSS/H, using the data collected in the previous step.

    There are also a number of software packages, such as iGrafx, Arena, and others, which enable modelers to translate their models into simple diagrams, such as a flowchart, before running the simulation process.

6. Verification: This step deals with the verification of whether the accurately written program truly reflects the translation of the systems model into the program. This step requires debugging the program carefully in order to remove any mistakes that exist in it. The result of this step should be a program that represents the behavior of the system that is presented by the model.

7. Validation: The validation step examines the model developed in order to find out whether it is a true reflection of the original real system. This can be achieved by performing a comparison between the model and the system concerned. Such a comparison could be carried out by testing the simulation model using tests already used from real processes in which the input data and the expected output data are known in advance.

8. Experimental design: In the experimental design step, the simulation team prepares different alternative scenarios for running the simulation process. These scenarios are developed on the basis of a complete understanding of the behavior of the system, generating different possible behavior possibilities of the system by using what-if questions, and trying to implement ideas for achieving improvements in the functioning of the system.

9. Runs and analysis: In this step, the simulation team deals with estimating and analyzing the performance results of the simulation in the prepared scenarios of the previous step. On the basis of the results of the previously completed simulation runs, the team may determine the need for conducting more simulation runs. New ideas may be considered in the context of making changes in the existing scenarios or new scenarios developed on the basis of the carefully analyzed output data, leading to the performance of new simulation runs on the system concerned.

14.4 Process Analytics

Section 14.2.3 introduced the four performance measures of quality, time, cost, and flexibility. These performance measures are usually considered to be generally relevant for any kind of business. Beyond this general set, a company should also identify specific measures. Often, the measures are industry-specific, like profit per square meter in gastronomy, return rate in online shopping, or customer churn in marketing. Any specific measure that a company aims to define should be accurate, cost-effective, and easy-to-understand. This subsection focuses on the four general performance measures of quality, time, cost, and flexibility. The question this section addresses is how to spot when a process does not perform well according to one of these dimensions. Event log is the data generated from the execution or effectively by the simulation of processes; event logs provide very detailed data that are relevant to process performance.

14.4.1 Quality Measurement

The quality of a product created in a process is often not directly visible from execution logs. However, a good indication is to check whether there are repetitions in the execution logs, because such typically occur when a task has not been completed successfully. Repetitions can be found in the sequences of task.

The loop of a rework pattern increases the cycle time of a task to

$$CT = \frac{T}{1-r}$$

in comparison to T being the time to execute the task only once.

The repetition probability r from a series of event logs would be

$$r = 1 - \frac{T}{CT}$$

Both CT and T can now be determined using the data of the event logs.

In some information systems, it might be easier to track repetition based on the assignment of tasks to resources. One example is helpdesk ticketing systems that record which resource is working on a case. Also, the logs of these systems offer insights into repetition. A typical process supported with ticketing systems is incident resolution. For example, an incident might be a call by a patient who complains that the online doctor's appointment booking system does not work. Such an incident is recorded by a dedicated participant—for example, a call center agent. Then, it is forwarded to a first-level support team who tries to solve the problem. In case the problem turns out to be too specific, it is forwarded to a second-level support team with specialized knowledge in the problem domain.

In the best case, the problem is solved and the patient is notified accordingly. In the undesirable case, the team identifies that the problem is within the competence area of another team. This has the consequence of that the problem is rooted back to the first-level team. Similar to the repetition of tasks, we now see that there is a repeated assignment of the problem to the same team. Accordingly, log information can be used to determine how likely it is that a problem is rooted back.

14.4.2 Time Measurement

Time and its more specific measures cycle time and waiting time are important general performance measures. Event logs typically show timestamps such that they can be used for time analysis. Time analysis is concerned with the temporal occurrence and probabilities of different types of events. The event logs of a process generally relate each event to the point in time of its occurrence. Therefore, it is straightforward to plot events on the time axis. Furthermore, we can employ classifiers to group events on a second axis. A classifier typically refers to one of the attributes of an event, like a case identification number (ID) or participant ID.

There are two levels of detail for plotting events in a diagram, as follows:

1. Dotted charts using the timestamp to plot an event: the dotted chart is a simple yet powerful visualization tool for event logs. Each event is plotted on a two-dimensional canvas, with the first axis representing its occurrence in time and the second axis representing its association with a classifier such as a case ID. There are different options to organize the first axis. Time can be represented either in a relative manner, such that the first event is counted as zero, or in an absolute manner, such that later cases with a later start event are further right in comparison to cases that began earlier. The second axis can be sorted according to different criteria. For instance, cases can be shown according to their historical order or their overall cycle time.

2. A timeline chart showing the duration of a task and its waiting time: the temporal analysis of event logs can be enhanced with further details if a corresponding process model is available and tasks can be related to a start and an end event. The idea is to utilize the concept of token replay for identifying the point in time when a task gets activated.

   - For tasks in a sequence, the activation time is the point in time when the previous task was completed.
   - For tasks after an AND-join, this is the point in time when all previous tasks were completed.
   - For XOR-joins and splits it is the point when one of the previous tasks completes.

Using this information, we can plot a task not as a dot but instead as a bar in a timeline chart. A timeline chart shows a waiting time (from activation until starting) and a processing time (from starting until completion) for each task. The timelines of each task can be visualized in a similar way as a dot in the dotted chart. The timeline chart is more informative than the dotted chart, since it shows the duration of the tasks and also the waiting times. Both pieces of information are a valuable input for quantitative process analysis.

When thousands of cases are available as a log, one can estimate the distribution of waiting time and processing time of each task, and:

1. Bottlenecks with long waiting times can be spotted.
2. What tasks are most promising to focus redesign efforts upon can be identified.
3. The execution times of running process instances, which is helpful for process monitoring, can be realized.

14.4.3 Cost Measurement

In a process context, cost measurement is mainly related to the problem of assigning indirect costs. Direct costs like the purchasing costs of four wheels that are assembled on a car can be easily determined. Indirect labor or machine depreciation are more difficult. In accounting, the concept of activity-based costing (ABC) was developed to more accurately assign indirect costs to products and services as well as to individual customers. The motivation of ABC is that human resources and machinery are often shared by different products and services as well as are used to serve different customers. For instance, the depot of BuildIT rents out expensive machinery such as bulldozers to different construction sites. On the one hand, that involves costs in terms of working hours of the persons working at the depot. On the other hand, machines like bulldozers lose value over time and require maintenance. The idea of ABC is to use activities in a manner so as to help distribute the indirect costs, e.g., those associated with the depot.

14.4.4 Flexibility Measurement

Flexibility refers to the degree of variation that a process permits. This flexibility can be discussed in relation to the event logs the process produces. For the company owning the process, this is important information in order to compare the desired level of flexibility with the actual flexibility. It might turn out that the process is more flexible than what is demanded from a business perspective. This is the case when flexibility can be equated with a lack of standardization. Often, the performance of processes suffers when too many options are allowed.

14.5 Summary

This chapter explained the rationale for modeling business processes with queuing theory. In business processes, each activity of the process is performed by a resource (i.e., either a human resource or machine resource); thus, if the resource is busy when the job arrives, then the job will wait in a queue until the resource becomes available. The benefits of applying queueing theory to analyze business processes is, first, they provide the analyst with insight into the performance of business processes and, second, the performance analysis can be conducted rapidly, allowing for the fast generation of alternative process designs. The second half of the chapter introduced simulation as a technique that enables defining and experimenting in the context of the imitation of the behavior of a real system in order to analyze its functionality and performance in greater detail. For this purpose, real-life input data are required and collected for use in running and observing the system's behavior over time and conducting for different experiments without disturbing the functioning of the original system.

15

EPMS for Business Process Improvement

Process improvement programs range right from disruptive to continuous improvement programs—the first of these corresponds to business process reengineering programs, while the latter corresponds to programs like lean, Six Sigma, and the Theory of Constraints (TOC). This chapter discusses a seven-step methodology that can be employed for both business process reengineering (BPR) and business process redesign.

The chapter discusses well-known continuous improvement programs like:

1. Lean, which is a proven approach for becoming an excellent operational system
2. Six Sigma, which is a program for attaining world-class quality improvement
3. The TOC, which is an unsurpassed tool for identifying and removing bottlenecks

The last part of the chapter focuses on the basic principle of time-based competition (TBC)—to react faster to changes in the environment and to be more flexible than competitors in order to grow faster; correspondingly, it also discusses activity-based costing (ABC) and time-driven ABC (TDABC).

15.1 Business Process Reengineering

Although, BPR has its roots in information technology (IT) management, it is basically a business initiative that has major impact on the satisfaction of both the internal and external customer. Michael Hammer, who triggered the BPR revolution in 1990, considers BPR to be a "radical change" for which IT is the key enabler. BPR can be broadly termed as the rethinking and change of business processes to achieve dramatic improvements in the measures of performance aspects such as cost, quality, service, and speed.

Some of the principals advocated by Hammer are as follows:

- Organize around outputs, not tasks.
- Place the decisions and control, and hence all relevant information, into the hands of the performer.
- Have those who use the outputs of a process perform the process, including the creation and processing of the relevant information.
- The location of user, data, and process information should be immaterial; it should function as if all were in a centralized place.

As will become evident when perusing the previous points, the implementation of enterprise systems, especially business process management (BPM), possesses most of the characteristics mentioned earlier.

The most important outcome of BPR has been viewing business activities as more than a collection of individual or even functional tasks; it has engendered the process-oriented view of business. However, BPR is different from quality management efforts like total quality management, International Organization for Standardization (ISO) 9000, and so on, that refer to programs and initiatives that emphasize bottom-up incremental improvements in existing work processes and outputs on a continuous basis. In contrast, BPR usually refers to top-down dramatic improvements through redesigned or completely new processes on a discrete basis. In the continuum of methodologies ranging from ISO 9000, total quality management (TQM), activity based management (ABM), and so forth on one end and BPR on the other, enterprise systems, especially BPM implementation, definitely lies on the BPR side of the spectrum when it comes to corporate change management efforts.

BPR is based on the principle that there is an inextricable link between positioning *and* capability/capacity. A company cannot position the enterprise to meet a customer need that it cannot fulfill without an unprofitable level of resources, nor can it allocate enhanced resources to provide a cost-effective service that no customer wants!

BPR in practice has developed a focus on changing capability/capacity in the short-term to address current issues. This short-term change in capability/capacity is usually driven by the need to:

- Reduce the cycle time to process customer orders
- Improve quotation times
- Lower variable overhead costs
- Increase product range to meet an immediate competitor threat
- Rebalance resources to meet current market needs
- Reduce work-in-progress stocks
- Meet changed legislation requirements
- Introduce short-term measures to increase market-share (e.g., increased credit limit from customers hit by recessionary trends)
- And so on

 Outsourcing is distancing the company from noncore but critical functions; as it is against this, reengineering is exclusively about the core.

An overview of a seven-step methodology is as follows:

1. Develop the context for undertaking the BPR and in particular reengineer the enterprise's business processes. Then, identify the reason behind redesigning the process to represent the value perceived by the customer.
2. Select the business processes for the reengineering effort.
3. Map the selected processes.
4. Analyze the process maps to discover opportunities for reengineering.
5. Redesign the selected processes for increased performance.
6. Implement the reengineered processes.
7. Measure the implementation of the reengineered processes.

The BPR effort within an enterprise is not a one-time exercise but rather an ongoing one. One could also have multiple BPR projects in operation simultaneously in different areas within the enterprise. The BPR effort involves business visioning; identifying the value gaps; and, hence, selection of the corresponding business processes for the BPR effort. The reengineering of the business processes might open newer opportunities and challenges, which in turn triggers another cycle of business visioning followed by BPR of the concerned business processes.

The competitive gap can be defined as the gap between the customer's minimum acceptance value (MAV) and the customer value delivered by the enterprise. Companies that consistently surpass MAVs are destined to thrive, those that only meet the MAVs will survive, and those that fall short of the MAVs may fail. Customers will generally take their business to the company that can deliver the most value for their money. Hence, the MAVs have to be charted in detail. MAV is dependent on several factors, including:

- The customer's prior general and particular experience base with an industry, product, and/or service
- What the competition is doing in the concerned industry, product, or service
- What effect technological limitations have on setting the upper limit

As mentioned earlier, MAVs can be characterized in terms of the critical value determinants (CVDs); only four to six value determinants may be necessary to profile a market segment. CVDs can be defined by obtaining data through

1. The customer value survey
2. Leaders in noncompeting areas
3. The best-in-class performance levels
4. Internal customers

A detailed customer value analysis analyzes the value gaps and helps in further refining the goals of the process reengineering exercise. The value gaps are as follows:

- Gaps that result from different value perceptions in different customer groups
- Gaps between what the company provides and what the customer has established as the minimum performance level
- Gaps between what the company provides and what the competition provides
- Gaps between what the organization perceives as the MAV for the identified customer groups and what the customer says are the corresponding MAVs

It must be noted that analyzing the value gaps is not a one-time exercise, and neither is it confined to the duration of a cycle of the breakthrough improvement exercise. Like the BPR exercise itself, it is an activity that must be done on an ongoing basis. Above all, selecting the right processes for an innovative process reengineering effort is critical. The processes should be selected for their high visibility; relative ease of accomplishing goals; and, at the same time, their potential for great impact on the value determinants.

15.2 Enterprise Business Process Redesign or Reengineering Methodology

In this section, we look at the full life cycle of an enterprise's BPR methodology.

 Outsourcing is distancing the company from noncore but critical functions; as against this, reengineering, which is associated with BPR, is exclusively about the core.

We present an overview of the seven steps in a BPR methodology. These steps are as follows:

1. Develop the context for undertaking the BPR and, in particular, reengineer the enterprise's business processes. Then, identify the reason behind redesigning the process to represent the value perceived by the customer.
2. Select the business processes for the design effort.
3. Map the selected processes.
4. Analyze the process maps to discover opportunities for design.
5. Design the selected processes for increased performance.
6. Implement the designed processes.
7. Measure the implementation of the designed processes.

The seven steps of the enterprise BPR methodology are shown in Figure 15.1.

The BPR effort within an enterprise is not a one-time exercise but instead an ongoing one. One could also have multiple BPR projects in operation simultaneously in different

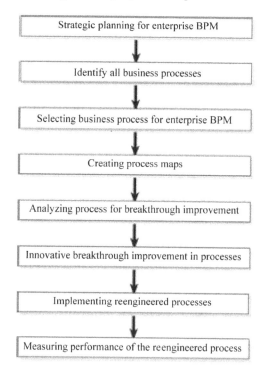

FIGURE 15.1
A cycle of enterprise BPR methodology.

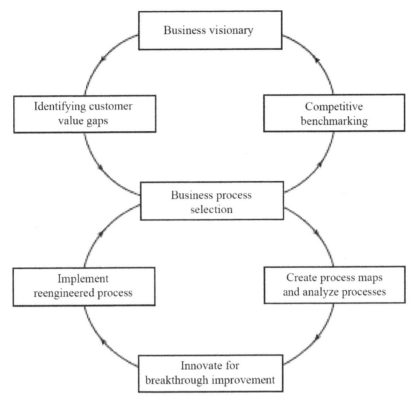

FIGURE 15.2
The alternate activities of business visioning and BPR.

areas within the enterprise. The BPR effort involves business visioning, identifying the value gaps and, hence, completing selection of the corresponding business processes for the BPR effort. The reengineering of the business processes might open newer opportunities and challenges, which, in turn, triggers another cycle of business visioning followed by BPR of the concerned business processes. Figure 15.2 shows the iteration across the alternating activities without end.

15.2.1 Strategic Planning for Enterprise Business Process Reengineering

All markets are fluid to some degree, and these dynamic forces and shifting customer values necessitate changes in a company's strategic plans. The significance of a process to the success of a company's business is dependent on the nature and extent of the value addition to a product or service. Consequently, as stated earlier, one can understand the competitive value gap in terms of the customer-expected level of value and the value delivered by the enterprise for the concerned product or service.

The competitive gap can be defined as the gap between the customer's minimum acceptance value (MAV) and the customer value delivered by the enterprise. Companies that consistently surpass MAVs are destined to thrive, those that only meet the MAVs will survive, and those that fall short of the MAVs may fail.

CVDs are those business imperatives that must happen if the enterprise wants to close the competitive gap and are similar to the critical success factors at the enterprise level. CVDs are expressed in terms of factors such as

- Time (e.g., lead time, cycle time)
- Flexibility (e.g., customization, options, composition, resource network interfaces)
- Responsiveness (e.g., lead time, duration, number of hand-offs, priority, number of queues)
- Quality of work (e.g., rework, rejects, yield)

Market segmentation is performed based on the customer value and the corresponding CVDs. Such a market division technique helps in suggesting corrective strategic and tactical actions that may be required, such as in devising a process-oriented strategic business plan. The strategic plan can in turn help to identify the major processes that support these critical value determinants that must be innovatively improved and reengineered.

15.2.1.1 Identifying the Business Processes in the Company

All business process in an enterprise are identified and recorded. A process can be defined as a set of resources and activities necessary and sufficient to convert some form of input into some form of output. Processes can be internal or external, or a combination of both. They cross functional boundaries; have starting and ending points; and exist at all levels within the enterprise, including the section, department, division, and enterprise levels. In fact, processes exist across enterprise boundaries as well. Processes evolve and degrade in terms of their efficiency and effectiveness.

A process itself can consist of various substeps. The substeps in a process may include:

- Value-added steps
- Non-value added steps
- Legal and regulatory steps (which are treated as value-added steps)

15.2.2 Selecting Business Processes for Business Process Reengineering

Selecting the right processes for an innovative process reengineering effort is critical. The processes should be selected for their high visibility; relative ease of accomplishing goals; and, at the same time, their potential for great impact on the value determinants.

Customers will take their business to the company that can deliver the most value for their money. Hence, the MAVs must be charted in detail. MAV is dependent upon several factors, such as:

- The customer's prior general and particular experience base with an industry, product, and/or service

- What the competition is doing in the concerned industry, product, or service
- What effect technological limitations have on setting the upper limit

As mentioned earlier, MAVs can be characterized in terms of the CVDs; only four to six value determinants may be necessary to profile a market segment. CVDs can be defined by obtaining data through the following:

1. The customer value survey
2. Leaders in noncompeting areas
3. The best-in-class performance levels
4. Internal customers

A detailed customer value analysis analyzes the value gaps and helps in further refining the goals of the process reengineering exercise. The value gaps are as follows:

- Gaps that result from different value perceptions in different customer groups
- Gaps between what the company provides and what the customer has established as the minimum performance level
- Gaps between what the company provides and what the competition provides
- Gaps between what the enterprise perceives as the MAV for the identified customer groups and what the customer says are the corresponding MAVs

It must be noted that analyzing the value gaps is not a one-time exercise; neither is it confined to the duration of a cycle of the breakthrough improvement exercise. Like the BPR exercise itself, it is an activity that must be done on an ongoing basis.

As a goal for the improvement effort, a clear, competitive advantage can be gained if best-in-class performance levels can be achieved in some key customer value areas and at least some MAVs can be achieved in all others.

15.2.3 Creating Process Maps

A process map documents the flow of one unit of work (the unit may be one item, one batch, or a particular service that is the smallest unit possible to follow separately) or what actually happens to the work going through the process. A process map is developed at several process levels, starting at the highest level of the enterprise. It documents both value-added and non-value-added steps. A process map could either be sequential or concurrent in nature.

A process could be mapped in the following two forms:

- Workflow chart form
- Work breakdown structure form

Process workflows fall into three categories: continuous workflows, balanced workflows, and synchronized workflows.

Workflow becomes nonsynchronized because of the following:

1. Steps or tasks being produced at different rates—that is, an imbalanced workflow
2. Physical separation of operations causing work to move in batches (i.e., a non-continuous workflow)
3. Working in batches, causing intermittent flow
4. Long setup or changeover times resulting in batched work along with associated problems
5. Variations in process inputs in terms of quality availability on time

All these add time and costs to the process and reduce flexibility and responsiveness.

Using the value-added workflow analysis of the process map, we can complete the following:

1. Identify and measure significant reengineering opportunities.
2. Establish a baseline of performance against which to measure improvement.
3. Determine which tools may be most useful in the reengineering effort.

Evidently, the major goal in reengineering the process is to eliminate non-value-added steps and wait-times within processes. A good rule of thumb is to remove 60%–80% of the non-value-added steps, resulting in the total number of remaining steps not being more than one to three times the number of value-added steps. Even this would be a credible goal for the first iteration of the BPM effort.

15.2.4 Analyzing Processes for Breakthrough Improvements

A enterprise's competitive strength lies in eliminating as many costly non-value-added steps and wait-times as possible. The key to eliminating non-value-added steps is to understand what causes them and then eliminate the cause.

For breakthrough improvements, the process maps are analyzed for the following:

- Enterprise complexity: Commonly organizational issues are a major deterrent to efficiency of the processes.
- Number of handoffs, especially those other than those associated with resource network interfaces.
- Work movement: Workflow charts are utilized to highlight move distances (i.e., work movements)
- Process problems: Several factors may have a severe effect on the continuity, balance, or synchronicity of the workflow. Examples are loops of non-value-added steps designed to address rework, errors, scraps, and so on. These may be on account of the following:

1. Long changeover times
2. Process input/output imbalances
3. Process variabilities
4. Process yields

These problems need to be identified, measured, analyzed, and resolved through innovative problem-solving methodology.

15.2.5 Innovative Breakthrough Improvement in Processes

The steps involved in innovative problem-solving methods are as follows:

1. Define a problem.
2. Find alternate solutions.
3. Evaluate the solutions.
4. Implement the best solution.
5. Measure and monitor the success.

The responsive process consists of the following components:

- Diagnosing customer need(s)
- Developing customized solutions specific to organizational interfaces
- Dynamically assigning work to the appropriate delivery unit
- Tracking performance as each task is completed

Business issues fall into three basic categories:

- System problems (e.g., methods, procedures)
- Technical problems (e.g., engineering, operational)
- People problems (e.g., skills, training, hiring)—these problems arise because of the concept of "if you change what a person does, then you change what he or she is"

15.2.6 Implementing Designed Processes

This involves the following:

- Reengineered vision and policies
- Reengineered strategies and tactics
- Reengineered systems and procedures
- Reengineered communication environment
- Reengineered organization architecture
- Reengineered training environment

15.2.7 Measuring the Performance of Designed Processes

Measuring the performance of any process is very important, because a lack of measurement would make it impossible to distinguish such a breakthrough effort from an incremental improvement effort of a total quality management program.

Measurements are essential because they are:

- Useful as baselines or benchmarks
- A motivation for further breakthrough improvements, which are important for future competitiveness

The measures for innovative process reengineering should be:

- Visible
- Meaningful
- Small in number
- Applied consistently and regularly
- Quantitative
- Involving the personnel closest to the process

Table 15.1 enlists tools and techniques for continuous improvement and Table 15.2 lists some of the advanced techniques.

TABLE 15.1

Tools, Techniques, and Benefits for Radical or Continuous Improvement

Tools or Technique	Use
External customer survey	To understand the needs of the external customers
Internal customer survey	To understand the perceptions of internal services
Staff survey	To obtain employee feedback on work environment
Brainstorming	To generate ideas for improvements
Cause and effect diagrams	To prompt ideas during brainstorming
Benchmarking	To compare similar processes to find the best practice
Service performance	To quantity the importance/performance of services
Activity data	To understand the allocation of time in processes
Activity categories	To obtain the level of core/support/diversionary activities
Activity drivers	To relate volumes of activity to causes
High–low diagram	To group objects using two variables
Force-field analysis	To show the forces acting for/against a variable
Histogram	To show frequency of a variable in a range
Scatter diagram	To view the correlation between two variables
Affinity analysis	To measure the strength of functional relationships
Bar chart	To plot the frequency of an event
Run chart	To show how a variable changes over time
Pie chart	To show the frequency of a variable in a range

TABLE 15.2

Advanced Techniques for Radical or Continuous Improvement

Tools or Technique	Use
Statistical process control (SPC)	SPC is a means to understand if a process is producing and is likely to produce an output that meets the specifications within limits
Failure mode and effects analysis (FMEA)	FMEA is a means to understand the nature of potential failure of components and the effect this will have on the complete systems
Quality function deployment (QFD)	QFD is a structured process to build
Taguchi methods	The design of experiments to create robust processes/products wherein final quality is subject to many variables

$$\text{Degree of Responsiveness}\,(\text{DOR}) = \frac{\text{Customer Fulfillment Cycle}}{(\text{Manufacturing Time} + \text{Distribution Time})}$$

15.3 Enterprise-Wide Continuous Improvement Programs

Operating strategy can be expressed in terms of the degree of responsiveness expected for an customer order. It can be defined as

$$\text{Degree of Responsiveness (DOR)} =$$

As an illustration, in the order of magnitude, the DOR can range from 0.01 to about 5, corresponding to

- Purchase from a retail outlet
- One-of-a-kind product or project

As an illustration, Figures 15.3 and 15.4 present, for different operating philosophies, a snapshot schematic of DOR versus product flow and planning techniques, respectively.

Lean is a proven approach for becoming an excellent operational system, Six Sigma is a program for attaining world-class quality improvement, and the TOC is an unsurpassed tool for identifying and removing bottlenecks.

15.3.1 Lean System

Lean System is based on the Toyota production system, which Toyota Motor Corporation (Toyota, Japan) has been perfecting for more than five decades. The Toyota production system was inspired by the Ford production system (Ford Motor Company, Dearborn, MI, USA). In 1950, when Toyota was in trouble, Eiji Toyoda went to Detroit to learn from the legendary Ford Motor Company about how to improve his family's business.

He spent three months in Detroit, studying Ford's manufacturing techniques in detail and looking for ways to transport them back to Japan. His conclusion was that, while

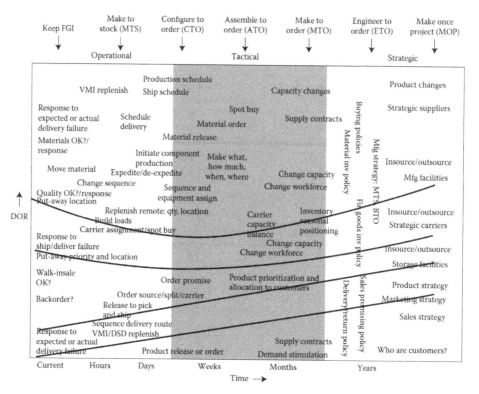

FIGURE 15.3
DOR, product planning techniques, and operating philosophies.

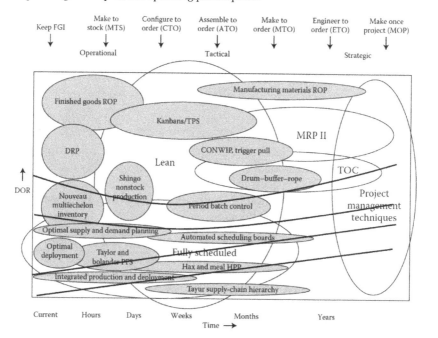

FIGURE 15.4
DOR, product flow decisions, and operating philosophies.

Henry Ford's concept of mass production was probably right for 1913, it was not responsive to the demands of the 1950s. The result was the design of a fundamentally different system, the Toyota production system, which enabled the Japanese automobile industry to overtake Detroit. Toyota is now recognized as a benchmark of superior performance among the world's best-run, most successful manufacturing companies.

The central organizing concept of Toyota can be described as multiproduct flow. The major difference between it and Ford, and it is a major one, is that Toyota is not constrained to one product. Toyota applied the principle of flow to a range of products: specifically, different models go down the same line without adversely affecting the goals of minimal throughput time and of low inventory targets. Toyota still achieved an inventory turn (ratio of sales divided by work in progress) approaching 300 [as compared with Ford's inventory turn of about 200 and General Motors' (Detroit, MI) inventory turns of about eight, respectively]. Toyota took Ford's challenge of synchronization two steps beyond Ford: the first step was to introduce multiproduct flow, while the second was equalization of the cycle times for every part.

Lean applies a unique process mapping approach called value-stream mapping. The current-state, value-stream map documents the materials and information flow. Value-stream mapping always starts with the customer and includes both materials and information flow. In addition, key information is gathered about each value-stream operation. The second step is the creation of a future-state, value-stream map, which is done by assuming that lean practices have been applied to the value stream. Projects are identified based on the changes needed to transform current-state processes into future-state processes. Lean tools are then applied to the improvement projects. When projects are completed, the process is repeated to create a new set of projects. This iterative process continues forever in the pursuit of perfection.

Lean identifies five key concepts:

- Value is defined by the customer.
- Value stream is the information and material flow from suppliers' suppliers to customers' customers.
- Flow is the synchronized continuous movement of material through the value stream.
- Pull is a product usage signal from the customer to other participants in the supply chain.
- Perfection is the neverending pursuit of zero waste.

The lean system is predicated on four clear values and seven principles, and has as its goals eliminating waste and increasing customer value forever by optimizing people, materials, space, and equipment resources. It specifies seven forms of waste to be eliminated:

1. Overproduction: making more than is needed
2. Transport: excessive movement of materials
3. Motion: inefficient movement of people
4. Waiting: underutilization of people
5. Inventory: material lying around unused
6. Overprocessing: manufacturing to a higher quality standard than expected by the customer
7. Defect correction: time spent fixing defects, including the part that gets thrown away and the time it takes to make the product correctly

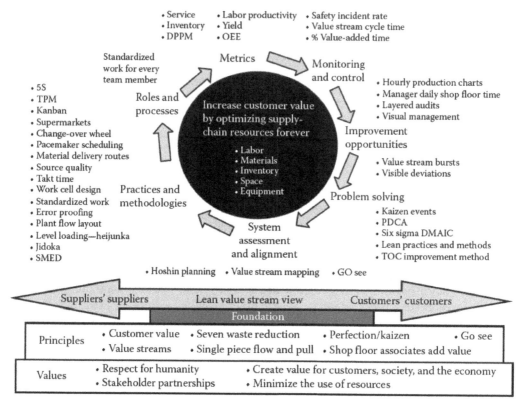

FIGURE 15.5
Lean system improvement cycle.

Figure 15.5 shows an overview of a lean system improvement cycle.

Lean is a holistic supply-chain operational system best practice with imbedded continuous improvement capability linked to customer value. The repetitive cycle of "standardize, level load, stabilize, and create flow" ensures continuous regeneration of improvement opportunities as perfection is pursued. Problem-solving in lean is a combination of prescriptive standard practices and scientific problem-solving; when none of the existing lean prescriptive solutions are directly applicable, this allows for the development of new solutions. Lean engages the entire enterprise in the improvement effort centering around the shop floor operators, so that continuous improvement is part of everyone's job. Finally, lean imparts the continuous improvement system and culture with a common language, tools, goals, and objectives.

Understanding lean philosophy fully is a challenge. Lean has been explained by a set of principles and concepts that tie its practices together into a system comparatively recently. Lean is not easily scalable: the fastest complete systems implementations take two to three years, as an enterprise absorbs an immense amount of specific knowledge and applies it to its value streams. Building a team of internal lean experts also takes two to three years before members have likely implemented all of the lean system practices. Lean implies a committed shop floor management team for sustained gains and to lead the next level of improvement, which can be very difficult to retain. Often, the early results from lean are difficult to map to bottom-line benefits. As such, it necessitates enlightened financial leadership to either change some of the financial operational measurements or educate their organizations as to how to look at the financial benefits created by lean. In fact, inventory reduction that results in improvement in working capital will likely cause a short-term reduction in output, which will reflect negatively on factory costs or cost of goods as a percentage of sales metrics.

15.3.2 Six Sigma

Six Sigma is a business improvement approach that seeks to find and eliminate causes of mistakes or defects in business processes by focusing on outputs that are of critical importance to customers. Six Sigma projects should be customer-focused. The key element of any customer–supplier relationship is a clear understanding of what the customer expectations are. The message received from gaining a clear understanding of customer expectations is sometimes referred to as the voice of the customer.

Six Sigma can be applied to any process that needs improvement. Potential projects are defined to fill gaps between current performance and the level required to achieve the success as envisaged in the annual business plan of the company. By targeting the areas of the business plan with the greatest critical gaps, organizational efforts can be focused and prioritized; projects are also identified by examining the defects affecting the achievement of business objectives or obvious variability in processes. Brainstorming and analysis of current processes are then often used for bottom-up generation of potential projects. Process performance may be compared to an entitlement level, a level of performance that may represent the best short-term performance ever achieved for such a process. Once the projects are defined, the five-step Six Sigma Define, Measure, Analyze, Improve, and Control (DMAIC) process is used.

DMAIC is the primary Six Sigma tool for reducing variability in existing processes. DMAIC, without doubt, has proven itself to be a very powerful tool for improvement at 3M (Maplewood, MN) and a number of other well-known companies. It is a rigorous process that relies heavily on statistical methodologies and techniques. Projects that follow the prescribed five-step process are completed within a specified time frame, resulting in a quick impact on the business. During the early stages of Six Sigma implementation, projects are often completed in four to six months; however, once the Master Black Belts and Black Belts gain experience and become more proficient, projects can get completed faster.

Six Sigma requires an investment in infrastructure, or the training of Master Black Belts and Black Belts. Most leading Six Sigma practicing companies have their own certification process, which requires successful completion of a certain number of projects. A Master Black Belt has the same technical skills as a Black Belt but is normally also trained in leadership and program management; thus, they are usually responsible for a number of Black Belts. Black Belts are intensively trained in all Six Sigma DMAIC skills and tools; they are expected to complete projects and coach Green Belts, who are leading their own projects.

For Six Sigma, it is imperative that strong management support exists. The efforts expended must have buy-in from management because various resources will be utilized and personnel will be called upon throughout the project to invest time and energy. The commitment needs to be there or the project is doomed to failure. In addition to management support, the personnel involved in the project need to be adequately trained in the methodology of Six Sigma in order to properly apply the tools. The level of training is commensurate with the role an employee plays in the Six Sigma scheme of things. The typical roles that exist in the world of Six Sigma are Black Belt, Master Black Belt, Green Belt, Executive Sponsor, Champion, and Process Owner.

The objective or focus of the project team needs to be related to the organizational goals and results aimed at providing a financial benefit to the company. In order to verify that the team's efforts have resulted in a financial benefit, it is imperative that effective metrics are evaluated. Once the project team screens through the maze of potential metrics and selects those most appropriate to the organizational goals, then the team is poised to initiate the project. A Six Sigma effort is a project that has a predetermined objective, a planned life cycle, and that requires the allocation of resources for completion. Therefore, many of the basic tenets of project management apply to the execution of a Six Sigma project, and its successful execution and monitoring of status are accomplished in the same fashion as any other project, e.g., using Gantt charts, Program Evaluation Review Technique charts, and so on.

The execution of a Six Sigma project uses a structured method of approaching problem-solving, i.e., DMAIC, which is primarily used for improving existing processes. In contrast, the Define, Measure, Analyze, Design, and Verify method is used for improving designs. The purpose of DMAIC is to improve growth, cost, or working capital performance of a business. It is a five-step improvement methodology based on the vigorous use of statistical methods. Potential improvement projects receive high priority when their elimination or improvement is necessary to achieve the annual business plan, for example, defects that result in customer dissatisfaction, high cost, high inventories, or other negative financial measures. Once the "hopper" of potential projects is identified, the projects are then prioritized to align with the business's priorities and started through the five-step process.

Six Sigma DMAIC is a methodology for reducing variation, decreasing defects, and improving quality when the root cause is unknown and not easily identifiable. The process turns input Xs into output Y; Six Sigma DMAIC identifies defects (Ys) in the output of processes that need improvement through better control of key input and process variables (Xs).

The five phases are as follows:

1. Define: this phase clearly defines the goal of the project by asking the following:

    What is the undesirable process variability or defect that must be eliminated?

    What is the benefit if there is zero waste and a well-defined project charter, which

    - Is driven by a business strategy and a business plan improvement goal?
    - Reflects the voice of the customer in project metrics?
    - Clearly defines project objectives?
    - Defines the scope of the project appropriately to ensure it can be accomplished in four to six months or less?

2. Measure: this phase clearly defines the current process, establishes metrics, and validates the measurement quality by asking:

    - What is the measurement of the output defects (Ys)?

        Many statistical tools are available to the Six Sigma professional, including probability analysis, box plots, scatter diagrams, and trend analysis. All of these measures will provide some understanding as to how the data are distributed, but a deeper grasp can be obtained with the probability density function and cumulative distribution function. Measurement system analysis is an evaluation of the amount of variability that is being introduced into your data values as a result of the measuring equipment you are using.

        Process flowchart, process mapping, or value-stream mapping gives a road map of potential opportunities to focus on.

3. Analyze: this phase clearly defines the root causes of variation:
   - Selecting enough input variables (Xs) to make analysis feasible
   - Using multiple-variable studies to determine which Xs have the most impact on the output defect(s) (Ys)
   - Planning initial improvement activities

   There are numerous statistical tools to analyze data, including simple linear regression, correlation coefficient, multivariable analysis, coefficient of determination, goodness of fit test, analysis of variance, nonparametric tests, the Spearman rank correlation coefficient, Kruskal–Wallis one-way analysis of variance by ranks, the Mann–Whitney U test, Levene's test, and Mood's median test. The challenge is to identify the most appropriate tool for the situation in order to make the best decision(s).

4. Improve: this phase clearly identifies relationships between critical Xs; the output defect(s) (Ys) are quantified and selected to verify the proposed solutions by:
   - Determining the effect critical Xs have on the output defect(s) (Ys) using designed experiments
   - Developing the sequence of experiments
   - Identifying the critical inputs that need to be controlled
   - Defining and piloting solutions to resolve problem root causes

   There are three primary methods that the Six Sigma professional may want to consider when beginning to attempt to improve a process: design of experiments, response surface methodology, and evolutionary operations. Experimentation performed without utilizing the design of experiments method effectively only looks at one factor at a time and may end up drawing erroneous conclusions because an interaction effect that may exist between factors goes unobserved; another consideration is that, without comparing various levels of all factors simultaneously, there may be no insight as to what the optimal combination of factor levels is. This is where design of experiments comes in. With design of experiments, one can look at multiple levels of multiple factors simultaneously and make decisions as to what levels of the factors will optimize the output.

   There are various types of experimental designs that can be drawn upon depending on what the user is trying to evaluate; these include randomized and randomized block designs, full factorial designs, fractional factorial designs, mixture experiments, and Taguchi designs.

5. Control: this phase ensures that the process maintains the gains achieved, is neutral or positive for customers, and controls the critical Xs through the following:
   - A well-executed control plan
   - The identification of the control plan process owner
   - Tracking of financial results for one year

There is a need to build an appropriate level of control into the process to assure that it does not backslide into an undesirable state. This can be achieved by tools such as statistical process control and some of the lean tools. Statistical process control is designed to provide the operator with real-time feedback as to whether or not a process is functioning in control.

There are a host of different types of charts that can be employed depending on the type of data collection desired including X-bar/R, X/MR, and Exponentially Weighted Moving Average (EWMA) as well as attribute charts including c, p, u, and np. Lean tools include the 5Ss, the kaizen blitz, kanban, poka-yoke, total productive maintenance, and standard work.

Six Sigma's major strength is that its project focus, measurable defect elimination, and direct financial benefits are easily understood by the business's leadership and aligned with their need to meet the annual business objectives. Rigorous control plans are established as a part of finalizing Six Sigma projects to ensure improvements become permanent and result in a good bottom-line profit for the business. Six Sigma should measure only hard savings, cost, or cash benefits that are actually tracked to an operating budget, inventory, accounts payable, or accounts receivable balance. This would ensure that some true net financial benefit will show up in the profit and loss statement.

Six Sigma creates a company-wide improvement methodology, allowing employee team members to engage in problem-solving and maximizing their improvement capacity. Six Sigma's fact-based problem-solving rigor gives a good level of confidence that true root causes are being addressed and prompts data-based thinking throughout the enterprise. Six Sigma necessitates the maintenance of a team of experts for implementation and ongoing support; however, since the training is focused on the deployment of the tool set, it is relatively easy to scale up quickly.

 Six Sigma identifies projects that resolve known process defects and variations or gaps between current performance levels and the requirements of the operating plan. What Six Sigma does not have is assessment tools that look at overall enterprise or plant processes to continuously generate opportunities and connect improvements to the entire system. Consequently, a few years of eliminating low-hanging fruit generally results in a declining number of Black Belt projects, making return on Six Sigma infrastructure investment more difficult to justify and sustain. Six Sigma has no process or tools for ensuring complete alignment of metrics and projects across the entire enterprise. Goal trees, also called Y-trees, are used to align projects with business goals. This method, however, is not effective in assuring the alignment of metrics across enterprises nor in prioritizing projects to meet the metrics. This can lead to less than optimum results at minimum, and potentially to projects that serve one function without contributing to overall business improvement. Six Sigma solutions are not prescriptive: solutions must be identified, developed, tested, and then implemented. Even using shared project databases and encouraging the replication of solutions are ineffective in creating prescriptive solutions.

15.3.3 Theory of Constraints

The TOC was developed by Eli Goldratt and collaborators. It became broadly known in 1984 when Goldratt's book, *Goal*, was published. The TOC views an enterprise as a system with resources linked together to meet the enterprise's goals. All systems have a constraint that limits the system's capacity to improve and better meet or exceed a goal. Enterprises have limited resources, so it is critical that resources be applied to reduce or eliminate constraints to maximize success. The TOC methodology includes improvement tools that use rigorous root-cause analysis to define the solution. The methodology also identifies all the assumptions and conditions needed to ensure the success of a proposed solution. These very conditions and assumptions become the basis for action items for implementation plans. TOC improvement tools are effective both for continuous improvement and breakthrough problem-solving.

Over the course of the 1980s, Goldratt introduced a powerful set of concepts that compose the TOC. The theory represents a philosophy of operations management, a management system, and a set of tools/principles to improve operations. Initially, TOC promotion focused around the fact that most manufacturing operations have a few bottleneck steps that limit the throughput of the plant under typical product mixes. The goal of planning, then, should be to schedule these bottleneck steps efficiently so as to achieve maximum throughput; to schedule steps before and after the bottlenecks in order to best support the bottlenecks; and to elevate the constraints by adding capacity there, thus shifting the binding constraints to elsewhere in the system. The drum–buffer–rope scheduling methodology was invented to support plant operations to exploit constraints to the maximum possible (i.e., get maximum throughput through them) and subordinate other manufacturing steps to the constrained ones. As the TOC evolved, greater emphasis was placed on the fact that the principles apply not only to manufacturing but also to supply-chain operations as a whole and even to non-supply-chain activities like project management.

These principles led to the following universal five-step methodology for business improvement:

1. Identify the system's constraints.
2. Decide how to exploit the system's constraints.
3. Subordinate everything else to the earlier decision.
4. Elevate the system's constraints.
5. If in the previous steps, a constraint has been broken, go back to step 1.

The TOC takes a holistic systems view of all operations of a plant or supply chain. Applied to a business, the TOC purpose is to increase profit. It focuses system improvement on increasing throughput as the best way to add more value. Improvement or elimination of a current constraint results in more throughput, at which point a new system constraint is typically identified. This continuous cycle drives performance improvement forever.

The TOC includes concepts used to schedule operations. The constrained operation is scheduled in a specific product sequence, aligning resource usage to meet customer demand. This system, termed as drum–rope–buffer scheduling, sets the pace for all other operations, as follows:

1. Upstream, raw materials are subordinated to the constrained operation to make sure materials are available when needed to support the constrained operations schedule.

2. Downstream operations must flow, and are therefore planned and run with sufficient capacity so that all products made by the constrained operation can be processed.

3. Time buffers are used upstream from the constraint so promised shipment dates are met, protecting promised dates from inevitable process variability. Work is released into production at a rate dictated by the drum and started based on a predetermined total process buffer length.

When sales is the constraint, the TOC has an approach for solving these problems, which includes the use of problem-solving tools in combination with the TOC accounting, market segmentation, and pricing strategies to identify what needs to change in order to increase sales. This is a unique feature of the TOC as compared with other problem-solving methodologies.

The metrics used in the TOC measure the value add produced. Key TOC metrics include:

T: Throughput value of sales less materials cost.

I: System's raw material inventory.

OE: Operating expenses.

Conversion ratio: Dividing T by OE gives a productivity measurement, or the rate at which operating expenses are converting raw materials into T.

Inventory turnover: This is determined by dividing T by I; dividing the money generated from sales by raw material inventory cost indicates inventory turnover.

15.3.3.1 Theory of Constraints Tools

The TOC employs five tools as follows:

1. What to change?

    Current reality tree: The current reality tree is a tool used to identify the root cause of a core problem that has no known solution in order to eliminate initial undesirable effects. The current reality tree is a type of flowchart that depicts the cause-and-effect relationships that exist for the object of interest. The tree is normally built using a storyboard-type approach, starting with a listing of the effects to be remedied. The contributing factors that perpetuate these effects are associated with them and listed accordingly. This type of analysis is performed again on the perpetuating factors and is continued until what in essence would be the root cause of the problem can be identified. This simplistic explanation can become quite convoluted in practice, especially when the situation under study has multiple effects to remedy and many associated contributing factors.

    One of the expected outputs of creating a current reality tree is to identify the root causes that are perpetuating the effects to be remedied. Once these causes are identified, they can then provide a focus for subsequent efforts.

2. Objective for change

    Evaporating cloud: The evaporating cloud identifies requirements that the solution must satisfy. The first step is to state the core problem and define what should replace it. The current core problem exists because it satisfies an organizational need or requirement. This means defined solutions must satisfy needs currently fulfilled by whatever caused the core problem and by whatever will replace it.

    Future reality tree: The future reality tree defines the desirable effects of the solution, which will become the improvement project objectives. Future reality trees create a complete picture of positive and negative consequences of the proposed solution defined in the evaporating cloud process. Each undesirable effect discovered in making the current reality tree is reviewed to define its opposite (i.e., desirable effect). These desirable effects become implementation plan objectives. They are also inputs examined using the prerequisite tree.

3. How to change?

    Prerequisite tree: The prerequisite tree defines conditions that need to be in place in order to achieve future reality tree-defined objectives. Prerequisite trees ensure that all necessary conditions are identified and objectives are set to ensure implementation plans meet them. Projects are implemented efficiently by defining the best sequence to meet these conditions and they are included as input to the transition tree.

Transition tree: The transition tree creates detailed plans to implement the objectives defined in the prerequisite tree. Intermediate objectives and action plans supporting them are delegated to teams or individuals. Teams use transition trees to break down the actions needed to achieve the assigned objectives. These transition tree objectives and actions are used in implementation reviews to ensure that overall project objectives are met.

Systems always have constraints to be eliminated, so the TOC will always regenerate opportunities for improvement. The heart of the TOC methodology is the focus on the system constraint, which ensures that all resources are applied to maximize the system improvement benefit. The TOC thinking process is based on the scientific method; that is, it identifies the root cause(s) of a problem and develops effective solutions. The thinking process is useful for making both incremental and breakthrough improvements.

 Understanding TOC thinking fully is a challenge. Becoming proficient in applying the TOC takes time because its language and rigorous improvement methodology are not easily understood. TOC thinking provides no prescriptive solutions but rather a very rigorous scientific method problem-solving process. It ensures focus on the most important defect as well as that the real problem is well-understood, that root causes are defined, and that implementation will treat all of the root causes and mitigate any unintended consequences. The entire company leadership team must be on board in leading the use of the TOC across the company because, at some point in the journey, the constraint will move to all of the operating functions in the organization. If the TOC is applied only in manufacturing and the supply chain without total organizational involvement, the maximum potential benefit will not be achieved. As in lean, the implementation of the TOC also requires an enlightened financial leadership team to change some of the financial operational measurements or educate the organization on how to look at the financial benefits created by the TOC.

15.4 Time-Based Competition

TBC was invented by George Stalk and his colleagues from the Boston Consulting Group (Boston, MA). TBC is defined as *the extension of just-in-time (JIT) principles into every facet of the value delivery cycle, from research and development through to marketing and distribution.* Both concepts, TBC and JIT, have the same goal: eliminate waste in the production or service delivery process. Waste is anything that does not add value to a product or a service. In many instances, waste involves activities that do not contribute to the value of the company. Through the elimination of waste time, more time can be spent on value-added activities. However, while JIT looks more at the operations function, TBC considers the whole value chain and focuses on the total time required to produce and deliver products and services.

 TBC gains significance because of the enormous opportunities for time reductions that can be achieved across processes: on average, 95% of the process time has been evaluated as being non-value-adding.

The basic principle of TBC is to react faster on changes in the environment and to be more flexible than competitors in order to grow faster. One of the key issues in TBC is regarding how to reduce the development time of new products and services. Shorter lead times generate many secondary effects, such as higher efficiency, higher supplier reliability, and flexibility. Besides the primary effect of being faster, TBC also generates secondary effects in costs and quality. A flexible operations process, a fast reaction, and innovation are the key elements needed in order to attract profitable customers. To this end, the company strategy should be the highest value for the lowest cost in the shortest time.

Time reduction essential for achieving TBC can be achieved through measures such as:

- Simplification, or removing process complexity that has accumulated over time
- Integration, or improving information flows and linkages to create enhanced operability and visibility
- Standardization, or using generic best-practice processes, standardized components and modules, and information protocols
- Concurrent working, or moving from sequential to parallel working by using, for example, teams and other forms of process integration
- Variance control, or monitoring processes, and detecting problems at an early stage so that corrective action can be taken to avoid problems with quality and waste
- Automation, which is applied to improve the effectiveness and efficiency of entities and activities within the supply-chain process
- Resource planning, or allocating resources in line with operational best practice; for example, a company can plan by investigating bottleneck activities and considering the use of multiskilled workforces to provide resource flexibility

Becoming a TBC is a strategy that goes hand-in-hand with total quality management. Eliminating non-value-adding activities or preventing rework from being done in order to work faster are strategies totally in line with quality management. Notably, there is a bilateral relationship between speed and quality: while quality is a necessary condition in order to produce or deliver goods or services quickly, speed can be considered as a component of quality because it contributes to the satisfaction of customers.

15.4.1 Activity-Based Customer Responsiveness

The customer-responsiveness of an enterprise is really dependent on the corresponding business processes or activities. In any enterprise, the focus is on flexibility—specifically, the flexibility to obtain the capability and capacity needed in order to respond sufficiently to a wide variety of individual customer requests. Customer responsive activities are used to find the best way to solve individual customer needs. In customer-responsive activities, the emphasis is on delivered solution effectiveness (i.e., how well are the individual problems communicated, diagnosed, and solved) and delivered solution efficiency (i.e., how few resources are required to solve the problems).

Enterprises that deploy customer responsive activities have the following objectives:

- Building relationships so that customers become "conditioned" to contact the enterprise first whenever they have a need

- Establishing the enterprise to provide effective diagnoses and responses whenever customers establish such contact with the enterprise
- Creating the capability and processes to enable customer-facing members to cultivate deep and long-term relationships with the customers and cost-effectively coordinate each individual delivery of benefits

Traditional mass marketing or the mass production approach has long considered a process to be a way to produce a product; it focuses on limitations (e.g., setup time, resource availability, capability of the existing workforce) and develops the most efficient process that can function within the constraints. The focus is on coping with internal limitations (often self-inflicted) instead of on becoming more responsive to customers and the changing business climate. The emphasis is on control rather than performance. In contrast to this, mass customization obtains its flexibility by viewing the process as a way of converting resources into products so that a single process can be used to produce many different products. The balance of control and power has shifted from producers to the customers. Mass customization develops processes to minimize or eliminate limitations (e.g., reduce setup time, locate alternative resources, expand capabilities of current workforce, develop a network of resources). Customer-responsiveness management develops numerous best-practice guidelines to guide front-line workers as they interact with customers to plan deliveries and enables them to modify the plans, if necessary, to improve the customer fit.

Therefore, for an enterprise to be totally flexible in responding to individual customers, the enterprise must develop the following three things:

- Process(es) for interacting with individual customers and defining their individual needs
- Conditional best-practice guidelines for defining how the organization will respond to various type of customer requests
- A dynamic assigning system that allows JIT assignment of work for delivery to resources with appropriate capability and capacity

15.4.2 Activity-Based Costing

ABC is a way of linking an enterprise's market positioning to its internal cost structure, i.e., capability. The basic premise is that activities that are realized via the processes consume resources and convert them into products and services that are usable by the customers. Thus, costs are the consequence of resource decisions and income is the consequence of the business processes that deliver value to the customers. In other words, the requirement is to improve resourcing decisions as a means of managing costs and to improve processes as a means of improving business effectiveness, leading to improved customer loyalty and, therefore, revenue.

The ABC data is useful as a source to support:

- Profitability management, such as costing and profitability analysis, customer and product mix decisions, and support for marketing decisions
- Revenue and performance management, such as resource to volume and service level changes, activity budgeting, and cost driver analysis

The principle of ABC is based on knowledge of activities, including the reason of their existence and the factors that drive them. The BPM effort helps in identifying a list of cost drivers that are allocated to the various activities. These could include:

- The volume of materials used, labor hours consumed, parts produced
- The number of new parts, new suppliers, new prototypes
- The number of customers, orders raised, invoices sent
- The number of design modifications, customer warranty claims, and so on

The database of activities can then be aggregated into "pools" of activities that have common cost drivers. By assigning such pools of activities to "objects" (e.g., products, distribution channels, customer groups), a proper allocation of product and customer costs is then derived.

To build up activity-based product costs, the total for any one product (or a group) would be the sum of:

$$\sum_{l=1}^{M} \{\text{activity-based product costs}\}_l = \sum_{l=1}^{M} \left\{ \begin{array}{l} \text{direct material and labor +} \\ \text{volume-dependent overheads +} \\ \text{variable cost driver-dependent overheads} \end{array} \right\}_l$$

Similarly, to build up activity-based customer costs, the total for a customer (or a group) would be the sum of:

$$\sum_{l=1}^{M} \{\text{activity-based customer costs}\}_l = \sum_{l=1}^{M} \left\{ \begin{array}{l} \text{activity-based product costs +} \\ \text{voulme-dependent customer costs (e.g.,} \\ \text{packging materials or cost of delivery) +} \\ \text{variable cost driver-dependent overheads} \end{array} \right\}_l$$

ABC provides the basis to understand product and customer profitability and allows the management to make decisions both on positioning and capability, which are the twin pillars of BPM. The understanding of product and customer costs that comes from using ABC proves its real value when the revenue resulting from the total activity within a business area is related to the costs of achieving that revenue.

It is usually possible to trace revenue to customers only if the enterprise operates a billing system requiring customer details or if there is a membership scheme in place, such as a store card or loyalty program. Costs vary from customer to customer on account of:

- Customer acquisition costs: sales calls and visits, free samples, engineering advice, and so on
- Terms of trade or transaction: price discounts, advertising and promotion support, extended invoice due-dates, and so on
- Customer service costs: handling queries, claims, and complaints; demands on sales persons and contact centers; and so on
- Working capital costs: the cost of carrying inventory for the customer, the cost of credit, and so on

15.4.3 Time-Driven Activity-Based Costing

The conventional ABC systems demonstrated many drawbacks in that they were expensive to build, complex to sustain, and difficult to modify. Furthermore, their reliability was highly suspect, as the cost assignments were based on individuals' subjective estimates of the percentage of time spent on various activities. They also made unrealistic assumptions, as follows:

- Identified activities (e.g., processing customers orders or enquiries) take about the same amount of time, without any clear variations for particular circumstances
- Resources work at full capacity without discounting for idle or unused time

Moreover, implementing an ABC system for realistic enterprise scenarios (e.g., a few hundred activities, a few hundred thousand cost objects, a time duration of a couple of years) quickly ended up facing computational challenges of gargantuan proportions, requiring huge computational resources that were beyond the capabilities of normal enterprises. As a result of the subjective, time-consuming surveying and data-processing costs of ABC systems, many enterprises either abandoned ABC entirely, localized it in isolated units, or ceased updating their systems, which left them with out-of-date and highly inaccurate estimates of the business process, product, and customer costs.

TDABC gives enterprises an elegant and practical option for determining the cost and capacity utilization of their processes and the profitability of orders, products, and customers. Based on this accurate and timely information, enterprises can prioritize for business process improvements, rationalize their offering variety and mix, price customer orders, and manage customer relationships.

TDABC avoids the costly, time-consuming, error-prone, and subjective activity-surveying task of the conventional ABC by skipping the activity definition stage and, therefore, the very need to estimate allocations of the departments' costs to the multiple activities performed by the department (Robert Kaplan and Steven Anderson).

TDABC defines activity costs with only two parameters:

1. Capacity cost rate for the department executing the activity or transaction
2. Capacity usage time by each activity or transaction processed in the department

Thus,

$$\text{Activity-based cost} = \text{capacity cost rate} * \text{capacity usage time}$$

where

$$\text{Capacity cost rate} = \frac{\text{cost of capacity supplied}}{\text{practical capacity of resources supplied}}$$

and

The cost of capacity supplied is the total cost of the department executing the activity or transaction

The practical capacity of resources supplied is the actual time employees, machines, and other pieces of equipment perform productive work

The capacity usage time is the observed or estimated time for performing the activity or transaction

TABLE 15.3

Conventional ABC versus TDABC

Conventional Activity-Based Costing	Time-Driven Activity-Based Costing
Tedious, costly, and time-consuming to build a model that is error-prone, difficult to validate, and localized	Easier, inexpensive, and faster to build an accurate and enterprise-wide model
Drives cost first to the activities performed by a department and then assigns the activity costs down to orders, products, and customers on the basis of subjective estimates (based on interviewing and surveying process) of the quantity of departmental resources consumed by various activities	Drives costs directly to the transactions or orders using specific characteristics of particular business processes, products, and customers
Complexity and variations are incorporated by adding more activities to the model, increasing its complexity and subjectivity and resulting in lower accuracy; creates an exploding demand for estimates data, storage, and processing capabilities	Incorporates complexity and variations that add accuracy at little additional cost and effort without creating and exploding demand for estimates data, storage, and processing capabilities
Calculates cost driver rates by taking into account the full rated capacity of resources without discounting for idle or unused resources	Calculates cost driver rates by taking into account only the practical capacity of resources supplied by discounting for idle or unused resources, rather than the full rated capacity of the resources

Both of these parameters can be estimated and validated easily and objectively. These estimates are not required to be precise; a rough accuracy is adequate. The cost of capacity includes the cost of all resources including personnel, supervision, equipment, maintenance and technology, and so on that are supplied to the department or business process. However, the practical capacity of resources supplied is usually lower as compared with the rated capacity because it excludes the cost of unused resources on account of scheduled breaks, training, meetings, setting time, maintenance, and so on.

Table 15.3 compares the conventional ABC and TDABC.

TDABC does not require the simplifying assumption, unlike in the case of conventional ABC, that all customer orders or transactions are the same and require the same amount of time for the processing. TDABC is not only more accurate but also granular enough to capture the variety and complexity of actual operations. For example, it allows time estimates to vary on the basis of particular requirements of individual customers, or orders such as manual or automated orders, orders for fragile or hazardous goods, expedited orders, international orders, or orders from a new customer without an existing credit record. It achieves this through the simple mechanism of altering the unit time estimates or adding extra terms to the departmental time equation on the basis of the order's activity characteristics. Thus, TDABC can readily incorporate many more variations and complexities (in terms of business process efficiencies, product volumes and mixes, customer order patterns, and channel mixes), which adds accuracy at little additional cost and effort and with fewer number of equations compared (i.e., without creating an exploding demand for estimates data or storage or processing capabilities), than conventional ABC can. TDABC models expand only linearly with variation and complexity by merely adding terms in the time equation; however, a department is still modeled as one process with one time equation.

Consequently, the expressions for the total costs presented in the previous section get modified to:

$$\sum_{l=1}^{M}\{\text{activity-based product costs}\}_{1} = \left\{(\text{capacity cost rate})*\left(\sum_{l=1}^{M}\text{capacity usage time}\right)_{1}\right\}$$

and

$$\sum_{l=1}^{M}\{\text{activity-based customer costs}\}_{1} = \left\{(\text{capacity cost rate})*\left(\sum_{l=1}^{M}\text{capacity usage time}\right)_{1}\right\}$$

 Regarding the importance of TDABC, TDABC plays an increasingly significant role in strategy and operations of an enterprise because of reasons including:

1. The fact that time is a decisive factor in all efforts for process improvements, BPR, enterprise performance management, balance scorecard, and so on because of the criticality of wait times, lead times, cycle times, handover processes across department boundaries, and so on. By contributing through increased accuracy at dramatically reduced complexity, efforts, resources, and costs, TDABC plays a determining role in enabling all such exercises.

2. Along the critical path of departmental business processes, any drastic imbalances in the capacity usage times of the various process or subprocesses will highlight the potential for dramatic improvements in terms of complexity, efforts, resources, materials, technology, costs, and so on and will become obvious candidates for detailed scrutiny. This will usually result either in a BPR initiative or even in a restructuring or reconfiguring of the department(s).

3. Based on the analysis of capacity cost rate, TDABC plays a crucial role in deciding the boundaries of an enterprise—that is, in the bifurcation of core activities (that get executed in-house) from noncore activities (that can get outsourced). TDABC is critical for addressing the issues of dramatically reduced response times, turn-around times, high throughputs, increased accuracy, and so on. Hence, it is for this reason that all customer-facing processes like call centers or contact centers, customer service or customer response desks, help desks, and so on are usually outsourced.

The TDABC model simulates the actual business processes deployed across the enterprise. In addition to addressing the improvement of inefficient processes and transforming non-profitable products and customers, an enterprise can also use TDABC to tackle the issue of excess capacity revealed by the application of this model. An enterprise can use the TDABC model as the core of its budgeting process to link its strategic plan as well as sales and production forecasts to the specific demands for capacity required to implement the plan and realize the forecast. Thus, TDABC can assist in deciding on the capacity the company needs to supply in the future.

15.4.4 Responsive Activity Pricing

For the sake of completeness, we will touch briefly on the issues related to the pricing of responsive activities for BPM.

Some of the relevant characteristics of customer-responsive activities are as follows:

- There is no standardized product for which there is a market price. As the delivered solution is customized to each individual customer's needs, the value of the delivered solution is determined by how well the solution solves the customer's needs and must be priced separately.

- There are no products that are tradable; delivery services are not tradable. Therefore, there is no market price for the delivery service.

- There are no products to inventory—only capacity that continuously perishes if it is not utilized to deliver benefits.

- Commitments to the customers are made on a real-time basis.

Thus, the emphasis must be on pricing in the immediate run to maximize the yield that can be obtained from the capacity scheduled in the short run that is minimizing wasted capacity (or maximizing capacity utilization) and maximizing the customer value of capacity. The objective must be not only to collectively cover the fixed capacity costs but also to profit through contributions from customers; or, in other words, the objective is to maximize contribution to fixed capacity and to profit from each sale. The price will range between the customer value at the upper limit and, at the lower limit, the larger amount of either the cost of delivery or the competitor's price.

However, the final price is determined by the customer's perception of a reasonable price in light of the corresponding hassles (to identify the right solution) and the risks. Evidently, the customer will pay a premium for response commitments like guaranteed-response, time-of-day, lead-time, response-level, and so on.

The front-line worker can make the pricing decision based on information like customer value, cost of delivery, competitor's charges, and alternative use of capacity.

15.5 Summary

Process improvement programs range right from disruptive to continuous improvement programs—the first corresponds to business process reengineering programs, while the latter corresponds to programs like lean, Six Sigma, and the TOC. This chapter discussed a seven-step methodology that can be employed for both BPR or business process redesign. BPR is associated with disruptive improvement, while business process redesign is associated with continuous improvement. Lean is a proven approach for becoming an excellent operational system, Six Sigma is a program for attaining world-class quality improvement, and the TOC is an unsurpassed tool for identifying and removing bottlenecks. The last part of the chapter focused on the basic principle of TBC—the idea of reacting faster to changes in the environment and being more flexible than competitors in order to grow faster. Since a business process is a set of activities, ABC would be the most appropriate approach for their assessment. The chapter culminates with a discussion on TDABC and a comparison between it and the more conventional ABC.

16

EPMS for Customer Conversations

Customer conversation or dialog systems are a technology aimed at sustaining conversations with users that could be considered natural and human-like. Proactiveness is necessary for computers to stop being considered tools and as real conversational partners instead. Proactive systems have the capability of engaging in a conversation with the user even when the user has not explicitly requested the system's intervention: this is a key aspect in the development of ubiquitous computing architectures in which the system is embedded in the user's environment and thus the user is not aware that he or she is interacting with a computer but rather perceives instead that he or she is interacting with the environment. To achieve this goal, it is necessary to provide the systems with problem-solving capabilities and context-awareness.

The chapter starts with an introduction to the approach of human interaction management (HIM), which was developed to deal with the human behavior in the organization, drawing ideas not only from process theory but also from biology, psychology, social systems theory, and learning theory. An interaction or interactive pattern is a sequence of actions, references, and reactions wherein each reference or reaction has a certain, ex-ante intended and an ex-post recognizable interrelation with preceding event(s) in terms of timing and content. Quality of experience (QoE) for interaction is dependent on various factors like effort, smoothness, pace, response ability, naturalness, attention, comprehension, and so on. Additionally, the interaction is influenced by three influence factors: human, system, and context. Based on the comprehensive understanding of interactions, an effective customer interaction system is envisaged to possess subsystems for automatic speech recognition, spoken language understanding, dialog management, natural language generation, and text-to-speech synthesis. This chapter explains all of these components of customer interaction systems.

16.1 Business Processes and Human Interactions

It has been observed that jobs that involve participating in interactions rather than extracting raw materials or making finished goods are becoming pervasive in developed economies. Raising the productivity of the workers who perform complex, nonroutine tasks can provide a company with competitive advantages that are much harder for competitors to copy than the advantages created by simply reengineering, automating, or outsourcing clerical jobs (Han et al. 2005; Harrison-Broninski 2005).

Businesses that want to stay competitive must put into place efficient systems for managing processes. Most often, these are computer systems for business process management (BPM). However, the existing process languages and tools are not applicable for complex processes involving human interaction as a core element, as they do not capture the human element crucial for these processes. The traditional process modeling approaches of BPM, such as Business Process Modeling Notation or Business Process Execution Language, are designed specifically for the description of regulated, routine, largely automatable activity with only occasional human involvement. However, when it comes to the processes driven by humans, such techniques are no longer applicable. The approach of HIM was developed to deal with the human behavior in the organization, drawing ideas not only from process theory but also from biology, psychology, social systems theory, and learning theory. HIM as an approach facilitates the following five main stages of human work: research, evaluation, analysis, constrainment, and task.

16.1.1 Human Interaction Management

Per HIM, there are two kinds of business processes, as follows:

1. Mechanistic business processes are for the most part implemented by machines, and human involvement in them is limited to key decision-making efforts and data entry points. They are routinized and often semi- or fully automated. Examples of mechanistic business processes include logistics, invoicing, purchase order approval, and stock level maintenance.
2. Human-driven processes differ from this in that they are fundamentally collaborative, dynamic, and innovative. These processes depend on interaction and are dynamically shaped by the participants. Examples of human-driven processes are product design, research, sales, marketing, and/or company growth/merger/divestment processes.

Human-driven processes are characterized by the following observations:

1. Intentionality: The intention of each process participant is important. These individuals may have different goals and their responsibilities may prevent certain actions from being taken.
2. Data: Data are typically maintained privately and may be expressed informally throughout the course of the process. There may also be some informal metadata attached to the shared information.
3. Mental work: Human-driven processes include activities that are investigative and analytic and which may not move the process along in a visible way.
4. People are not robots: People do not operate like a conventional program that follows a procedural workflow. Activities can be controlled by pre- and postconditions, but any number of them can be true at once; that is, the persons participating in a process may freely choose the tasks to execute as long as the preconditions are valid.
5. Process dynamism: A large part of the process is about defining what will happen next and thus agreeing on the rest of the process. For process management, this implies that how an agreement is gained, described, and shared needs to be determined.

The five main features of HIM are:

1. Connection visibility: A human process creates meaningful connection between participants with varying skills, with each participant in the process requiring to know who the other participants are and what they do in order to efficiently work

with them. A representation of the process participants is thus needed, showing the roles they play and the private information resources they have access to.

2. Structured messaging: Messaging is an essential part of human–computer interaction, but it typically results in both efficiency gains and losses. As an example, consider the large amount of email received by office workers and the difficulties related to determining the relevance and priorities of the messages. The interactions between process participants must thus be structured and under process control.

3. Mental work: A large part of human work does not have a concrete output that could be measured by existing management techniques or computer systems. However, the amount of time and mental effort invested in this nonmeasurable work—for example researching, comparing, and making decisions—is a critical part of the job of an interaction worker and should thus be supported by the systems they work with.

4. Supportive rather than descriptive activity management: Humans do not sequence their activities in the way computer programs do—that is, "after doing x, I either do y or z, depending on the outcome of x"; people work differently on different days, depending on their coworkers, the resources to which they have access to, and their own mood.

   However, activities do have preconditions (a state in which the activity can be performed) and postconditions (a state in which the activity is seen as completed). People should be allowed to carry out any activity for which the precondition is true at any time, disregarding what activity they have completed previously. Similarly, any activities that do not fill the postconditions should be regarded as completely undone, so as to prevent them from derailing the entire process.

5. Processes change processes: Human activities are often concerned with solving problems or making something happen. Before such an activity is started, some planning is must be done on how to carry out the activity, which methodology to use, which tools are required, which people should be consulted, and so on. Process definition is in fact a part of the process itself; this definition does not happen only the first time the process is carried out but continuously throughout the life of the process.

   In other words, in human-driven efforts, processes are continuously changed by their actions and interactions. They effectively separate management control (day-to-day facilitation of human activity, ongoing resourcing, monitoring, and process redesign) from executive control (authority over the process as well as determination of its primary roles, interactions, and deliverables). Process evolution can be implemented under management control with the agreement of the related process participants, these agreements are generally documented and shared within the organization.

16.1.2 Human Interaction Management System

The concept of a HIM system as a process modeling and enactment system supports the five main elements of HIM in the following ways:

- Connection visibility: Role and User objects, both instances and types, each with its own properties and responsibilities.

- Structured messaging: Interaction objects, in which there are multiple asynchronous channels, each for a different purpose.

- Support for mental work: Entity objects that can be created, versioned, and shared in a structured way.

- Supportive rather than prescriptive activity management: State objects that can both enable and validate Activity objects, along with the Roles that contain them.

- Processes change processes: The ability to manipulate not only objects but also user interfaces and integration mechanisms via the process that contains them.

The HIM system is used to manage the work and separate it into "levels of control" to support the organizational strategy. A process requiring human knowledge, judgment, and experience is divided into Roles and assigned by an HIM system to an individual or group that is to be responsible for a certain part of the process. A certain Role may be responsible for several activities and tasks; additionally, the Roles have interactions with each other. A business process is modeled using role activity diagrams; the activities and other Roles related to a certain role are depicted in the role activity diagrams.

16.1.3 Comparing Human Interaction Management and Business Process Management

There is a marked difference between the approaches of BPM and HIM. HIM as a concept offers an alternative perspective to business processes, but it does not represent a contrarian view to BPM; instead, it represents a complementary view to process management.

While both BPM and HIM have a way to model a process and the rules it should follow, BPM assumes that a process can be fully planned in advance and controlled during execution, whereas HIM admits that unexpected events can occur and that the process may not go exactly as planned (though it will stay within the guidelines). Some processes follow the rules and conditions set for them without any variation at all, whereas, in others, it is impossible to avoid the phenomenon of processes straying away from the set rules and conditions. BPM recognizes human participation in a process, but gives humans a role more akin to that of a machine—it assumes that all humans have perfect knowledge and make rational decisions. BPM also assumes that humans are only a part of the automated process, taking on the tasks that are too complex for machines to perform, yet it does not recognize the fact that there may be processes that are primarily driven by humans.

Ultimately, both BPM and HIM aim to improve business processes. In BPM, the goal of "improving the business processes" implies optimizing the activities conducted within the process to increase customer value, whereas, in HIM, "improving the business processes" is regarded as facilitating and supporting the human interactions within the process to increase customer value. In other words, BPM focuses on improving the outcomes of the actions, whereas HIM focuses on improving the way the actions are carried out. HIM does not address how a process is or should be carried out but rather what types of interaction and information exchange is essential for the process and which actors participate in them. In other words, HIM does not focus on optimizing business processes—that is, completing activities in an optimal way—but instead focuses on optimizing the environment for enabling the execution of these processes by facilitating the exchange of information.

16.1.4 HumanEdj Human Interaction Management Systems

Internet tools have made basic communication quicker, but they have not made collaboration more efficient; human work is the only competitive differentiator left, and such work depends fundamentally on collaboration. This is why people need to collaborate better—they need to adopt a simple, general approach that meets both individual and organizational needs.

HumanEdj is an software application founded directly on the principles of HIM. It helps the user to carry out all of the work activities in which they are engaged, facilitating complex tasks and interactions. Furthermore, HumanEdj aims to help users to structure their activities, interactions, and resources so that they can manage them more efficiently. HumanEdj is a complete replacement for user's standard desktop. It provides access to all computing resources that the user may need (e.g., programs, files, network access) in a structured way. HumanEdj is a personal desktop tool with the objective of helping collaboration among humans through support for business rules, multi-agent system functionality, speech acts, Extensible Markup Language schemas, ontology, Web services, scripting languages, Web browsing, and external document access. It is available free of charge for all standard computing platforms and devices. It runs on the client machine(s) of each process participant and does not require any server installations (HumanEdj webpage).

To use HumanEdj, the user has to first create a Book. Regarding the Book:

1. It is the view to one's entire working life. The user can add as many Books as he or she wants. The Book files are encrypted and may be opened only with a password defined by the user. A Book consists of Stories and Identities.

2. Stories describe collaborations that the user is involved in, while an Identity includes the user's personal name and email account. Each Identity may have several messaging accounts attached—one for chatting, one for the mobile phone, and so on—and the user may have several Identities.

3. The main objects inside a Story are the Roles that represent participants in the work process; in a development project, for example, the roles could be Project Manager, Designer, Quality Assurance, and Business Analyst. Other types of collaborative work process will include different Roles.

4. In addition to Roles, a Story may contain Users and Interactions. Users are the people who will play the Roles. The ability to define User types allows control over the sort of people that are assigned to particular Roles. Interactions describe how Role instances send information to one another. This information may be, for example, a document, structured data, or a Web link.

An individual HumanEdj user goes usually through three stages:

1. HumanEdj for messaging: This stage uses the software to simplify and structure one's communications with colleagues. HumanEdj offers an email account with full capabilities of sending and receiving messages. However, the beta version of HumanEdj that was explored in this study does not have all of these email capabilities. Instead, it is only able to pick up messages directly from an email server.

2. HumanEdj for work: At this stage, the user use the software to coordinate and automate all his or her working tasks, including document creation, Web searching, use of other enterprise systems, data maintenance, calculations, and so on—even tasks that are not themselves conducted using a computer.

3. HumanEdj for HIM: This stage involves using the software to organize and manage one's work (and those of colleagues) via standard principles and patterns. The developers of HumanEdj emphasize that the software on its own is not enough to fully transform one's working life. As an example, having a computer-aided design tool will help to plan an office layout, but its use does not qualify anybody to design an aircraft. However, by gradually adapting the use of HumanEdj, it could massively reduce the daily effort one expends on work, resulting in larger personal efficiency. However, this can happen only when the user adopts the principles of HIM.

16.2 Interactions and the Quality of Experience

Interaction can only take place if certain interactive acts are performed by at least two actors communicating with each other. An interaction or interactive pattern is a sequence of actions, references, and reactions wherein each reference or reaction has a certain, ex-ante intended and ex-post recognizable interrelation with preceding event(s) in terms of timing and content. The most common feature constituting the exchange of interactive acts and thereby interactivity is the recurring characteristic of the request–response pattern (Figure 16.1).

The surface structure of an interactive conversation between two partners A and B may formally be described as a sequence of four states. These states are a result of each speaker alternating between active and passive periods that can be numbered according to their temporal order. Together with the delay added by the transmission channel, on each speaker's side, this leads to a sequential chain made up of four states:

"A" if speaker A is active (only)

"B" if speaker B is active (only)

"Double talk" if both speakers are active

"Mutual silence" if none of them is active

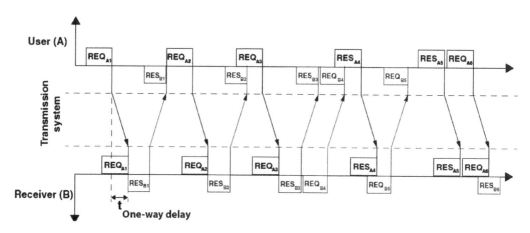

FIGURE 16.1
An interactivity constituting a request–response pattern.

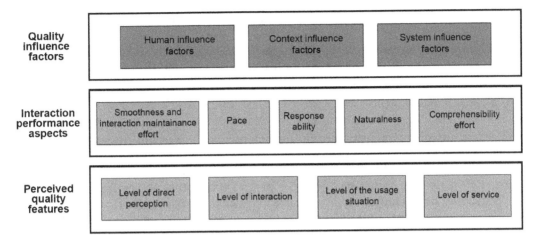

FIGURE 16.2
Taxonomy of influence factors, interaction performance aspects, and quality features.

For defining the interactivity metric, it must not make a difference whether it is calculated based on the interaction pattern as seen by A or B (symmetry criterion).

Figure 16.2 shows the influence interactivity has on the quality of experience via a taxonomy of influence factors, interaction performance aspects, and quality features.

The process of interaction between two or more entities and their perception of this process on several dimensions is depicted in Figure 16.2 and described as follows:

1. Smoothness and interaction maintenance effort is how fluent and effortless the users experience the conversational flow. Typically, interaction has an inherent pace it establishes, thereby keeping the maintenance efforts of the interaction parties minimal. However, due to system impairments, the interaction pace can be changed, thereby accordingly demanding additional user effort in order to adapt to the changed pace. For human-to-machine interaction, this can severely impact the flow experience or the experienced smoothness, whereas, for human-to-human interaction, the conversational rhythm can be impaired.

2. Pace is the users' perceived promptness of the interactional acts and respective actions by the other entity.

3. Response ability denotes if it is possible to issue a response following a prior message or a response from the system or other user. Response abilities through interruptions in human-to-human interactions can be severely obstructed by transmission delays, as interruptions may not arrive in time and are not able to interrupt in the way originally intended. In terms of browser-based applications, the modality type of the response can be a source of difficulty, but is rather caused by the website content in this application type.

4. Naturalness is related to the inherent knowledge about how an interaction takes place in a nonmediated or ideal case.

5. Comprehension effort is required to understand either the other interlocutor (in the case of human-to-human interaction) or needed to interpret the response from the machine. Comprehension can be distorted by, for example, double talk or non-rendered portions of the webpage, which might be needed for navigation or information retrieval.

When interacting with or via a system, the initial situation is composed of:

1. A human (or humans) having perceptions, emotions, motivations, and behaviors that are built on the human's personality, experiences, and the current state
2. A system providing a certain quality of service
3. A context (or contexts)

To illustrate the role of interaction from the viewpoint of a user, the process of interaction can be understood as a tool for him or her to infer the quality provided by the system of interest. In the case of human-to-human communication, interaction problems experienced by the user can either be due to the person at the other end or due to the system. For some cases, the identification is obvious; for instance, if background noises are falsely amplified, it may be difficult to maintain a fluent conversation, but it can easily be identified as a technical problem. The quality can be rated low accordingly.

In the human-to-machine context, the interaction quality directly provides information to the user on the quality of the system. The gathered information—for example, how comprehensible messages are, how easy it is to respond, or how fluently an interaction can be maintained—can directly be transferred into a judgment on the quality. Interaction measures can therefore be considered to have a direct link to QoE. However, for other cases, the reason—that is, whether it is the other person or the system that is responsible for a low performance—is not clearly identifiable. When response times are rather long, it can for example either be due to a long transmission delay or to a slowly responding person at the other end. Similarly, inappropriate timing of utterances can be due to either the system sending out messages at an incorrect time or to someone being inattentive or impolite and not getting the timing right.

16.2.1 Factors Influencing Quality of Experience

The influence factor can be understood as any characteristic of a user, system, service, application, or context whose actual state or setting may have influence on the QoE for the user.

QoE can be subject to a range of complex and strongly interrelated factors and falls into three categories of human, system, and context influence factors, respectively. With regard to human influence factors, we discuss variant and stable factors that may potentially bear an influence on QoE, either for low-level (bottom-up) or higher-level (top-down) cognitive processing. System influence factors are classified into four distinct categories, namely, content-, media-, network- and device-related influence factors. Finally, the broad category of possible context influence factors is decomposed into factors linked to the physical, temporal, social, economic, task, and technical information contexts (Table 16.1).

1. Human influence factors: A human influence factor is any variant or invariant property or characteristic of a human user. The characteristic can describe the demographic and socioeconomic background, the physical and mental constitution, and/or the emotional state of the user. Human influence factors may bear an influence on a given experience and how it unfolds, as well as on its quality. They are highly complex because of their subjectivity and relation to internal states and processes. This makes them rather intangible and therefore much more difficult to grasp. In addition, human influence factors are strongly interrelated and may

TABLE 16.1

Overview and Examples of Potential Influence Factor

IF	Type	Examples
HIF	Low-level: physical, emotional, mental constitution	Visual/auditory acuity and sensitivity; gender, age; lower-order emotions; mood; attention level
	High-level: understanding, interpretation, evaluation	Sociocultural background; socioeconomic position; values; goals; motivation; affective states; previous experiences; prior knowledge; skills
SIF	Content-related	Audio bandwidth, dynamic range; video motion and detail
	Media-related	Encoding, resolution, sampling rate, frame rate; synchronization
	Network-related	Bandwidth, delay, jitter, loss, error rate, throughput: transmission protocol
	Device-related	Display resolution, colors, brightness; audio channel count
GIF	Physical context	Location and space; environmental attributes; motion
	Temporal context	Time, duration and frequency of use
	Social context	Interpersonal relations
	Economic context	Costs, subscription type, brand
	Task context	Nature of experience; task type, interruptions, parallelism
	Technical/informational context	Compatibility, interoperability; additional informational artifacts

also strongly interplay with the other influence factors described in this chapter. As a result, the influence of human factors on QoE cannot only be considered at a generic level.

a. *Low-level processing and human influence factors*: At the level of early sensory—or so-called low-level—processing, properties related to the physical, emotional, and mental constitution of the user may play a major role. These characteristics can be dispositional (e.g., the user's visual and auditory acuity, gender, age) as well as variant and more dynamic (e.g., lower-order emotions, the user's mood, motivation, attention). At the same level, characteristics that are closely related to human perception of external stimuli might bear the strongest influence on QoE.

b. *Higher-level processing and human influence factors*: Top-down—or, so-called higher-level—cognitive processing relates to the understanding of stimuli and the associated interpretative and evaluative processes. It is based on knowledge, i.e., "any information that the perceiver brings to a situation." As a result, a wide range of additional human influence factors are important at this level. Some of them have an invariant or relatively stable nature. Examples in this respect include the sociocultural and educational background, life stage, and socioeconomic position of a human user.

2. System influence factors: System influence factors refer to properties and characteristics that determine the technically produced quality of an application or service.

a. *Content-related system influence factors*: The content itself and its type are highly influential to the overall QoE of the system, as different content characteristics might require different system properties. For auditory information, the audio bandwidth and dynamic range are the two major system influence factors and their requirements vary with the content itself (e.g., for voice/spoken content versus musical content).

When it comes to visual information, the amount of detail as well as the amount of motion in the scene is important. To a large extent, this has to do with human influence factors such as contrast sensitivity and visual masking, but also with the fact that current compression techniques are affected by these. Furthermore, it is also influenced by the content itself, as well as influenced by the higher-level processing. In three-dimensional image and video content, the amount of depth is an aspect that also influences the quality and especially the viewing comfort.

b. *Media-related system influence factors* refer to media configuration factors, such as encoding, resolution, sampling rate, frame rate, and media synchronization. They are interrelated with the content-related system influence factors. Media-related system influence factors can change during the transmission due to variation in network-related system influence factors.

In most cases, the resources for distributing media are limited. There are both economical- as well as hardware-related reasons for limiting the size of media. This is usually accomplished by applying compression, which can be either lossless or lossy. Lossy compression gives higher compression rates at the cost of quality. However, the influence depends on the principle that the lossy coding is built upon. For instance, for images and video, block-based compression techniques such as via JPEG or MPEG4/ AVC a.k.a. H.264 are the most common. For stronger compression, these will usually give visible blocking (rectangular-shaped) distortions and blurring, whereas wavelet-based techniques mostly give blurring distortions, as seen in JPEG 2000.

For audio, the coding also depends on the content type and service/ application scenario.

c. *Network-related system influence factors* consider data transmission over a network. The main network characteristics are bandwidth; delay; jitter; loss, error rates, and distributions; and throughput The network-related system influence factors may change over time or as a user changes his location and are tightly related to the network quality of service. Network-related system influence factors are impacted by errors occurring during the transmission over a network. Especially in case of delay, the impact of system influence factors also depends on whether the service is interactive or more passively consumed, as, for instance in the case of telephony versus radio broadcast or video conferencing versus streaming video. In an interactive, for example, conversational service, delay may have a negative impact on QoE. Most often, the video is deliberately delayed by using strategically placed buffers in order to be more resilient towards network capacity variations and errors.

The popularity of over-the-top streaming video, for example YouTube or Netflix, has increased very rapidly. The distribution method is Transmission Control Protocol- and Hypertext Transfer Protocol-based and, here, the influence of packet loss and bandwidth limitations is quite different. Network problems will result in freezes without loss of content in the video. Freezing also has a bad influence on the experienced quality, but can be avoided by using adaptive or scalable codecs in conjunction with over-the-top video services.

d. *Device-related system influence factors* refer to the end systems or devices of the communication path. The visual interface to the user is the display. Its capacity will have a tremendous impact on the end-user experience, but the content and signal quality will interact with it. For instance, if a high-quality, high-resolution (here meaning in terms of number of pixels) image is shown on a low-resolution display with few colors, most of the original intent of the image might be lost. However, if a low-resolution image is shown on a large, high-resolution display, most likely a very blocky and blurry image will be displayed, but the end result will be highly dependent on the final image scaling procedure.

The main progress in the area of input devices is the increased usage of touchscreens, which are addressing the human tactile modality. The touch-screen as an input device can present a limitation if the user needs to input a larger amount of information. The existing state-of-the-art mobile devices with multi-core processors and advanced graphics processing units can deliver a substantial amount of computational power, but at the cost of autonomy. Mobility, which is a context influence factor, thus strongly influences various characteristics of devices.

3. Context influence factors: Context influence factors are factors that embrace any situational property to describe the user's environment.

a. *Physical context* describes the characteristics of location and space, including movements within and transitions between locations; spatial locations (e.g., outdoor or indoor or in a personal, professional, or social place); functional places and spaces; sensed environmental attributes (e.g., peaceful place versus a noisy place, lights and temperature); movements and mobility (e.g., sitting, standing, walking, or jogging); and artifacts.

b. *Temporal context* is related with temporal aspects of a given experience, for example, time of day (e.g., morning, afternoon, or evening), week, month, season (e.g., spring, summer, fall, or winter) and year; duration and frequency of use (of the service/system); before/during/after the experience; actions in relation to time; and synchronism.

c. *Social context* is defined by the interpersonal relations existing during the experience. Hence, it is important to consider if the application/system user is alone or with other persons as well as how different persons are involved in the experience, namely including interpersonal actions. Moreover, the cultural, educational, professional levels (e.g., hierarchical dependencies, internal versus external), and entertainment (dependent of random or rhythmic use) also need to be considered. The social context becomes very important at the recommendation level. Content recommendation based on the gathered context information allows guaranteeing better user experience. Collaborative recommendations, wherein the user recommends items that are consumed by other users with similar preferences, can also be made possible.

d. *Economic context*: Costs, subscription type, or brand of the application/system are part of the economic context. Network cost information (e.g., relative distances between the peers), jointly with some physical and social factors, can be used to enable network optimization strategies for media delivery.

e. *Task context* is determined by the nature of the experience. Depending on this, three situations may arise: multitasking, interruptions, or task type.

An additional task does not have an influence on the perceived quality, independently of the difficulty (hard or easy) of that task, as stalling did affect the perceived quality to a similar extent under both task conditions.

f. *Technical and information context* describes the relationship between the system of interest and other relevant systems and services including: devices (e.g., existing interconnectivity of devices over Bluetooth or nearfield communication); applications (e.g., availability of an application instead of the currently used browser-based solution of a service); networks (e.g., availability of other networks than the one currently used); or additional informational artifacts (e.g., additional use of pen and paper for better information assimilation from the service used). Characteristics like interoperability, informational artifacts, and access as well as mixed reality also need to be considered.

16.2.2 Features of Quality of Experience

This subsection describes how the factors of the user, system, and context of use, which influence QoE, are perceived by the user. For this purpose, the notion of a feature—that is, a perceivable, recognized, and nameable characteristic of an experience—is deployed. Such a feature can be considered as a dimension of the perceptual space and the nature and dimensionality of this space can be analyzed. The characteristics of the individual's experience is analyzed by decomposing it into so-called quality features.

Quality can be understood as the outcome of an individual's comparison and judgment process, requiring perception, reflection, and description processes to take place. Knowledge about these characteristics is however necessary when investigating why a specific experience is suboptimum, i.e., not judged with the highest-possible rating, and what can be done in order to improve the situation (quality diagnosis).

A perceptual event is triggered by a physical event, or the physical signal reaching the individual's sensory organs in a specific situation. The physical event is first processed by the low-level sensation and perception processes, resulting in a perceptual character of the event. This perceptual character is then reflected by the individual during the quality judgment process, resulting in the perceptual event, which is characterized by its decomposing features. Thus, a feature can be seen as a dimension of a multidimensional perceptual event, in a multidimensional perceptual space. As a perceptual event is always situation and context-dependent, a feature also depends on the situation and the context it has been extracted in. Thus, an empirical analysis of features commonly reveals only those features that are perceivable and nameable in that respective context (the others cannot be discerned).

The concept of a feature space can be helpful for explaining the relation between features and the quality of a perceptual event. The (integral) quality is a scalar value that can in general not directly be represented in the feature space. However, functional relations can be established by mapping the feature values of perceptual events onto corresponding quality scores. Depending on the form of this mapping, the nature of the features with respect to quality can be analyzed.

The perceptual event that a physical stimulus provokes can be conceived as being located in a multidimensional feature space. In this feature space, each of the underlying axes corresponds to one feature of the perceptual event. The perceptual event can mathematically be described by a position vector, where its coordinates correspond to specific feature values of the perceptual event. If the underlying axes of this space and, thus, the features are orthogonal, then the features can also be referred to as *perceptual dimensions*. The number of the dimensions—that is, the nameable perceptual features that are orthogonal to each other—corresponds to the dimensionality of the feature space.

Once the perceptual features have been identified, they can be mapped to integral quality judgments obtained for the same physical events and trigger hopefully the same perceptual events. This way, it becomes possible to identify the weighting or importance of each perceptual feature for the integral quality. This process is called *external preference mapping*, and the resulting weights can be used for modeling overall quality on the basis of features.

16.2.2.1 Feature Levels

When referring to a service that is potentially interactive, wherein the individual usage situation spans over a delimited period of time and/or which is being used regularly over a longer time, there are additional features that may play a role for the global quality, utility, and acceptability of the service.

Features are grouped on five levels:

1. *Level of service*, which is related to the usage of the service beyond a particular instance. This category includes features like appeal, usefulness, utility, and acceptability.

2. *Level of the usage instance of the service*, which includes also the physical and social usage situations. Examples of such features are the learnability and intuitiveness of the service, its effectiveness and efficiency for reaching a particular goal during the current usage instance, and the ease of using the service as well as non-functional features such as the "personality" of the interaction partner (human or machine) or its aesthetics.

3. *Level of interaction*, or the level that includes the constant exchange of actions and reactions, be it between humans (human-to-human interaction) or between humans and systems (human-to-machine interaction), includes features like responsiveness, naturalness of interaction, communication efficiency, and conversation effectiveness.

4. *Level of action*, or the level that relates to the human perception of his/her own actions, may include involvement and immersion and the perception of space (as far as this is supported by the user perceiving his/her own motions in the virtual space) as well as the perception of one's own motions in the case of video services. In the case of speech services, this may include talking-only features such as the perception of sidetone, echo, or double-talk degradations.

5. *Level of direct perception* summarizes all quality features that are related to the perceptual event and which are created immediately and spontaneously during the experience. These features may be related to individual sensory channels, such as visual features, auditory features, or tactile features, but may also be linked to the perception via multiple senses in parallel

(e.g., audio–visual features). For the visual channel, examples include sharpness, darkness, brightness, contrast, flicker, distortion, and color perception. For the auditory channel, example features of audio-streaming services are localization and timbre, while example features of speech-transmission services include coloration, noisiness, loudness, or continuity. For services that address multiple sensory channels simultaneously, relevant features are, for example, balance and synchronism.

16.3 Customer Interaction Systems

Traditional graphical interfaces may not be appropriate for all users and/or applications; for this reason, spoken dialog systems are becoming a strong alternative. Speech and natural language technologies allow users to communicate in a flexible and efficient way while also enabling access to applications when traditional input and output interfaces cannot be used (e.g., in-car applications, access for disabled persons, etc.). Also, speech-based interfaces work seamlessly with small devices (e.g., smartphones and tablets) and allow users to easily invoke local applications or access remote information (Griol et al. 2017).

Spoken dialog systems are computer programs that receive speech as input and generate information as output synthesized speech, engaging the user in a dialog that aims to be similar to that between humans:

1. Automatic speech recognition (ASR): The goal of speech recognition is to obtain the sequence of words uttered by a speaker. Once the speech recognizer has provided an output, the system must understand what the user said.

2. Spoken language understanding module: The goal of spoken language understanding is to obtain the semantics from the recognized sentence. This process generally requires morphological, lexical, syntactical, semantic, discourse, and pragmatic knowledge.

3. Dialog manager module: The dialog manager decides the next action of the system, interpreting the incoming semantic representation of the user input in the context of the dialog. In addition, it resolves ellipsis and anaphora, evaluates the relevance and completeness of user requests, identifies and recovers from recognition and understanding errors, retrieves information from data repositories, and decides about the system's response.

4. Natural language generation (NLG) module: Natural language generation is the process of obtaining sentences in natural language from the nonlinguistic, internal representation of information handled by the dialog system.

5. Text-to-speech module: Text-to-speech transforms the generated sentences into synthesized speech.

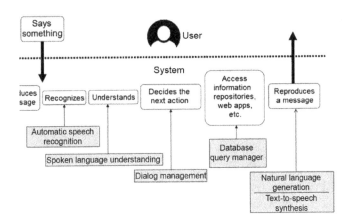

FIGURE 16.3
Customer conversation systems.

Figure 16.3 shows the schematic of a customer conversation system.

16.3.1 Spoken Language Recognition

Speech recognition is the process of obtaining the text string corresponding to an acoustic input. Since the output of the ASR is the starting point of the other modules in a spoken dialog system, it is important to try and detect and correct errors generated during the ASR process.

The complexity of the recognition task arises because of reasons like:

- The acoustic variability (each person pronounces sounds differently when speaking)
- Acoustic confusion (many words sound similar)
- The coarticulation problem (the characteristics of spoken sounds may vary depending on neighboring sounds)
- Out-of-vocabulary words and spontaneous speech (e.g., interjections, pauses, doubts, false starts, repetitions of words, self-corrections)
- Environmental conditions (e.g., noise, channel distortion, bandwidth limitations)

Consequently, ASR systems are classified according to the kind of users supported (user-independent or user-dependent systems); the style of speech supported (recognizers isolated words, connected words, or continuous speech); vocabulary size (small, medium, or large vocabulary); and so on.

The field of automatic speech recognition has progressed from the recognition of isolated words in reduced vocabularies to continuous speech recognition with increasing vocabulary sets. These advances have made communication with dialog systems increasingly more natural. Among the variety of techniques used to develop ASR systems, the data-based approach is currently the most widely used. In this approach, the speech recognition problem can be understood as:

Given a sequence of acoustic data A, finding the word sequence W uttered by the user determined by

$$W = \max_{W} P(W|A)$$

Using Baye's rule,

$$P(W|A) = \frac{P(A|W)P(W)}{P(A)}$$

where:

P(A|W) is the probability of the acoustic sequence A when the word sequence W has been uttered (acoustic model)

P(W) is the probability of word sequence W (language model)

The probabilities of the rules in these models are learned from the training data. Since, P(A|W) and P(W) are not dependent on each other,

$$W = \max_{W} P(A|W)P(W)$$

The acoustic model is created by taking audio recordings of speech and their transcriptions and then compiling them into statistical representations of the sounds for the different words.

Acoustic modeling has been implemented mostly by means of hidden Markov models (HMMs). The success of the HMM is mainly based on the use of machine learning algorithms to learn the parameters of the model, as well as in their ability to represent speech as a sequential phenomenon over time. Multiple models have been studied, such as discrete models, semicontinuous or continuous, as well as a variety of topology models.

 In more recent times, deep neural networks have largely replaced HMM models. Deep neural networks are now used extensively in industrial and academic research as well as in most commercially deployed ASR systems. Various studies have shown that deep neural networks outperform HMM models in terms of increased recognition accuracy. Deep learning algorithms extract high-level, complex abstractions as data representations through a hierarchical learning process. A key benefit of deep learning is the analysis and learning of massive amounts of unsupervised data, making it a valuable tool for big data analytics wherein raw data are largely unlabeled and uncategorized.

Learning a language model requires the transcriptions of sentences related to the application domain of the system. The language model is one of the essential components required to develop a recognizer of continuous speech. The most used language models are based on regular or context-free grammars, and n-grams. Grammars are usually suitable for small tasks, providing more precision based on the type of restrictions. However, they are not able to represent the great variability of natural speech processes. N-grams models allow for the collection more easily of the different concatenations among words when a sufficient number of training samples is available.

16.3.2 Spoken Language Understanding

Once the spoken dialog system has recognized what the user uttered, it is necessary to understand what the user said. Natural language processing is a method of obtaining the semantics of a text string, and generally involves:

1. Lexical and morphological: Lexical and morphological knowledge divides words into their constituents by distinguishing between lexemes and morphemes as follows: lexemes are parts of words that indicate their semantics and morphemes are the different infixes and suffixes that provide different word classes.

2. Syntactical: Syntactic analysis yields the hierarchical structure of the sentences. However, in spoken language, phrases are frequently affected by difficulties associated with the so-called disfluency phenomena, such as filled pauses, repetitions, syntactic incompleteness and repairs.

3. Semantic: Semantic analysis extracts the meaning of a complex syntactic structure from the meaning of its constituent parts.

4. Discourse and pragmatical knowledge: In the pragmatic and discourse processing stage, the sentences are interpreted in the context of the whole dialog; the main complexity of this stage is the resolution of anaphora; and ambiguities are derived from phenomena such as irony, sarcasm, or double entendre.

The process of understanding can be comprehended as a change in language representation, from natural language to a semantic language, so that the meaning of the message is not changed. As in the speech recognizer, the spoken language understanding module can work with several hypotheses (both for recognition and understanding) and confidence measures. The major approaches to tackling the problem of understanding are:

- Rule-based approaches extract semantic information based on a syntactic semantic analysis of the sentences, using grammars defined for the task, or by means of the detection of keywords with semantic meanings. In order to improve the robustness of the analysis, some analyzers combine syntactic and semantic aspects of the specific task. Other techniques are based on an analysis at two levels, in which grammars are used to carry out a detailed analysis of the sentence and extract relevant semantic information. In addition, there are systems that use rule-based analyzers automatically learned from a training corpus using natural language processing techniques.

- Statistical models learned from data corpus: Statistical methods are based on the definition of linguistic units with semantic content and attainment of models from labeled samples. This type of analysis uses a probabilistic model to identify concepts, markers, and values of cases in order to represent the relationship between markers of cases and their values and to decode semantically the utterances of the user. The model is generated during a training phase (learning), wherein its parameters capture the correspondences between text entries and semantic representation. Once the training model has been learned, it is used as a decoder to generate the best representation.

16.3.3 Dialog Management

The core logic of the conversational application is encapsulated within dialog management, which mainly consists of tasks like:

- Updating the dialog context
- Providing a context for sentence interpretation
- Coordinating invoking of other modules
- Deciding the information to convey to the user and when to do it

The design of an appropriate dialog management strategy is at the core of dialog system engineering. Users are diverse, which makes it difficult to foresee which form of system behavior will lead to quick and successful dialog completion, and speech recognition errors may introduce uncertainty about their intention. The selection of a specific system action depends on multiple factors, such as the output of the speech recognizer (e.g., measures that define the reliability of the recognized information); the dialog interaction and previous dialog history (e.g., the number of repairs carried out so far); the application domain (e.g., guidelines for customer service); knowledge about the users; and the responses and status of external back-ends, devices, and data repositories.

Statistical approaches for dialog management present several important advantages with regard to traditional rule-based methodologies. Rather than maintaining a single hypothesis for the dialog state, they maintain a distribution over many hypotheses for the correct dialog state. In addition, statistical methodologies choose actions using an optimization process, in which a developer specifies high-level goals and the optimization works out the detailed dialog plan. The main trend in this area is an increased use of data for automatically improving the performance of the system. Statistical models can be trained with corpora of human–computer dialogs with the goal of explicitly modeling the variance in user behavior that can be difficult to address by means of handwritten rules. Additionally, if it is necessary to satisfy certain deterministic behaviors, it is possible to extend the strategy learned from the training corpus with handcrafted rules that include expert knowledge or specifications about the task.

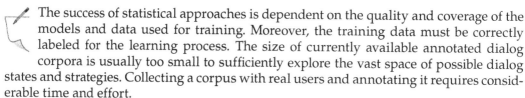

The success of statistical approaches is dependent on the quality and coverage of the models and data used for training. Moreover, the training data must be correctly labeled for the learning process. The size of currently available annotated dialog corpora is usually too small to sufficiently explore the vast space of possible dialog states and strategies. Collecting a corpus with real users and annotating it requires considerable time and effort.

Automating dialog management is useful for developing, deploying, and redeploying applications and also reducing the time-consuming process of handcrafted design. In fact, the application of *machine learning* approaches to dialog management strategy design is a rapidly growing research area. Machine learning approaches to dialog management attempt to learn optimal strategies from corpora of real human-computer dialog data using automated "trial-and-error" methods instead of relying on empirical design principles.

The most widespread methodology for machine learning of dialog strategies consists of modeling human–computer interaction as an optimization problem using Markov decision processes and reinforcement methods. The main drawback of this approach is that the large state space of practical spoken dialog systems makes its direct representation intractable. Partially observable Markov decision processes often outperform Markov decision process-based dialog strategies, since they provide an explicit representation of uncertainty. This enables the dialog manager to avoid and recover from recognition errors by sharing and shifting probability mass between multiple hypotheses of the current dialog state.

16.3.4 Natural Language Generation

Natural language generation is the process of obtaining texts in natural language from a nonlinguistic representation. It is important to obtain legible messages, optimizing the text using referring expressions and linking words and adapting the vocabulary and the complexity of the syntactic structures to the user's linguistic expertise.

Traditional natural language generation consist of the following five steps:

1. Content organization
2. Content distribution in sentences
3. Lexicalization
4. Generation of referential expressions
5. Linguistic realization

The approaches for natural language generation are:

- Default text generation, which uses predefined text messages for example error messages and warnings.
- Template-based generation, in which the same message structure is produced with slight alterations. The template approach is used mainly for multi-sentence generation, particularly in applications whose texts are fairly regular in structure, such as business reports.
- Phrase-based systems, which employ what can be considered as generalized templates at the sentence level (in which case, the phrases resemble phrase structure grammar rules) or at the discourse level (in which case, they are often called text plans). In such systems, a pattern is first selected to match the top level of the input and then each part of the pattern is expanded into a more specific one that matches some portion of the input. The cascading process stops when every pattern has been replaced by one or more words.
- Feature-based systems, which represent the maximum level of generalization and flexibility. In feature-based systems, each possible minimal alternative of expression is represented by a single feature; for example, whether the sentence is either positive or negative, if it is a question or an imperative or a statement, or its tense. To arrange the features, it is necessary to employ linguistic knowledge.
- Corpus-based natural language generation, which stochastically generates system utterances.

 Natural language generation has traditionally been modeled as a planning pipeline involving content selection, surface realization, and presentation. Early NLG systems were rule-based and consequently quickly grew complex to maintain and adapt to new domains and constraints.

Some related important aspects are given in the following:

1. Collaboration: In an interaction, no participant's contributions stand alone—the process of constructing the discourse is a collaboration. This is true even if the participants are disagreeing or attempting to deceive one another—collaboration on an underlying task is not necessary for collaboration in the interaction process. Each contribution is shaped by the needs to fit into what has come before and to maximize the chances of success of what will follow. These constraints influence content selection, surface realization, and production. In addition, the collaboration causes additional language behaviors not present in noninteractive situations; these include interaction maintenance behaviors such as turn-taking.

2. Reference: A problem that is key to any interactive system is the understanding and production of references to entities states as well as activities in the world or in the conversation. Reference influences or is influenced by every dialogue task, from the recognition of user input through to production of user output. Referring expression generation, in particular, is the core of the NLG problem, for everything that a dialogue participant does is aimed at describing the word as it is or as the participant wishes it to be.

3. Uncertainty: Grounding and alignment behaviors help to minimize uncertainty related to each conversational participant's model of the interaction so far, but do not drive the interaction further. There is another type of uncertainty relevant to NLG, which is the construction of a "right" contribution to drive the next step of the interaction.

4. Engagement: Any agent that produces language, whether for interactive or noninteractive contexts, will be more successful if it is engaging. An agent will engage a user if it is informative, relevant, clear, consistent, and concise. However, it is easier to be engaging for a particular (known) audience than for a general audience and, in a conversational interaction, the participants are constantly giving each other information about themselves (what will best inform and engage them) and feedback about the success of the interaction so far. In particular, conversational participants give evidence of their culture and personality.

Another area in which engagement affects the performance of dialog systems is when they are used to provide assistive and augmentative communication services.

 As communication aids become increasingly multimodal, combining speech with image and video input, so also to is natural language generation evolving to produce multimodal contributions. One such multimodal generation mechanism is to use an avatar or a virtual agent. In the realm of multimodal communication, the intent of the message is carried not only by words but also by the prosody of speech and by nonverbal means including body posture, eye gaze, and gestures. These paralinguistic means of communication take on a different dimension when contextualized by the cultural backgrounds of the conversational participants.

5. Evaluation: With the increasingly multimodal nature of human–machine conversation, where humans interact with devices endowed with cameras, the efficacy of conversation can be hugely improved by taking into account different factors beyond just the speech input/output to/from the system.

16.3.5 Text-to-Speech Synthesis

Text-to-speech synthesizers transform a text into an acoustic signal. A text-to-speech system is composed of two parts:

1. The front-end

    a. Converts raw text containing symbols such as numbers and abbreviations into their equivalent words. This process is often called text normalization, preprocessing, or tokenization.

b. Assigns a phonetic transcription to each word and divides and marks the text into prosodic units (i.e., phrases, clauses, and sentences). The process of assigning phonetic transcriptions to words is called text-to-phoneme or grapheme-to-phoneme conversion. The output of the front-end is the symbolic representation constituted by the phonetic transcriptions and prosody information.

2. The back-end (often referred to as the synthesizer) converts the symbolic linguistic representation into sound in two ways:

   a. Speech synthesis based on human speech production: parameters such as fundamental frequency, voicing, and noise levels are varied over time to create a waveform of artificial speech. This is further subdivided into:

      - Parametric synthesis which simulates the physiological parameters of the vocal tract
      - Formant-based synthesis, which models the vibration of the vocal chords
      - Articulatory synthesis, which is based on physiological models and refers to computational techniques for synthesizing speech based on models of the human vocal tract and the articulation processes

   b. Concatenative synthesis employs prerecorded units of human voice. Concatenative synthesis is based on stringing together segments of recorded speech. It generally produces the most natural-sounding synthesized speech; however, differences between natural variations in speech and the nature of the automated techniques for segmenting the waveforms sometimes result in audible glitches in the output. The quality of the synthesized speech depends on the size of the synthesis unit employed.

      Unit selection synthesis uses large databases of recorded speech. During database creation, each recorded utterance is segmented into some or all of the following: individual phones, syllables, morphemes, words, phrases, and sentences. Unit selection provides the greatest naturalness, because it applies only a small amount of digital signal processing to the recorded speech. There is a balance between intelligibility and naturalness of the voice output or the automatization of the synthesis procedure. For example, synthesis based on whole words is more intelligible than the phone-based but for each new word it is necessary to obtain a new recording, whereas the phones allow building of any new word.

   - Domain-specific synthesis concatenates prerecorded words and phrases to create complete utterances. It is used in applications in which the variety of texts produced by the system is limited to a particular domain, such as transit schedule announcements or weather reports.

   - Diphone synthesis uses a minimal speech database containing all of the diphones (sound-to-sound transitions) occurring in a language. The number of diphones depends on the phonotactics of the language: for example, Spanish has about 800 diphones, while German has about 2,500. In diphone synthesis, only one example of each diphone is contained in the speech database.

- HMM-based synthesis is a method in which the frequency spectrum (vocal tract), fundamental frequency (vocal source), and duration (prosody) of speech are modeled simultaneously by HMMs. Speech waveforms are generated from the HMMs themselves, based on the maximum likelihood criterion.

16.4 Implementing Customer Interaction Systems

The following modules cooperate to perform the interaction with the user: ASR, Spoken Language Understanding module, Dialog Manager, NLG, and text-to-speech synthesizer.

Each one of these has its own characteristics and the selection of the most convenient model varies depending on certain factors, such as the goal of each module, the possibility of manually defining the behavior of the module, and/or the capability of automatically obtaining models from training samples.

16.5 Summary

The chapter started with an introduction to the approach of HIM, which was developed to deal with the human behavior in the organization by drawing ideas not only from process theory but also from biology, psychology, social systems theory, and learning theory. The chapter then introduced the concept of interaction or interactive pattern as a sequence of actions, references, and reactions wherein each reference or reaction has a certain, ex-ante intended and ex-post recognizable interrelation with preceding event(s) in terms of timing and content. The resulting or consequent QoE for interaction is dependent on various factors including effort, smoothness, pace, response ability, naturalness, attention, comprehension, and so on. Additionally, the interaction is influenced by three influence factors, namely, human, system, and context. The latter half of this chapter presented the components of an effective customer interaction systems, namely, automatic speech recognition, spoken language understanding, dialog management, natural language generation, and text-to-speech synthesis.

Epilogue: Digital Transformations of Enterprises

An enterprise's business model reflects the design of value creation, delivery, and capture mechanism that a firm deploys: it describes about how a firm has organized itself to create and deliver value in a profitable manner. In other words, a firm's behavior reflects its management hypothesis about what customers want; how they want it; and how the enterprise can organize itself to best meet those needs, get paid for doing so, and make a profit. Companies competing in the same industry may deploy dissimilar business models from one another. For example, 7-Eleven (Irving, TX, USA) and Tesco Lotus (Bangkok, Thailand) have completely different business models. 7-Eleven makes a profit from selling fewer items to its customers, who typically demonstrate frequent visits. Its profit is driven by a smaller number of shelf items, a high inventory turnover at each store, and products that are easy to carry and consume. It chooses to spread its chain of stores throughout the city and sells franchises to building owners located in high-pedestrian traffic areas. Tesco Lotus, in contrast, realizes its profit from selling a broad range of products with different inventory turnovers. The company builds large-scale malls to attract infrequent shoppers who spend more during each store visit. The two companies have different store designs, supply-chain configurations, and ownership structures. Because the two companies target different customer segments with different value propositions, they consequently deploy two distinct business models.

E.1 Business Model

As a conceptual tool, a business model is a simplified representation of how the business of any company works. To achieve this, it contains elements describing different parts of a business and their relationships with each other; in effect, it states the business logic of a firm.

With the business model concept, we can depict the following:

- Which kind of value is offered to which customers
- Which kinds of resources, activities, and partners are needed
- How the value offered to customers is captured and transferred back to the company through revenue

E.1.1 Osterwalder and Pigneur's Business Model Canvas

Business model canvas is an easy-to-use tool for business model development and proposes an business model framework consisting of nine elements grouped in four pillars (Osterwalder 2004; Osterwalder and Pigneur 2010), as follows:

1. *Product pillar* describes the business of a company, its offerings, and the value propositions it offers to the market.

a. *Value proposition* describes an overall view of a company's bundle of products and services that represent value for a specific customer segment, and is packaged and offered to fulfill customer needs. Moreover, it describes how a company differentiates itself from its competitors.

2. *Customer interface pillar* identifies who a company's target customers are, how it delivers products and services to them, and how it builds strong relationships with them; in particular, it specifies the path of how a company goes to the market, reaches its customers, and interacts with them.

   b. *Customer segments* define the types of customers a company wants to offer value to. A company selects its target customers by segmenting the potential customer base according to different criteria, techniques, or approaches.

   c. *Channels* describe the means of getting in touch with customers. They are the conduits or connections between a company's value proposition and its target customers. Channels include communication, distribution, and sales channels that deliver value propositions to customers. The sales channels can be further divided into company-owned direct and indirect sales channels and partner-owned indirect sales channels.

   d. *Customer relationships* describe the kinds of links a company establishes between itself and its customers. All of the interactions between a company and its customers determine the strength of the relationships. As interactions come with cost, a company carefully defines the kinds of relationships it wants to maintain and the kinds of customers it wants to establish these relationships with.

3. *Infrastructure management pillar* addresses the question as to how a company executes its business and creates value. It describes how a company efficiently performs infrastructural and logistical issues, with whom it performs these issues with, and the kind of *network enterprise or business* it operates (Kale 2017). Thus, it defines what capabilities and capacities the company needs to provide its value proposition and to maintain its customer interface. It specifies the capabilities and resources that are needed in a business model and the executors of each activity, as well as their relationships with each other.

   e. *Key resources* describe the arrangement of assets required to create value for the customer. They are inputs in the value-creation process and sources of capabilities, which a company needs to provide its value propositions. Resources can be categorized into physical, intellectual, human, and financial resources.

   f. *Key activities* describe the actions a company performs to help realize the business model. A business model framework helps in configuring key activities both inside and outside of a company. This is done in accordance with the logic of the company's value chain or value network.

   g. *Key partnerships* describe the network of suppliers and partners needed to realize the business model. They are a result of cooperative agreements for outsourcing activities and acquiring resources from outside the company.

4. *Financial aspects* define the company's revenue model and cost structure, resulting in profitability. Such defines a business model's economical sustainability in terms of the configuration of all other elements.

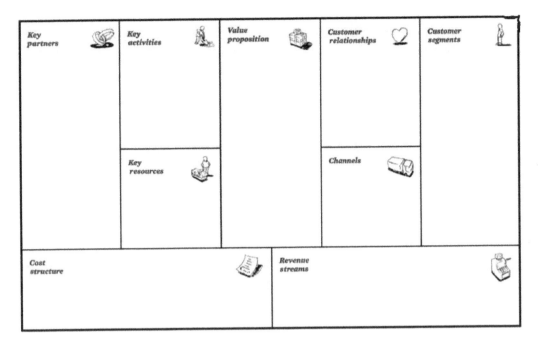

FIGURE E.1
Business model canvas.

h. *Revenue streams* describe how a company makes money through a variety
   of revenue flows resulting from value propositions offered profitably to customers. Revenue streams result directly from pricing models chosen by the
   company.

i. *Cost structure* is the representation of costs resulting from the operation of a
   business model, which is to create, market, and deliver value to customers. It
   monetizes the various elements of a business model—that is, it sets a price tag
   for the other elements of a business model.

Figure E.1 presents the schematic of a business model canvas.

E.1.2 Design Thinking for Business Model Design

Scientific inquiry means reasoning, questioning, and considering alternatives, thus induc-
ing the deliberative mindset; this is especially so when one considers the classic, philosoph-
ical, and truth-oriented perspective on scientific enterprise. However, the pragmatic view
on science reveals scientific enquiry as a paradigm oriented toward envisioning new possibilities resulting from the scientific findings. In 1877, Charles S. Peirce proposed a pragmatic view on scientific inquiry. Following his notion of human reasoning, he described
inquiry as attempts to eliminate problems, doubts, and dissatisfaction related to them and
to replace them with a satisfactory and calm belief that one can act upon (Hartshorne
and Weiss 1931). He effectively criticized the view that science is the ultimate search for
fundamental truth. Almost 100 years later, Thomas S. Kuhn proposed another pragmatic
view of science; he stressed the fact that the primary activities of scientists focus on solving

particular problems (i.e., on "puzzle-solving") rather than on the testing of fundamental theories (Kuhn 1970a, 1970b). Peirce's and Kuhn's perspectives on scientific enquiry highlight the problem-solving aspects of the enquiry and, as such, they open pathways for design-oriented approaches to general inquiry, including design thinking.

Information systems (IS) is a specific field of scientific research encompassing the development, use, and application of IS by individuals, organizations, and society as a whole.

IS research strategies are of the following two types (Hevner and Chatterjee 2010):

1. *Behavioral research* is rooted in psychology science and thereby has its roots in the natural sciences. Behavioral research seeks to develop and justify theories (i.e., principles and laws) that explain or predict organizational and human phenomena surrounding the analysis, design, implementation, management, and use of IS. Behavioral science starts with a hypothesis and researchers subsequently collect data to either prove it right or wrong. Eventually, a theory is developed. The behaviorist approach underlies logical positivism, which would not consider the hypothesis as acceptable scientific knowledge as long as it had not been allowed for being tested through observations (Popper 2002).

2. *Design science research* (DSR) is construction-oriented and is in which a designer answers questions relevant to human problems via the creation of innovative artifacts, thereby contributing new knowledge to the body of scientific evidence. An *artifact* is a solution made by humans with the intention to solve a problem. Unlike the natural sciences, DSR is fundamentally a problem-solving paradigm whose final goal is to produce an artifact that must be built and then evaluated. The knowledge generated by this research informs us, specifically with regards to how a problem can be improved and/or why the developed artifact is better than existing solutions, and can help us to more efficiently solve the problem being addressed.

Table E.1 shows a comparison of the behavioral research and DSR strategies.

Frameworks like DSR address problems encountered in the domain of IS. DSR aims to solve a defined problem and meet identified needs through the artifacts produced and addresses research relevance by the clear linkage of a solution to an identified problem. Design science is a good fit wherein the research focus is on gaining both knowledge and understanding of a defined problem and its solution, while creating and applying the artifacts identified (Hevner et al. 2004).

Hevner et al. (2004) provide seven guidelines for good DSR within the IS discipline, based on the fundamental principle that understanding and knowledge of a problem are acquired by building and applying artifacts. These guidelines include the following requirements:

1. Creation of an artifact
2. Usefulness of an artifact for a specified problem or problem domain
3. Ascertaining the usefulness of an artifact by performing a rigorous evaluation
4. Contribution of the artifact through a new and innovative solution to the problem domain
5. Construction and evaluation of the artifact based on the existing knowledge base in the problem domain

TABLE E.1

Comparison of Behavioral and Design Science Research Strategies

	Behavioral Research	Design Science Research
Goal	Description and declaration of the reality with the aid of theories (*focus on reality*)	Changing the reality by developing and using artifacts (*focus on benefits*)
Perception of reality	There exists an ontic reality that is responsible for perceiving a subject (*realism*)	There exists an ontic reality that is bound to a subject that creates distortions (*relativism*)
Knowledge evaluation	Differentiation between knowledge development and application Methodological principles and procedures guarantee knowledge quality (*positivism*)	A logical separation between knowledge development and knowledge application is either not possible or not desired; only a few methodological standards; the grade of knowledge is determined by the quality of the argumentation (*pragmatism*)
Knowledge structure	It is assumed that sociotechnical coherences are explicable by empirical data (describe, explain, and predict) (*reductionism*)	Data form a basis for constructing an artifact but are not applicable for drawing conclusions within the overall context, which is called the contextual knowledge, about the artifact (*emergence*)
Knowledge development process	Inquiry, evaluation, interpretation, and generalization (*sequence*)	Problem analysis and formulation, development and adaptation of concepts, evaluation and recalibration synthesis (*iteration*)
Interaction with the object of research	Actions that have an influence on the object of research should be omitted (*observer*)	Affecting opportunities for target-oriented modification of the environment are actively used (*participant*)

6. Design science, being an iterative search process, involves a cycle of designing, building, and testing of the solution
7. Communicating the research clearly to both technical and managerial audiences

The design science method offers a framework to perform a DSR project in structured way (Johannesson and Perjons 2014). It consists of the following five main activities:

1. The first activity is *Explicate Problem*, which is the investigation and analysis of a practical problem. In this activity, the problem should be formulated to highlight its significance and general interest and even explain the underlying causes.
2. The second activity is Outline Artifact and Define Requirements, where the solution to the defined problem is outlined as an artifact. The problem is transformed into defined requirements for the proposed artifact.
3. The third activity is *Design and Develop Artifact*, wherein an artifact is designed and created to solve the explicated problem by fulfilling the requirements that were defined.
4. The fourth activity is *Demonstrate Artifact*, which aims to use the resulting artifact in a scenario to demonstrate or prove that the artifact does solve the explicated problem.

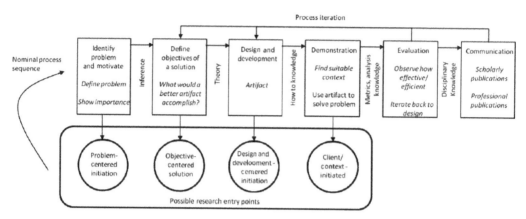

FIGURE E.2
Design science research methodology.

5. The fifth and final activity is *Evaluate Artifact,* which aims to determine how the artifact fulfills the requirements and how it addresses or solves the practical problem that was identified in the first step.

A corresponding DSR methodology for information systems is shown in Figure E.2 (Peffers et al. 2008).

E.1.3 Business Model Design and Organizational Architecture

The main drawbacks of the business model canvas framework relate to its inability to address the context, or the environment in which the business model is to be applied. The business environment as a background concept also allows for taking into account the special characteristics that the product-service system context sets for business model development. With it, the overall orientation of the business logic of the company can be addressed and the business model can be designed according to it. At this point, organizational structure and culture, which are closely related to the aforementioned aspects, can be addressed in order to build a better organizational fit for the business model.

Adaptability of business models, responsiveness to market changes, and the increasing digitalization are acknowledged factors for competitiveness on globalized markets. Enterprises can be understood as complex and highly integrated systems, which are composed of a set of elements such as goals, processes, organizational units, information, and supporting technologies, with multifaceted interdependencies across their boundaries. Enterprises become more complex in the context of strategic changes, e.g., digitalization of products and services, establishment of highly integrated supply chains in global markets (with suppliers), and mergers and acquisitions including global interoperability or increased outsourcing. The economic success of an organization can only be achieved when an enterprise is able to handle upcoming challenges and complex changes as fast as possible, without generating new problems and challenges.

As discussed in Chapter 3, Subsection 3.3.2, enterprise architecture (EA) enables the maintenance of flexibility as well as the cost-effectiveness and transparency of the infrastructure, information systems, and business processes. EA enables, supports, and manages the alignment of business strategy and information technology (IT); furthermore, it enables the coordination of business and IT activities, thereby assisting with strategic decisions,

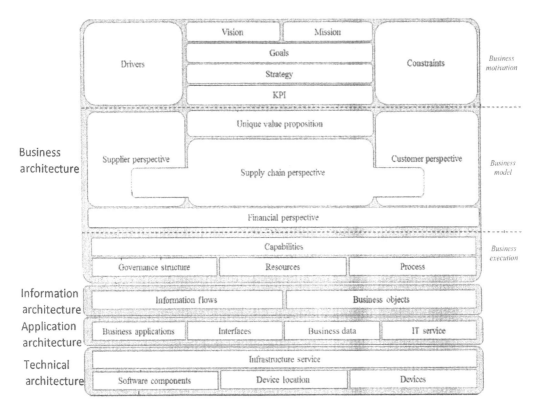

FIGURE E.3
Enhanced business model design.

accompanying its implementation in collaboration with IT, and enabling informed strategy control. In particular, EA determines how IT has to reconfigure according to the changing needs of the business, as well as how business has to reframe strategy driven by new opportunities enabled by newer technologies.

An enhanced business model relevant for undertaking digital transformation initiatives is shown in Figure E.3 (Simon et al. 2014; WiBotzki 2018).

E.2 Digital Transformation of Enterprises

In the past few years, new firms have grown from start-ups to international multibillion-dollar companies, with much of their success credited to their innovative business models and smart use of the digital environment. Customers have begun to expect services to perform at a level comparable to the front-runners of digitalized companies. Firms increasingly need to maintain, on an ongoing basis, a variety of innovation efforts to operate more efficiently, as well as to continuously strive to deliver greater and greater value to their customers. To stay competitive, this has led to an increased focus on keeping the firm's business model current in line with the leading digitalized companies, in other words, for the digital transformation of enterprises, such involves the digital transformation of business models, architectures, and processes.

Digitization refers to the process of converting or switching from analog to digital format. Digitalization refers to the waves of change that empower society through the increased utilization of digital technology. *Digital transformation* refers to the adaptations that firms make in order to thrive in an increasingly digital world; it incorporates the effects that digitalization has upon businesses.

Digital transformation can be accomplished through the following:

1. *Business model innovation* along the dimensions of value propositions, customer segments, channels, customer relationships, key activities, key resources, key partners, cost structure, and revenue streams

2. *Enterprise architecture evolution* along the dimensions of integration and interoperability, availability and scalability, performance and reliability, and access and security

3. *Business processes improvement* programs ranging right from disruptive programs like business process reengineering to continuous improvement programs like lean, Six Sigma, and Theory of Constraints.

References

Hartshorne, C., and P. Weiss (Eds.), *Collected Papers of Charles Sanders Peirce* (Cambridge, MA: Harvard University Press, 1931).

Hevner, A., and S. Chatterjee, *Design Research in Information Systems: Theory and Practice* (New York: Springer, 2010).

Hevner, A., S. March, J. Park, and S. Ram, Design science in information systems research. *MIS Quarterly* 28(1):75–105, 2004.

Johannesson, P., and E. Perjons, *An Introduction to Design Science* (New York: Springer, 2014).

Kale, V., *Agile Network Businesses: Collaboration, Coordination, and Competitive Advantage* (Boca Raton, FL: CRC Press, 2017).

Kuhn, T. S., Logic of discovery or psychology of research? In: I. Lakatos and A. Musgrave (Eds.) *Criticism and the Growth of Knowledge* (Cambridge, UK: Cambridge University Press, 1970a), pp. 1–23.

Kuhn, T. S., *The Structure of Scientific Revolutions*, 2nd ed. (Chicago, IL: Chicago University Press, 1970b).

Osterwalder, A., *The Business Model Ontology: A Proposition in a Design Science Approach*, Doctoral Dissertation (Lausanne, Switzerland: University of Lausanne, 2004).

Osterwalder, A., and Y. Pigneur, *Business Model Generation: A Handbook for Visionaries, Game Changers, and Challengers* (Hoboken, NJ: Wiley, 2010).

Peffers, K., T. Tuunanen, M. Rothenberger, and S. Chatterjee, A design science research methodology for information systems research. *Journal of Management Information Systems* 24(3):45–77, 2008.

Popper, K., *The Logic of Scientific Discovery* (London, UK: Routledge, 2002).

Simon, D., K. Fischbach, and D. Schoder, Enterprise architecture management and its role in corporate strategic management. *Information Systems and e-Business Management* 12(1), 5–42, 2014.

WiBotzki, M., *Capability Management Guide: Method Support for Enterprise Architectures Management* (Wiesbaden, Germany: Springer, 2018).

Appendix A: Business Process Execution Language

The development of the Business Process Execution Language (BPEL) was guided by the requirement to support service composition models that provide flexible integration, recursive composition, separation of composability of concerns, stateful conversation and life-cycle management, and recoverability properties. BPEL has now emerged as the standard to define and manage business process activities and business interaction protocols comprising collaborating Web services. This is an Extensible Markup Language (XML)-based flow language for the formal specification of business processes and business interaction protocols. By doing so, it extends the Web service interaction model and enables it to support complex business processes and transactions. Enterprises can describe complex processes that include multiple organizations—such as order processing, lead management, and claims handling—and execute the same business processes in systems from other vendors.

BPEL as a service composition (orchestration) language provides several features to facilitate the modeling and execution of business processes based on Web services. These features include the following:

1. Modeling business process collaboration (through <partnerLink>s)
2. Modeling the execution control of business processes (through the use of a self-contained block and transition-structured language that support the representation of directed graphs)
3. The separation of abstract definition from concrete binding (static and dynamic selection of partner services via endpoint references)
4. The representation of participants' roles and role relationships (through <partnerLinkType>s)
5. Compensation support (through fault handlers and compensation)
6. Service composability (structured activities can be nested and combined arbitrarily)
7. Context support (through the <scope> mechanism)
8. Spawning off and synchronizing processes (through <pick> and <receive> activities)
9. Event handling (through the use of event handlers)

BPEL can also be extended to provide other important composition language properties such as support for Web service policies and security and reliable messaging requirements. In this section, we summarize the most salient BPEL features and constructs.

A.1 Background of Web Services Description Language

BPEL's composition model makes extensive use of the Web Services Description Language (WSDL). It is therefore necessary to provide an overview of WSDL before going into the details of BPEL itself. A WSDL description consists of two parts: an abstract part defining the offered functionality and a concrete part defining how and where this functionality may be accessed. By separating the abstract from the concrete, WSDL enables an abstract component to be implemented by multiple code artifacts and deployed using different communication protocols and programming models.

The abstract part of a WSDL definition consists of one or more interfaces called port-Types in WSDL. PortTypes specify the operations provided by the service and their input and/or output message structures. Each message consists of a set of parts; the types of these parts are usually defined using XML schema. The concrete part of a WSDL definition consists of three parts: first, it binds the portType to available transport protocol and data-encoding formats in a set of one or more bindings. Additionally, it provides the location of endpoints that offer the functionality specified in a portType over an available binding in one or more ports. Finally, it provides a collection of ports as services.

A.2 Business Process Execution Language for Web Services

BPEL for Web Services is a workflow-based composition language geared toward service-oriented computing and layered as part of the Web service technology stack. BPEL composes services by defining control semantics around a set of interactions with the services being composed. The composition is recursive; a BPEL process itself is naturally exposed as a Web service, with incoming messages and their optional replies mapped to calls to WSDL operations offered by the process. Offering processes as services enables interwork flow interaction, higher levels of reuse, and additional scalability.

Processes in BPEL are defined using only the abstract definitions of the composed services—that is, the abstract part (portType/operations/messages) of their WSDL definitions. The binding to actual physical endpoints and the mapping of data to the representation required by these endpoints is intentionally left out of the process definition, allowing the choice to be made at deployment time, at design time, or during execution. Added to the use of open XML specifications and standards, this enables two main goals: flexibility of integration and portability of processes.

The BPEL language is designed to specify both business protocols and executable processes. A business protocol, called an abstract process in BPEL, specifies the flow of interactions that a service may have with other services. For example, one may accompany a WSDL description with an abstract BPEL process to inform parties using it in what order and in what situations operations in the WSDL should be called (e.g., a call to a "request for quote" operation must precede a call to a "place order" operation). An executable process is similar to an abstract process, except that it has a slightly expanded BPEL vocabulary and includes information that enables the process to be interpreted, such as fully specifying the handling of data values, and includes interactions with private services that one does not want to expose in the business protocol. For example, when an order is placed, the executable BPEL process might have to invoke a number of internal applications wrapped as services (e.g., applications related to invoicing, customer relationship management, stock control, logistics), but these calls should not be visible to the customer and would be omitted from the abstract process the customer sees. In the executable variant, the process can be seen as the implementation of a Web service. Most work in BPEL has been focused on the executable variant of the language.

A.3 The Business Process Execution Language Process Model

BPEL has its roots in both graph- and calculus-based process models, giving designers the flexibility to use either or both graph primitives (nodes and links) and complex control constructs to create implicit control flow. The two process modeling approaches are integrated through BPEL's exception handling mechanism. The composition of services results from the use of predefined interaction activities that can invoke operations on these services and handle invocations to operations exposed by the process itself. The unit of composition in BPEL is the activity. Activities are combined through nesting in complex activities with control semantics and/or through the use of conditional links. In contrast to traditional workflow systems in which dataflow is explicitly defined using data links, BPEL gives activities the read/write access to shared, scoped variables. In addition to the main forward flow, BPEL contains fault handling and rollback capabilities, event handling, and life-cycle management.

The role of BPEL is to define a new Web service by composing a set of existing services through a process-integration-type mechanism with control language constructs. The entry points correspond to external WSDL clients invoking either input-only (request) or input/output (request–response) operations on the interface of the composite BPEL service. BPEL provides a mechanism for creating implementation- and platform-independent compositions of services woven strictly from the abstract interfaces provided in the WSDL definitions. The definition of a BPEL business process also follows the WSDL convention of strict separation between the abstract service interface and service implementation. In particular, a BPEL process represents parties and interactions between these parties in terms of abstract WSDL interfaces (by means of <portType>s and <operation>s), while no references are made to the actual services (binding and address information) used by a process instance. Both the interacting process and its counterparts are modeled in the form of WSDL services. Actual implementations of the services themselves may be dynamically bound to the partners of a BPEL composition, without affecting the composition's definition. Business processes specified in BPEL are fully executable portable scripts that can be interpreted by business process engines in BPEL conformant environments.

BPEL distinguishes five main sections:

1. The message flow section of BPEL is handled by basic activities that include invoking an operation on some Web service, waiting for a process operation to be invoked by some external client, and generating the response of an input/output operation.

2. The control flow section of BPEL is a hybrid model principally based on block-structured definitions that has the ability to define selective state transition control flow definitions for synchronization purposes.

3. The dataflow section of BPEL comprises variables that provide the means for holding messages that constitute the state of a business process. The messages held are often those that have been received from partners or which are to be sent to partners. Variables can also hold data that are needed for the holding state related to the process and which are never exchanged with partners. Variables are scoped, and the name of a variable should be unique within its own scope.

4. The process orchestration section of BPEL uses partner links to establish peer-to-peer partner relationships.

5. The fault and exception handling section of BPEL deals with errors that might occur when services are being invoked with handling compensations of units of work and dealing with exceptions during the course of a BPEL computation.

BPEL consists of the following basic activities:

receive: The receive activity initiates a new process when used at its start or does a blocking wait for a matching message to arrive when used during a process.

reply: The reply activity sends a message in reply.

invoke: The invoke activity calls a Web service operation of a partner service. This can either be a one-way or a request–response call. One way means that the called service will not send a response, whereas request–response blocks the process until a response is received.

assign: The assign activity updates the values of variables or partner links with new data.

validate: The validate activity checks the correctness of XML data stored in variables.

wait: The wait activity pauses the process, either for a given time period or until a certain point in time has passed.

empty: The empty activity is a no-operation instruction for a business process.

Another element of the Web Services BPEL (WS-BPEL) language is a variable. BPEL supports both global (i.e., process level) and local (i.e., scope level) variables. BPEL variables may be typed using an XML schema (XSD) type or element, or a WSDL message. For initializing or assigning variables, BPEL provides the "assign" activity. Each assign consists of one or more copy statements. In each copy, the *from* element specifies the assignment source for data elements or partner links, while the *to* element specifies the assignment target.

Additionally, there are several basic activities that deal with fault situations:

throw: The throw activity generates a fault from inside the business process.

rethrow: The rethrow activity propagates a fault from inside a fault handler to an enclosing scope, where the process itself is the outermost scope.

compensate: The compensate activity invokes compensation on all completed child scopes in a default order.

compensateScope: The compensateScope activity invokes compensation on one particular (completed) child scope.

exit: The exit activity immediately terminates the execution of a business process instance.

Furthermore, WS-BPEL offers structured activities. Structured activities can have other activities as children; that is, they represent container activities. WS-BPEL consists of the following structured activities:

flow: The activities contained in a flow are executed in parallel, partially ordered through control links. A flow activity represents a directed graph. Note that cyclic control links are not allowed.

sequence: The activities contained in a sequence are performed sequentially in lexical order.

if: The if activity represents a choice between multiple branches. However, exactly one branch is selected.

while: The contained activity of a while loop is executed as long as a specified predicate evaluates to true.

repeatUntil: The contained activity of a repeatUntil loop is executed until a specified predicate evaluates to true.

forEach: The activity contained in a forEach loop is performed sequentially or in parallel, controlled by a specified countervariable. This loop can be terminated prematurely by means of a completion condition.

pick: The pick activity blocks and waits either for a suitable message to arrive or for a time out, whichever occurs first.

scope: A container that associates its contained activity with its own local elements, such as variables, partner links, correlation sets, and handlers (please see the following).

To handle exceptional situations, WS-BPEL offers four different handlers, as follows:

1. catch and catchAll: Fault handlers for dealing with fault situations in a process. A fault handler can be compared to the catchpart of a try{}... catch{}-block in programming languages like Java.

2. onEvent and onAlarm: Event handlers for processing unsolicited inbound messages or timer alarms concurrently to the regular control flow.

3. compensationHandler: A compensation handler undoes the persisted effects of a successfully completed scope.

4. terminationHandler: A termination handler can be used for customizing a forced scope termination, for example, as caused by an external fault.

In addition to concepts introduced already, there are three more concepts for communication: partner links, correlation sets, and (variable) properties. These are defined as follows:

1. PartnerLinks describe the relationship between a process and its services. A partner link points to a Web service interface the process provided via a myRole attribute. Consequently, a partnerRole attribute points to the Web service interface that is required from the partner. A partner link can only have one myRole attribute (inbound partner), only one partnerRole attribute (outbound partner), or both attributes (bidirectional partner).

2. CorrelationSets are of help in identifying (stateful) process instances. Each process instance will get one or more unique keys based on business data, which are used to correlate a process instance with an incoming message. A correlation set consists of one or more properties.

3. A property is business data that creates a name that has a semantic meaning beyond an associated XML type, for example, a social security number versus a plain XML schema integer type. Therefore, properties help to isolate the process logic from the details of a variable definition. Such typed properties are then mapped (aliased) to the parts of a WSDL message or an XSD element.

 BPMN is a notation used to graphically depict business processes. The language provides users with the capability to capture their internal business procedures in a graphical notation. In other words, BPMN is a graph-oriented visual language that allows one to model business processes in a flowchart-like fashion. Such a standardized graphical notation for business processes allows one to explain and exchange processes in a standard manner and to better understand collaborations and business transactions between organizations.

Basically, the BPMN language consists of four core elements:

1. Flow objects are the nodes of the BPMN graph. There are three kinds of flow objects: activities, events, and gateways.

2. Connecting objects are the edges of a BPMN graph. BPMN allows three different kinds of connecting objects: sequence flow, message flow, and association.

3. Swim lanes are used to group other modeling elements in two distinct ways: a pool represents a single process, or it can be divided up into multiple lanes, where each lane is a subpartition of that process and is used to organize and categorize activities (e.g., activities that are performed by the same department are grouped in the same lane).

4. Artifacts. As an example, a data object is an artifact that represents the data that an activity requires before it can be performed or that an activity produced after it has been performed. For the sake of completeness, there are two more artifacts mentioned in the BPMN standard: text annotation and group.

BPMN is discussed in detail in Chapter 11.

Appendix B: Interaction Architectures

The interaction-oriented software architectures decomposes the system into the following three major partitions: data module, control module, and view presentation module. Each module has its own responsibilities, as follows:

1. The data module provides the data abstraction and all core business logic on data processing.
2. The view presentation module is responsible for visual or audio data output presentation and may also provide user input interface when necessary.
3. The control module determines the flow of control involving view selections, communications between modules, job dispatching, and certain data initialization and system configuration actions.

The key point of interaction architecture is its separation of user interactions from data abstraction and business data processing. Since there may be many view presentations in different formats, multiple views may be supported for the same dataset.

Even for a specific view presentation, the interfaces or views may need to change often, so loose coupling between data abstractions and presentations is helpful and is supported by this style. The loose coupling connections can be implemented in a variety of ways such as explicit method invocation or implicit registration/notification method invocation.

The control module plays a central role that mediates the data module and view presentation modules. All three modules may be fully connected.

B.1 Presentation–Abstraction–Control

Presentation–abstraction–control (PAC) was developed to support the application requirement of multiple agents in addition to interactive requirements. In PAC, the system is decomposed into a hierarchy of cooperating agents. Each agent has three components (Presentation, Abstraction, and Control). The Control component in each agent is in charge of communications with other agents. The top-level agent provides core data and business logics. The bottom-level agents provide detailed data and presentations. A middle-level agent may coordinate low-level agents. Within each agent, there are no direct connections between the Abstraction component and Presentation component (Figure B.1).

The Presentation is the visual representation of a particular abstraction within the application and is responsible for defining how the user interacts with the system.

The Abstraction is the business domain functionality within the application.

The Control is a component that maintains consistency between the abstractions within the system and their presentation to the user, in addition to communicating with other Controls within the system.

PAC is suitable for any distributed system in which all of the agents are distantly distributed and each agent has its own functionalities with data and interactive interface. In such a system, all agents need to communicate with other agents in a well-structured manner.

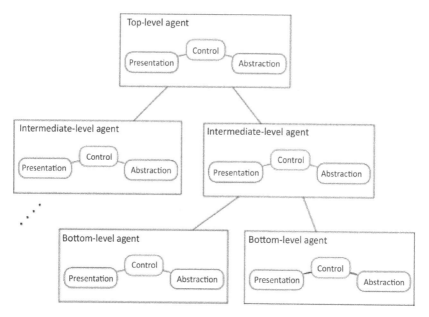

FIGURE B.1
Presentation–abstraction–control (PAC) architecture.

PAC is also used in applications with rich graphical user interface components when each of them keeps its own current data and interactive interface and needs to communicate with other components.

The PAC architecture is the right choice for distributed applications of wireless mobile communication systems, since each device needs to have its own data and its own interactive interface but also needs to communicate with other devices. A typical PAC software design is a networked traffic control management system that requires many mobile agents to monitor traffic and get data; display the analyzed data in graphics; coordinate the data from agents; and complete many other management tasks.

B.2 Model–View–Controller

The model–view–controller (MVC) pattern was first described in 1979 by Trygve Reenskaug, then working on Smalltalk at Xerox. The original implementation is described in-depth in the influential paper "Applications Programming in Smalltalk-80(TM): How to use Model-View-Controller."

The Model module provides all of the core functional services and encapsulates all data details. The Model module does not depend on other modules nor does it know which views are registered with or attached to it.

The View module is responsible for displaying the data provided by the Model module and updating the interfaces whenever the data changes are notified.

The Controller manages the user input requests; controls the sequence of user interactions; selects desired views for output displays; and manages all initializations, instantiations, and registrations of the other modules in the MVC system (Figure B.2).

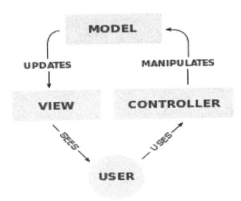

FIGURE B.2
Model–view–controller (MVC) architecture.

JSP Model 2 (or MVC 2) is Sun's attempt to wrap Java Server Pages (JSP) within the MVC paradigm. It's not so much a product offering (or even an application program interface) as it is a set of guidelines that go along with Sun's packaging of Java-based components and services under the umbrella of J2EE.

Most web developers are familiar with the MVC architecture because it is widely adopted for web server site interactive application designs such as online shopping, surveys, student registration, and many other interactive service systems. MVC architecture is specifically used in applications wherein user interfaces are prone to data changes. MVC also typically supports "look and feel" features in graphical user interface systems.

B.3 Data Context Interaction

While MVC separates the parts of a program that are responsible for representing the information in the system and the parts that are responsible for interaction with the user, data context interaction (DCI) minimize(s) any gap that might exist between the programmer's mental model of their program and the program that is actually stored and executed in the computer. In particular, it concretizes how the system realizes system operations as networks of communicating objects.

The goal of DCI is to separate the code that represents the system state from the code that represents system behavior. This separation is related to but different from MVC's split between data representation and user interaction.

Ordinary object-oriented programming lumps *what-the-system-is* and *what-the-system-does* interfaces together. However, these two interfaces change at different rates and are often managed by different groups of people. DCI separates the architecture into a data part (the domain part, or what the system *is*) and an interaction or feature part (what the system *does*) (Figure B.3). The interaction part becomes connected to the data part on an event-by-event basis by an object called the Context. The architecture can be viewed as Data and Interaction code dynamically connected together by a Context—hence, the name "data, context, and interaction," or DCI.

Object roles are collections of related responsibilities that accomplish their work through each other's responsibilities. When a system event occurs, code in the environment (often in

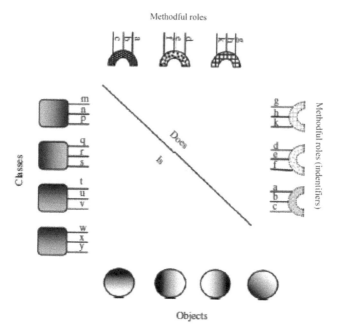

FIGURE B.3
Data context interaction (DCI) architecture.

the MVC Controller object) finds a Context object that understands the object-role-to-object mapping for the use case that corresponds to the event. That allows each domain object to play an object role. The Controller passes control to the Context object, which "wires up" the object roles to the objects and then kicks off the execution by invoking the object role method that initiates the use case; this is called the trigger. In general, each object may play several object roles, and a given object role may be played by a combination of several objects together.

B.4 Micro-Service Architecture

The shortening of product cycles coupled with personalization of customer preferences has led to a surge in virtualization technology applications, enabling rapid changes and continuous delivery of business applications. This has been possible only because of the concomitant transformation of traditional monolithic architecture to micro-service architecture (MSA) that can cater to an increasing number of and changes in services.

The MSA is an architectural pattern that advocates the partitioning of a single application into a small set of services that provide the ultimate value to the user by coordinating and cooperating with each other. Each service runs in its own process, with lightweight communication mechanisms between services usually via a Representational State Transfer-conforming application program interface based on the Hypertext Transfer Protocol. Each service is built around the specific business and can be deployed independently to production environments, deployment environments, and so on (Figure B.4).

The core benefits of the MSA concept include: small and focused services implementation, independent processes, lightweight communication mechanisms, loosely coupled distributed data management, and independent deployments tasks.

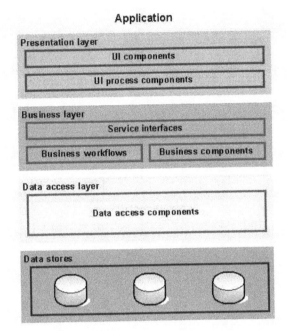

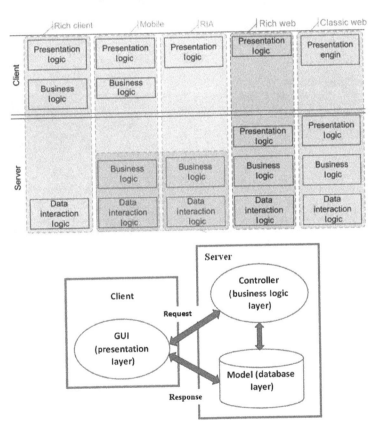

FIGURE B.4
Micro-service architecture (MSA).

Bibliography

Anthony, R. C. *Systems Programming: Designing and Developieng Distributed Applications* (Burlington, MA: Morgan-Kaufmann, 2016).

Bass, L., P. Clements, and R. Kizman. *Software Architecture in Practice* (Boston, MA: Addison-Wesley, 3rd Ed. 2013).

Bean, J., *SOA and Web Services Interface Design: Principals, Techniques and Standards* (Burlington, MA: Morgan Kaufmann, 2010).

Bilay, J. M., and R. V. Blanco. *SAP Process Orchestration: The Comprehensive Guide* (Quincy, MA: Rheinwerk Publishing, 2nd Ed. 2017).

Boyer, J., and H. Mili, *Agile Business Rule Development: Process, Architecture and JRules Examples* (Berlin, Germany: Springer, 2011).

Bridgeland, D., and R. Zahavi, *Business Modeling: A Practical Guide to Realizing Business Value* (Amsterdam, the Netherlands: Elsevier, 2008).

Bubenko Jr., J. A., A. Persson, J. Stirna, *User Guide of the Knowledge Management Approach Using Enterprise Knowledge Patterns, deliverable D3, IST Programme project Hypermedia and Pattern Based Knowledge Management for Smart Organisations*, project no. IST-2000-28401 (Stockholm, Sweden: Royal Institute of Technology, 2001).

Burgess, M., *In Search of Certainty: The Science of Our Information Infrastructure* (Charleston, SC: CreateSpace, 2013).

Ceri, S., and P. Fraternali, *Designing Database Applications with Objects and Rules: The IDEA Methodology* (Harlow, UK: Addison-Wesley, 1997).

Cervesato, I. *The Deductive Spreadsheet* (Berlin, Germany: Springer, 2013).

Chang, J. F., *Business Process Management Systems: Strategy and Implementation* (Boca Raton, FL: Auerbach Publications, 2006).

Cunningham, H. C., Y. Liu, and J. Wang. Designing a flexible framework for a table abstraction. In: Y. Chan, J. R. Talburt, and T. M. Talley (Eds.), *Data Engineering: Mining, Information and Intelligence* (Berlin, Germany: Springer, 2010).

Damij, T., *Tabular Application Development for Information Systems: An Object Oriented Methodology* (New York: Springer, 2001).

Damij, N., and T. Damij, *Process Management: A Multi-Disciplinary Guide to Theory, Modeling and Methodology* (Berlin, Germany: Springer, 2014).

Davenport, T. H., and J. E. Short, The new industrial engineering: Information technology and business process redesign, June 1990, CISR WP No. 213, Sloan WP No. 3190-90.

Davenport, T., and J. Short. The new industrial engineering: Information technology and business process redesign, pp. 11–27. *Sloan Management Review* (Cambridge, MA: Massachusetts Institute of Technology, Summer 1990).

Dawson, P., *Organizational Change: A Processual Approach* (London, UK: Paul Chapman, 1994).

Deitz, J. L. G., *Enterprise Ontology: Theory and Methodology* (Berlin, Germany: Springer, 2006).

Dori, D., *Object-Process Methodology: A Holistic Systems Paradigm* (Berlin, Germany: Springer, 2002).

Dumas, M., W. M. Van der Aalst, and A. H. Ter Hofstede (Eds.), *Process Aware Information Systems: Bridging People and Software through Process Technology* (Hoboken, NJ: Wiley, 2005).

Dwyer, B., *Systems Analysis and Synthesis: Bridging Computer Science and Information Technology* (Amsterdam, the Netherlands: Morgan Kaufmann, 2016).

Embley, D. W., and B. Thalheim (Eds.), *Handbook of Conceptual Modeling: Theory, Practice and Research Challenges* (Berlin, Germany: Springer, 2011).

Erl, T. *Service-Oriented Architecture: A Field Guide to Integrating XML and Web Services* (Upper Saddle River, NJ: Prentice-Hall, 2004).

Ferreria, D. R. *Enterprise Systems Integration: A Process Oriented Approach* (Berlin, Germany: Springer, 2013).

Finkelstein, C., *Information Engineering: Strategic System Development* (Sydney, Australia: Addison-Wesley, 1992).

Finklestein, C., *Enterprise Architecture for Integration: Rapid Delivery Methods and Technologies* (Irvine, CA: BookPal, 2011).

Gardner, R. A., *The Process-Focused Organization: A Transition Strategy for Success* (Milwaukee, WI: ASQ Quality Press, 2004).

Gasavic, D., D. Djuric, and V. Devedzic, *Model Driven Architecture and Ontology Development* (Berlin, Germany: Springer, 2006).

Goldin, D., S. A. Smolka, and P. Wegner (Eds.). *Interactive Computation: The New Paradigm* (Berlin, Germany: Springer, 2006).

Graham, I., and P. L. Jones, *Expert Systems: Knowledge, Uncertainty and Decision* (London, UK: Chapman & Hall, 1988).

Graham, I., *Requirements Modelling and Specification for Service Oriented Enterprise* (Chichester, UK: Wiley, 2008).

Griol, D., J. M. Molina, and Z. Callejas, Big data for conversational interfaces: Current opportunities and prospects. In: F. Pedro, G. Márquez, and B. Lev (Eds.), *Big Data Management* (Cham, Switzerland: Springer, 2017).

Gustavo, C., and J. Macazaga, *The Process-Based Organization: A Natural Organization Strategy* (Amherst, MA: HRD Press, 2005).

Hammer, M. Reenginering work: Don't automate, obliterate. *Harvard Business Review*, 90(4): 104–112, 1990.

Han, Y., A. Kauranen, E. Kristola, and J. Merinen, *Human Interaction Management – Adding Human Factors into Business Processes Management* (Espoo, Finland: Helsinki University of Technology, 2005).

Harrison-Broninski, K., *Human Interactions: The Heart and Soul of Business Process Management* (Tampa, FL: Meghan Kiffer Press, 2005).

Hendriks, P. *Asymmetries between Language Production and Comprehension* (Berlin, Germany: Springer, 2014).

Hentrich, C., and U. Zdun, *Process-Driven SOA: Patterns for Aligning Business and IT* (Boca Raton, FL: CRC Press, 2012).

Herbst, H., *Business Rule-Oriented Conceptual Modeling* (New York: Physica-Verlag, 2000).

Hernes, T., *Understanding Organization as Process: Theory for a Tangled World* (London, UK: Routledge, 2008).

Hernes, T., *A Process Theory of Organization* (Oxford, UK: Oxford University Press, 2014).

Ifukube, T., *Sound-Based Assistive Technology: Support to Hearing, Speaking and Seeing* (Cham, Switzerland: Springer, 2017).

Josuttis, N. M. *SOA in Practice: The Art of Distributed System Design* (Newton, MA: O'Reilly, 2007).

Juric, M., and K. Pant, *Business Process Driven SOA Using BPMN and BPEL* (Birmingham, UK: Packt Publishing, 2008).

Jungerman, J. A., *World in Process: Creativity and Interconnection in the New Physics* (New York: State University of New York Press, 2000).

Kale, V., *Guide to Cloud Computing for Business and Technology Managers: From Distributed Computing to Cloudware Applications* (Boca Raton, FL: CRC Press, 2015).

Kale, V. *Big Data Computing: A Guide for Business and Technology Managers* (Boca Raton, FL: CRC Press, 2017).

Kaschek, R., and L. Delcambre (Eds.), *The Evolution of Conceptual Modeling: From a Historical Perspective towards the Future of Conceptual Modeling* (Berlin, Germany: Springer, 2011).

Khisty, C. J., J. Mohammadi, and A. A. Amekudzi. *Systems Engineering: with Econimics, Probability and Statistics* (Ft. Lauderdale, FL: J. Ross Publishing, 2nd Ed. 2012).

Kossak, F., C. Illibauer, V. Geist, J. Kubovy, C. NatschlRager, T. Ziebermayr, T. Kopetzky, B. Freudenthaler, and K. D. Schewe. *A Rigorous Semantics for BPMN 2.0 Process Diagrams* (Berlin, Germany: Springer, 2014).

Kossak, F., C. Illibauer, V. Geist, J. Kubovy, C. NatschlRager, T. Ziebermayr, T. Kopetzky, B. Freudenthaler, and K. D. Schewe. *Hagenberg Business Process Modelling Method* (Berlin, Germany: Springer, 2016).

Kirby, P., *The Process Mind: New Thoughtware For Designing Your Business on Purpose* (Boca Raton, FL: CRC Press, 2015).

Kirchmer, M. *High Performance through Business Process Management: Strategy Execution in a Digital World* (Berlin, Germany: Springer 3rd Ed. 2017).

Khoshafian, S., and M. Buckiewicz, *Introduction to Groupware, Workflow and Workgroup Computing* (New York: John Wiley & Sons, 1995).

Koa, L. Y., *The Five Breakthroughs of Business Process Management: One Standard, One Table, One Database, One Process System, One Management System* (Charleston, SC: CreateSpace, 2013).

Koskinen, K. U., *Knowledge Production in Organizations: A Processual Autopoietic View* (Cham, Switzerland: Springer, 2013).

Krumnow, S., and G. Decker, A concept for spreadsheet-based process modeling. In: J. Mendling, M. Weidlich, and M. Weske (Eds.), *Business Process Modeling Notation Second International Workshop, BPMN 2010* (Berlin, Germany: Springer, 2010).

Laguna, M., and J. Marklund, *Business Process Modeling, Simulation and Design* (Boca Raton, FL: CRC Press, 2nd ed. 2013).

Loucopoulos, P., V. Kavakli, N. Prekas, C. Rolland, G. Grosz, and S. Nurcan, *Using the EKD Approach: The Modelling Component* (Manchester, UK: UMIST, 1997).

Luvkham, D., *The Power of Events: An Introduction to Complex Event Processing in Distributed Enterprise Systems* (Boston, MA: Addison-Wesley, 2009).

Maier, M. W., and E. Rechtin, *The Art of Systems Architecting* (Boca Raton, FL: CRC Press, 2009).

Magalhaes, R., and R. Sanchez, *Autopoiesis in Organization Theory and Practice* (Bingley, UK: Emerald Group Publishing, 2009).

Maturana, H. R., and F. J. Varela, *Autopoiesis and Cognition: The Realization of the Living* (Dordrecht, the Netherlands: D. Reidel, 1980).

Maula, M., *Organizations as Learning Systems: 'Living Composition' as an Enabling Infrastructure* (Oxford, UK: Elsevier Science, 2006).

McCormack, K. P., and W. C. Johnson, *Business Process Orientation: Gaining the E-Business Competitive Advantage* (Boca Raton, FL: St. Lucie Press, 2000).

McCormack, K. P., and W. C. Johnson with W. T. Walker, *Supply Chain Networks and Business Process Orientation: Advanced Strategies and Best Practices* (Boca Raton, FL: St. Lucie Press, 2003).

McTear, M., Z. Callejas, and D. Griol, *The Conversational Interface: Talking to Smart Devices* (Cham, Switzerland: Springer, 2016).

Minoli, D. *Enterprise Architecture A to Z: Frameworks Business Process Modeling, SOA and Infrastructure Technology* (Boca Raton, FL: CRC Press, 2008).

Muller, G., *Systems Architecting: A Business Perspective* (Boca Raton, FL: CRC Press, 2011).

Nalepa, G. J. *Modeling with Rules Using Semantic Knowledge Engineering* (Berlin, Germany: Springer, 2018).

Niapolitan, R. E., *Probabilistic Reasoning in Expert Systems: Theory and Algorithms* (Charleston, SC: CreateSpace, 2012).

Olive, A., *Conceptual Modeling of Information Systems* (Berlin, Germany: Springer, 2007).

Oquendo, F., J. Leite, and T. Batista. *Software Architecture in Action: Designing and Executing Architectural Models with SysADL Grounded on the OMG SysML Standard* (Berlin, Germany: Springer, 2016).

Pastor, O., and J. Molina, *Model-Driven Architecture in Practice: A Software Production Environment Based on Conceptual Modeling* (Berlin, Germany: Springer, 2007).

Perroud, T., and R. Renversini, *Enterprise Architecture Patterns: Practical Solutions for Recurring IT-Architecture Problems* (Berlin, Germany: Springer, 2013).

Ponniah, P., *Data Modeling: Fundamentals: A Practical Guide for IT Professionals* (Hoboken, NJ: Wiley-Interscience, 2007).

Reichert, M., and B. Weber, *Enabling Flexibility in Process-Aware Information Systems: Challenges, Methods, Technologies* (Berlin, Germany: Springer, 2012).

Rescher, N., *Process Philosophy: A Survey of Basic Issues* (Pittsburgh, PA: University of Pittsburgh Press, 2000).

Rindler, A., B. Hillard, S. McClowry, and S. Mueller, *Information Development Using MIKE2.0* (Motion Publishing, 2013).

Ross, R. G., *Principles of the Business Rules Approach* (New York: Addison-Wesley, 2003).

Rozanski, N., and E. Woods. *Software System Architecture: Working with Stakeholders Using Viewpoints and Perspectives* (Boston, MA: Addison-Wesley, 2nd Ed. 2012).

Russell, N., W. M. P. van der Aalst, and A. H. M. ter Hofstede, *Workflow Patterns: The Definitive Guide* (Cambridge, MA: The MIT Press, 2016).

Sandkuhl, J. et al., *Enterprise Modeling: Tackling Business Challenges with the 4EM Method* (Berlin, Germany: Springer, 2014).

Shahzad, K., M. Elias, and P. Johannesson, Towards cross language process model reuse—A language independent representation of process models. In: A. Persson and J. Stirna (Eds.), *The Practice of Enterprise Modeling* (Berlin, Germany: Springer, 2009).

Shoval, P., *Function and Object-oriented Analysis and Design: Integrated Methodology* (Hershey, PA: IGI Global, 2006).

Smith, H., and P. Fingar, *Business Process Management (BPM): The Third Wave* (Tampa, FL: Meghan-Kiffer, 2003).

Stiehl, V. *Process Driven Applications with BPMN* (Berlin, Germany: Springer, 2014).

Szyperski, C., *Component Software: Beyond Object-Oriented Programming* (New York: Addison-Wesley, 2002).

ter Hofstede, A. H. M., W. M. P. van der Aalst, M. Adams, and N. Russell (Eds.). *Modern Business Process Automation—YAWL and its Support Environment* (Berlin, Germany: Springer, 2010).

Tran, H., T. Holmes, U. Zdun, and S. Dustdar, Modeling process-driven SOAs: A view-based approach. In: J. Cardoso and W. van der Aalst (Eds.), *Handbook of Research on Business Process Modeling* (Hershey, PA: IGI Global, 2009).

Tregear, R. *Reimagining Management: Putting Process at the Center of Business Management* (2016).

van der Aalst, W. M. P., and K. M. Van Hee, *Workflow Management: Models, Methods and Systems* (Cambridge, MA: MIT Press, 2002).

van der Aalst, Wil M. P. *Process Mining—Discovery, Conformance and Enhancement of Business Processes* (Berlin, Germany: Springer, 2010).

Vernadat, F. B., *Enterprise Modeling and Integration: Principles and Applications* (London, UK: Chapman & Hall, 1996).

Verissimo, P., and L. Rodrigues. *Distributed Systems for System Architects* (South Holland, Netherlands: Kulwer Academic Publishers, 2001).

Vissers, C. A., L. F. Pires, D. A.C. Quartel, and M. van Sinderen. Architectural Design: Conception and Specification of Interactive Systems (Berlin, Germany: Springer, 2016).

vom Brocke, J. and M. Rosemann (Eds.). *Handbook on Business Process Management (1 & 2): Introduction, Methods, and Information Systems Strategic Alignment, Governance, People and Culture* (Berlin, Germany: Springer, 2nd Ed. 2014).

Von Halle, B., *Rules Applied: Building Better Systems using the Business Rules Approach* (New York: Wiley, 2002).

Walden, K., and J. M. Nerson, *Seamless Object-Oriented Software Architecture: An Analysis and Design of Reliable Systems* (New York: Prentice-Hall, 1995).

Walford, R. B., *Business Process Implementation for IT Professionals and Managers* (Norwood, MA: Artech House, 1999).

Weske, M., *Business Process Management: Concepts, Languages and Architectures* (Berlin, Germany: Springer, 2nd ed., 2012).

Whitehead, A. N., *Process and Reality* (New York: Free Press, 1978).

Zachman, J. A., A framework for information systems architecture. *IBM Systems Journal* 26(3):276–292, 1987.

Zikra, I., J. Stirna, and J. Zdravkovic, Bringing enterprise modeling closer to model-driven development. In: P. Johannesson, J. Krogstie, and A. L. Opdahl (Eds.) *The Practice of Enterprise Modeling* (Berlin, Germany: Springer, 2011).

Index

Note: Page numbers in italic and bold refer to figures and tables respectively.